Fanny
Kembl

A sketch inspired by Sir Thomas Lawrence's portrait

Fanny Kemble

THE RELUCTANT CELEBRITY

REBECCA JENKINS

LONDON • SYDNEY • NEW YORK • TORONTO

First published in Great Britain by Simon & Schuster UK Ltd, 2005
This edition published by Pocket Books, 2006
An imprint of Simon & Schuster UK Ltd
A Viacom Company

1 3 5 7 9 10 8 6 4 2

Simon & Schuster UK Ltd
Africa House
64-78 Kingsway
London WC2B 6AH

www.simonsays.co.uk

Simon & Schuster Australia
Sydney

A CIP catalogue record for this book is available
from the British Library.

ISBN 0-7434-0399-1
EAN 9780743403993

Typeset by M Rules
Printed and bound in Great Britain by
Cox & Wyman Ltd, Reading, Berks

Picture Credits
Plate Section
1, 3: Garrick Club/Art Archive; 2: Mary Evans Picture Library; 4: National Portrait Gallery; 5, 6, 7, 8, 13: Private collection, by kind permission of the owner; 9: Mander & Mitchenson; 10: Folger Shakespeare Library; 11: Detroit Institute of Art; 12: Boston Atheneaum; 14: Historical Society of Pennsylvania; 15: Lenox Library Association; 16: Hulton Archive
Part Openers
1: Mary Evans Picture Library; Frontispiece, 2: National Portrait Gallery; 3: Brooklyn Museum of Art

For my parents, who taught me to love words

CONTENTS

PART III

A QUEST FOR SUBSTANCE –

The Making of Mrs Frances Anne Kemble

The Kemble Line

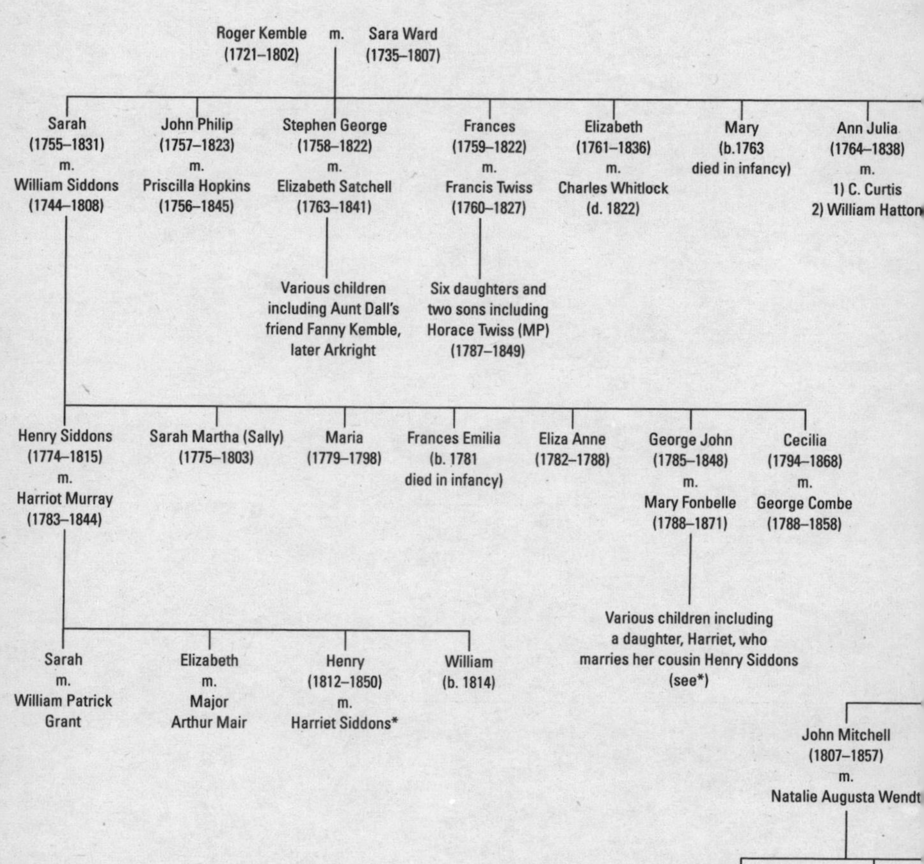

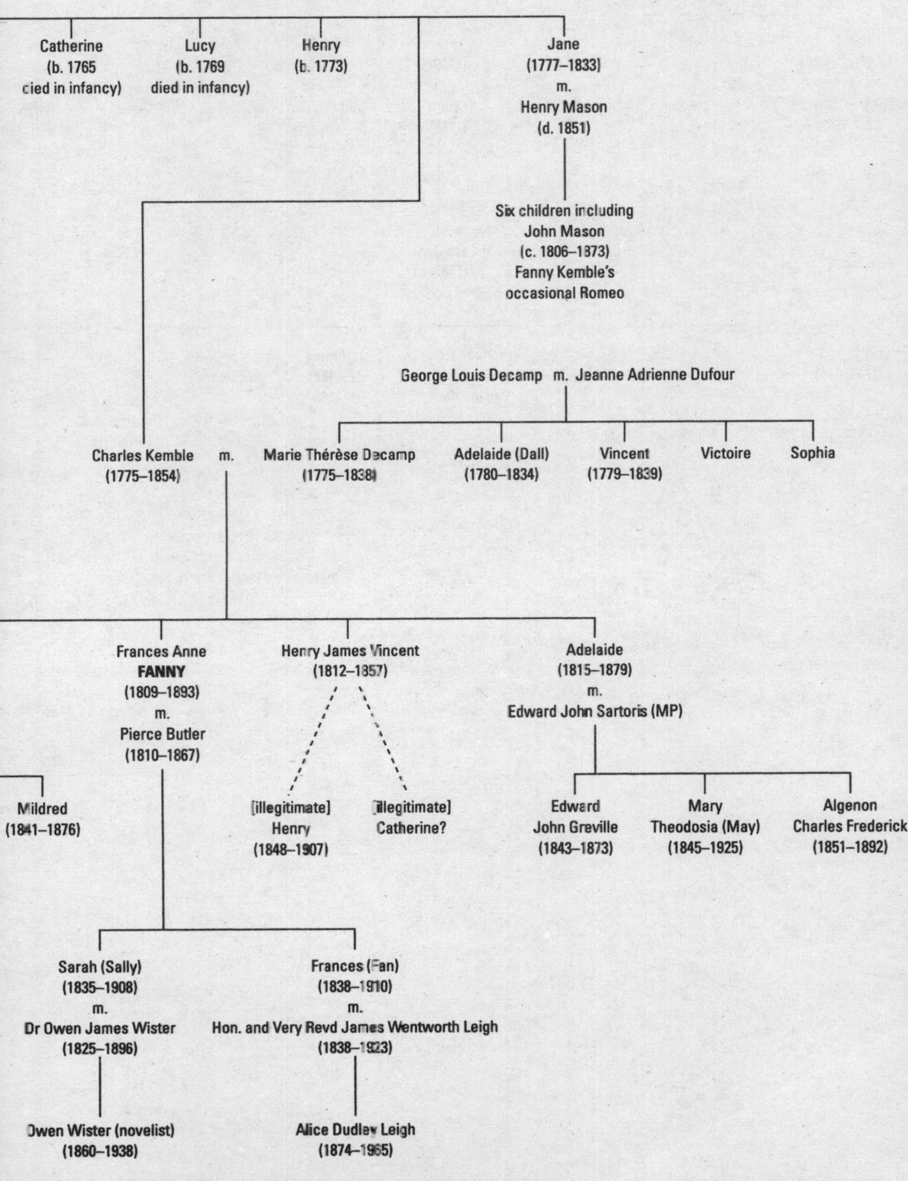
Catherine (b. 1765 died in infancy)
Lucy (b. 1769 died in infancy)
Henry (b. 1773)
Jane (1777–1833) m. Henry Mason (d. 1851)
Six children including John Mason (c. 1806–1873) Fanny Kemble's occasional Romeo
George Louis Decamp m. Jeanne Adrienne Dufour
Charles Kemble (1775–1854) m.
Marie Thérèse Decamp (1775–1838)
Adelaide (Dall) (1780–1834)
Vincent (1779–1839)
Victoire
Sophia
Frances Anne FANNY (1809–1893) m. Pierce Butler (1810–1867)
Henry James Vincent (1812–1857)
Adelaide (1815–1879) m. Edward John Sartoris (MP)
Mildred (1841–1876)
[illegitimate] Henry (1848–1907)
[illegitimate] Catherine?
Edward John Greville (1843–1873)
Mary Theodosia (May) (1845–1925)
Algenon Charles Frederick (1851–1892)
Sarah (Sally) (1835–1908) m. Dr Owen James Wister (1825–1896)
Frances (Fan) (1838–1910) m. Hon. and Very Revd James Wentworth Leigh (1838–1923)
Owen Wister (novelist) (1860–1938)
Alice Dudley Leigh (1874–1965)

ACKNOWLEDGEMENTS

This book has taken four years to write. Its existence owes much to the contribution of others – the friends and family who fed me, bailed me out, listened to my endless theories, and never failed to remind me that I had to finish one day. So thank you to my parents, Mollie and David Jenkins; to Debba Jenkins and Ivor Stolliday, who never gave up on me; to Diane Roberts, for her analysis, constructive criticism and the many fruitful conversations over the years; to Jessica Purkiss and Sebastian Knowles who generously took the time to read raw chapters; to Gail Jordan, Gail Goodall, Fiona McCleod and Dan Lafayeedney and all those who encouraged and sustained me through the long haul.

I am extremely grateful to Peter Siddons and Margaret Sharman who gave me their time, shared their expertise and their fascinating collections of papers and pictures relating to the Kemble and Donne families. All biographers rely on the work of others – this book would not have existed but for the careful research of those who went before. I was very lucky to be given the opportunity to read the unfinished manuscript about Fanny Kemble left by Robert Bernard Martin, the biographer of Tennyson and Edward Fitzgerald. I have benefited greatly from the scholarship of others. I would like to thank the Garrick Club for allowing me access to their wonderful collection of books and pictures.

This book was financially supported by a travel grant from Northern Arts and an exceedingly timely grant from the Society of

Authors which enabled crucial research. I would also like to thank Claire Malcolm of New Writing North for her practical assistance and encouragement.

I am very grateful to those without whom *Fanny Kemble: A Reluctant Celebrity* would never have seen the light: to Helen Gummer who first commissioned the project at Simon & Schuster UK and helped nurture its early development; to my editor Andrew Gordon, for his good sense and admirable patience; to Edwina Barstow for her efficiency, hard work and unfailing courtesy and to Martin Bryant. And finally, thank you to my agent, Christopher Sinclair-Stevenson, for his unshakeable support through many years.

INTRODUCTION

A Reluctant Celebrity

There is one enduring picture attached to the name of Frances Anne Kemble – the Sir Thomas Lawrence drawing. It was the most famous marketing image of her in her day and it markets her still. Within weeks of his death, the courtly Sir Thomas sketched Miss Kemble as a young girl of nineteen soon after she became a theatrical sensation in autumn 1829. Portrayed with the hallmark Lawrence finish and charm, she sits for posterity, cosseted in the billowing folds of her dress, a sleek, doe-eyed young lady looking out to the viewer with a modest confidence.

It is said that the Irish feminist Lady Sydney Morgan was the first to record the word 'celebrity' in print, that same year of 1829, in reference to the peculiar status of famous British personalities. Fanny Kemble was one of the very first cross-Atlantic examples of the breed. Before Victoria was Queen and when the Republic of the United States of America was barely a half a century old, fans collected her picture, mimicked her hairstyles and followed details of her personal life in the columns of newspapers from London to New York.

Ours is a peculiarly visual age. Today as we watch our celebrities on television we like to think that we can assess their humanity from the way they present themselves, but we know in our heart of hearts that much of what we see is honed for a particular demographic. In contrast, we tend to regard our ancestors, before the invention of the forensic eye of the camera, as quaint, simple folk. Here is a portrait. This is the face of our subject. Many likenesses were taken of Fanny Kemble as a young woman at the height of her theatrical career and all were used for commercial purposes. Laid side by side, the extremes of the spectrum are hardly recognizable as the same person. 'I do wish they would leave off trying to take my picture,' she exclaimed at the age of twenty-one. 'My face is too bad for anything but nature, and never was intended for still life.'[1]

Since Fanny Kemble's death in 1893 some dozen biographers have been inspired to write about her and yet, again and again, the melodrama of her life has obscured the person who lived it. It is hard not to be caught up in the dramatic outline of her story – the actress who left career and country to marry for love. Fanny Kemble had her principal residence in the United States for the greater part of her adult life and her biographers, in the main, have been Americans. Given the importance of the Civil War in that country's history, it is hardly surprising that Fanny's account of the time she spent among her husband's slaves, recorded in her *Journal of a Residence on a Georgian Plantation*, should provide their focus. Fanny married at the age of twenty-four. At twenty-four the basic elements of our characters are set. In later life Mrs Kemble liked to exclaim: 'Je suis la plus anglaise des anglais, moi!'* The statement, and the fact that it was invariably made in French, is telling. The perspective from the American record of her life tends to overlook Fanny's European roots.

The parable of the Civil War within a marriage divided over abolition is a neat one, but to my mind it fails to encompass the real story. Fanny Kemble's is not a simple love story; it is the uneasy quest for self-respect of an outsider in society – a story with resonances for anyone who has tried to pursue their own identity when the community demands that they conform.

I first came across Fanny Kemble in a rubbed and cracked leather-

*I am the most English of the English!

bound edition of her *Records of a Girlhood*, her three-volume memoirs of her early life. From the outside, the books promised yet another ponderous Victorian memoir of respectability, but inside the narrative sprang off the desiccated pages. Here was a writer who opened out her world to the reader in an entirely modern way. She described places and people, she made jokes; she conveyed her feelings, her passions, her moments of prejudice and ill-humour with equal honesty; this long-dead woman had left the impression of a soul in a book.

Fanny Kemble's account takes the reader into the world of the Napoleonic War generation, that pivotal generation in which the Georgian age gave way to the Victorian. Fanny was born into the world of Jane Austen, lived through the end of the Napoleonic Wars and through the American Civil War, and died at last a mere eight years before Queen Victoria. She rode on the *Rocket* with George Stephenson and lived to see railways transform the landscape. In a lifetime of travelling between England and the United States she experienced the transition from sail to steam and the two continents brought closer as crossing times shrank from four weeks to seven days.

The history of this period is liberally documented. It is easy enough to compile a chronology of events. Maps lay out the lines of the streets; prints illustrate buildings and interiors; the fixed likenesses of faces are animated by letters, anecdotes and newspaper accounts. But the sense of what it was to live in such a society, to be part of such a culture – a sense of the then common belief, of conventional manners – these things are much more difficult to reconstruct. Charles Mathews (1776–1835), a mimic and satirist and one of the first stand-up comedians, liked to say that 'the stage is the real picture of life and manners'.[2] The picture has elements of caricature, but stage performances and the life of actors off it are no less informative for that.

During this period, actors provide an interesting barometer of social change and the Kemble family particularly so. As a Kemble, Fanny was born into a family that aspired to gentility. In the oligarchical society of George III, which liked to assign the badge of gentility to a combination of family connection, manners and landed wealth, the Kemble clan sought to build their social standing on their professional talents and manners alone. Fanny Kemble's aunt was the great tragic actress Sarah Siddons and her uncle, John Philip Kemble, was the most successful actor-manager of his generation. Actors – as Charles Mathews implies – entertain the society they serve by reflecting back images of itself. Towards the end of the eighteenth century Sarah Siddons and John Philip Kemble became cultural icons, projecting on stage (with the collaboration of some of the leading artists of their day) images of aristocratic nobility that flattered and inspired the ruling elite. For a couple of decades Kemble and Siddons – purveyors of taste to the aristocracy – made an unstable transition from stage to social gentility, but then times changed.

The end of the Napoleonic Wars in 1815 released the full impact of advances in manufacturing techniques, transport and commercial organization, that had been building through the eighteenth century. With bewildering speed, the forces of the industrial revolution crashed through Georgian society to produce the Victorian age. The flows of the new prosperity remodelled the intimate, nobility-dominated culture of eighteenth-century London – that elite which for a time adopted Mrs Siddons and her elegant brother John Philip as junior members. As the Georgian era gave way to the Victorian, the aspiration to gentility was transformed into a middle-class desire to be genteel. The standards of 'taste' set by the cosmopolitan aristocracy of the Enlightenment gave way to sentiment and, above all, the dominance of that very British concept – respectability.

The physical transformation of society during Fanny's lifetime is illustrated by the growth of London, then the cultural capital of the English-speaking world. Fanny Kemble was born on 27 November 1809 into the city that Wordsworth described as he stood on Westminster Bridge seven years earlier –

Ships, towers, domes, theatres & temples lie
Open unto the fields . . .

When she died in 1893, the fields were gone, covered by a population that had quadrupled to over four million.

The London of Fanny's childhood was a city still loosely tethered to its Tudor past. Remnants of the medieval London Bridge spanned the Thames at Southwark.* The Kings Mews, where Henry VIII had housed his falcons, still stood by Charing Cross on a site that was to become part of Trafalgar Square a couple of decades later. This was the old capital of rural England, strung on the two allied webs of patronage and family allegiance spreading out from the aristocracy and court in Westminster, and the merchants of the ancient corporation of London in the City. The growth of the metropolis was confined within walking distance of its centre. When she was a child, Fanny's father, Charles, would finish his performances at Covent Garden†, wipe off his greasepaint and walk three miles through the night over dirt roads to the family's home in what was then the garden suburb of Bayswater on the edge of London. Village developments of elegant, flat-fronted terraces were just beginning to be built amid the market gardens and open fields of Camberwell and Hammersmith, but Belgravia, for instance, was still swamp land, and Islington a popular village to which city dwellers liked to stroll on a mild evening to enjoy the stars and open country.

During Fanny's childhood and teens, newly cash-rich speculators began to tear up and build over this old London of Dr Johnson. The urban sprawl expanded as the first horse omnibus was introduced in the year of Fanny's theatrical debut, 1829, and exploded with the establishment of the railway thirty years later. A German immigrant, the artist George Scharfe, who moved from lodging to lodging in the first decades of the century, has left us evocative sketches of the London streets around him as buildings were torn down, streets relaid and old timber houses gave way to stucco and

---

*Demolished in the 1820s; the new bridge was opened in 1831.

†The Covent Garden theatre of Fanny's childhood was the second theatre, reconstructed after the fire of 1808. It incorporated the site of the present Royal Opera House, standing with its back to the Covent Garden piazza; its grand entrance opened on to Bow Street.

brick. Out of the chaos and brick dust emerged the first metropolis of the industrial age. The cultural style of the Victorian era was epitomized by the Thames Embankment, completed in 1870. The river was held back behind a solid granite wall to create a 100-foot-wide roadway running along the north bank of the Thames between Blackfriars and Westminster Bridge. Statues dotted among the trees lining the Embankment celebrated the heroes of the new age – men such as Robert Raikes, the founder of Sunday Schools, William Tyndale, who by his English translation gave the Bible to the people, and the colonizing general Sir James Outram, credited for subduing rebellious natives, thus enabling the appropriation of the wealth of India. At night the Embankment's smooth curve of regular gas-lamps shone out in the night, a testament to the Victorian ideals of ordering and harnessing both nature and human beings.

The glamour of the Lawrence sketch of Fanny disguises the prejudice she experienced all her life as an actress. Even at the profession's high point at the end of the eighteenth century, her most successful relatives never entirely broke free from the notion that public performance was a sordid occupation pursued by the naturally immoral. This was not just a matter of lingering Puritanism. There was a deep-rooted unease about players' ability to impersonate: to fool audiences and – what was more material to their own moral health – to persuade themselves, into believing sham to be real.

Today when we routinely spend so many hours watching sophisticated dramatizations on television, we have lost a sense of the intoxication of live drama. The power the charismatic performer held over his or her audience in the days before moving images led moralists to fear the seduction of the theatre. The intellectual atmosphere of the Enlightenment contributed to the lifting of that prejudice among the cultural elite. For a brief period actors such as David Garrick, Mrs Siddons and John Philip Kemble elevated the stage – and in particular the performance of tragedy – as a platform for morally instructive exploration of human emotions.

Gradually Jean-Jacques Rousseau's philosophy that too much

civilization corrupted natural goodness amplified a concern to distinguish artificial sentiment from sincere feeling. During the eighteenth century artifice might be admired as a display of skill, but by the nineteenth century it implied an intent to deceive. Actors in general, and the Kembles in particular, fared badly from Romanticism. In the light of 'nature' and 'sincerity' the Kemble manners became mannerisms and their art, artifice. So Fanny Kemble was born into a family that regarded itself as belonging to an aristocracy of artists, and yet lived in an age that increasingly discounted the histrionics of the stage as vulgar and degrading.

In Fanny Kemble the passionate heart of Romanticism struggled to conform to the evangelical soul of Victorian respectability. As Henry James, a close friend in her later years, put it, she was a moralist out of a theatrical nest. In her *Records of a Girlhood*, she expressed the unease of living within that tension. 'Only in England [is] the full bitterness of such experience . . . felt, for what knows the foreign artist of the inexorable element of Respectability.' 'That English moral climate . . . that neutral and temperate tone' that by its 'omnipotent compression, repression, and oppression' preserved the artist class of England from 'the recklessness bred of insecure means and obscure position.'[3]

A central theme of Fanny's adult life was a quest for substance. She wanted to anchor her identity to some purpose less superficial – more 'sincere' – than her celebrity born of an ability to mimic emotion. As much as she aspired to be an artist, she never felt she touched that ideal. 'The finest actor is but a good translator of another man's work,' she wrote, at the height of her theatrical career, 'but he creates nothing, and that seems to me the test of genius, after all.'[4] She never believed in her own worth. It took others to recognize it.

In her time Fanny Kemble made a great impact on the living. This book is not a 'life' in the traditional sense; it is an attempt to retrieve something of what Henry James, that most sentient of observers, described as 'that intense presence . . . that simply continues to impose itself'.[5]

It is my belief that the key to understanding Fanny Kemble lies in the complexity of her family inheritance. Therefore I make no apology for spending my first chapters on her parents' generation. It is important to sketch Fanny's artistic progenitors, Mrs Siddons and particularly John Philip Kemble. The Kemble style articulated the principles of late eighteenth-century aristocratic English culture. That style and its accompanying celebrity was carried over into the next generation – arguably beyond its time – by John Philip Kemble's faithful brother and emulator, Charles. The significance attached to the Kemble name was an inescapable element throughout Fanny's life. Her own actual success on the boards scarcely lasted five years, yet at the end of her eighty-three years, her obituary still began with the claim that 'her name will for ever be associated with the stage'.[6] The family image-makers of the previous generation were so successful in marketing their renown to posterity that the Kemble fame was debatably more potent as myth than in its contemporary reality.

Towards the end of the nineteenth century, Mrs Richmond Ritchie, daughter of the novelist William Makepeace Thackeray and a family friend of several Kembles, wrote that,

> The Kembles strike one somehow as a race apart . . . they seem divided from the rest of us by a more dominant nature, by more expressive ways and looks; and reading of them, one is reminded sometimes of those deities who once visited the earth in guise of shepherds, as wanderers clad in lion skins, as muses and huntresses, not as Kembles only.[7]

Mrs Ritchie's words conjure up the myth wreathed around the Kemble story. That myth was a testament to Fanny's uncle, John Philip, and the professionalism with which he, with the aid of his siblings, constructed the family name.

PART I

THE IMPORTANCE OF BEING A KEMBLE –

The History of a Theatrical House

1

The House that Jack Built

This is the manager, full of scorn, who raised the prices to the people
forlorn,
And directed the thief-taker, shaven and shorn,
To take up John Bull with his bugle-horn,
Who hissed the cat engaged to squall to the poor in pigeon-holes over
the boxes
Let to the great that visit the house that Jack built.

(Anti-Kemble parody printed in *The Chronicle*
at the time of the Old Price Riots.)

On the night of 4 October 1809, John Philip Kemble – actor-manager, leading tragedian of his generation and 'Black Jack' to his enemies – stood on the apron of his stage at the Covent Garden Theatre in London. A veteran of fifty-three, his years of experience enabled him to appear calm, but his palms were sweaty and his pupils contracted with the opium he took to ease his nerves. Before him, the brightly lit auditorium heaved with humanity. Well-dressed tradesmen shook dustmen's bells, young gentlemen of the town halloo'd, whistled, stamped and whirled watchmen's rattles. All around, banners festooned the earthy-pink box-fronts: 'No Kembles', 'Britons be firm', 'Be silent. Mr Kemble's head AITCHES', 'The House that Jack Built'. Up the five galleries to the very ceiling the theatre resounded to the cry: 'OLD PRICES!'[1]

The noise died down to let the manager speak. In his distinctive, measured diction Kemble begged his public's indulgence. Wrapped up in the round-about courtesies of the eighteenth century, his words acknowledged what everyone knew – that his patrons disputed the management's right to raise the prices of admission to one of their favourite theatres. The proprietors contended that the new prices were dictated by the expense of building the fine new theatre in which they stood. Since the opposition was so violent, a committee of 'impartial persons' had been appointed to examine the books. The committee was made up of men of public stature, including the Governor of the Bank of England and the Solicitor General. These gentlemen had now reported. They were satisfied that, were the proprietors to sustain the old prices, in view of the debts incurred in building the new theatre, they would lose three-quarters of a per cent on their investment every year. John Philip Kemble looked down his Roman nose and trusted that men of reason would allow the proprietors their moderate rise in prices.

With a 'Yoikes!' and a 'Tally-ho!' the rattles sounded, bells rang, hundreds of pairs of feet thundered on the floor, and the crowd roared back: 'Old Prices!' To a resounding chorus of 'Britons never will be slaves!' the gentlemen of the pit climbed on their benches and turned their backs to the stage.

The riots had been raging for nearly three weeks. The Riot Act had been read from the stage. It had been howled down. The management imported shaven-headed hard men, professional boxers and Bow Street runners (the 'thief-takers' of the songs) to arrest the leading trouble-makers, but they only prompted more fights. The Italian singer, Mme. Catalani, who had been a major favourite for many seasons, and was engaged at great expense for the opening of the new theatre, hid herself from the mob that shouted abuse about 'Mme. Cat'. John Kemble and his even more famous sister, Sarah Siddons, the stars of the company, also removed themselves from performing to insults after the very first night. Instead, they left the junior members of the family to face the outcry that met any Kemble who continued to perform.

Marie-Thérèse Decamp was one of the newer members of that

family. She had become Mrs Charles Kemble three years previously. Marie-Thérèse was thirty-four and a popular comedienne of French extraction. On the evening of 4 October she was performing as Lucy Lockitt in *The Beggar's Opera*. She was a petite, dark-haired woman with a fine nose and sparkling eyes, her cheeks scarred by small-pox. She had begun her career as a dancer and was known for her grace and good figure – though that figure was temporarily misshapen. Like the character she played that night, Marie-Thérèse was pregnant; seven months pregnant indeed.

Act II, Scene II began. The highwayman, Macheath, in the portly person of the ballad singer Incledon, sat alone in Newgate Prison on a stage littered with scraps of paper on which the letters OP stood out. Lucy swept on:

> 'You base man, you! How can you look me in the face after what hath passed between us?'

She might as well have mimed the words. The crowd roared on cue and a shower of apples hit the stage. Marie-Thérèse, bending as gracefully as her belly would allow, collected up the apples, tossing them off at the wings as she went on with her part. Out in the horse-shoe-shaped auditorium, the rioters pressed to the sides to make a free channel and the more sporting young men ran races over the benches, shredding the new green cloth covers with their heels.

After this night Marie-Thérèse withdrew from the theatre to the family home in Newman Street where she gave birth to the baby she carried on 27 November 1809. Her husband, Charles Kemble, John Philip's handsome little brother (for all he was six foot tall) was left alone among the family to face the mob. Night after night they hooted, mewed, whistled and barked at him – only cheering and stamping when he died as the tyrant Dionysius in the sombre tragedy of *The Grecian Daughter*. Nevertheless, he continued to don the costumes and make-up and go out on that stage to the bitter end.*

---

*John Philip Kemble finally capitulated to the rioters in December 1809.

The baby born in the midst of such strife was Frances Anne Kemble. The third child born to Marie-Thérèse, she came into a world where her uncles, aunt and father represented the Theatrical Establishment. The Kemble clan had achieved this position through hard work, ambition and talent, but also sheer numbers. In an essay she published in late middle-age, Fanny Kemble pointed out that twenty-eight immediate members of her aunt's – Mrs Siddons's – family had been professional actors.[2] When baby Frances made her appearance, her Uncle John Philip had managed one of London's two principal theatres – Covent Garden, for six years, having managed the other at Drury Lane for fifteen years before that. Her Uncle Stephen was also a manager of Theatres Royal in Newcastle and Edinburgh. Numerous aunts and cousins on her father's side were actors of repute in tragedy and comedy, and towering above the whole clan was Mrs Siddons.

Sarah Siddons was a star of such commonly acknowledged talent that at the height of her career she was frequently acclaimed as the greatest actress of all time and the very personification of the Muse of Tragedy. The journalist and theatre critic Leigh Hunt, who was not easy to please, wrote that 'to write a criticism of Mrs Siddons is to write a panegyric, and a panegyric of a very peculiar sort, for the praise will be true.'[3] Even the sourly disposed theatrical journalist Oxberry had to admit that Mrs Siddons on stage 'was a wonderful being, for whom we felt awe, veneration and a more holy love; she was so great in her sufferings, her soul never seemed subdued'.[4]

John Philip Kemble did not share his sister's unique talent for communicating dramatized emotion but he had an intuitive sense for both staging and self-promotion. It was the combination of this brother and sister, and their mutual support and drive, that created the Kemble fame. John Philip and Sarah were the eldest and closest of nine children.* They were both tall and well-proportioned, with thick dark hair and handsome features dominated by soulful brown eyes. Above all,

*Nine children, that is, who survived to adulthood. Sarah and Roger Kemble had another three children who died in infancy.

they had great presence both on and off the stage, carrying themselves with what contemporaries called a 'noble bearing'.

After working her apprenticeship in the provinces, Sarah Siddons became a London star with her heart-wrenching portrayal of the much put-upon heroine Isabella in Thomas Southern's tragedy of *The Fatal Marriage* in October 1782. Within a year she had used her influence to bring her favourite brother to join her at Drury Lane.

John Philip became another overnight success in tragedy, this time in the classic part of Hamlet in 1783. Once Sarah and John Philip were performing side by side in London, their ambition and mutual confidence forged them into a formidable team. The rest of their performing brothers and sisters acted and managed up and down the country and one sister, Mrs Whitlock, crossed the Atlantic to become 'the American Mrs Siddons', but none of them shared in the magical alliance of this pair – until Charles grew up.

Charles Kemble, Fanny Kemble's father, was among the babies of his family. John Philip never had any children, and in some sense Charles's relationship to him was more that of a son or favourite nephew than of a brother. Charles suited the partnership well. His nature was compliant and he was no threat to John Philip's pre-eminence in tragedy, being by ability and physique the 'walking gentleman' type. Charles looked charming in those male lead roles that did not suit his brother – the romantic and light comedy parts such as Romeo or Charles Surface in Sheridan's *School for Scandal*. He too was tall, perhaps even more classically handsome than his brother, and most important of all – he looked like, and had been educated as, a gentleman.

Sarah and John Philip were determined to raise their status in the world. John Philip in particular was fervently ambitious that he and his chosen family would not remain mere actors but be accepted in society as professional gentry.

In the second half of the eighteenth century actors had an uncertain status. Many towns welcomed the entertainment that a troupe of travelling players brought, but if a local magistrate wished to be petty, actors could be locked up as 'rogues and vagabonds', fined and deported to their natal parish under the provisions of the Elizabethan Act of Settlement. Legitimate drama resided in the Theatres Royal.

In London, a monopoly established under the Licensing Act of 1737 meant that Drury Lane and Covent Garden were the only two theatres with the right, enshrined in their Royal Patents, to stage plays. As musical performances were exempted from the licences, managers of other theatrical venues in the capital took refuge behind the convention that the audience was paying for a concert and any drama was performed 'gratis' sandwiched between musical items. London's 'minor theatres' broke up their plays with music, dance, and pantomime – a piece of make-do that contributed to the evolution of a new form, melodrama, which became increasingly popular in the early decades of the nineteenth century. After 1745, when it was used to close the popular but unlicensed theatre at Goodman's Fields, the Licensing Act was strictly enforced in London – apart from one amendment by which the Haymarket Theatre was granted special dispensation to perform plays while the Patent Theatres were closed during the summer.*

For all the rigid social codes we are familiar with from television dramatizations of Jane Austen's novels and the like, the Georgian era was an age of aspiration and social movement. Appearances were important. A social climber must look like a gentleman and behave like a gentleman. Actors were by their profession ideally equipped to adopt the right outward appearances; however, while John Philip Kemble and Mrs Siddons were growing up the player remained an outsider in society. As Samuel Richardson quipped, acting was 'the trade where a Man may represent a gentleman, yet never can be farther from that character'.

John Philip Kemble, when drunk, once told Walter Scott that his family had been 'ruined' for their Royalist sympathies during the Rebellion.[5] This was a story calculated to appeal to the author of Jacobite romances but it was more aspirational than true. To bolster his social status John Philip liked to imply a blood connection to a

*After 1767.

Captain Richard Kemble who had fought for King Charles in the Battle of Worcester. As the story goes, the valiant captain lost a castle near Monmouth rather than sacrifice his honour by submitting to the Parliamentarians. The captain was particularly remembered for claiming the remains of his martyred uncle, another John Kemble. This seventeenth-century John Kemble was a Catholic priest who, at the age of eighty, became caught up in the anti-Catholic hysteria of 1678. Accused of complicity in the so-called 'Titus Oates plot' to assassinate King Charles II, the priestly John Kemble was condemned and executed despite his age and the lack of evidence against him.

Apart from their being Catholics, no one seems to have been able to turn up concrete proof that there was any real connection between the gallant Royalist captain and the acting Kembles. Roger, John Philip's father, came from Catholic stock and raised his sons in his faith (although the daughters followed their mother in the Protestant Church). Roger Kemble's family did spring from Herefordshire, as did the Royalist captain, but there were several groups of Kembles clustered around that county in the late sixteenth and early seventeenth centuries, and numerous families of the same name resided in the Welsh Marches throughout the eighteenth century.

John Philip's story makes skilful use of his Catholic faith. It implied that his bloodline did not spring from a rootless band of strolling players, but rather from a dispossessed member of England's original landed gentry. Walter Scott, with his sense of romance, must have appreciated the association of the foremost interpreter of nobility on stage with a real-life example of heroic gentility in history. The fact that the Kemble family was proud to declare an ancestral connection to this Catholic martyr shows that they envisaged themselves among the genteel classes.*

Being a Catholic under King George III complicated a man's status. To the landed Catholic families with long pedigrees that persisted

*When Mrs Siddons and Charles Kemble visited the grave of the martyred John Kemble during a 'genteel' holiday, they ensured that the item was reported in the society news.

particularly in the North of England, it gave a certain blue-blooded cachet. From 1786 adherence to the 'Romish faith' acquired an additional gloss in London circles, when that leader of the fashionable world, the Prince of Wales, took up a Catholic mistress, Mrs Fitzherbert, with whom he lived for several years. However, to be poor and landless, as well as Catholic, was likely to carry a stigma and a whiff of treachery. Anti-Catholic feeling was still associated in popular culture with John Bull's traditional enemies, the Catholic powers of France and Spain – and in particular with the rebellious Scottish Jacobites who had been crushed so viciously in 1745. Although prejudice was not always overt, it could still coalesce into significant violence – as in the Gordon Riots of 1780. Then several people died in the capital during disturbances orchestrated by Protestant opposition to a Catholic Relief Bill. Up until 1829, legislation prevented Catholics from holding public office, or sitting in Parliament.* Therefore, in the second half of the eighteenth century the legitimate London stage provided one of the few routes to a public reputation for a talented and ambitious young Catholic without money or land.

The acting branch of the Kemble family was founded by Frances Anne Kemble's grandfather, Roger Kemble. He was born in Hereford in 1722, the seventh child of a barber and periwig maker, a freeman of the city. The family was sufficiently well-off to send their son to a 'very respectable' seminary nearby. There Roger received an education which sparked in him aspirations beyond the following of his father's trade. He completed his training as a barber but then, in conformity with the best acting memoirs, disgraced his family and became a strolling player.

After an undistinguished beginning, Roger Kemble's fortunes improved when he married his manager's daughter, Sarah Ward, in

*Unless they were prepared to deny their faith by receiving the Anglican sacrament and rejecting the doctrine of transubstantiation.

1753. He was thirty-one and she a fresh and determined seventeen-year-old. According to the recollections of the couple's somewhat unreliable daughter, Ann Kemble Hatton, his new in-laws thought that Roger Kemble's 'person was his only recommendation, it was obvious to them he had no talent for the stage'.[6] Roger, however, thought he knew how to make the best of his handsome presence. His years at the seminary and then barbering upper-class clients had taught him the manners of a gentleman and he made that manner his trademark. The couple were not long married before the bride's parents felt secure enough to retire. They sold their theatrical properties and wardrobe to their son-in-law in return for an annuity, and Roger Kemble became master of his own company.

Like many of the groups of strolling players at that time, this company was a family affair. Sarah Kemble bore twelve children. Of the nine that survived to adulthood, eight had stage careers. During the fifteen or more years that it toured the western counties of England, Roger Kemble's company built up a reputation for respectability at a time when the popular image of the strolling player was that of John O'Keeffe's 'Rover' in his play *Wild Oats*.* That is, a rogue dressed in tattered finery, who could be relied upon to charm the locals before absconding without paying the bill and possibly carrying off a chicken for good measure. Thomas Holcroft, a playwright who was once a member of their company, described Roger Kemble as easygoing and gentlemanly, while his wife Sarah was the efficient disciplinarian.

Roger Kemble was ambitious that his sons should improve their social status. As soon as he was able to scrape the money together Roger sent his eldest son, John Philip, aged eleven, to a Catholic seminary and then to college in France. Until Gladstone abolished University Religious Tests in 1871, practising Catholics were excluded from attending the English universities. It was Roger Kemble's intention that his son should become a priest, but the English seminary at Douai in France was also traditionally used by

*First performed at Covent Garden in 1791.

English Catholics to give their young men the classical education provided to Anglicans at Oxford and Cambridge.

John Philip's education developed the strong sense of self he gained from his close family upbringing. From his earliest adulthood he displayed a self-confidence and sense of his own dignity that was frequently interpreted by others as unwarranted arrogance in a mere player. (The banker and wit Samuel Rogers used to joke that he could make a fortune by buying Kemble at other people's valuation and selling him at his own.)

The priesthood held no attractions for John Philip. It was hard to imagine any public fame – apart from martyrdom – that a Catholic priest could aspire to in a resolutely Protestant kingdom. When he returned from school in 1775, John Philip defied his father and went on stage. He had a grasp of French, a leaning towards pedantry and a sufficient grounding in the Latin and Greek classics. In addition, he was able to portray priestly roles on stage with striking conviction. As Michael Kelly, a famous Irish tenor and composer and a colleague at Drury Lane, liked to exclaim, John Philip Kemble became the best theatrical priest in the business and 'his Cardinal Wolsey, in *Henry VIII*, was a masterpiece'.[7]

John Philip embarked on his career at a time when the definition of an English gentleman was shifting. As the century progressed the English middle classes blossomed in the flood of mercantile and manufacturing prosperity. The idea of an English gentleman centred less around breeding and bloodlines, and became more a matter of education, wealth and leisure. As one foreign commentator observed: 'The title of gentleman is commonly given in England to all that distinguish themselves from the common sort of people by a good garb, genteel air or good education, wealth or learning'.[8] The way was open for a man of education and culture to make himself a gentleman.

The prejudices against actors were still hard set, but during the middle of the century the mould was – if not broken, distinctly cracked – by one charming individual, Dr Johnson's old pupil and friend, 'Davy' Garrick.

From the time he sprang into public notice with his performance of

Richard III at Drury Lane in October 1741, David Garrick made himself into The Actor of his generation. He was versatile – an outstanding success in both tragedy and comedy – and a gifted entrepreneur. During the 1760s he consolidated his fame as part-proprietor and actor-manager of Drury Lane. Having first walked to London with Dr Johnson from their home town of Lichfield with a couple of pounds in his pocket, Garrick made himself a fortune unparalleled by any English actor who had gone before. A measure of his impact was that during his famous tenure at Drury Lane he lifted the status of the whole of the legitimate theatre. In the words of one newspaper commentator:

> Few while living have arrived at such eminence in their professions as Mr Garrick, and indeed it may be said that while the art has advanced him he has no less advanced the art. What before was considered by our law as a trade taken up by vagrants, is now considered, through his great merits, as a profession tending to promote decency and inspire virtue.[9]

When Garrick retired in 1775 it was to a country estate on the Thames at Hampton. The walls of his villa there were hung with portraits of himself and his wife painted in the style of a gentleman and his lady. In his gardens, in aristocratic fashion, he built a temple to house a specially commissioned statue of Shakespeare (a statue whose features bore a remarkable similarity to Garrick's own). When he died, little Davy Garrick was buried in Westminster Abbey – one of the very few of his profession to be accorded that honour. His monument in Poet's Corner recorded the means by which the actor achieved this elevation.

> *To paint fair Nature, by divine command,*
> *Her magic pencil in his glowing hand,*
> *A Shakespeare rose: then, to expand his fame,*
> *Wide o'er this breathing world a Garrick came.*

In the course of the reformulation of British national identity following the Glorious Revolution of 1688, English nationalism harked back to the self-confidence and pride of the Elizabethan era. The distinguishing feature around which this new sense of English culture coalesced was Shakespeare. Ever since the 1730s and the days of the Shakespeare Ladies' Club when fashionable ladies banded together to promote the Bard's plays as a moral alternative to the decadence of Restoration comedies and imported Italian operas, Shakespeare was put forward as the standard of good English taste. In 1741 – the year of Garrick's London début – the Bard of Avon was officially enshrined in Westminster Abbey with a statue in Poet's Corner. Soon afterwards it was decided that since Shakespeare was baptized on the 26 April it was reasonable that he should have been born on the feast day of St George, 23 April. From then on the patron saint of England and the patron poet of Englishness could be commemorated together.

Garrick built his fame by convincing his contemporaries that 'if nature wrote through Shakespeare, the poet in his turn spoke best through Garrick'.[10] In 1769 he organized his famous pageant in Stratford-upon-Avon to celebrate Shakespeare's jubilee. The event itself was very nearly rained off, but it confirmed the ascension of Shakespeare as National Poet. The jubilee was followed by a rash of cheap publications of the plays, one of the most popular series being that of Shakespeare's plays 'As they are now Performed in the Theatres Royal in London'.[11]

This was the age of the actor. The period from Garrick's management to the close of John Philip Kemble's career came to be looked back on by subsequent generations as a golden age of the English theatre. This was partly because, for the London audiences of the late eighteenth century, Shakespeare represented more than a skilful dramatist and an outstanding poet. He was, as Dr Johnson wrote,

> above all writers, at least above all modern writers, the poet of nature; the poet that holds up to his readers a faithful mirrour of manners and of life.[12]

The legitimate theatre acquired status as a place of moral instruction as well as entertainment. William Robson, self-declared Kemble 'clansman', wrote lyrically in his memoirs *The Old Playgoer* about the impact the performances of John Philip Kemble and Sarah Siddons had on him:

> Images of beauty and feeling! . . . ye helped me to love the lovely, to understand the intellectually grand.[13]

When culture was largely the province of the aristocrats revolving around the Royal Court, people were just as likely to read plays as see them performed, but the more business-like gentleman of the late eighteenth century was less inclined to waste his leisure hours poring over texts. As James Boaden, John Philip Kemble's biographer, noted:

> The bulk of mankind have neither leisure nor faculties for very accurate study; they must be content with the interpretation of actors.

In short, John Philip Kemble arrived in London just as Garrick's retirement opened up the possibilities for a gentlemanly successor. If the model of English genius was Shakespeare, then the actor, his chief interpreter, could similarly be raised by the Aristocracy of the Word. Armed with his gentlemanly education, his noble figure and his ambition, John Philip set out to become an arbiter of classic taste for his generation.

2

An Aristocracy of the Word

When John Philip Kemble arrived in the West End in 1783 to join His Majesty's servants at 'Garrick's House', the Theatre Royal Drury Lane, he was just another public entertainer. In the nightly programme of the two Patent theatres (Drury Lane and Covent Garden), drama competed for attention with farces, pantomimes and ballets. Even a successful play would only normally be repeated for a few nights. As stock members of the Drury Lane company, Sarah Siddons and John Philip Kemble sang songs, danced and played both comic and tragic parts. Under such conditions it was hard for an actor to project the dignity of an artist.

Their first advantage was that the elder Kembles *looked* noble. Like his sister, John Philip Kemble was made for tragedy. Even towards the end of his career, the journalist and leading theatre critic Leigh Hunt would wax lyrical about Kemble's 'manly and dignified' figure. The actor's features, he said, were 'strongly marked with what is called the Roman character, and his head altogether . . . the heroic head of the antiquary and the artist'. At a time when actual royalty was embodied in a shy and soon-to-be mad king, and a selfish and dishonourable prince, Mrs Siddons and John Philip Kemble portrayed noble humanity on stage in a way that soothed the British spirit. During the years of the Napoleonic Wars, in the words of one historian, theatre-going was enhanced as 'an informal act of mass public patriotism, a chance to luxuriate in the display of English virtue'.[1] When John Philip played Coriolanus or Mrs Siddons *was* Queen Katherine, the audience could sing with confidence that 'Britons never shall be slaves', however much the rumblings of Revolution across the Channel – followed in 1793 by out-and-out war with France – might threaten their island security.

Like Garrick, both brother and sister projected their dignified personas beyond the stage through the medium of portraits. Their striking good looks made them attractive sitters for artists but they were additionally fortunate in that their careers coincided with a vibrant period in British painting. The foundation of the Royal Academy in 1768 under the patronage of George III had given artists a firm place in the British establishment. The Academy's annual Summer Exhibition provided a prominent venue for art, opening up public access to painting. Exhibitors gained celebrity – along with rich commissions. The portrait in oils became fashionable as Gainsborough, Reynolds, Romney, Hoppner and others competed against one another.

Sir Joshua Reynolds, the first President of the Royal Academy, paralleled Garrick in his determination to raise the status of his art. Whereas Garrick sought validity as an interpreter of Shakespeare, it was Reynolds's vision to elevate portraiture by establishing a canon of rules drawn from the Old Masters. He marked his presidency with a famous series of lectures, his *Discourses*, in which he set out his definition of the classical principles of colour and composition; principles he hoped would be further disseminated through the drawing studios of the Royal Academy. Naturally, other artists challenged his authority – one of the most acute rivalries being that between Reynolds and Gainsborough.

At the time of the Royal Academy Summer Exhibition of 1785, Gainsborough chose the thirty-year-old star of Drury Lane to make his point. His portrait of Mrs Siddons was a deliberate refutation of the conservative doctrines of Reynolds. Sir Joshua followed the studio tradition – that is, he regularly employed other artists to create drapery and landscape elements within his paintings. The president liked to depict his female sitters in classical drapery, believing that it elevated his subject. In his eighth *Discourse* he had made a point of pronouncing against the use of cold colours – blues, greys and greens – in the 'masses of light in a picture'. So when Gainsborough presented Mrs Siddons in a luxuriant blue dress in the height of contemporary fashion, demonstrating his superior skill in handling all the details, even down to the fur on her foxskin muff, the challenge to Sir Joshua was obvious and much relished by commentators.

Mrs Siddons's celebrity greatly benefited from the publicity. Through the next decade she and her brother carefully cultivated relationships with fashionable artists. Whereas the common run of actors around them were recorded in the crude outlines of theatrical prints, the King and Queen of tragedy were memorialized in canvases of genuine artistic merit. Thomas Beach painted them in oils as *Macbeth and Lady Macbeth*. Sir Joshua Reynolds himself immortalized Mrs Siddons as *The Tragic Muse*. These were paintings exhibited to fashionable society and reproduced in innumerable prints and engravings. However, beyond the lavish portrayals of stage roles, the portraits most significant to their legend were those that portrayed them in their private character, as persons of education and consequence. In this respect, their most fruitful artistic collaboration was with Thomas Lawrence.

Thomas Lawrence, it is said, first set eyes on Mrs Siddons as a young boy of ten, when the twenty-six-year-old star of the Bath stage stopped at the Black Bear in Devizes, the inn kept by his father in the late 1770s. She was building her career towards her triumphant success in London in 1782 and he was a child prodigy, flaunted before guests by an exuberant father for his skill in sketching likenesses. The boy – sensitive to beauty even at that young age – was enchanted by the star's presence. For the rest of his life Lawrence cherished an odd combination of mother-fixation and adoration of Mrs Siddons as muse, painting and sketching her again and again, and even falling in love with both of her elder daughters in turn.

When John Philip Kemble died, his widow told Lawrence of the pride he had felt in 'having conviction that by your aid he would be remembered'.[2] Over a lifetime association Lawrence painted and sketched all the key members of the Kemble and Siddons families – Mrs Siddons and her daughters, John Philip and Charles, and even their parents. By Lawrence's skill Roger and Sarah Kemble acquired an oak-aged dignity that transformed the travelling player and his wife into ancestors worthy of a genteel dynasty.

Lawrence explained his approach to portraiture by a passage from Aristotle's *Poetics* that describes good portrait painters as artists who while preserving a resemblance, yet made it more beautiful. As John Philip Kemble and Sarah Siddons portrayed elemental passions on stage, so Lawrence sought to reflect the qualities of innocence, vivacity, dignity, bravery, pride and so on that his imagination perceived in his sitters. His style was an appropriate artistic match for the persona John Philip established in his early years at Drury Lane. There he honed a statuesque deportment – haughty, intense, invulnerable and contained. (Hazlitt suggested ironically that Kemble's tendency to hold poses partly grew out of his fine figure – knowing that he could stay still 'in the same posture for half an hour' confident that 'his figure would only excite admiration'.)

John Philip's supporters liked to call him 'the Last of the Romans'. Contemporaries particularly admired his performance as Coriolanus, personifying a patrician full of haughty dignity, 'energy of will and unbending sternness of temper throughout'.[3] It was these elements, blended with an overweening arrogance, that Lawrence captured in his *Kemble as Coriolanus*. This 'half-history picture' as the painter described it, was one of the successes of the 1798 exhibition – the *True Briton* declaring it to be painted 'with a powerful hand . . . suitable to the elevated character of a historical portrait'.[4]

John Philip Kemble was a born networker. With the assistance of his ambitious wife, Priscilla, he gathered around his table men of wit and talent; a company that in turn attracted a range of aristocratic acquaintances.

In the mid 1780s Drury Lane was under the control of the playwright Richard Brinsley Sheridan. Sheridan, along with two partners, had bought a half-share in the patent from David Garrick on the latter's retirement in 1775. That year Sheridan had two runaway successes with *The Rivals* and *The Duenna*. *School for Scandal* followed in 1777, by which time Sheridan was the most fashionable playwright of his generation. But after this meteoric beginning, he frittered away much of his creative energies in pursuit of his social ambitions and political career.

Success in the fashionable world of late eighteenth-century London was a face-to-face business. David Garrick, Richard Sheridan and John Philip Kemble stood out as men of talent who won the friendship of noble patrons who, in turn, publicly endorsed them as natural gentlemen – men of sense and education as well as wit and polish. The fact that aristocrats opened their houses to these actors – and more particularly, accepted their hospitality in return – was a highly prized sign of intimacy. Nonetheless, the relationship remained a delicate one, and the wise social climber knew not to presume on it.

The relationship between Kemble and Sheridan was uneasy. Sheridan, the son of an Irish actor-manager, played the gentleman so well that he could almost make his blue-blooded friends forget his origins. He was nonetheless conscious of the fragility of his social position. Sheridan kept his distance, as far as possible, from his actors. John Philip Kemble, however, was determined to follow Sheridan into the inner circles of the fashionable set grouped around the Duke and Duchess of Devonshire and the Prince of Wales. It took him a decade but by 1796 the biographer James Boaden would observe John Philip and his wife Priscilla 'playing the great worldly games, and strengthening themselves by splendid connexion'[5] as they welcomed the fashionable aristocracy to their country house at Harrow Weald.

Off stage, John Philip created his social persona with a meticulous eye for detail, cultivating the air of a scholarly gentleman.* He

---

*William Robson, who, it must be admitted was an ardent fan, described in *The Old Playgoer* the role John Philip played in private life: 'with somewhat stately carriage, a little stooping forward withal . . . and his apparent perpetual thoughtfulness, there was a blandness, a kindness, a suavity, that spoke him to be the character I am sure he coveted as much as he did that of a great actor – a good man and a gentleman', p. 24.

anticipated the dress code of a contemporary who also rose from obscure origins to become an arbiter of taste – Beau Brummel.

> In his cloaths and dress Mr Kemble preserved the Ciceronian medium, a perpetual cleanliness, without the appearance of pains; free from the affectation of singularity; and avoiding the extremes of rustic negligence and foppish delicacy.[6]

Early on in his London career he published a carefully considered essay on *Macbeth*.* During the 1790s he began to collect a significant dramatic library. He cultivated the society of literary celebrities, particularly the more scholarly ones such as Edward Malone and Isaac Reed, who were leading authorities on Elizabethan literature. More of a pedant than a poet, Kemble's learning was of the dry kind. He enjoyed compiling lists of snippets about stage history. For instance, he copied out one hundred and thirty pages of extracts from the Dublin *Journal* concerning the history of that city's Theatre Royal.[7]

The unkind might suggest that Kemble's interest in literature was 'minute, grammatical and verbal' and that he only began his library in a desire to outclass Garrick's collection of 'dramatic curiosities', but his collection of early English drama became celebrated. 'No man knows more, or better, whatever relates to the History of the Drama; no man possesses more copies, more valuable materials; no man communicates what he knows and possesses, to his friends, with greater or more agreeable facility.'[8] By the time his library was sold at his retirement it held over 4000 English plays and 40 volumes of playbills.

After five years at Drury Lane John Philip had established his reputation as the leading male tragedian of his day, but his vision for the Drama required that he move into management. He became

*Sarah Siddons was later to do the same, publishing an essay on the role of Lady Macbeth. In the next generation, Fanny Kemble was to maintain the family tradition with her *Notes on Some Characters in Shakespeare's play of* Macbeth – 1867.

Sheridan's acting manager at Drury Lane in the autumn of 1788. Delivering a combination of tested stock pieces and a series of acclaimed Shakespearean revivals (spiced up with Sheridan's flare for introducing eye-catching stage effects) the new actor-manager made the most of an excellent company of actors. He built a reputation for a high standard of artistic production. It was likely that Drury Lane might have achieved financial solvency – but for Sheridan's monstrous debts.

By the late 1790s Sheridan was becoming increasingly difficult to work with. Although his attention was mostly on his political career, he would not loosen his hold on Drury Lane. The theatre's treasury was his piggy bank. Sheridan was shameless about spending other people's money. He frequently swept in to carry off the box-office receipts, slipping out of a back door to avoid the anxious actors and stage personnel queuing outside the treasurer's office for their wages.

John Philip was determined to become a proprietor. Only then could he gain the freedom to mount the productions he dreamed of and cap his career as the true successor to Garrick. By the end of the 1801–2 season, he had had enough. He walked out of Drury Lane taking his sister, Mrs Siddons, and their brother Charles with him.

John Philip then negotiated with Thomas Harris, the manager of Covent Garden, to transfer his services and those of Mrs Siddons to the rival house. He was now forty-six, and he was taking a calculated risk. Management more often than not led to bankruptcy – a fact he had plenty of time to contemplate during his association with Sheridan – but the possession of property was the only way for a man of talent to cement his position as a gentleman. After several months of negotiation, he acquired a sixth share of the Covent Garden patent and assumed the artistic management of that theatre. The Kemble House was ready to make its début.

3

Covent Garden: The Kemble House

During 1803 the new alliance between the Kemble clan and Covent Garden was the talk of London as the play-going public anticipated the transfer of the 'seat of tragedy' to the rival theatre. For several years the Garden had been trailing the Lane in that department, being associated more with comedy and farce. Excitement was in the air. Covent Garden was spruced up, the auditorium repainted 'chastely dead white and gold' and the insides of the boxes in 'party-coloured green'. Through the summer carpenters had been at work carving sixteen new private boxes out of the public space. These were decorated and gilded to attract the cream of society at an annual rent of £300. John Philip Kemble was bringing several aristocratic patrons with him to his new house. Despite his somewhat unbending manner (unless drunk) he was popular with aristocratic ladies – the Duchesses of Northumberland and Devonshire (the 'divine Georgiana'), the Marchioness of Abercorn and Lady Holland. In short, he stole away some of Sheridan's most glittering supporters.

On 24 September 1803 John Philip made his first appearance at Covent Garden under the new management in *Hamlet*. Three days later Mrs Siddons followed him as Isabella in *The Fatal Marriage*. As if to underline the point that tragedy had moved to the Garden, both repeated the roles they had first made their names with at Drury Lane.

In his first season (1803–4) John Philip brought out eleven Shakespeare plays in six months, staging lavish revivals of, among others, *King John* and *The Tempest*. Much though he might display himself as a 'scholar and a ripe one', Kemble continued to follow the eighteenth-century fashion of adapting Shakespeare, mauling the original texts to make a good show. His production of *The Tempest or The Enchanted Island*, for instance, was a spectacular mish-mash of Dryden and Shakespeare, all dressed up with music by Purcell and Arne. It featured Dryden's additional secondary couple of Miranda's younger sister Dorinda 'who never saw a man' and her beau Hippolyto 'who never saw a woman' – no doubt because the audience liked their slightly saucy sideshow. The production was a great hit with audiences but some of John Philip's scholarly friends expressed reservations. They also carped about his handling of the text in his splendid revival of *Henry VIII* in April 1805.

As the years passed these contemporary quibbles were glossed over. In the next decade Henry Harlow confirmed the production's fame by using *Henry VIII* as inspiration for his large historical canvas *The Trial of Queen Katherine*.* History painting in the grand manner normally featured biblical or mythological subjects. Here the leading members of the Kemble clan were memorialized for posterity as the dramatic embodiment of a piece of English history. Mrs Siddons as Queen Katherine forms the focal point of the picture, looking straight out at the observer. Charles Kemble sits behind the table as Cromwell, and behind him, his brother Stephen, seated on a raised throne, is King Henry. And to the left sits the figure of John Philip, bulky in his red robes, his features framed by his cardinal's hat as Wolsey.

It is worth noting that John Philip's understanding of 'authenticity' in relation to staging Shakespeare was not about

*Exhibited at the Royal Academy in 1817.

historical accuracy. As the historian of the Georgian playhouse, Richard Southern, explains, 'to the Georgian mind any conception of scenery as factual background to action was wholly unmeaning and indeed alien'.[1] When a pedantic acquaintance, the respected historian Francis Douce, pointed out to Kemble that his production of *Coriolanus* should be set amongst the unadorned brick buildings of Republican Rome,* John Philip exclaimed in horror, 'If I did . . . they would call me an antiquarian!'[2] John Philip's idea of historical staging was to reproduce classicism as depicted in the canvases of Poussin and Claude. His reputation for bringing scholarship to his productions was enhanced by his association with the painter William Capon. Capon, well known as an illustrator of medieval architecture, was commissioned to paint a series of stage drops for him at both Drury Lane and Covent Garden. In these were accurate representations of Tudor and medieval buildings. But Capon never designed a whole production; his drops and wings were basic pieces interspersed with other stock. Similarly, in costume, John Philip's innovations 'rendered them more picturesque, but added little to their propriety'.[3] Once at Covent Garden, he did away with such things as Garrick's habit of dressing Macbeth as a British general officer of around 1770, introducing an equally historically inaccurate, but more appropriate, Highland dress complete with kilt. Generally speaking, Kemble's innovations were so that 'enough should be done . . . to prevent the illusion being too roughly disturbed, but not enough to distract attention from the essentials'.[4] In his Shakespearean tragedies, the actor was still the main focus – and not the scenery or costumes.

He did, however, parade his pedantry in what he convinced himself were 'authentic' Shakespearean pronunciations. Leigh Hunt complained that John Kemble's great fault was a 'laborious and almost universal preciseness'. The tragedian suffered from asthma

*That is, because according to history it was the first Emperor, Caesar Augustus, who boasted that he found Republican Rome clothed in brick and left her dressed in marble.

and he overcame breathing difficulties by projecting his voice in a higher register than normal in a measured and distinct delivery. It made him vulnerable to parody. Hunt mocked that 'his words now and then follow one another so slowly, and his face all the while assumes so methodical an expression, that he seems reckoning how many lines he has learnt by heart'.[5] According to Kemble a beard was pronounced a 'bird'; a heart was not pierced but 'pursed', and he pronounced the 'my' in 'smashed my hat' exactly in the same manner as the 'me' in 'knocked me down'. This latter, at least, reflected the dialect of the Devonshire House set, so although his ostensible reason for the habit was scholarship it also implied his familiarity with the most fashionable and aristocratic Whigs.

His most famous débâcle over pronunciation arose around his revival of *The Tempest* at Covent Garden. He insisted that Prospero, at the end of Act I, Scene I, should threaten Caliban that he would 'fill all his bones with aches' – pronouncing the latter word 'aitches'. Scholars then and now have agreed that it is perfectly proper to give the word two syllables, but the pitites howled him for it. Never one to yield to the mob in matters of taste, John Philip persisted. 'Mr Kemble' wrote Leigh Hunt severely,

> does not use this pronunciation from a regard either for Shakespeare or the audience; we must attribute it of that self-possession or self-confidence which in all ages has enabled great men to be perfectly satisfied with themselves, though the whole world were unable to tell why.[6]

Despite such rebukes, Leigh Hunt's criticism was in itself a measure of John Philip's success. During his management at Covent Garden theatrical criticism emerged as a serious exercise in aesthetics. The theatre critic – as Sheridan's comedy *The Critic* makes clear – was a familiar character in the late eighteenth century. However, occasional columns in the press were recognized as 'puffery', a debased journalism allied to paid publicity. Starting with Leigh Hunt's *Critical Essays on the Performers of the London Theatres* (published in book form in 1807), writers such as Hunt and then William Hazlitt developed the genre with literate essays that discussed acting as a legitimate branch of the arts.

As the century approached its end, the 'men of taste' appeared to be in firm control of the Drama. But the record of oil paintings and essays can be deceptive. Times were changing. In 1794 Henry Holland renovated Drury Lane, doubling its capacity. Now the cavernous space held just over 3500 spectators. Covent Garden was gradually expanded to follow suit. The shift in size meant that the business on stage now had to be intelligible to spectators who could be sitting a hundred feet from the actors. Effects that were telling in an intimate playhouse holding 500 people were lost to half the seats in the new auditorium. Spectacle and 'novelties' became increasingly necessary. High tragedy needed to be sandwiched between animal acts, tight-rope walkers and 'prodigies' such as Master Betty, the thirteen-year-old who sing-songed his way through grand tragedy parts to considerable financial success through two seasons from autumn 1804.

John Philip knew how to trim his ambitions to the prevailing wind. His vision was on a grand scale. His production of *Coriolanus* at Covent Garden, for instance, included a triumphal procession in which over two hundred extras paraded as a succession of vestals, lictors, soldiers, senators, silver-eagle bearers, drummers, trumpeters, priests and dancing girls.[7]

However successful he might be in adapting to the taste of the times, John Philip continued to insist on his status as a gentleman. In 1806 while he was playing Coriolanus, Mrs Siddons, in the part of the majestic matriarch Volumnia, was struck by an apple thrown from the galleries. Kemble stopped the performance. Striding to the front of the stage he declared, 'We cannot proceed this evening unless we are protected, especially when ladies are thus exposed to insult.' He was heckled and booed, but stood his ground. In cold fury he announced that the management offered a hundred guineas to whoever would give up 'the ruffian who has been guilty of this act'.

'I will raise my voice, and the galleries *shall* hear me. This protection is what the audience owe it to themselves to grant, and what the performers, for the credit of their profession, have a right to demand.'

The hecklers were silenced.

It looked as if John Philip might be on course for a tomb near Garrick's in the Abbey. Then, on the evening of 19 September 1808, during a performance of Sheridan's *Pizarro*, wadding from a gun fired during the performance became lodged in some scenery and smouldered. During the night fire broke out and by six o'clock the following morning the theatre was gutted. The tragedy was compounded when passers-by and firemen tackling the blaze were crushed by falling roof timbers. Eleven people died in the rubble and eleven more succumbed to their injuries. The theatre fire consumed John Philip Kemble's capital and sealed the fate of the Kemble family for two generations.

James Boaden gives an account of his visit of condolence to John Philip's house in Great Russell Street on the morning of 20 September. Charles Kemble sat shocked in smoke-saturated clothes, having been called out to the scene of the disaster in the early hours of the morning when the theatre was already all but gone. The bird-like 'Pop', John Philip's wife, Priscilla, hovered around her husband who stood half dressed in front of the mirror.

While he shaved himself John Philip addressed the company with a peculiar oration:

> Yes, it has perished – that magnificent theatre. It is gone with all its treasures of every description . . . That library which contained all those immortal productions of our countrymen prepared for the purpose of representation. That vast collection of music, composed by the greatest geniuses in that science, by Handel, Arne and others. That wardrobe, stored with the costumes of all ages and nations, accumulated by unwearied research, and at incredible expense. Scenery, the triumph of the art, unrivalled for its accuracy, and so exquisitely finished . . . Of all this vast treasure, nothing now remains but the

arms of England over the entrance of the theatre and the Roman eagle standing solitary in the market-place.[8]

James Boaden was a journalist and playwright who wrote several 'lives' of famous actors. John Philip was well aware of his presence. He was making a statement about the artistic priorities for which he wished to be remembered. First he speaks of the library – he is not just a player but a scholar. The lost music is no collection of popular songs; it is a treasured cultural archive, including original scores by Handel and Arne (the author of the music for 'Rule Britannia' – 'Britons never shall be slaves!' – and perhaps the most famous English composer of his generation). The lost wardrobe is no clutter of pasteboard crowns and tattered finery, these are pieces of historic reconstruction, 'accumulated by unwearied research'. The scenery too is elevated from routine backdrops. These stretches of canvas are 'a triumph of art', 'unrivalled for accuracy'. The whole picture is finished off with the striking image of the Roman eagle standard rising above the destruction – reminding posterity that he, John Kemble, the 'last of the Romans' and the dramatic heart of Covent Garden, still stood proud. As a piece of PR the self-promotion is masterly. Perhaps his greatest skill was in leaving dramatic vignettes, whether in print or on canvas, on which the Kemble myth could be founded.

The destruction of Covent Garden was like a family home burning down. Mrs Siddons lost her entire theatrical wardrobe – all the many pieces she had collected over her illustrious career. Valuable items, such as a veil of point lace that had once belonged to 'the poor Queen of France' Marie-Antoinette and all the stage jewels accumulated over thirty years. And as for John Philip, as his sister put it, 'my poor dear brother had to begin the world again' – not an easy challenge for a man of fifty-two.

John Philip showed his mettle. His sister described him to a friend as bearing his misfortunes 'most nobly with manly firmness, hope and even cheerful resignation'.[9] He set to work to raise the money to rebuild his theatre. The old building had been under-insured. The proprietors were only awarded £45,000, far short of the costs of reconstruction. However, the time and trouble John Philip and Priscilla had put in to wooing the aristocracy over the years paid off. The Duke of Northumberland set the subscriptions rolling in with a hand-out of £10,000 and the rebuilding fund mounted up. The first stone of the new theatre was laid by the Prince of Wales on 30 December 1808 with great state and Masonic ceremony (John Philip, a stickler for detail as ever, having been admitted to the Masonic Lodge the night before).

Far from being cowed by his misfortunes, John Philip seized this opportunity to build a new temple of drama worthy of his conception of his art. The proprietors found an energetic young architect by the name of Richard Smirke. Smirke was twenty-eight and had returned from a continental tour four years previously in the grip of Greek revivalism. His designs for the new Covent Garden, which drew heavily on the Parthenon, matched John Philip's formal and stiff classicism to perfection.

The main contractor, Alexander Copland, had made his reputation for speed and solid construction putting up barracks at the height of the Invasion scare four years before. In double-quick time there was a grand new entrance facing on to Bow Street, its solemn Greek portico resting on four hefty Doric columns. The bas-reliefs that ran along the front of the building signalled the proprietors' cultivation and classical taste. On the south side sat Shakespeare with his poet's lyre, with the masks of comedy and tragedy at his feet and surrounded by figures from *The Tempest* – this enchanted isle. John Philip had his temple.* The upshot was that the proprietors opened their new theatre carrying debts that had risen to the region of £209,000.

All at once the rumblings of the anti-Kemble feeling that had built up through the years of the family's supremacy began to break out in earnest. The theatre historian and commentator Genest, who

*Significantly, only two contemporary actors were memorialized in the fabric of the theatre. Sarah Siddons and John Philip Kemble had their portraits moulded in bas-relief, a classical form that signalled their enduring fame.

was never a Kemble supporter, complained that after such a loss, the proprietors should have exercised economy in building their replacement. He labelled the overspending on the new theatre as being 'for the gratification of Kemble' rather than the 'accommodation of the public'. He complained that the price of the boxes had risen from 5 to 6 shillings only seventeen years before and now were raised again to 7 shillings (these were the days before inflation). Not only that, but the proprietors were also raising the price of admission to the pit by sixpence to 4 shillings.

As has been mentioned, when John Philip first became a proprietor at Covent Garden in 1803, there had already been a refit with sixteen boxes being added. The trick had worked before, so this time he built more boxes. By squeezing the public galleries he added a whole new circle, raising the number to twenty-eight exclusively reserved for private subscribers. These boxes each had a small antichamber veiled from the public gaze. Not only that, but they were reached by a separate private entrance and staircase. This and the grand saloon reserved for the private subscribers meant that, for the first time, the rich could patronize the theatre without ever having to rub shoulders with the vulgar masses. The advocates of the ordinary playgoers, who were thus squeezed into what they called the 'pigeon holes' of the cramped upper galleries, resented this further example of Kemble 'avarice and pride'.

The newspaper commentators suggested that the only possible reason for such privacy in the boxes could be to veil immoral acts. This was a revival of 'French' aristocratic decadence. Leigh Hunt protested in the *Examiner* that it was against British principles of democracy to remove an entire tier from 'lovers of theatre' to 'make privacies for the luxurious great'.[10]

As the opening night of the new theatre approached, rumours circulated that £25,575 had been spent on the salaries and benefits of the Kembles, Mrs Siddons and the Italian singer Mme Catalani alone. For several years journalists, disappointed rivals and others had carped about the 'avarice' of the Kemble clan. The professional ambitions of Mrs Siddons and her brother had not inclined them to make friends among their fellow performers. The actor turned journalist Oxberry claimed to represent the Green Room when he wrote that,

> We were always too afraid of John Kemble. Mrs Siddons, too, was awful . . . even Charles, gentle Charlie, had a disdainful look, a scornful brow, and his affability always bore the air of condescension.[11]

On the afternoon before the grand opening of the new Covent Garden Theatre James Boaden was worried. As he made his rounds, collecting the gossip at the newspaper offices and coffee houses, he was struck by the level of indignation against the new prices:

> I saw a prospect of annoyance, such as made me tremble for my friends. I told Mr Kemble what I knew; but he smiled at my terrors – and so late as two o'clock on the day of opening, I saw him in Bow-Street, quite perpendicular and confident, with a heap of papers under his arm, which he was himself going to deliver to the offices of our journals.[12]

That evening of 18th September 1809, Kemble, resplendent in his 'superb' costume as Macbeth, stepped to the front of his stage to speak the opening address in his brand new theatre and was halted in his tracks. The riots had begun – and they were to run for sixty-seven nights.

For all his gentlemanly friends, his aristocratic patrons, his scholarly library and pursuits, John Philip Kemble found himself unprotected. His friend Mrs Inchbald exclaimed in frustration –

> The favourite song of the rioters is, *Britons never shall be slaves* – but they seem to think the managers of a theatre are to be condemned to the vilest slavery – the will of the mob. As players were out of the pale of the Church under the late government in France, so WE would now exclude them from the protection of our laws.[13]

John Kemble was attacked from all sides. Even *The Times*, supposedly a supporter of the proprietors during the days to come, reported gleefully on the disturbance:

> It was a noble sight to see so much just indignation in the public mind, and we could not help thinking, as Mr Kemble and Mrs Siddons stood on the stage, carrying each £500 in clothes upon their backs, that it was to feed this vanity, and to pay an Italian singer, that the public were screwed.

The player king and queen had got above their station and were to be put in their place. This was spelled out in no uncertain terms. As a placard from the night of 21 October recorded by Stockdale makes clear:

> *King John of old, by sturdy barons aw'd,*
> *Our British rights in Magna Carta sign'd;*
> *To stage crown'd John, in insolence and fraud,*
> *Shall our dramatic rights be now resign'd?*
> *From British favour has thy pseudo king*
> *His fame, his wealth, his impudence, deriv'd.*
> *By British spirit let this empty thing*
> *Of all his borrow'd feathers be deprived.*

The anger of the mob was fuelled to some extent by party politics. Drury Lane too burnt down five months after Covent Garden* – fires being all too common a risk when auditoriums were constructed in wood and canvas to maximize acoustic qualities and lit by candles. Due to the financial chaos of Sheridan's affairs, the rival patent theatre was not to be rebuilt until October 1812. The temporary crippling of the competition might have made John Philip's speculation in the new Covent Garden a runaway success, but for the riots – a fact that tends to support Boaden's belief that the

*On 24 February 1809.

disturbances were orchestrated by supporters of Sheridan. Certainly the newspapers divided along party-lines, the Tory papers of *The Times* and the *Post* supporting Kemble and the Whig *Chronicle* opposing him.

William Cobbett, the outspoken advocate of the Ordinary Englishman, might 'rebuke the vulgar cry so often heard of calling Kemble and his sister "upstarts" – those great artists who had been before them so many years,'[14] but the Old Price opposition reminded John Philip that he was an actor who played gentlemen and not the real thing. His scholarship and his genteel taste were mocked as delusions of grandeur. An anonymous correspondent published in *The Times* of 4 October derided Kemble's obsession with 'historically accurate' costume –

> Imagine that Cardinal Wolsey must of necessity, to give effect to the character, have a pocket-hankerchief of the finest cambric trimmed with lace at four, five or six guineas a yard!!! . . . Thus it is possible that imagination might . . . persuade an Acting Manager that he was in reality the King or Cardinal he was to personate.

It was a hard lesson. Kemble capitulated to the rioters in December 1809. He agreed to do away with the new private boxes and restored the pit prices to the old levels. He had to make a series of humiliating apologies to his tormentors from his own stage and then he was permitted to get on with his business.

For weeks Old Price agitators made disturbances outside John Philip's house in Great Russell Street after the play. The authorities took the threat sufficiently seriously to put a party of military on alert near by. Priscilla Kemble was so frightened she kept a ladder outside her bedroom window and a bag packed in case the household might need to make a quick getaway through the garden. As Mrs Siddons told a close friend, Kemble's nerves were much shaken – nerves that he controlled with increasing resort to opium.

The patrons of Covent Garden were soon restored to good

humour (in fact many of the rioters had been having a fine old time anyway). But for John Philip Kemble the consequence of that autumn of rioting was slow, seeping financial ruin that undermined his security and that of his heirs well into the 1840s.

It turned out that 'Little Davy' Garrick came nearer to achieving the status of gentility than any actor that followed him until the career of Henry Irving, who became the first theatrical knight in 1895. John Philip Kemble never made it into the Abbey. He and Priscilla were forced to economize and retired to an uneventful middle-class life in a villa in Switzerland. He died there in February 1823 and was buried among a row of graves with broad, flat tombstones bearing English names, overlooking the beautiful blue water of Lac Leman. The family struggle to be respected on and off the stage was passed on to Frances Anne Kemble and the next generation.

4

'To Charm the Sportive Throng'

If you were able to step into a Bond Street print shop in 1800 a certain picture might have caught your eye. It portrays a scene from one of the biggest stage hits of that year – the melodramatic pantomime *Obi, or Three Fingered Jack*. Charles Kemble, blacked up in the title role of Three Fingered Jack, the rebel slave leader, lolls on a chair, his fine torso displayed through a scanty Grecian drapery. Rosa approaches him timidly from the left – a slight figure with curly cropped hair, cross-dressed in pantaloon trousers and a snug jacket falling open to reveal well-developed breasts. The actress is Marie-Thérèse Decamp. The sexual undertones are unmistakable. This is not high art, this is melodrama.

What many accounts of the Kemble-Siddons family have overlooked is that even the dignified John Kemble and Mrs Siddons postured and swooned as the Gambler and Mrs Beverley, or the Stranger and Mrs Haller, to more audiences than ever saw their acclaimed portrayals of Macbeth and his lady. The everyday performances of the Kemble dynasty were occupied with melodrama more than Shakespeare. Fanny Kemble's parents, in particular, made their careers in popular rather than high-brow drama.

This was a matter of box office. When one patron of the arts was approached for his support in lobbying for a third patent theatre in

London in 1801, he replied that there was no demand for it. The fancy of the day, he wrote, was for,

> A five-act farce composed of such characters as never did yet exist, intermixed . . . with some forced or sickly sentiment, supported by grimace or buffoonery, with the motley train of processions, battles, spectres, pantomimes and Scaramouch ballets.[1]

However much men of culture might bemoan the decline of 'taste', the growth market of the entertainment business lay among the energetic classes that were filling the new suburbs of London. The expanding audience of clerks and prospering tradesmen appreciated physical as well as intellectual talents – skills such as those parodied by Dickens in his vignette from the life of Mrs Vincent Crummles in *Nicholas Nickleby*.

> 'The very first time I saw that admirable woman, Johnson,' said Mr Crummles, drawing a little nearer, and speaking in a tone of confidential friendship, 'she stood upon her head on the butt-end of a spear, surrounded with blazing fireworks.'
>
> 'You astonish me!' said Nicholas.
>
> '*She* astonished *me!*' returned Mr Crummles with a very serious countenance. 'Such grace, coupled with such dignity! I adored her from that moment.'

An important clue to understanding Fanny Kemble lies in the tension between the public face of her family celebrity (that veneration of Shakespeare and high art) and the actual origins the celebrity image sought to conceal. Fanny's mother in particular was a dancer, a mime, a singer and a low comedienne.

When she wrote her memoirs in her sixties, Fanny described her mother as if she were some Rousseau-esque child of nature:

> To the fine senses of a savage rather than a civilized nature, she joined an acute instinct of correct criticism in all matters of

> art, and a general quickness and accuracy of perception, and brilliant vividness of expression, that made her conversation delightful. Had she possessed half the advantages of education which she and my father laboured to bestow upon us, she would, I think, have been one of the most remarkable persons of her time.[2]

It was important to emphasize her mother's natural genius. Fanny was always sensitive about potential accusations of vulgarity. Nonetheless, two of the strongest characteristics she inherited from her impulsive and sharp-tongued mother were courage and honesty. She begins her public account of herself in her *Records of a Girlhood* by identifying strongly with her mother.

> The great actors of my family have received their due of recorded admiration; my mother has always seemed to me to have been overshadowed by their celebrity; my sister and myself, whose fate it has been to bear in public the name they have made distinguished, owe in great measure to her, I think, whatever ability has enabled us to do so not unworthily.[3]

Marie-Thérèse Decamp had the self-confidence and authority that came from supporting herself and her family from an early age. As her father died when she was twelve years old, until she married her wages were her own.* For a couple of decades she knew a measure of control over her own life that was singularly rare among 'respectable' women of her time. During her early childhood, Fanny grew up with a mother who had a public career just as her father did. Marie-Thérèse retired from the stage when Fanny was nine, but she continued to give acting lessons for some years after that and remained respected by colleagues for her knowledge of the business of the theatre.

Marie-Thérèse was born in Vienna in January 1775 – the year

*Until the Divorce Act of 1857 any money a married woman earned or inherited belonged legally to her husband.

Garrick retired. By Fanny's account, Marie-Thérèse's father, Captain Decamp, was a French military adventurer who, as part of the revolutionary army invading Switzerland, fell in love and married a girl from a farming family near Berne. The couple then went to Vienna and named their new daughter Marie-Thérèse after the Empress whose birthday coincided with their child's arrival. The charming captain, according to his granddaughter, made friends with a tourist, Lord Monson (later the Earl of Essex), who encouraged him to come to England –

> where [his] talents as a draughtsman and musician, which were much above those of a mere amateur, combined with the protection of such friends as he could not fail to find, would easily enable him to maintain himself and his young wife and child.[4]

Fanny was probably repeating a version of the story her mother told her. Marie-Thérèse and her brother Vincent, who was also an actor, used to tell their Drury Lane colleagues that their father was the grandson of a French aristocrat, the Marquis de Fleury. In their version, George Decamp's father had been disinherited for marrying the daughter of a Berne innkeeper and had been forced to change his name to Decamp. The truth of this story is unproven. As for the rest – Marie-Thérèse's father might have been a soldier at some time but he was a generation too early to take part in the revolutionary armies of France. He died in 1787, two years before the French Revolution took place. As Peachum, the receiver of stolen goods in *The Beggar's Opera* points out, 'captain' was a title frequently appropriated by adventurers wishing to pass among the nobility.

In fact, Fanny's mother was the eldest of the six children of a French musician, George Louis Decamp, and his wife, Jeanne Adrienne Defour, who hailed from Nancy in France. Before coming to England, George Decamp was employed in the Imperial opera house at Vienna where his brother was ballet master.[5] Many members of the extended family were performers, musicians and dancers. Marie-Thérèse's father was principally a flautist. Her uncle, aunt and cousins were dancers, sufficiently well known to be commemorated in theatrical prints. Her brother and two of her sisters had stage careers, and one dancing cousin seems to have ended up as an equestrienne circus performer in Bristol in the 1790s.[6]

In 1776, as the American colonists declared their independence, George Louis Decamp brought his family to England. His brother-in-law and sister, dancers by the name of Simonet, had already emigrated, so perhaps he moved to London to join them. George Louis played his flute in several theatre orchestras, taking work where he could get it. The family was poor and George Louis suffered from ill health, so Marie-Thérèse began her working life early. Her uncle Louis Simonet taught her to dance. The same year that John Philip Kemble made his Drury Lane debut as Hamlet – 1783 – little Miss Decamp, aged eight, made her first stage appearance across town at the King's Theatre (also known as the Italian Opera). She danced as a diminutive cupid in a ballet by Noverre called *Les Ruses de L'Amour* that followed the main opera. Her uncle and aunt and her eight-year-old cousin, Theresa, were named on the same bill.

Fanny mentions none of these details but she must have known some of them. Two of her mother's sisters, Adelaide – called Dall by the family – and Victoire, were members of the Kemble household during Fanny's childhood and youth.* What Fanny chooses to recall for public consumption emphasizes the Dickensian picture of the poor child battling courageously to keep her family fed.

There was considerable mobility between the Continent and London among dance and musical performers before the French Revolution, but the immigrants kept themselves apart as a distinct community. Marie-Thérèse did not speak English until her early teens and she learnt her first stage lines by rote. Though later she became remarkably fluent in her adopted language, she never lost her French accent.

---

*Dall lived with them from the time Fanny was a baby until she died in the early 1830s. Victoire was part of the household while Fanny was acting in England in the early 1830s; she was with her sister when Marie-Thérèse died in 1838 and stayed on to housekeep for her widowed brother-in-law, Charles.

For three years, from 1783 to 1786, young Marie-Thérèse danced in the minor theatres of London as part of a family group along with her Aunt Simonet and three cousins. She appeared on the bills as a pupil of Monsieur Simonet, and performed as Cupid and other parts that took advantage of a slight build that made her appear even younger than she was.

In January 1786 Marie-Thérèse turned eleven. She was a lively, dark-haired little girl, with a strong sense of responsibility. Her father was ailing and the child knew that her family depended on her earning ability. She began to perform outside the family group. Her sparkle and grace caught the eye of Le Texier, a Frenchman who directed a troupe of French émigré children at his theatre in Lisle Street. All things French were popular with the Prince of Wales's set at the time, and the engagement with Le Texier was a lucky one for Marie-Thérèse.

George Decamp's health gave way due to a disease of the lungs. He was forced to give up playing his flute. He tried to earn a living by giving drawing lessons but the family was in dire straits. Early in 1786 it seems that his wife Jeanne took a position as a housekeeper to a nobleman in the Prince of Wales's social circle.[7]

Fanny Kemble recounts a favourite family story about her mother. When Marie-Thérèse was 'about six years old', she used to dance in a drawing room for the Prince of Wales. (Though the story is more affecting when told of a child aged six, Fanny was writing forty years after her mother's death and the natural exaggeration of family legend had shaved five years off Marie-Thérèse's actual age. Fanny also failed to recall that her grandmother was a housekeeper.)

In the 1780s the Prince of Wales was still in his honeymoon period with the English public, when they called him Prince Florizel and gossiped over his romantic escapades rather than his debts and dishonourable behaviour. Marie-Thérèse would tell her children how she was petted by the Prince's mistress (and titular wife) Mrs Fitzherbert. The Prince himself would take his 'little French fairy' on his knee, and exclaim over her lack of appetite, pressing bon-bons on her. The housekeeper's dancing daughter was enough of a favourite for the occasion to be repeated more than once. Prince George even had a laborious 'joke' whereby he would put a large glass dome, designed to display *objets d'art*, over the child while she posed. (It is not recorded how long he left her there. Luckily it seems that Marie-Thérèse did not suffer from claustrophobia.)

Whereas nowadays this behaviour might be regarded as bordering on child abuse, the Prince's favour was a turning point. Marie-Thérèse cherished her memories of the corpulent Prince's magnificence and condescension for the rest of her life. (An obituary published at her death recounted the story that as a child she had danced for the Prince with the snide rider: 'a circumstance she has herself not infrequently mentioned'.[8])

Looking back from the vantage point of a Victorian matron, Fanny Kemble saw this period of her mother's life in dark colours. She focused on the 'cruel contrast' between the desperate family life of poverty dominated by the distress of an ailing father (who was only thirty-four) and the business of being a child-sized diversion for bored aristocrats. For Fanny it was 'impossible to imagine anything sadder' than the family's efforts to scrape together enough to trick out their little girl to charm the idle great with her childish joie de vivre. As a child of eleven Marie-Thérèse had lived with the 'fear of offending . . . the fastidious taste of the wealthy and refined patrons' whose gratuities paid for the food on her family's table.[9]

Fanny described her mother as a 'frank, generous, and unworldly woman', but she was also temperamental, depressive, and passionate. A difficult woman to live with. Her daughter suspected that her early experiences contributed to her mercurial and vehement temper. The daughter discerned moral damage arising from such whimsical exposure to all the wealth of a class to which neither girl nor woman could ever belong.

In the summer of 1786 Mr Coleman engaged young Miss Decamp to play at the Haymarket, a step up for the little French fairy. According to Marie-Thérèse, the Prince had put in a word for her. Up until now she had been playing in the rough equivalent to vaudeville.

Marie-Thérèse began in a small way, dancing *The Nosegay* with

Master James Harvey D'Egville in the presence of the Royal Family on 14 June 1786. In September the German tourist Sophie v.la Roche recorded in her diary a confident Marie-Thérèse singing a song as 'The Chair Mender':

> A twelve-year-old girl dressed as a poor boy who walks around with a bundle of rushes, straw and reeds to patch up old chairs, then really sits down to work on one, sang and played unusually well; indeed, was obliged to give two encores; the third time, however, announced with dignity and candour that it would not be possible, and that she feared she might be unable to take her part the next day; which would grieve her excessively, as she liked having her modest talents appreciated and applauded. Everyone clapped and praised her aloud. She is beautiful, and deserves to be the nation's darling, and will certainly become a great actress, competent to keep her voice, gesture and features in complete control, never using her talents wrongly or producing exaggerated effects.[10]

On 24 October, Marie-Thérèse appeared as Julie in the afterpiece of *Richard, Coeur de Lion* at Drury Lane. This was the first time she shared a stage with John Philip Kemble, now thirty and a major star. *Richard, Coeur de Lion*, was one of the hits of that season, and Kemble, who was unable to carry a tune, was the – regrettably singing – lead as Richard. Marie-Thérèse, on the other hand, proved she had a good voice as well as a talent for dance and mime.

On 7 October 1787 the Royal Society of Musicians received a petition that George Louis Decamp, thirty-five, with a wife and six children, 'by a violent disorder is totally unable to perform on any instrument'. The plea was a last desperate throw. George returned alone to Vienna to die. His departure left his pregnant wife and eldest daughter to support the family – Vincent, who was eight, Adelaide (Dall) who was seven, Victoire aged five and Sophy, a toddler of two.

For the next six years Marie-Thérèse spent her adolescence supporting herself and her family as a dancer with gradually increasing acting roles and some singing parts. Managers began to pick her for dramatic singing and comic soubrette parts for which 'an ear naturally correct – and very sedulous application to the science of music' recommended her. This was not the whole story. Her excellent figure, her vivacity and the grace with which she moved made her popular in 'breeches parts'. She was known for her 'sprightliness'. As one admirer put it:

> *To thee, DE CAMP, to thee belong*
> *The powers that charm the sportive throng;*[11]

Sometimes the press would scold her for some saucy outfit cut 'to display the symmetry of her person', but a generation of men remembered her fondly as a delightful dark-eyed girl who filled out her costume so charmingly when dressed as a boy.

This is not the way a respectable Victorian wishes to remember her mamma and partly explains Fanny's difficulty in dealing with her mother's career in her memoirs. In November 1862, Edward Fitzgerald, who remained one of her correspondents all his life, wrote to their mutual friend W.B. Donne about an old theatrical print he had come across.

> I wish you could have seen a sketch, and a very clever one, of Mrs C. Kemble in *very tight Men's Clothes*, by De Wilde – all whose Portraits are good. I have not dared to buy it: but I almost think it *should* be bought up. However, don't suppose it's absolutely indecent: but only so as one certainly would not wish one's Mother to be represented.[12]

However risqué some of Marie-Thérèse's roles may have seemed to her daughter's generation, in her personal life she preserved her reputation in a way that belied her pert stage image. She lived with her mother and sisters and always had members of her family about her. In November 1792 her thirteen-year-old brother, Vincent, joined the Drury Lane company; later two of her sisters had brief engagements, and occasionally her cousins Rosine and Leonora would be on the bill in a speciality act. By the late eighteenth century certain individual and married actresses – and in particular Sarah Siddons – had achieved a hard-won respect as models of admirable and unassailable womanhood.* A handful of titled men in the Prince of Wales's set even took a stage favourite for their wife. The elegant and elfin blonde Miss Farren was a celebrated example when the turf-mad Earl of Derby made her his second wife and a countess. But these were examples of aristocratic self-confidence rather than a measure of the respect that actresses might expect. (Elizabeth Farren had been the Earl's established mistress long before his first wife died.) Society in the reign of George III lived by harsh and hypocritical rules. If an actress managed to preserve her public reputation and snagged the prize of marriage to a gentleman, she might make 'a lady'. But – no matter her personal probity – if an actress fell, or was pushed, into some indiscretion she could expect no mercy. As a rule an actress was treated as a near-relation to a prostitute and fair game without the constant protection of family members.

This vulnerability of unchaperoned actresses was demonstrated by an incident at Drury Lane in January 1795. Marie-Thérèse, who had just turned twenty that month, went to discuss some piece of business with the manager in his office. She found the usually stately John Philip Kemble somewhat the worse for drink. Perhaps unsurprisingly, Kemble would occasionally relieve the strain of maintaining his image by getting gloriously drunk. (The Sheridan set was notoriously hard drinking in an age of formidable drunkards.) There are some appealing stories told of the lofty Kemble wandering about Covent Garden Market in the hours before dawn being uncharacteristically chatty with the porters. However, he normally kept his drinking out of the theatre. On this occasion the thirty-eight-year-old manager was sufficiently unbent by alcohol to

*'Make love to her! To that magnificent and appalling creature?!' the playwright Sheridan is reported to have exclaimed with reference to Sarah Siddons; 'I should as soon have thought of making love to the Archbishop of Canterbury!'

make a grab for his lithe young *soubrette*. Her loud protests brought her young brother Vincent crashing through the door, a crowd gathered and Miss Decamp's reputation was saved.

Such assaults were fairly common. John Philip Kemble's great friend Mrs Inchbald – an established actress and playwright, and a prettily stammering redhead – used to regale the Green Room* with a story of Thomas Harris, the co-proprietor of Covent Garden. Harris once leapt on her while she was trying to discuss a play with him. She escaped by pulling his hair, the punchline of her story being: 'I d-d-don't know wh-what I would have done if he had w-worn a w-w-wig.' What was different in this case was that, as soon as he had sobered up, Kemble rushed to print a statement in the press that Miss Decamp's 'conduct and character had in no instance authorized his unjustifiable behaviour'.[13] This was the one sexual scandal of his London career. Of all the attacks that were made on him, his enemies did not portray John Philip as a womanizer.† His aristocratic friends might have thought the tale merely deliciously amusing but – perhaps conscious of the sensibilities of his middle-class patrons – John Philip felt it necessary to make an immediate apology for his 'uncharacteristic' behaviour.

*There were three Green Rooms at the Covent Garden and Drury Lane Patent Theatres during this period – one for the ballet and chorus, one sitting-out room for the 'supernumeraries' (what we might call 'extras' today) and the 'first' Green Room. This latter not only served as a rehearsal room and a place where the leading actors could wait for their cues, but as a drawing room where stage-struck gentlemen, many with titles, would 'lounge' flirting with the prettiest actresses and swapping *bon-mots* with the stars. Visitors would not be admitted unless in full evening dress.

†It is significant that the story told of Kemble wandering inebriated about Covent Garden – then notorious as the residence of sex workers – highlights his conviviality with porters not prostitutes.

5.

Thérèse and Charles: A Melodrama

Fanny's father, Charles Kemble, was the eleventh child of Roger and Sarah Kemble. Born in Brecon in South Wales, on 25 November 1775 – nine months after his future wife – he arrived in the world just after his eldest sister, Sarah Siddons, had given birth to her first daughter,* while his elder brother, John Philip, was eighteen. As Charles grew up Roger and Sarah gradually passed their parental duties over to his successful older brother.

When Charles was thirteen, in 1788, John Philip sent him over to France to attend his old college. While Marie-Thérèse Decamp was building her career dancing as a succession of fairies at the Haymarket and performing juvenile roles at Drury Lane, Charles was closeted in the Catholic Seminary at Douai. According to his own account he acquired 'a knowledge of Pagan and Christian wisdom' under the careful tuition of monks who 'wafered over with blank paper, any page which might tend to awaken the passions'.[1] It is perfectly possible that he was exaggerating his youthful isolation from poetry and the feminine sex. Once he was in London, it seems Charles rapidly recognized the powerful attraction to women of a touch of bashfulness in a handsome young man.

---

*Sarah Martha, known as Sally.

After three years at Douai Charles fell ill. It was 1791 and the tremors of the Revolution were spreading across France. The Kemble family was sufficiently concerned for John Philip to cross the Channel to fetch him home. His elder brother meant to steer him into a respectable occupation, but the sixteen-year-old was not impressed by the 'modest situation' selected for him at the Post Office. Within the year Charles had struck off up North to try his talent on the boards. He was not a resounding success. He was just capable enough – or his Kemble connections were strong enough – for him to be cast in secondary parts through two winter seasons on the northern circuit.

John Philip relented and brought Charles out at Drury Lane in April 1794 as Malcolm to his Macbeth. The encouraging reviews from the press may have said more about his elder brother's influence than Charles's actual performance. The waspish theatrical journalist Oxberry described Charles at this time as

> a tall, awkward Youth, with what is termed a hatchet face, a figure badly proportioned, and evidently weak in his limbs; his acting was even worse than his appearance.

Others – most notably young women – however, found Charles Kemble decidedly handsome. Sally and Maria, Mrs Siddons's two lively and popular daughters, rejoiced in their attractive uncle. Jane Porter (later to become the author of a successful novel, *The Chieftains*) and her playwriting elder sister, Maria, were very taken with him. He had the Kemble soulful brown eyes defined by attractively long lashes and a classical nose. Although his lower lip was rather too full for modern taste, to susceptible females of his own generation his was the model mouth of a man of sentiment. He soon adopted the trademark Kemble bearing, arousing the savage resentment of one critic who fulminated against

> the pride of this family who rise from a low origin. We remember, a few years since, meeting this young man with a stick

> over his shoulder, on which was a bundle, walking unabashed through the streets. He is now, without merit to apologize for it, as proud as any of his relations.[2]

Family history in the next generation related how John Philip 'imposed upon the young debutant a probation as strict and regular as he was in the habit of prescribing to the least gifted of his associates'.[3] Charles was determined to fulfil his brother's expectations. Through the second half of the 1790s he worked his passage at Drury Lane, learning his craft in a succession of secondary roles.

During this period, Marie-Thérèse and Charles were both members of the summer theatre at the Haymarket. There, away from the oppressive weight of the Kemble ambition at Drury Lane, their relationship blossomed. James Boaden recalled a melodrama of his called *The Italian Monk* that was a success at the Haymarket in the summer of 1797. Miss Decamp was his lead as Rosalba and Charles Kemble her hero in the part of Vivaldi. The pair were twenty-two and twenty-one years old respectively, youthful and good-looking. It was a particularly happy time. To Boaden's eyes, Charles Kemble was obviously smitten. Through that heady summer the Green Room gossips speculated how long it would be before an engagement was announced.

The gossips were to be kept guessing for some time. Marie-Thérèse was in no hurry to lose her independence. A married woman had no legal entity; she was regarded as of a piece with her husband and it was his right to do what he pleased with all she owned. So there was little incentive for Marie-Thérèse to 'make herself a property'.[4] She starred in a string of popular comedies and spectacles in the late 1790s. In 1798 she created the role of Irene in the melodrama of *Blue Beard*. It was a second-rank part, but she made her mark in it. This extravaganza featured complicated stage machinery, including a dramatic perspective of distant mountains over which a mischievous boy called Edmund Kean rode on a plaster and board elephant as Blue Beard. The machinery failed on the first night at a crucial dramatic climax and Marie-Thérèse earned the composer Kelly's undying gratitude by saving the show with her vivid contribution to 'I see them galloping!' 'She gave it with such irresistible force of expression,' recalled Kelly fondly, 'as to call from the audience loud and continued shouts of applause.'[5] Her attitude in that piece became a classic. Over a decade later Grimaldi the Clown was still able to bring the house down with his burlesque of Miss Decamp's action and manner in 'I see them galloping'.[6] As late as 1832 a writer in *Blackwood* magazine recalled the impact of this 'delightful dark-eyed girl whose motion was itself music ere her voice was heard'.

Charles too scored the occasional hit. His portrayal of the drunken lieutenant Cassio in *Othello* was well received. The theatre critic Leigh Hunt was later to applaud his 'very happy mixture of the occasional debauchee and the gentleman of feeling'.[7] With such performances Charles began to construct a reputation. 'Who ever played a drunken gentleman as he did?' wrote Robson. 'His efforts to pick up his dress hat in Charles Oakley were the most laughable, the most ridiculous, the most natural that can be imagined.'[8]

As the relationship progressed, Marie-Thérèse proved herself not only a gifted comedienne but a playwright as well. Her first dramatic piece at Drury Lane in May 1799 was a five-act comedy called *First Faults* and Charles took the lead opposite Mrs Jordan. The play was not strong enough to be repeated but, performed for Miss Decamp's Benefit*, it drew a good house, making a highly respectable £447 and 8 shillings. But Charles was catching up. By 1800 both actors were paid £9 a week each. And that July, in the midst of a successful run as Three-Fingered Jack in the new hit pantomime *Obi*, Charles brought out his first play, *The Point of Honour*. It was an adaptation of a French melodrama rather than an original work but this play proved more successful than *First Faults*. It continued to be performed on and off for a couple of decades.

---

*Benefit performances were held each season to raise a bonus for the principal members of a company. The performer whose Benefit it was took the lion's share of that night's takings. Benefits were also used to raise funds for fellow performers in distress and sometimes for local charities.

One evening at the Haymarket, during a performance of *Obi*, Charles came crashing to the ground during a nightly leap from a precipice. The stage crew had been negligent and he injured his back so severely that he was unable to perform for the rest of the summer. Luckily his injuries were interesting rather than disfiguring and he took advantage of the crisis to declare his love. Thérèse – as he called her – was moved to confess hers and in August the couple at last became engaged.

As a couple of play-actors they might have known that the path of true love would not run smooth. When Charles 'all rapture' told his elder brother the news, John Philip played his full melodramatic part. He was violently against the match. The Kemble elders closed ranks, threatening their youngest son with 'everlasting displeasure' if he went ahead with his choice.

In the personal apology John Philip wrote to Miss Decamp after the unfortunate incident in his office in 1795 he assured her that 'I shall always endeavour, by the most respectful means, to Prove my high opinion of your exemplary Conduct, in every regulation of Life.'[9] Five years later this high opinion did not extend to his approval of her marrying his brother. Both he and Sarah Siddons were appalled by the connection. They had no objection to Charles marrying a player – they had both done so. But Marie-Thérèse was from a different class of performer entirely. Not only was Marie-Thérèse herself a low comedienne but her family made no secret of the fact that they were among the foot soldiers of the entertainment business. They had none of the Kemble clan's artistic and social pretensions.

Her family's poverty during her childhood meant that there had been no money for Marie-Thérèse's schooling. She was twelve before a philanthropic viscountess took up a copy of Milton's *Paradise Lost* and taught her her letters. She learned to read but she disliked Milton ever after. Despite this, she admitted to no mental inferiority to the men about her. She had clear opinions and articulated them fluently. Indeed, she acquired a reputation as a brilliant conversationalist. Maria Porter, Jane's elder sister, describes Marie-Thérèse at their first meeting:

> I can see no point of her character or manners, that can unite with the softness, and dignity of Kemble's. She is lively, free, commanding, and self-assured. Exactly what she appears on the stage, only losing twenty per cent in the person, as you approach nearer. This person, tho' well shaped and of fine contour, is coarse and unfinished: it seems like the statue of an exquisite figure, which the sculptor has yet to chisel into the smooth polish of grace and beauty.[10]

In short, not only was Marie-Thérèse a reminder of an embarrassing incident John Philip preferred to forget, but also she was not the kind of polite helpmate designed to promote the family's rise towards gentlemanly status.

The problem was that Charles was determined. As a junior member of a family distinguished by several powerful and managing females, he was undeterred by Marie-Thérèse's independence and spirit. (While the fact that his stately and superior brother had been so firmly repulsed may well have served as an added attraction.) He refused to break his commitment to Thérèse. Eventually the family worked out a compromise. The conditions were stringent. 'All visiting at her house should be laid aside.'[11] The pair could meet as fellow performers and acquaintances but Charles must wait five years until he was thirty. Then, if his feelings remained unchanged, he could marry without opposition. Marie-Thérèse saw the imprudence of marrying in the teeth of the 'displeasure of all his friends', and she agreed to wait. In romantic fervour, the lovers swore fidelity to each other and determined to serve out their probation.

The engagement period demanded by John Philip put the young couple under considerable strain. Our principal witness to their story is Jane Porter. In 1800, Jane and Marie Porter were the twenty-something sisters of the artist Robert Kerr Porter, a painter of military scenes and orientalist who later attained a knighthood. Both sisters had literary ambitions and towards the end of 1800 Maria had a play awaiting production at Covent Garden. When the Porters were introduced to Charles Kemble by a mutual acquaintance, Jane was immediately taken with him. In her diary she recorded her strong interest in the handsome young actor.

Early in 1801 gossip was circulating about Marie-Thérèse and Charles's broken love affair. Their engagement being secret, the pair were assumed to have quarrelled. The sisters wondered about Kemble, whom they considered 'one of the best young men in the world' with 'the most tender and delicate of hearts' being attracted to the lively French actress. They had been told that Miss Decamp was 'violent in temper, and in disposition an avowed coquette'.[12] Maria met Charles's 'enchantress' first. By the third visit she was won over. Marie-Thérèse was,

> . . . animated, ardent and affectionate; a masculine understanding, united with an independent spirit and an apparently feeling heart seems to have fallen to her share. I no longer wonder at Charles Kemble having loved her – how could he *cease* to do so?

When her younger sister, Jane, met the actress in her turn, she was not so quickly impressed. Marie-Thérèse lacked modesty and was clearly open to accusations of 'lust for praise'. One evening in March Jane was invited to a supper at Miss Decamp's. She expected her hostess to put herself out to charm, but instead:

> Herself appeared the first person in her thoughts; to display her figure, her hair, and her elegant movements, was all that she attended to! I contemplate with amazement the total want of that nice politeness which I had so largely expected . . .

The comedienne flirted openly with Charles Moore,* who was supposed to be engaged to Sally Siddons at the time. Jane was disgusted by her 'freedom of manner' in calling Moore by his first

*Charles Moore was the younger brother of the military hero Sir John Moore who died at Corunna.

name in public, considering her to be playing cruelly with both his and Charles Kemble's feelings. Evidently, the French coquette was not behaving in a 'polite' manner. She was careless of other people's opinions – too open and, it might be said, too sincere. Worse still, Marie-Thérèse spoke of Charles Kemble 'always bitterly, both with voice and looks'. The disgruntled Jane decided that Miss Decamp was an artful woman who liked to play with 'the uncomfortable dupes of her schemes'.

Miss Porter's opinion was confirmed the following week when Charles came to pay the sisters a morning visit. The young actor conformed to all their ideals of politeness and sensibility. Their delightful tête à tête went on until mid-afternoon as Charles basked in the sisters' adoring attention. He expounded sentimentally on the 'subject of friendships and the affections. He had suffered perfidy; and the circumstance at which we guessed, gave a particular pathos to his words and manner'. The sisters blushed with pleasure as Charles described the kind of woman he would choose to marry. 'Her beauty should not be of the obtrusive kind; her dress should be quiet; her manners retiring; and her temper the gentlest of the gentle; for a bad temper was horror to him.' As soon as their visitor took his leave, the sisters hatched a plan for their brother to join the younger Kemble on a tour of German states that summer.

It is hard not to see something of Jane Austen's insinuating cad George Wickham in Charles Kemble's behaviour. The best that can be said for him is that poor Jane became entangled in the middle of the secret lovers' efforts to make one another jealous. It is a testament to Marie-Thérèse's charisma that she swiftly managed to neutralize her potential rival for Charles's affections. Within weeks she had not only charmed Jane out of her prejudices but also converted her into a principal confidante to her troubles with the Kemble Clan. She told her new friend about the secret engagement and how she had agreed to wait for the five years specified by Charles's brother. Thérèse's dramatic nature did not appreciate the grace with which Charles bowed to his family's wishes. He was altogether too reserved.

At first he would send me two or three letters in the day; but he never sought to meet me at the theatre, where he knew he might. This piqued me much.

It was the old story – from the moment that Charles had obtained her acknowledgement that she loved him, 'he relaxed all those little attentions which he had formerly shewed, and which she was solicitous to shew him'. The Kembles, exclaimed Thérèse, were remarkable for coldness. Charles would appear all ardour and then 'when occasions presented themselves to excite his fire, he suddenly stopped short, and was frozen into ice'. (Her complaints recall Leigh Hunt's criticism that Charles's Romeo was occasionally so languid that 'his attention to his mistress appears to be a painful effort, and instead of being tender from amatory feelings betrays a kind of civil pity for the poor lady'.)

With such suppressed emotions electrifying the atmosphere, it is a measure of the professionalism of all concerned that John Philip, Charles and Marie-Thérèse continued to work successfully together. In February 1801 they were on stage in *Deaf and Dumb*, a popular musical drama written by Thomas Holcroft. John Philip – the best theatrical priest in the business – was the Abbé de L'Epée, Charles, as usual, was the romantic hero while Marie-Thérèse created one of her most famous roles as Theodore, a part that featured her skills as a mime.*

Behind the scenes, the expressive Thérèse was resorting to Lydia Languish-style efforts to prompt a suitably romantic reaction from Charles. She poured her troubles into Jane's half-sympathetic, half-appalled ears. One day she had lingered after rehearsals hoping to speak to Charles, only to see him walk off with his elder brother. She was so 'enraged' at this, that she rushed home to write to Charles that,

*James Boaden described how her '*expression*, in look and gesture was even more intelligent than speech; it was the lightening of the mind, and reduced the labour of disclosure to a point, and the detection of villany to a glance'. Boaden, *Memoir of Mrs Inchbald*, vol. II, p. 50.

> He knew very well the offer he had made me of himself was not my wish . . . In Heaven's name, let us give up the engagement between us entirely – let us be free – and go on in the same friendly terms as formerly.

If bad temper and scenes were indeed a horror to Charles, then this love affair was yet more evidence to support the cliché that opposites attract. There was some gossip at the time that *Deaf and Dumb* – yet another play pilfered from the French – was the work of Marie-Thérèse and Charles. One night in the Green Room the actor Bannister thought to tease her by saying, 'You and Charles have made a good thing between you.' 'Indeed,' Marie-Thérèse snapped back, 'Charles and I will never make any thing between us.'

Then she received Charles's response to her angry letter. His dear Thérèse, her lover wrote in melodramatic despair, had confirmed his suspicions that her affections 'have never been equal to mine for you'. He who had sworn to love her for ever would abide by his oath, 'unless I possess you, to go single to my grave'. After discussion with Jane, Thérèse decided that this avowal was sufficiently romantic and the engagement held. Jane pondered the troubles that lay ahead for Charles. Despite all Marie-Thérèse's 'attractive sweetness and affectionate manner' she wondered whether her 'spirit is too vain and violent to make the felicity of Kemble'.

That summer Marie-Thérèse abandoned the Haymarket for engagements in the provinces while Charles went abroad. 'Mr Charles Kemble,' the press announced, 'does not accept any theatrical engagements for the summer. He proposes to take a continental excursion, and to reside chiefly at Vienna, for the purpose of acquiring a complete knowledge of the German language.' His companion was to be Robert Porter, 'the painter of Seringapatam'.

'How preciously tired they will be of each other, before they return!' quipped Marie-Thérèse, on learning of these travel arrangements. 'Kemble sits for hours without looking at or speaking to anybody.'[13]

She knew she was secure in Charles's affections. Poor Jane could only grumble to her diary that her troublesome new friend 'risks her own respectability by setting the man she loves in a ludicrous light'.

When John Philip Kemble initiated his family's move from Drury Lane to Covent Garden in 1803, the professional relationships between the Kembles' triumvirate were shifting. Real-life tragedy was distracting Sarah Siddons from her career. In 1798 she had already lost one daughter, Maria, to consumption. In March 1803 her eldest daughter Sally followed her sister to the grave. Sarah Siddons was devastated. She began to talk privately about amassing sufficient money to enable her to retire and maintain her remaining household in her old age. Charles was now in his late twenties. He had carved out a niche portraying gallant gentlemen such as Falconbridge in Shakespeare's *King John*, or, in light comedy, Charles Surface in *School for Scandal*. His easy-going manner masked a hard worker who was ambitious to prove himself. In particular, he hankered to make his mark in tragedy.

But the 'possession of parts' was a well-established convention of the Georgian theatre. An actor had the exclusive right – so long as he remained with the company – to a part in which he had established himself. At Drury Lane the first parts in tragedy were his elder brother's prerogative. His sense of dissatisfaction accentuated by his family's interference in his private life, Charles grew restless. As a concession, John Philip stepped aside to allow his brother to give his first performance as Hamlet in Spring 1803. According to the *Monthly Mirror* Charles 'greatly increased his reputation, before deservedly high, by his chaste and animated performance'. But his chaste style of acting was never going to rival his stately brother in tragedy. It was clear that Charles's ambitions were blocked, and yet he lacked the confidence to break free from his brother's dominating presence and strike out on his own.

The first years of the nineteenth century saw Marie-Thérèse at the height of her career. She began 1804 with a striking success at Drury Lane as Cinderella, dancing for fifty-one nights amid 'profusely splendid . . . scenery, machinery and decorations'. Songs she sang became favourites 'found on every piano-forte' and – the greatest sign of popularity – were taken up by the ballad singers who worked the streets of the capital.

Across at the Kembles' new 'House', Covent Garden, Charles went about his business with his customary good manners and reserve. The pressure he was under was reflected in bouts of ill-health. After the back injury of 1800, his season at the Haymarket in 1802 had to be abandoned once more due to illness. In 1804, as soon as the summer came he escaped the pressures of his work, family and love life by leaving the country again – this time bound for Russia. 'Mr Charles Kemble put himself into a ship that was bound for St Petersburgh about three months ago, thinking he should be returned by the opening of the theatre, but we hear nothing of him,' wrote Sarah Siddons to a friend in September. He turned up eventually, a month late, to resume his second-rank roles once more, playing Laertes to John Philip's Hamlet on 22 October.

That winter the Master Betty phenomenon hit London and Charles had the dubious honour of introducing the teenage prodigy to a packed house at Covent Garden. William Henry West Betty was a rosy-cheeked thirteen-year-old from Belfast whose confidence and competence on the stage was turned into lucrative celebrity by his wily father. The Georgians were given to episodes of fervent worship of youth and beauty. The late eighteenth century saw many juvenile performers but the rage for Master Betty was exceptional. He arrived in London on the back of provincial triumphs that have been described as 'national hysteria'. After fierce competition with Sheridan, Harris secured his London début at Covent Garden on 1 December 1804. The town was convulsed by the sight of this precocious boy spouting the lines of its favourite tragic heroes. It is said that some of the capital's newspapers were so taken up with their coverage of the 'Infant Roscius' (Garrick had been the English Roscius) that they almost forgot to mention the coronation of

Napoleon that took place on the 2nd of that month. Not every lover of drama was so taken with the boy. Mrs Inchbald probably articulated the opinion of her professional colleagues with her languid comment that 'this is a clever little boy, and had I never seen boys act, I might have thought him exquisite'.[14] Still, the wider public took two seasons to wake up from their enchantment.

The reign of Master Betty was not a comfortable time for the Kemble clan. The king and queen of tragedy were forced to weather the humiliation of taking a back seat to a sing-songing boy. According to Mrs Inchbald, who was fretting about a play she had in production at the Garden, John Philip Kemble was sustaining himself on opium, while Mrs Siddons suffered some painful injury, perhaps a trapped nerve, that caused a bout of semi-paralysis down one side.

Marie-Thérèse turned thirty. She demonstrated her confident maturity as a performer and author with a short burlesque, *Personation or Fairly Taken In*. Designed as a vehicle for her own talents, and in particular her ability to do a proper French accent, she gave an 'exquisitely humorous performance' in the principal role as Lady Julia. This farce was to become her personal showcase, associated with her for the rest of her career. The following May she was back entertaining the sportive throng as a jockey in a musical entertainment entitled *Youth, Love and Folly*. She played the part with such vivacity, 'dressed it, and looked it, so completely that she might have passed as having been brought up at Newmarket'. She was earning the highest salary among the actresses at Drury Lane; at £15 a week only three male actors were paid more. But, Marie-Thérèse's happy association with the Drury Lane theatre was about to end.

John Philip's five-year probation was over. Marie-Thérèse's temper and love of dramatic scenes had not dissuaded Charles from his choice. He had proved he was tenacious – if not stubborn – once he had made up his mind. For her part, Thérèse confessed that there was no other man she could conceive of marrying. Although it was a love match, Marie-Thérèse did not surrender herself in any wild passion. She explained to Jane Porter that it was the companionship that had developed as they starred opposite each other in show after show during those long summers at the Haymarket that had initially drawn her to Charles. 'We were comfortable in each other's society every day, which was all I wanted,' she said.[15]

On 2 July 1806, seven months after the expiration of his stipulated period, and four months before Charles's thirty-first birthday, John Philip Kemble bowed before the inevitable.

> Yesterday morning a marriage long expected in theatrical circles took place at St George's, Bloomsbury, between Mr Charles Kemble and Miss De Camp. Mr John Kemble was present at the ceremony and gave the bride away.[16]

Marie-Thérèse left her 'true home' at Drury Lane – 'her departure . . . regretted by all'[17] and moved into the penumbra of her husband's family at Covent Garden.

It did not suit John Philip to have a sister-in-law celebrated for her ability to impersonate a jockey. Marie-Thérèse was tried out in Shakespearean parts – Ophelia in *Hamlet* and Dorinda in *The Tempest*. Soon the experiment was abandoned and she was largely confined to genteel comedy and such second-rank parts as the 'Jealous Lucy Lockitt' in *The Beggar's Opera*. ('Miss Decamp's real character, if we may say so, in more senses than one,' as one cutting journalist remarked.[18]) As befitted a husband – Charles's salary exceeded hers for the first time. A week and nine months after the wedding, at the age of thirty-two, she gave birth to their first child, John Mitchell Kemble.* Her baby kept her from the stage for several months but within the year the new mother was back creating another breeches role as Edmund in *The Blind Boy*. This was to be the last of her celebrated mime parts. Now she donned boy's clothes to wring the hearts of the audience in touching and 'artistic' melodrama; the days when she delighted the sportive throng were over.

---

*Born 11 April 1807.

During the following year, both Charles and Marie-Thérèse brought out plays, but they also lost their second son, Philip, who died at a few weeks old. The subject of Marie-Thérèse's comic interlude, *The Day After the Wedding, or A Wife's First Lesson*, was something of an irony considering her reputation for short temper. It was an adaptation of a French farce entitled *La Jeune Femme Colère*, a competent but conventional piece, along the lines of *Catherine and Petruccio* – Garrick's softened version of *The Taming of the Shrew* in which Marie-Thérèse had been regularly cast opposite John Philip in the 1790s. Marie-Thérèse's hero was a playful homage to her new husband. In a play-actor's ideal of gentility, Colonel Freelove, the new bridegroom, is represented as 'surrounded by faithful servants, enjoying a princely fortune; possessing an amiable, beautiful and accomplished' bride. His new wife, the noble and youthful Lady Elizabeth, has a temper 'impatient of restraint, quick, and irritable'. The gentlemanly Colonel – who, naturally, is 'mild, gentle and affectionate' – proceeds to tame his new wife by pretending to an even worse temper than hers. She sees the light, like Kate, in the last act. The wife's first lesson, in the mouth of Colonel Freelove, the forebearing but firm husband, is that:

> 'Tis not an easy task to reform our characters suddenly; I expect to find you now and then relapsing into your former error: but you have experienced the evil effects of it; and reflection cannot fail to convince you, that affection and gentleness are the brightest ornaments of your sex, and the surest source of Domestic Felicity.

One wonders whether Charles had any sense of foreboding as he played his part. The considered opinion of his younger daughter, Adelaide, looking back from the hard-won maturity of adulthood, was that her father was a 'mild and gently amiable person of cultivated tastes and refined habits – with a great deal of natural tenderness, but a man of the world without one particle of romance or passion – and utterly incapable of answering or comprehending a nature'[19] such as that of his wife. The Kemble children grew up in a household where their mother's impulsive outbursts were regularly circumvented by her phlegmatic husband. It was a model that was to prove profoundly influential in the course of Fanny's own marriage.

Despite the reservations of Charles's family, the bond between Fanny's parents survived through separation, hard times and repeated infidelity on Charles's part, until Marie-Thérèse's death in 1838. Perhaps unsurprisingly, given Marie-Thérèse's strength of character, of the four children she bore to Charles who survived to adulthood, it was their two daughters who continued the family tradition on the stage.

Marie-Thérèse was in many ways a remarkably modern mother. She brought up her daughters to believe that they had choices beyond marriage – that conventional fate for all 'respectable' women in the nineteenth century. But Fanny also struggled with her mother's 'savagery' and the volatile, passionate temperament she inherited from her. She observed that her mother's natural abilities had not been sufficient to gain her widespread respect among her contemporaries. Marie-Thérèse had suffered from her lack of 'finish'. From her, Fanny acquired early experience both of the virtues of independence and the price of being an outsider.

M Gauci Lith.

PART II

CONFESSIONS – AN ACCOUNT OF A ROMANTIC EDUCATION

(or How Frances Anne Became Miss Kemble)

6

Childhood

In November 1809 Fanny's parents were living in rented lodgings in Newman Street, a road that ran off the north side of Oxford Street opposite Soho Square. It was an area occupied by the skilled craftsmen and working classes who supplied the grand houses of Mayfair. The home was a modest one. Charles Kemble might keep a maid or two, but he could not afford a horse or carriage, and his wife and her sisters* cooked for the household as well as making and mending most of their clothes.

The streets around Fanny's first home were the narrow, winding ones of the Elizabethan city. Nash was yet to transform the capital, there was no Regent Street cutting its elegant swathe southwards from the New Road†, marking out the boundary of the residences of beau monde in the West End. Regent's Park was yet to be fashioned out of open fields in Marylebone. Indeed, there was no Regent. King George III was to hang on to his sanity for another two years yet. The Thames, its waters crowded with white sails, was the main thoroughfare and focus of the city. The pillory stood at Charing

---

*As well as Aunt Dall, Victoire, a younger sister, was also intermittently a member of the household.

†Now Marylebone / Euston Road.

Cross and at night the streets were patrolled by super-annuated parish watchmen with their long staffs and lanterns crying out the hour. Nonetheless signs were appearing of social change. Fashion might dress women in high-waisted empire gowns that recalled the classicism of the previous century, but male dress reflected the values of the new-moneyed classes. In 1809 the arbiter of fashion was Beau Brummel, a self-made man who prescribed cleanliness, dark coats and practical trousers strapped under the foot to keep them wrinkle-free. Gone were the silk brocade coats of those pre-revolutionary days when the Town delighted in the antics of Prince Florizel and Mrs Fitzherbert. The Beau declared moderation to be the soul of elegance – 'if John Bull turns round to look after you, you are not well-dressed, but either too stiff, too tight or too fashionable'.

From the very first, Fanny was reliant on the support of an extended family. Her mother was back at the theatre two months after her daughter's arrival. She never breast-fed any of her children but passed her baby to a wet nurse, and left her along with her brother John in the care of their aunt, Adelaide Decamp.

Adelaide – Dall, as her toddling nephew John Mitchell christened her – was twenty-nine the year Fanny was born. In her late teens and early twenties she had performed as part of Stephen Kemble's company, then based at Durham. There she had formed a close friendship with Stephen Kemble's daughter Fanny. Together they giggled and joked their way through several happy years until they both fell in love. Fanny – whose 'lovely countenance', marked by a serene sweetness and a child-like simplicity, rendered her ballad singing particularly effective – made a 'most advantageous' marriage to the heir to an industrial fortune, Mr Arkright of Derby. Her more lively friend, however, failed to fit the same angelic mould. Dall's young man could not bring himself to marry an actress. Her feelings at her disappointment are not recorded. She gave up her acting life, returned to London and became an indispensable part of Marie-Thérèse's household. Although similar physically to her sister, being petite and dark, unlike her elder sibling, Dall was resolutely calm and sunny-tempered. Fanny recalled that the only sign the family ever had that her aunt might be out of sorts was her habit of singing to cheer herself up whenever she felt dispirited.

Dall made Fanny's early childhood secure, despite frequently absent parents and the lack of a fixed home. Although Charles Kemble was always careful not to run up personal debts, he never amassed the capital to invest in a house. The family regularly moved from lodgings to rented houses and back again. Nevertheless Fanny grew up a confident little girl – albeit a handful (as intelligent toddlers with erratic parents are apt to be).

The senior manager-proprietor of Covent Garden, Thomas Harris, retired passing his share of the management to his son, Henry. The young manager had a good sense of what appealed to a generation that had grown up at war with the French. Jolly tars and patriotic songs were the lures laid out to fill the pit. *King John* was the favourite Shakespeare. Just as Laurence Olivier's *Henry V* caught the national mood in 1944, John Kemble's production of *King John* resonated with the nation at war. Charles Kemble was a particular hit bounding across the stage as the chivalric Falconbridge, rousing his audience with the closing rallying cry:

Come the three corners of the world in arms
And we shall shock them: Nought shall make us rue,
If England to itself do rest but true.

The country was in need of unity. The war was not going well and in 1811 the pressures of crippled trade and developments in mechanization resulted in eruptions of machine breaking in the cloth districts of the Midlands and the North. 'People here and everywhere are desponding: trade is ruined and poverty universal; and it seems to increase every hour,'[1] wrote Aunt Dall's friend, the comedian Charles Mathews, from Yorkshire. London audiences needed cheering up. Marie-Thérèse was back in her popular part of Irene as

John Philip revived *Blue Beard*, dressing up the production with sixteen live horses.*

Off stage the Charles Kembles were sociable and popular. Marie-Thérèse had little time for her children, but Charles was erratically indulgent. It was said that when his wife was away, he kept a becoming lace cap to hand in the drawing room in which to display his daughter to his visitors. (His practical wife told him off for encouraging vanity in his offspring.) But both parents were restless. Despite her occasional successes, Marie-Thérèse could feel her career slipping away. In 1812 the popular comedian Jack Bannister, who was planning a move into management of the new Drury Lane that autumn, put out feelers to see whether he might woo Marie-Thérèse to play opposite him in all his favourite farces. Charles too opened correspondence with the rival house. Salary was 'but a secondary consideration'; what the younger Kemble was after was the promise of 'a certain line of characters'. At thirty-seven, Charles knew that his 'future prospects would entirely depend upon the estimation in which I am to be held for the next [few] years'.[2] But Drury Lane was not to be the answer. Charles's negotiations fell through and Marie-Thérèse's dreams of a come-back collapsed when she discovered that she was pregnant again. It is no wonder that her temper became notoriously short. She was forced to face the fact that in marrying she had committed herself to being swallowed up by the Kemble family professionally as well as personally.

That summer all the attention focused on Sarah Siddons as she took her leave of the stage aged fifty-six. For some years critics had been carping that the Great Siddons was growing stout, but now all that was forgotten. Her retirement gave rise to a swell of popular feeling and newspaper commentators wrapped her in an almost mythical mantle of superlatives. Her farewell performance was as Lady Macbeth. The capacity audience honoured her by insisting that the performance be ended with her last exit. Mrs Siddons reappeared before her adoring

*The theatre historian Genest complained that the smell was such that when you sat in the first row of the pit you might as well be sitting in a stable.

fans dressed in white to deliver a farewell address composed by her nephew, Horace Twiss. This theatrical epitaph glossed over her many years as Mrs Beverly in *The Gamester*, or Mrs Haller in *The Stranger*, or even Isabella in *The Fatal Marriage*. Mrs Siddons was to be remembered as a semi-divine communicator of Shakespeare:

> *Perhaps your hearts, when years have glided by,*
> *[. . .]May think on her whose lips have poured so long,*
> *The charmed sorrows of your Shakespeare's song.*[3]

In December 1812 Fanny acquired a new little brother, Henry. She was now walking and displaying all the hallmarks of an intelligent and strong-willed child. She was extrovert and utterly determined and the adults around were no match for her: 'I never cried, I never sulked, I never resented, lamented or repented either my ill-doings or their consequences.'[4] The antics of their lively toddler convinced the Kembles that they needed more space. In 1813 they moved from their lodgings in Newman Street to a rented house in the rural suburb of Westbourne Green, not far from the Paddington Canal. To Marie-Thérèse's great pleasure there was a garden. She had always yearned for the country life. Even before she was married, she had rented a little cottage beyond the city's congestion which she would walk to whenever she had a day free from the theatre.

One day, some misdeed led the adults to put a large fool's cap on Fanny's head. Blithely ignoring the advice to go and hide her disgrace, the little girl bounded off down the drive to meet her friend the postman so that he might admire her new 'helmet'. Scrambling up a nearby bank the histrionic child joyfully invited the passers-by to come and admire. By the time she was retrieved she had gathered quite a crowd. They tried her on bread and water. Fanny expressed pleasure: 'Now I am like those poor dear French prisoners that everybody pities so.' Mrs Siddons, who lived next door, was even called in. She took the small girl on her knee, and, summoning the great tragic voice that had made grown men weep, sketched the consequences of such evil ways to the admiration of the rest of the family who had assembled to watch. The awful speech ended. The silence was broken by Fanny. 'What beautiful eyes you have,' she observed, clearly fascinated. Mrs Siddons smothered a smile and let her go unrepentant. Fanny's problem was decided opinions rather than malice. When an interfering friend of her aunt's suggested that she pray to God to make her better, Fanny shook her head seriously and replied, 'So I do, but he makes me worse and worse.'

At the close of the winter season in June 1813, Charles finally made up his mind and resigned from the Covent Garden company. He and Marie-Thérèse left London to tour wherever provincial managers would offer him the first-rank roles he coveted. For the next two years they starred up and down the country to mixed reviews. March 1814 found them performing in Dublin at the Crow Street Theatre. One anonymous Irish spectator recorded his opinion that neither was 'brilliant' – Charles's impact as Hamlet suffering from the fact that while exiting from his impassioned scene with Ophelia (played by his wife) he 'bumped hard into the door and got a bloody nose'.

In Newcastle that year, the couple came across a young actor who was to feature large in the professional lives of both Charles and, later, his daughter Fanny. William Charles Macready was the star of a Newcastle theatre company. A sturdy twenty-one-year-old, Macready was a life-long diary-writer and famously sour about everyone around him. In his diary, Macready pompously dismissed Charles the established star: 'On the other hand, his Richmond was chivalrous and spirited, and his Cassio incomparable. He was a first-rate actor in second-rate parts.'[5] Young William suggested that the Kembles' visit was something of a wash-out, but the takings must have been lucrative enough, because the London stars were invited back for race week for the sizeable fee of £100.

In Westbourne Green Fanny's childhood unfolded happily enough. The constant Dall was always at hand and the house was a popular calling place for the stars of the day – convivial souls such as the charming Charles Young, whose black hair, Grecian profile and melodious voice cast him as a tragedian although his natural preference was for comedy. He was a great pal of the mimic Charles

Mathews – a comedian Adelaide Decamp had worked with in her acting days with Tate Wilkinson's company in Yorkshire. Dall had been a bridesmaid at Mathews's marriage to his second wife, Ann, in 1803, and the Matthews were staples of the Kemble family's social circle, along with the Covent Garden comedian Liston and his wife. They were a lively bunch with a reputation for practical jokes and amusing conversation. Young liked children and he often went up to the nursery to play. He taught four-year-old Fanny to cross her small arms and, creasing her face into an awful frown, lisp Lady Macbeth's line: 'My hands are of your colour.' Her most successful attempt: 'My handth are of oo tolor', became a family catchphrase.

After twenty-one years, the war with France finally approached its end and the family moved again, this time to within a stone's throw of the churchyard of Paddington parish church, where Fanny liked to play with her brother John, dining off the flat tombstones on bits of fruit and cake supplied by their nursemaid.

As she grew more articulate, the busy adults found the strong-willed little girl an increasing handful. When her mother became pregnant for the fifth time during 1814, Fanny was dispatched to stay with her godmother in Bath. John Mitchell, now seven, thoughtfully supplied his little sister with a collection of children's books to amuse her on the long journey. His sister proved an ungrateful little heathen; having read them too soon it occurred to her that the books might give her additional entertainment. Soon after her arrival at her godmother's, she made a bonfire of her brother's gift. She was immediately caught and reprimanded – an inauspicious start to her stay that was probably a protest at being sent away. However, the Twiss family, whose own children were in their teens, took the five-year-old to their hearts and Fanny became the family pet.

Mrs Frances Twiss, Fanny's godmother, was one of Charles's elder sisters. A softer, more retiring version of Mrs Siddons in looks, she had left an undistinguished stage career to marry a scholarly lawyer. She ran a 'fashionable establishment for the education of young ladies' in Camden Place, a classical Georgian terrace on the slopes above the Roman Baths. Trading heavily on her connection with Mrs Siddons, Mrs Twiss instructed her pupils in the social graces in the Pump Room, supplemented by such arts as shoe-making, bread-seal manufacturing and screen painting (these being considered at the time fashionable accomplishments for young ladies). Despite the frivolous nature of this curriculum, the Twiss family brought Fanny into early contact with models of female learning. Mr Twiss was a progressive father and he made sure that his three girls were competent in Latin and mathematics, as well as generally well-informed and well-read.

Across the Channel Napoleon broke out of his confinement to set the Continent in uproar with his Hundred Day Adventure but little Fanny was happily oblivious in Bath. She enjoyed her time at Camden Place – whether struggling to keep up as her tall cousins swept about in the discarded stage robes of Aunt Whitlock,* or being taken to see her first Shakespeare – a puppet version of *Macbeth* performed in the spacious hall of a local country house. Among her cultured elder cousins, Fanny developed a liking for words that displayed itself in an early love of puns.

While she was an energetic and cheerful child, at six Fanny began to exhibit signs of her mother's nervy temperament. On her birthday she was presented with her first real doll – 'a gorgeous wax personage' dressed in white muslin with cherry ribbons. Fanny was drawn to the splendour of her new charge's clothes but the waxy pallor of the doll upset her.

> I had a nervous dislike, not unmixed with fear, of the smiling simulacra that girls are all supposed to love with a species of prophetic maternal instinct.[6]

Perhaps, being small and rather doll-like herself, she did not like the association with an inarticulate and powerless object. The Twiss cousins had a large elder brother who was studying to be an

*The aunt who looked most like Mrs Siddons, but lacking her talent, crossed the Atlantic to make her career in America beyond the reach of odious comparisons.

engineering officer (he grew up to become a general). When he came home for the holidays, this hearty teenager liked to use the diminutive Fanny as a prop. He would give his version of –

> my Uncle John's famous rescue of Cora's child in *Pizarro*, with me clutched in one hand, and exalted to perilous proximity with the chandelier, while he rushed across the drawing rooms, to my exquisite terror and triumph.[7]

Weeks, then months, passed pleasantly in Bath. Across the Channel the momentous Battle of Waterloo put an end to Napoleon's adventures at last. In spring 1816 Fanny was brought back to London to the Kembles' new lodgings in Covent Garden Chambers near the theatre. She was met with a shock. No longer the pet of her godmother's family, she now faced another rival for her household's attention – a new sister, Adelaide, who had been christened the previous November.

Fanny was determined to find ways to win her parents' notice. The family liked to tell the story of how Talma, the famous French actor, called one day when Charles and Marie-Thérèse were out. Fanny, who answered the door with her nursery maid, received the great man with composure. When – somewhat pompously – he told her to be sure to remember his name and to tell her parents that Talma, the great French tragedian had called, the six-year-old replied that,

> my father was also a great tragedian, and my uncle was also a great tragedian, and that we had a baby in the nursery who I thought must be a great tragedian too, for she did nothing but cry, and what was that if not tragedy?[8]

It was a performance befitting a princess of a great acting dynasty. However, out in theatre-land a revolution was taking place. In 1814 the dramatic map had changed. The scamp, who had ridden the plaster and board elephant in *Blue Beard* all those years ago at Drury

Lane, emerged to conquer the Town with his impassioned style of acting. Edmund Kean had arrived.

After the fire of 1809, it took three years to rebuild the rival Patent Theatre of Drury Lane. In the meantime, Covent Garden had assembled a first-rate company whose popularity with audiences seemed unassailable. For a time the Drury Lane committee considered shutting up shop completely. Then in January 1814 the management put forward as Shylock a short, black-eyed tragedian who had been making a stir in the provinces. No one was anticipating anything great. Only three critics bothered to attend. Luckily for Edmund Kean, Hazlitt was one of them. Hazlitt was riveted and declared Kean 'the first gleam of genius breaking athwart the gloom of the stage'.

As the pressure of more than two decades of conflict lifted, signs of change that had been fermenting at home during the war years rose into view. The period from 1811 to 1819 saw a succession of disturbances across England, culminating in the Peterloo Massacre in Manchester, as working men protested against oppression from their manufacturing masters, and the middle-classes pushed against the aristocratic establishment. Young intellectuals and poets were exploring new forms and new ideas, groping for ways to articulate the spirit of the new age.

William Hazlitt was one such intellectual. Having given up his early ambitions to be a painter (as he decided he would never become a great one), Hazlitt arrived in the capital in 1812 to take up a career in journalism. His first break was to be made drama critic of the leading Whig daily, the *Morning Chronicle*, in September 1813. His strikingly literate essays had just begun to attract notice when Kean appeared. With such an invigorating subject, Hazlitt's articles took off.

Hazlitt said of himself that 'the only faculty I possess is that of a certain morbid interest in things'.[9] His self-atomizing sensibility caught the imagination of the Napoleonic War generation. The pendulum had swung against the clipped formality of classicism towards the worship of untrammelled nature and glorification of sincere feeling that characterized the Romantics.

The Romantics were passionate about Shakespeare – he was the poet of sympathy who unlocked the secrets of the human heart. However, they tended to think that performance trivialized Shakespearean tragedy. In 1811 Hazlitt's good friend Charles Lamb published an essay – 'On the Tragedies of Shakespeare' – in which he argued that an actor only projected a counterfeit 'symbol of the emotion' whereas Shakespeare's genius was to enter into the emotion itself. In an actor's performance, wrote Charles Lamb,

> we find to our cost that instead of realizing an idea, we have only materialized and brought down a fine vision to the standard of flesh and blood. We have let go a dream, in quest of an unattainable substance.

Lamb was reacting to the cult of the actor initiated by Garrick and his mangled playhouse texts, and then developed by John Philip Kemble. Both Lamb and Hazlitt were lovers of the theatre, but they yearned for a 'natural' actor. Just as Shakespeare entered into his characters, so should the ideal actor be able to so enter into the role that they would be 'beside themselves'. Only such an actor could embody the Romantic principle of sympathy. Mrs Siddons had been such an actress, but she had had no successor – until now.

Kean became a sort of poster-boy for the young English Romantics. He represented 'genius' and 'romance' in a coldly rational age. 'Kean! Kean!' wrote Keats. 'Cheer us a little in the failure of our days! For romance lives but in books. The goblin is driven from the heath, and the rainbow is robbed of its mystery.'[10] Like Sarah Siddons, Kean was supposed to be an original.

> Kean was not the copyist of any other, nor the pupil of any school, not a mannerist, but an actor who found all his resources in nature, who delineated his passions only from the expression that the soul gives to the voice and features of a

man . . . The wonderful truth, energy, and force with which he struck out and presented to the eye this natural working of the passions of the human frame, excited the emotions and engaged the sympathy of his spectators and auditors.[11]

Far from handsome – being short and swarthy, with the compact body of a tumbler – Kean was forced to rely on his energy for his effects. His intense black eyes and expressive mobile features made a vivid impression on his audience. His voice was harsh and husky (the opposite of the genteel standard of 'melodious' tones) but to the disquiet of moralists, women were stirred by its sensuality.

Not having any figure to begin with, Kean was not afraid of making himself grotesque. He would roar out certain lines then plummet to a whisper. He varied his pace – racing through passages he thought insignificant – to concentrate the audience's attention on crucial moments (called 'hits' by the profession). His style made his performances uneven – 'he seemed to be husbanding his powers for a point, or for an outburst of impassioned feeling'.[12] As Coleridge put it, to see Kean act was 'like reading Shakespeare by flashes of lightning'.[13] It was a showy technique suited to the vast theatres. It caught the attention of the audiences who found the contrast of his emotional style with the prevalent gentility electrifying. 'Other actors are continually thinking of their sum-total effect,' wrote Keats. 'Kean delivers himself up to the instant feeling, without the shadow of a thought about anything else.'*

The Romantics were anti-class insofar as they celebrated individual genius and self-determination. Taking the common experience of nature for their inspiration, they meant to speak in language intelligible to the uncultivated as well as the cultured. In the Lake District Wordsworth (whom Hazlitt, Lamb and Keats much

---

*Keats's review of Kean in *The Champion*, 21 December 1817, quoted in Bate, *Shakespeare and the English Romantic Imagination* pp. 165–6. Keats left the theatre inspired to 'make as great a revolution in modern dramatic writing as Kean has done in acting' – he too would enter into his characters as Kean entered into his roles and thus revive dramatic poetry in the tradition of Shakespeare as Kean had revived the performance of Shakespeare on stage.

admired) was initiating a revolution in poetry writing (as he put it) about 'incidents and situations from common life . . . as far as possible in . . . language really used by men'.

The height of Kean's celebrity mirrored the years of the radical protests – 1814 to 1819. Hazlitt represented him as the democrat and populist against the old, outmoded patrician style of Kemble. The class distinction was important. To the 'classical school' led by the Kembles at Covent Garden, Kean was vulgar and his advent threatened all those 'artist' actors whose taste served as a passport to genteel society. Kean's style depended on outbursts of feeling and emotion. Gentility was dependent on manners and self-control. 'Mr Kean's acting proves to be "sound and fury, signifying nothing",' wrote William Robson, the committed Kemble clansman. 'He wanted finish, he wanted study; his mind was not cultivated. I don't think he ever sat half an hour . . . in the presence of an educated gentleman, in his life.'[14] Kean never aspired to be anything other than an actor. He was not interested in management, or in adapting texts, and he could not care less about social aspirations – indeed he delighted in keeping 'low company'.

Kean's success damaged the status of the profession that the Kembles had fought so hard to build up. In their eyes, and those of their supporters, Kean 'could not be called an artist in the highest sense of the word'.[15] They were offended by both his frivolity and his technique, honed as a fairground showman. Kean had a habit of coming off stage from a moment of the highest emotion and performing a backflip (an ironic reminder of his early days as a tumbler). He was candid about the tricks he used – as he himself put it – to make 'the house rise to him'. Charles Young's son, Julian, spoke for the classicists when he circulated a piece of Regency gossip about the new star.

> . . . when Kean discovered that his imitation of the hysterical sob under powerful agitation caused ladies to faint, and Byron to weep, from nervous sympathy, he was perpetually indulging in it, not only when it was inappropriate but where its manifestation became absolutely ludicrous . . . one night, when he had been playing before a very intelligent audience, and had been

indulging in the propensity referred to, and had been lustily hissed in consequence, he whispered to Ralph Wewittzer as he retreated behind the scenes, 'By Jove, old fellow! They've found me out. It won't do any more. I must drop my hysterics.'[16]

Once acting was measured by its mob appeal, the classicists knew that the actor lost any status as a man of literature and a potential gentleman. As William Robson wrote in disgust,

> Contrast John Kemble in his library in Russell Street, at his own table, surrounded by the intellectual and refined; or at the board of the patrons of literature and the arts, sitting among the magnates of the land as a fellow and a cherished guest; contrast this, I say, with Kean in his beastly orgies.[17]

However much they might wish him away, the old guard could not ignore the parvenu. The impact of Kean's success began to be financially troubling. By autumn 1814, John Kemble was playing Cato to barely half-filled houses, 'many of the dress-boxes literally empty'.[18] There was nothing to be done but engage the rival head-on; the contest revived the flagging interest of the audiences in Covent Garden. When Kemble played Hamlet in direct opposition to Kean's portrayal of the Prince of Denmark on the very same night, both theatres overflowed.

That summer Charles headed back to rejoin the Covent Garden company. Rising forty, he anticipated inheriting his brother's roles. Even with the town agog at Kean, his hopes were high. At last he was to have his chance. John Philip (somewhat grudgingly) stepped aside to allow his younger brother to give London a sight of the Macbeth and Hamlet he had been honing in the provinces.

Charles's minute attention to detail was lost in the vastness of Covent Garden. His problem was that his interpretations were *too* considered. 'I have heard him give so many reasons for particular renderings of certain passages in Shakespeare,' said one acquaintance ruefully, 'that his notes on the text, if printed, would probably have surpassed it in bulk.'[19] Poor Charles had worked so hard at his gentlemanly performances only to discover that what audiences wanted was vulgar emotion. His great-niece, Lizzie Siddons, explained that Uncle Charles's attempts at the great tragic roles showed a 'deficiency of passion . . . I do not think that he was ever carried away by intense feeling'.[20] The management tactfully steered him back towards genteel comedy, his second-rank roles in tragedy, and into playing Romeo to the Juliet of the elegant new leading lady, Miss O'Neill.

While Charles – for all his natural good temper – must have been cruelly disappointed, his wife was sinking into depression. In the 1815–16 season Marie-Thérèse only appeared in one role at Covent Garden – playing nine times as Lady Emily Gerald in a comedy she wrote herself called *Smiles and Tears, or The Widow's Stratagem*. She took time to pick up from the birth of her last child, Adelaide – a process of recovery hindered by the death of her mother, Jeanne, in February 1816. She began to take to her bed with mysterious ailments – possibly episodes of manic depression.

Fanny returned home from her godmother's to a household straining to accommodate its increasingly unstable mistress. One day, pretty, curly-haired little Henry, a stubborn three-year-old, wandered away from his nurse and became lost in the London streets. Charles and Aunt Dall were frantic for several hours until the boy was found curled up fast asleep in his brown holland pinafore on the doorstep of a grand house in St James's Square. Throughout the crisis the household was on tenterhooks in case Marie-Thérèse, secluded in her darkened bedroom, should get wind of the alarm.

The details of what went on in that household have melted away into oblivion. The indications are that as her career trailed off Marie-Thérèse did not find solace in motherhood. When she was in her late seventies Fanny wrote a novel in which she replayed several memories in fictional guise. Her story features a persuasive portrayal of a wilful, opinionated daughter in conflict with a rigid and angry mother. One scene in particular springs out as being drawn from life. The fictional little girl, aged six, persists in her demands to be allowed to wander away from the house. The mother, losing her temper, ties the little girl to a bedpost so that she can get on with her housework. The father, coming home unexpectedly, finds his small daughter, her face 'purple with suppressed rage and crying, and wrists and arms red and swollen with ineffectual struggles to set herself free'.[21] The father is shocked. He releases the child but significantly says nothing to his wife who, externally controlling a passionate anger quite equal to that of her child, merely states: 'That child is good for nothing and will grow up good for nothing.' Having intervened so far and no further the father leaves to return to his work once more. The child immediately stops crying. She stands scowling, pulling and wrenching at the weave of a cloth covering the table. Twice her mother stops her housework to tell her to stop spoiling the cloth. The child merely deepens her scowl. Finally the mother comes up and forces her small hands from the fabric –

'*Let it alone!*'

'*Why must I?*'

'*Because I bid you and because it is mine!*'

'*Yes*,' the small girl replies forcefully, '*the tablecloth is yours and the table is yours, and everything in the room is yours, except me, and I'm my own.*'

Whether or not this scene actually took place between Fanny and her mother, it seems that the passionate temperament they both shared made for many a clash of wills between them. In Fanny's story the even-tempered father and his passionate daughter share an unspoken alliance in face of the 'irritable temper' of the mother. It is probable that her star-status gone and her gamine attractions blurring under the weight of middle-age, Marie-Thérèse resented the unquestioning affection her daughter shared with her father. It must have contrasted painfully with the caution with which her husband met her own outbursts of emotion.

Business continued to fall off at Covent Garden. John Philip – almost as if he had convinced himself that he *was* the Last of the Romans – continued stoically on through his stately rotation of parts, ignoring the mounting signs that he had held on a couple of years too long. 'The very tone of Mr Kemble's voice has something retrospective in it,' wrote Hazlitt. 'It is an echo of the past.'[22] The Great Man even suffered the humiliation, on the occasion of his last performance as Sir Giles Overreach (once one of his most celebrated parts), of the audience demonstrating its clear preference for the after-act, a pretty Italian tight-rope walker. Still John Philip clung grimly to his mission to bring taste to the capital. In April 1816 bills pasted up across town trumpeted a 'wonderful celebration' of the 200th anniversary of Shakespeare's death. In a deliberate echo of Garrick's famous jubilee, John Philip played Coriolanus, followed by a grand pageant of all the poet's great characters. The audience enjoyed the spectacle and left. The Golden Age was over. The Last of the Romans had become passé.

The Covent Garden management decided that their theatre needed more fire power to combat the tremendous draw of Kean at Drury Lane. In autumn 1816 they signed a deal with Macready, who drove a hard bargain to reserve for himself the best roles before he arrived in town to appear as Orestes in *The Distressed Mother*. Even before his brother had retired, here was a new aspirant to the tragic throne to whom Charles would have to give way.

The following June the whole family gathered in town. Even Marie-Thérèse came out of her seclusion to play Beatrice opposite Charles's Benedict in *Much Ado about Nothing* for her husband's Benefit. The Kemble clan and their supporters prepared for the momentous event of John Philip's farewell to the stage.

On the historic night of 22 June 1817 the Great Kemble gave his last performance as Coriolanus. The theatre was full and the audience threw themselves into the spirit of the occasion. When the curtain fell the pit rose up in a body, waving hats, handkerchiefs and laurels for several minutes. John Philip, with a fine show of reluctance, came forward for one last time.

> Whatever talents I am master of, whatever exertions I have made as an actor or a manager in improving the propriety of costume, and giving increased splendour to the representations, particularly those of Shakespeare, they have been

> rendered delightful to me on account of the favour with which you witnessed them.[23]

He bowed, wreaths of laurels falling about him, and the Last of the Romans retired.

John Philip had scarcely set off for his Swiss retreat before the fights broke out over who was to fill the vacuum he left behind. One day, on the stage during rehearsals, Henry Harris, son of Thomas Harris, the senior proprietor, even threw a punch at Charles 'for alleged heartless and irritating conduct'.[24] Despite the draw of Macready – who was turning in intelligent performances – audiences continued to melt away and everyone was frustrated.

In the midst of all these stresses, Marie-Thérèse decided that she was unable to cope with her unruly and opinionated seven-year-old. Fanny's parents felt that fluency in French was an indispensable foundation for a cultivated young woman and they selected a school in Boulogne. Fanny was told that this was because Boulogne was really quite near her home. In truth, their choice probably acknowledged the fact that as the daughter of a Catholic actor and a French comedienne, Fanny would face less prejudice on the Continent than in an equivalent English school. Besides, it was cheaper. Boulogne at this time was a fashionable refuge for English expatriates escaping their debts. It was quite usual for fashionable Londoners passing through to recognize the faces of old acquaintances in the main street.*

Sensible Aunt Dall might paint the delights of France and the excitement of making new friends, but the fact that she was sent away while her brothers and little sister stayed at home branded Fanny with a sense of rejection. At the tender age of seven she faced her first exile from the protective circle of her extended family.

---

*The town was so familiar to the English that the locals nicknamed Boulogne's prison 'L'Hôtel d'Angleterre' – see Lennox, *Fifty Years of Biographical Reminiscences*, vol. II, p. 266.

7

'Cette diable de Kemble'

By sending their seven-year-old daughter away to school in France, the Kembles were doing their best to obtain for her that 'finish' – the education and polite manners – that would be her passport to gentility. The school they chose was on the oddly named 'Rue tant perd tant paie',* a steep winding street in the older part of Boulogne. The tall town-house was owned by a weathered, vivacious and impatient Frenchwoman by the name of Mme Faudier, who ran her establishment with the help of her daughter, Mademoiselle Flore. Fanny described the daughter as a figure out of Dickens – 'a bouncing, blooming beauty of a discreet age' with a 'florid complexion, prominent black eyes, plaited and profusely pomatumed black hair, and a full, commanding figure'.[1] Her memories of her time in their care were similarly Dickensian.

Fanny arrived in Boulogne resentful and determined not to conform. She knew no one, she had little experience of mixing with other children, and besides she was the youngest member of the school. She was recalcitrant by day and cried to herself at night. Through ignorance or dislike, Mme Faudier met Fanny's

*'Rue tant perd tant paie' roughly translates as 'the street of who loses pays'.

disobedience with brutality. Her first punishment was to lock the little girl in an attic. Left to her own devices, the resourceful child found her way on to the roof, where she entertained herself admiring the view. A passer-by noticed a small figure dancing on the leads. Mme Faudier recaptured 'cette diable de Kemble' and locked her in a cellar without even a candle. Fanny spent the whole ordeal sobbing, huddled at the top of the dank staircase as she tried to draw comfort from a glimmer of light that seeped in under the door. It was an experience that was to stay with her for many years and gave substance to her later portrayals of terror on stage.

It was not long before she transgressed again. Eventually Mme Faudier went to the lengths of having Fanny taken to witness a public execution under the pretext of frightening her out of her disobedience. Fanny wrote subsequently that she did not know whether it was done deliberately, but she and her escort arrived in the square after the event. The spattered guillotine and the smell of the gutters running with blood imprinted themselves on the child's memory. Such cruel treatment was not that unusual for boarding schools at the time, but it was no less traumatic – and there was no appeal. Fanny's parents and Aunt Dall were beyond reach. At an early age Fanny was taught a hard lesson in self-reliance.

Fanny reacted to the trauma with Kemble steel. She became a high achiever within the limited curriculum on offer at Mme Faudier's. The emphasis was on social fluency in languages – French and Italian – music and dancing. As her parents intended, young Fanny learnt to speak French so well that in the future natives would compliment her on her lack of accent. Fanny won more than her share of the prizes at the end of year celebrations. Neither Aunt Dall nor her parents could get away to witness her triumph, but they ensured that a friend of the family was present to see the short, black-eyed little girl climb the podium to receive her awards. The applause of the local dignitaries and parents gathered in that sunny courtyard was balm to her battered spirit. With puritanical self-analysis, the adult Fanny later commented that 'abundant seeds of vanity, self-love, and love of display, were sown' that day.[2]

After nearly two years away, in the summer of 1818, Fanny was allowed to return home to London. Marie-Thérèse was preparing for her final engagement at Covent Garden. Since John Philip's retirement, Henry Harris and his advisors – the playwright Reynolds and Mr Fawcett the stage manager – refused to cast Marie-Thérèse in her traditional roles, arguing that she was too old and too stout for them. She did not give in gracefully. Her last years at Covent Garden were marked by constant quarrels with the management, and while Fanny was away at school she hardly worked at all. Employing all the resources of her famously 'severe and sarcastic'[3] tongue, Marie-Thérèse fought to the last to retain the gamine parts in which she had made her name. As a woman, in theatrical terms she had had a good run for her money, but it must have been galling to witness the contrasting development of her husband's career. When Charles courted her, she was the star. Now she was at the periphery of everyone's vision – an irritation and a nuisance. Meanwhile her husband was looking to follow his brother into management.

Marie-Thérèse was miserable and misery highlighted the 'savage' side of her nature. Her furious outbursts and episodes of depression became more severe. She was increasingly suspicious of her husband's interest in other women – with good cause. The jealous tempers she parodied so charmingly in her *Day After the Wedding* became tedious and embarrassing in a middle-aged mother of four. Social acquaintances attending the parties the Charles Kembles held noted the strains between the couple. One of their habitual guests, the aristocratic Green Room lounger and enthusiastic amateur actor, Lord William Pitt Lennox, recorded Marie-Thérèse's outbursts with amusement. While her once sprightly figure had acquired pounds with each childbirth, her handsome husband only seemed to grow more attractive to women. Many of the pretty actresses who decorated the Green Room were open in their attentions. Like a large cat, Charles always enjoyed being petted. Marie-Thérèse became so well-known for her domestic scenes, that the management at one point took advantage of the gossip to cast the pair opposite each other in

The Jealous Wife. 'Never was a comedy played with more spirit,'[4] as Lord William put it slyly.

The couple were no longer 'comfortable in each other's society every day' as during their young days at the Haymarket. Bored with the confrontations, Charles froze his wife out. He rented a second home in the semi-rural setting of Craven Hill in Bayswater. Aunt Dall explained to the children that Mamma suffered from the London fogs. The dense 'pea soupers' that were created by the coal fires that heated the capital affected her breathing and oppressed her spirits. During the last year of her career Marie-Thérèse frequently stormed off to their 'country' house, leaving both husband and management unsure as to when she would return.

The house at No. 3 Craven Hill stood in a row of villas, some of some pretension, others less so, each with pretty gardens, verandas and balconies hung with flowering creepers. Craven Hill was about a mile from Tyburn Gate, the tollgate marking the junction of the Oxford and Edgware Roads. In the 1820s, agents for the Bishop of London, who owned much of the land, began to develop residential suburbs in the area known as Tyburnia, but when the Kembles rented No. 3 Craven Hill the stretch between the Tyburn Turnpike and Bayswater was covered with open fields. There was a carriage road in front of the house with a border of elm trees, beyond which meadows and nursery gardens ran down to the Bayswater Road and Kensington Gardens. The setting was rural enough to delight Marie-Thérèse while retaining a measure of civilization. Their next-door neighbours included the large, bearded Italian Egyptologist Benzoni on one side, and the dashing Mrs Blackshaw, a sister of Beau Brummel, on the other. (The Beau himself had been driven into exile on the Continent by his debts in 1816.)

To outward appearances, at Craven Hill the Kemble children enjoyed a normal middle-class upbringing. John Mitchell was sent to school in Clapham. His master, Mr Richardson, was a scholar who supplemented his income by taking pupils while he completed his true work – the compilation of a dictionary. He employed his more gifted pupils to assist him in the task and this, according to Fanny, gave her elder brother the fascination with language that would lead to his adult career as a philologist.* Henry, who was seven, attended a day school in the neighbourhood. There were no schools for their sisters, however. Fanny, aged nine, and her sister Adelaide, aged three, were left under the supervision of Aunt Dall. Aunt Dall had had little formal schooling. She had been apprenticed to a musician at the age of fourteen.[5] There were few lessons; most of the time the two girls were left to amuse themselves. The three-year-old doted on her big sister and Fanny was fond, in the detached way of older siblings, of her small audience and acolyte. The girls revelled in their Bayswater garden after the smoky streets of London. A favourite treat was to be taken to a nearby nursery to spend their pocket money on pots of violets and seeds for their particular patches of earth.

During the 1818–19 season both parents were regularly absent working in London. Now that they knew she was retiring, the management allowed Marie-Thérèse several roles, including a re-creation of her 'Irene' in yet another revival of *Blue Beard*. In June 1819 Dall brought the children up to London for her sister's farewell performance, which was to take place at her husband's Benefit on Wednesday, 9 June. Typically, Charles's family could not even allow Marie-Thérèse to shine on her own last night. Battered by Kean's success at Drury Lane, the Kemble Clan gathered their big guns. Mrs Siddons herself came out of retirement 'for one night only' to support her brother at his Benefit.

Sarah Siddons was cast as Lady Randolph in the tragedy of *Douglas*. She was now sixty-four and everyone knew that this would be the last opportunity to see the legendary actress on stage. The excitement was intense and Fanny pestered her father to such effect that that afternoon he took her in his arms to see the vast crowd waiting patiently for the doors of the theatre to be opened, aiming to convince her that there would be no room in the auditorium for her. The dense mass of theatregoers filled the whole Piazza. At the last

*John Mitchell's fascination with the roots of language eventually led him to become a leading authority on Anglo-Saxon.

minute her indulgent father gave in to his favourite, and Fanny was there that night to see her famous aunt dressed in funereal black acknowledging the tremendous roar of applause. The child was particularly struck by her aunt's melancholy face and dress, and the terrifying barrage of sound from the audience. It was the only time she ever saw the great actress on stage.

Despite the enthusiasm of the crowds the performance itself was not an unmitigated success. The 26-year-old Macready, who took the role of Glenarvon opposite Mrs Siddons that night, wrote snidely in his diary that the great actress only managed 'a gleam of her original brightness'. As for Marie-Thérèse – her last appearance as Lady Julia in the after-piece – her own farce *Personation* – was nothing but a footnote to the evening.

For all the reams printed about the celebrated Kembles, the theatrical historian Genest distilled Marie-Thérèse's thirty-six-year career in four short paragraphs under her married name as Mrs Charles Kemble. He summed up her theatrical epitaph in a bare couple of lines. She was 'a very good actress – no person understood the business of the stage better – no person had more industry'.[6]

The excitement was over. Charles Kemble took up his regular engagement at the Haymarket for the summer and Marie-Thérèse retreated to the suburbs. Charles became a weekend commuter, making the three-mile walk out to see his family each Saturday, and returning to London the same way on Monday morning.

Marie-Thérèse threw herself into domesticity with manic energy. She might not like the bother of young children, but she had a talent for arranging a comfortable home on a budget. As one acquaintance put it, she was 'fond of management and . . . carried her talents for it into all her domestic arrangements'.[7] She toured sales, picking up bargain pieces of furniture to smarten up their shabby, ready-furnished rented rooms. She was a good cook, and bottled and preserved fruit from the garden, made jellies and jams, and created a pastille to lubricate her husband's voice that was the envy of fellow actors. There was a frantic note in her occupations. She was always struggling to keep depression at bay, and as she explained to a friend once, furniture moving was her favourite way of defeating the 'blue devils'.

> We never knew when we might find the rooms in a perfect chaos of disorder . . . while my mother, crimson and dishevelled with pulling and pushing was breathlessly organizing new combinations.[8]

Whatever Marie-Therese did to rearrange her rooms, she was powerless to rearrange her life. Her career gone, her passionate nature worried away at her loss of her husband's attention. And the more passionate she became, the more he slid away from her with the polite affability of a Cheshire Cat. While Dall continued to hold the household together with her usual even temper, her sister was increasingly cast as the family invalid. All her homemaking efforts were in vain. When her husband arrived at the weekend, he would generally pull a face as he looked around, chanting the refrain, 'Why, bless my soul! What has happened to the room, again!'

Despite the tensions within her marriage, Marie-Thérèse still retained her famous charm and her presence attracted friends and family to Craven Hill. Aunt Whitlock came to stay for several months. A legend in the family, as far as the children were concerned, Aunt Whitlock, now widowed, had retired from a reasonably lucrative stage career. An eccentric figure, a raw-boned version of Mrs Siddons – like a bad copy in an auburn wig that frequently slipped – she would play cards interminably with Marie-Thérèse. While members of the Kemble side of the family were usually marked by their 'quiet dignity and reserve of manner', Aunt Whitlock was a hoot. Her conversation was

> like that of people in old plays and novels; for she would slap her thigh in emphatic reinforcement of her statements (which were apt to be upon an incredibly large scale), not infrequently prefacing them with the exclamation, 'I declare to God!' or 'I wish I may die!'[9]

Her irreverent younger brother Charles called her Queen Bess.

Such relatives contributed to Fanny's gallery of powerful female role models. Aunt Whitlock, for all her comical eccentricity, had earned her living travelling across America at a time when it was still considered a wild and inaccessible continent. The children would sit wide-eyed, and somewhat sceptical, as she told them of Indians following her through the streets of Philadelphia and of flights of birds that almost darkened the sun.

While the London residence was 'principally inhabited by my father and resorted to by my mother as a convenience', during the winter season when Covent Garden was in operation, the children would spend several weeks in town. Charles had moved the family lodgings to 35 Gerard Street, Soho. The handsome old building, standing opposite Anne Street, had once belonged to the 'wicked Lord Lyttleton', who had famously been forewarned of the premature end of his rakish career by the ghost of a scorned mistress. The house now belonged to a picture dealer. His smoky Old Masters loomed over the corridors, and Fanny would always pass them at a run, fearful of the 'ill-defined and ill-discerned faces' lurking under the cracked varnish.

In these lodgings the Kembles kept up appearances amid the faded grandeur of broken-down aristocracy. Marie-Thérèse's pupils – the young *ingénues* to whom she gave acting lessons – walked through a rococo anteroom with mirrored double doors and ceiling to reach her oval drawing room. Charles put up shelves in the lofty dining room and called it his library. Fanny remembered him at that time sitting in his armchair there, enchanting her with his delivery of 'the sonorous melody' of *Paradise Lost*. No matter if the fine plaster mouldings were chipped. As actors the Kembles had long experience of contriving the illusion of gentility against shabby sets.

There was plenty of room in the old building for the parents to lead their own lives while Dall supervised the children. Again, there were few lessons, although Fanny was sent out to a music teacher. As no one was willing to supervise her piano practice in detail, a sort of harness, a 'chiroplast', was purchased. This invention strapped a brass brace around the child, tying metal rods to her arms so that

Fanny's small hands would be held in the proper position over the keys. It was supposed to prevent her falling into bad habits.

It was a lonely existence and in later life Fanny was nostalgic about the times when the family was all together. The little girl particularly admired her elder brother. When he was home for the holidays, John Mitchell added excitement to the house. He set up chemistry apparatus in an out-of-the-way spare bedroom – exacerbating his mother's chronic fear of sudden death with nightmares of being blown up by her son's experiments. Toy theatres were then very much in vogue and the Kemble children spent many happy hours cutting out and colouring the printed sheets, and pasting them carefully on to card. John Mitchell, who was by now in his early teens, was a handy boy. Their little theatre had a real blue silk curtain that could be rolled up and down, and proper burning footlights. The neat figures were fastened by the feet into a groove at the end of a stick and manipulated about the miniature boards through memorable productions such as *The Gypsy's Curse* and the great favourite – a toy version of a Haymarket hit – *The Miller and His Men*. A musical melodrama in the tradition of Schiller's *The Robbers*, it featured lots of people in disguise, imperilled lovers, a villainous miller (who is secretly the robber chief) and several rousing choruses. The Kemble children delighted in their production, particularly as John Mitchell used his chemistry set to concoct a mixture of resin, brimstone and salt that produced a 'diabolical splutter and flare' as the mill blew up at the climax of the play.

Encouraged by this success, John Mitchell went on to organize their friends to put on a proper play. During the London season, Fanny and her brothers and sister mixed with the offspring of other Covent Garden stars, such as the sons of Charles Mathews, Charles Young and the comedian Liston. The children put on a popular operatic burlesque, a hit at Drury Lane that season, called *Amoroso, King of Little Britain*.* They performed the entire piece, complete with songs, for their amused parents. It was Fanny and Adelaide's first

---

**Amoroso, King of Little Britain* was the first professionally performed piece of the dramatist J. R. Planché who had a long and productive career through the first half of the nineteenth century and was to become an important colleague of Charles Kemble's during his management of Covent Garden.

dramatic appearance and they were proud to be taken notice of with such warmth.

It was not thought seemly for Fanny to attend Covent Garden (the last appearance of Mrs Siddons being a special exception), but she was taken as a treat to Astley's Amphitheatre on the Westminster Bridge Road in Lambeth. Astley's, which had begun life as a riding school, before developing into a circus and then a theatre, was a much-loved institution among Georgian children. It specialized in 'grand spectacles and pantomimes wherein numerous horses are seen in what has every appearance of real warfare'.[10] The treat that filled the sawdust ring to Fanny's delight was 'a Highland horror called *Meg Murdock, or The Mountain Hag* and a mythological after-piece called *Hippolyta, Queen of the Amazons*'.[11] She was much impressed by the stage Amazons, who wore unconventionally short, shiny tunics and burnished breastplates, and engaged in choreographed battle sequences.

The audiences at Covent Garden grew alarmingly thin as the new decade dawned. The weight of debts hanging over from the reconstruction in 1809 were brought into crushing focus. Charles Kemble as Macbeth opened the 1819–20 season – 'a part which his best friends considered him unsuccessful in'.[12] The manager, Harris, told a friend that times were so black he was ready to shoot himself. Macready took advantage of the crisis to demonstrate his reliability. Unlike Edmund Kean, Macready had his eyes set on being a successful actor-manager. For a few weeks the theatre was only able to open its doors because Macready organized a postponement of the actors' salaries until the Christmas pantomime season could boost receipts.

The company limped through Christmas before another blow fell. In January 1820 George III died and the theatres were closed for a three-week period of official mourning. When they reopened, once again Macready saved the day. He brought a hit to the Garden in the shape of a new tragedy, *Virginius*, by a then unknown Irish playwright, Sheridan Knowles.* The play had been written for Kean but

*Sheridan Knowles, a cousin of Richard Brinsley Sheridan, went on to become one of the most admired British dramatists of the nineteenth century.

that mercurial genius had rejected it. Macready, in contrast, shrewdly identified both the dramatic talent of Knowles and a star vehicle for himself. *Virginius* became a comforting financial success and underlined Macready's position as the leading tragedian of Covent Garden.

In October 1820 old Thomas Harris died. As the majority shareholder, he had been the official patentee of Covent Garden. On his death, his son did not inherit his authority. The right to choose the manager reverted to the four remaining proprietors.

That November John Philip Kemble, now a stately, white-haired sixty-three-year-old, arrived from his Swiss retreat to stay at Gerard Street. Ostensibly in town to attend Harris's funeral, he took the opportunity to transfer his sixth share of the Covent Garden patent to Charles.

He did not make this gift out of pure generosity. He did it to preserve his remaining assets from being 'swept into the ruin which had fallen upon Covent Garden Theatre'. He seems to have had little conscience about saving himself at his brother's expense. Having passed over the poisoned chalice, he retired, with his 'beautiful and benign face', to live and die in peace at Beau Site, his house above the lake at Lausanne.

Charles received his brother's gift with 'cheerful courage, and not without sanguine hopes of retrieving [Covent Garden's] fortunes'. He remained spellbound by the ghost of his brother's dream, yet for others the dream was broken – as Hazlitt had predicted back in 1816:

> We wish we had never seen Mr Kean. He has destroyed the Kemble religion; . . . an old and delightful prejudice is destroyed, and no enthusiasm, no second idolatry comes to take its place.[13]

Fanny approached her teens a bored and unhappy little girl. At eleven years old she was 'a tragically desperate person',[14] vainly striving to catch her parents' attention. She was hypersensitive and still resentful of Adelaide, the little sister who was never sent away. She even considered poisoning her younger sibling by strewing privet berries in her path. Her intention was to make her parents suffer rather than her sister (she imagined Adelaide making a smooth transfer to heaven). In the event she did no more than confess the fact to Aunt Dall, who very sensibly refused to take the dramatic admission seriously.

Her impatient parents decided to pack their eldest daughter off to school once more. Fanny reacted with dramatic desperation; she contemplated suicide. When the pond she had selected to drown herself in proved to be covered with unattractively slimy green weeds, she ran away instead. Her plan was to reach London and seek an engagement at one of the theatres. As she reassured herself – 'nobody with talent need ever want for bread'. She was hardly a mile or so down the road before Aunt Dall caught up with her.

The adults' response was – as ever – somewhat theatrical. Every day for a week Fanny was confined to a shed in the garden, fed only on bread and water and left alone to meditate on her sins. Rather than admit her distress or sue for forgiveness, she sang at the top of her voice every time she heard a footstep on the gravel.

All her protests were in vain. On a hot summer day in 1821, as the capital resounded to the coronation of George IV, Marie-Thérèse, accompanied by her friend Mrs Charles Mathews, set out with Fanny on the journey to France. A few days later they placed her in a school in the Rue d'Angoulême off the Champs Élysées in Paris.

8

The Schoolgirl

The headmistress and proprietor of Fanny's new school was well chosen to guide an imaginative and wilful child. Mrs Rowden, an Englishwoman, had begun her career teaching in a fashionable school in Hans Place in London. There, a generation before, Mrs Rowden had under her care two young women who provided contemporary pendant portraits of alternate good and bad fates awaiting girls with lively imaginations. On the one hand, there was Lady Caroline Lamb – the scandalous lover of Byron – who brought herself to disaster by her indulgence in riotous passion. On the other – Mary Russell Mitford, the spinster authoress who willingly sacrificed her life to the domestic comfort of her clergyman father, and who was celebrated as much for being a dutiful daughter as for her successful writing career.*

In the eyes of contemporaries Fanny Kemble was at high risk in her passage from girlhood to womanhood. As the weaker sex, females were considered to be in danger from their thoughts and feelings. As one educator expressed it later in the century, the emotional female imagination was 'the weak part of woman; the breach

*Mary Russell Mitford had some success with plays, but she is perhaps best known as the author of *Our Village* a series of vignettes about her idyllic home near Reading.

in the wall by which the enemy often enters into the city'.[1] It was a popular assumption that over-indulgence in imagination, passion and the wrong sort of literature led a girl to ruin. Too many play-books caused Polly Peachum to throw herself away on a highwayman. Gothic novels made a fool of Jane Austen's Catherine Morland in *Northanger Abbey*, while Sheridan's Lydia Languish is the epitome of the silly miss, her brain addled by the sentimental novels she borrows from the circulating library.

Under the careful eye of Mrs Rowden girls were prepared to become the wives of rational men – the kind of partner suited to upper-middle-class professionals, such as civil servants, diplomats or well-connected clergymen. And if it were not their lot to find a husband, her pupils would be equipped to earn their living as governesses. Mrs Rowden had once been a great playgoer who still nursed something of a crush on Fanny's handsome uncle, John Philip. She had since found religion and turned 'methodistical' – but in spite of her renunciation of the theatre she was prepared to welcome a niece of the great John Kemble.

Under Mrs Rowden Fanny was given a grounding in Latin; she learnt the Greek alphabet; she acquired a familiarity with the French classical authors – Racine, Corneille, and even Voltaire – and she developed her Italian to encompass a fair knowledge of the poetry of Dante. She and her fellow pupils were schooled in music and dancing for polish, and dressmaking and mending for practicality. By the time she left the school she was a confident young girl, capable of carrying on a conversation in educated company, able to present herself in a ballroom with propriety, and still make her own dresses if necessary.

It was an above average education for a girl of her generation. But perhaps more importantly Mrs Rowden, and in particular her principal teacher Mademoiselle Descuillès, provided a happy and secure atmosphere.

The school building had once been a grand private hotel in the old-fashioned Parisian style, with a *porte cochère* and inner court. Mlle Descuillès, the 'active and efficient partner in the concern', was a warm, intelligent woman in her thirties who elicited affection from her pupils. Under her eye, Fanny prospered. She remained an independent soul. She formed no close life-long friendships although she developed a crush on an older girl. Elizabeth P—— was elegant, reserved and genteel, with a scholarly bent (Fanny took Latin and learnt the Greek alphabet for her sake). It was an admiration that set a pattern for subsequent intense friendships later in her life. Conscious of her impulsive temperament, Fanny would always look up to poised women with graceful manners and intelligence.

During her three years at Mrs Rowden's Fanny was schooled in the benefits of rule over riot. She particularly loved the convivial, domestic Saturday mornings when the girls would bring their sewing into a ground-floor classroom. The long glass doors open on the inner courtyard to let in the breeze, the pupils would mend and make clothes while Mademoiselle sang medieval French ballads to them, recounting tales of chivalry when knights and troubadours went off to war dreaming of their lady-loves.

In one respect Fanny's Paris education reproduced a weakness that had impeded her mother's social success: although most of her girls were from the United Kingdom, all classes were conducted in French. French became 'the language in which I habitually wrote, spoke and thought, to the almost entire neglect of my native tongue'.[2] Although she later taught herself from books Fanny would never be completely confident of her English grammar. She returned home stamped with a touch of 'foreign-ness' that would always mark her out in sober Anglo-Saxon society.

However, for recreation the girls would read books sent from home; Fanny's favourite author was Sir Walter Scott, the first British literary celebrity of the nineteenth century. In 1805, Scott published the *Lay of the Last Minstrel*, a 'romance' based on a Border legend about a goblin, which became an instant bestseller influencing a whole generation. Fanny loved the riding rhythms of the *Lay* and its successor, the stirring tale of *Marmion*, featuring the noble knight Lochinvar –

> *So faithful in love and so dauntless in war*
> *There never was a knight like the young Lochinvar.*

Stimulated by Scott's 'stirring, chivalrous stories, and spirited picturesque verse' she began to write poetry 'without stint or stopping – a perfect deluge of doggerel'. She was further inspired by her Italian teacher, a political exile with 'wild melancholy eyes', who communicated his enthusiasm for Dante by teaching his pupils Italian from his copy of *The Divine Comedy*.

The enthusiasm for poetry at the turn of the nineteenth century was an early sign of the broadening readership engendered by industrialization. By the second decade Sir Walter's somewhat staid celebrity was rivalled by that of Lord Byron. When the publication of the narrative poem *Childe Harold* made Byron famous in March 1812, the sale of an edition of 500 copies in three days made him 'the talk of London'. Two years later, *The Corsair* sold out its entire run of 10,000 copies on the very day of its publication. Byron himself might cherish his lionizing by the Whig aristocrats he met at Holland House but his celebrity was made among the same people who revelled in the 'debased' taste for melodrama – the aspiring middle classes. Byron was the James Dean of his day. Young women swooned in their provincial parlours while rebellious young apprentices tousled their hair and left their collars undone as they adopted the world-weary pose of their hero.

One of Fanny's most acute memories from her Paris schooldays was of her first encounter with Byron's verse. She was half asleep in the headmistress's drawing room one evening, under the portrait of her famous uncle, when an older girl showed her a volume of Byron's poetry. Fanny claimed that she read only one couplet,

> *It is the hour when from the boughs*
> *The nightingale's high note is heard*

and she was so moved that she snatched the book from its owner, insisting that she be allowed to take it away to read properly. Later that night, Fanny was so worried by her possession of such a 'dangerous' work, that she stuffed it under her mattress and had the owner come to collect it unread the next day.

Now that his name is cemented into the wall of the English literary heritage, the acute danger of Byron's poetry may not be immediately obvious. For all his posthumous classification as a leading Romantic, Byron's poetry was rooted in the aristocratic mind-set of the eighteenth century. His art was said to express his life (rumours abounded that *Childe Harold* was the real man's fictional persona and that the indiscretions paraded in verse were his own). In aristocratic circles, with their malleable morality and 'refined' wit, the poet's weary worldliness was as much titillating as shocking. But the readership was broadening and women were on their way to becoming the 'great dictating portion of the reading world'.[3] The 'ordinary' reader peeped into Byron's libertine world with an awareness of sampling forbidden fruit.

The couplet Fanny absorbed in the somnolent warmth of her headmistress's drawing room that evening opens the lurid tale of *Parisina*. The nightingale sings as the adulterous wife Parisina waits, bosom heaving and ears straining, for the whispered words of her lover Hugo. The added frisson is that Hugo is the bastard son of her husband, Prince Azo. The guilty lovers are exposed when Parisina breathes Hugo's name as she lies asleep in her husband's arms. Her jealous spouse, being a prince and unforgiving, dispatches his treacherous son in a public execution. Handsome Hugo goes to his end with noble composure and Parisina goes mad and is immured in a living death. Although their sin is paid for by madness and annihilation, the poet's sympathies are clearly with the guilty lovers –

Who that have felt that passion's power
Or paused, or fear'd in such an hour?

As Fanny recalled the incident she barely consumed a few lines, but had she read so far, the advocacy of sensation and lust would have rung alarm bells in any morally conscious girl. She described the effect of Byron's verse had upon her as being 'like an evil potion taken into my blood'.

The respectable, god-fearing folk busy weaving the moral fibre of a progressive civilization after the defeat of Napoleon (who provided an object lesson in the consequences of the romantic glorification of the individual) were acutely conscious of the poet's way with words. Among educators Byron's work was regarded in much the same light as good church-going parents in 1950s America feared Rock 'n' Roll. The poet was a Pied Piper calling the youth away to a freedom beyond laws. His sexual misdemeanours, his disruptive opinions, the sensuality of his verse, were part and parcel of his abandoning God's word in favour of his own self-made rules. Byron's poetry represented the 'evil potion' that could be distilled from unbridled Romanticism. The pursuit of 'instant feeling' could – if not tempered by the guiding hand of God – become an addiction that led to moral degradation.

By a concentrated act of will Fanny denied herself Byron's seductive verses; she returned for the time being to the safe ground of Scott's novels. They were full of 'healthful delight', peopling her imagination and giving her 'for companions and friends, men and women of such peculiar individual nobleness, grace, wit, wisdom and humour'.[4]

Under Mrs Rowden's care Fanny learned to feel self-conscious about her lack of religious education. Mrs Rowden's pupils were drilled in the regular use of the Bible. They recited passages by heart before breakfast and read sections aloud before bedtime. Fanny wrote in her memoirs that the greatest benefit she gained from her Paris schooling was this intimate familiarity with the Scriptures. Day by day she absorbed the rule of self-denying discipline and the soothing mechanism of piety. She came to regard these as an anchor, a defence against the riot of her unruly temperament and the uncertainty of her tempestuous home life.

By this time Charles had dropped any hint of his Catholic origins. He learned from his elder brother to avoid any singularity in either politics or religion. His religious observance was all that was sufficient to maintain a gentlemanly demeanour and little more. If he happened to be home at their bedtime, the children would be paraded to kneel before him as he sat in his library chair so that he could lay a hand on each head and repeat: 'God bless you! Make you good, happy, wealthy and wise.' His daughter described her home as one of 'average English Protestants of decent respectability'. Marie-Thérèse was a regular member of the Swiss Protestant Church and would read the Bible to the family before breakfast. Dall taught the children their catechisms and collects. They were taken to church every Sunday and brought up to say morning and evening prayers. Nonetheless, it was a light-handed religion, 'quite without enthusiasm'.*

Mrs Rowden's religion, on the other hand, was full of enthusiasm. Her pupils not only attended two or three services on Sundays, they were taken to hear fashionable preachers in the private salons of wealthy hosts. There, seated in satin and gilt armchairs, the select company would thrill to the admonitions of some impressive touring preacher. It was stimulating and exciting. It was not just inspiring – this was God-sanctioned entertainment. Each Sunday evening the girls wrote a summary of the sermons they had heard, and one girl was chosen to read her account aloud to the rest of the school. If memory failed, a girl might be allowed to choose a text and make up her own address. Fanny made herself popular by composing suitable sermons for her less imaginative friends. As Fanny herself admitted, she acquired 'rather an inclination for preaching' – it was a legitimate outlet for her penchant for performance; a way for a girl to 'put herself forward' without being blamed for it.

The engraving from Lawrence's portrait of John Philip Kemble as Coriolanus that hung in the headmistress's drawing room illustrated the celebrity that was largely responsible for Fanny's presence in the school. At the same time, Mrs Rowden's attitude made it clear to her that the theatrical life was an immoral one. In France – Fanny was informed – actors were not even allowed the dignity of burial in consecrated ground, being classed by convention alongside suicides and murderers.

---

*Echoing the famous epitaph for a late eighteenth-century Anglican Bishop – 'he was a good man, quite without enthusiasm'.

On the other hand, Mrs Rowden's recent distaste for the theatre did not prevent a distinctly theatrical bias among the male teachers she employed. French and Latin were taught by a 'clever, ugly, impudent, snuffy, dirty little man, who wrote vaudevilles for the minor theatres, and made love to his pupils'.[5] The dancing master was assisted by his son, a rather self-conscious youth who was a member of the corps de ballet at the Paris Opera. Fanny's first music teacher, Mr Shaw, had been a band leader at both Covent Garden and Drury Lane, while his replacement, Adolphe Adam, had a glowing theatrical future as the composer of the archetypal Romantic ballet, *Giselle*. For a growing girl, the signals were conflicting.

While the headmistress publicly pretended to disapprove of her pupils' dramatic efforts, all the while she 'winked at' the plays that the girls got up under Mlle Descuillès. Fanny shone in these productions. In one prophetic piece of casting, she was given a lead in a didactic piece by Mme De Genlis called *L'Isle Heureuse*. Her role was as the multilingual princess who is passed over as ruler of the island in favour of

> the tender-hearted young lady who, in defiance of all sound systems of political and social economy, always went about attended by the poor of the island . . . to whom she distributes . . . a perpetual stream of charity.[6]

The moral was clear: brains in a woman do not lead to success. Self-effacing piety – the serving angel role – was the one to win a girl approval. So it was that when Fanny caused a stir in a production of *Andromaque*, 'electrifying' both the audience and herself in the part of Hermione, Mrs Rowden stepped in quickly to dampen her enthusiasm. 'Ah my dear, I don't think your parents need ever anticipate your going on the stage; you would make but a poor actress.' Her snub still rankled with Fanny fifty years later, but she could not shake the underlying message. The status of a respectable woman, a feminine woman, was incompatible with a talent for public performance, however much the audience might applaud. And yet, the heady distinction of celebrity remained.

In the summer, when the Covent Garden season was finished, it was Charles Kemble's habit to travel to Paris to scout the French theatres for suitable plays to transfer to his stage.* Naturally, he took the opportunity to visit his daughter. When her handsome, famous father descended on the school, charming the teachers and fascinating the girls, Fanny knew that she was the envy of all her fellows.

Charles enjoyed squiring his pretty pocket-sized daughter, with her vivacious dark eyes, and rosy cheeks. Far from the irritating influence of her mother, Fanny blossomed in the light of her father's attention. 'Pleasant days of joyous camaraderie and flanerie! – in which everything, from being new to me, was almost as good as new to my indulgent companion.'[7] For Charles these Paris holidays were a welcome break from the cares of work and his troubled marriage. In 1822, just as he wrested the management of Covent Garden from Henry Harris, the rumours about his relations with young actresses crystallized in a piece of scandal printed by Oxberry in his monthly journal. The story was that Marie-Thérèse had discovered her husband at Howe's Royal Hotel in Margate in bed with another woman whom he had registered as his wife.

Charles and his daughter toured the usual sights – the Tuileries and the Palais Royal – and some more suitable to a mistress than a daughter. They shared 'déjeuner à la fourchette at the Café Riche', and little suppers in 'the small cabinet at the Trois Frères' before going on to the theatre to see the leading French stars of vaudeville and comedy on 'the small stages of the Porte St Martin, the Variétés, and the Vaudeville'.

During those Parisian holidays with his daughter, Charles personified what early nineteenth-century audiences conceived of as the perfect gentleman: that charming, handsome, flirtatiously asexual 'gay companion' who never existed before literature invented him. To his blooming daughter he was just like one of Scott's ideal characters – a

---

*The first decades of the nineteenth century suffered from a total lack of decent British playwrights. So English managers would hop over the Channel to Paris to seek out the best French material to translate and adapt for the London stage.

man of 'peculiar individual nobleness, grace, wit, wisdom and humour'. These golden days confirmed the special bond between the pair.

In Fanny's second year, Mrs Rowden moved her school to an even better address – a substantial stone house, standing behind high iron gates a few hundred yards back from the Champs-Élysées. The property was said to have once belonged to Robespierre. There was a deep well in the corner of their playground about which the girls told gruesome stories of victims the tyrant had drowned there. At break times, memories of Astleys Amazons still lingering in her mind, Fanny staged mock battles with her school fellows under the linden trees while Mlle Descuillès sat sewing in a comfortable chair in the shade.

During her three years in Paris she never went home. Her school holidays were spent as a guest of the family of a *petite bourgeois* rentier, a friend of her mother's, who owned a pretty house with green shutters and an orchard on the road from Paris to Versailles. Her hosts were kind to her. They took her to her first ball at the age of fourteen.

The pleasant afternoons spent mixing with the fashionable crowds on the Boulevard in company with her elegant father had given Fanny an eye for clothes. In clothes as elsewhere, the Romantic spirit was blowing away the severity of classicism – the column of the empire dress vanishing as waists drew in to accentuate bust and hips. It was a good time to be a teenage girl. Female fashions were becoming exuberant and eye-catchingly feminine. Fanny went to her first ball a pretty, confident young girl proud of the white muslin frock nipped in at the waist by a vivid red sash that contrasted so charmingly with her dark eyes and hair.

The ball was held at the school of her hosts' eldest son. Among the youths she was introduced to that night, uncomfortable in their cravats and pumps, she met a quiet, handsome lad of nineteen or twenty. Reserved and gentlemanly, with dark good looks reminiscent of her Uncle John, he was on his way to a commission in the English army and a posting in Gibraltar. She discovered he shared her love of Dante. They parted well pleased with one another. His name was Augustus Craven.

In spring 1824 word reached Paris that Byron had died at

Missolonghi. Fanny was more moved by the news than when she had been informed of the death of her Uncle John Philip months before. Change was in the air. She had lost interest in childish games under the linden trees. On the Boulevards hats were mushrooming, waists diminishing and skirts flaring above a daring glimpse of ankle. Elizabeth P—— left Mrs Rowden's and then, as summer approached, Fanny's father arrived to take her home.

In the French capital Charles Kemble was at his happiest and most confident – the cosmopolitan gentleman socializing with the managers of the leading Paris theatres and checking out the latest acts with his friend Charles Young and the playwright Planché. The latter accompanied Kemble and his daughter as they set off back to London, providing Fanny with the opportunity to make the acquaintance of the author of the piece in which she had made her dramatic debut (that childish production of *Amoroso, King of Little Britain*).

The journey was uneventful except that, as she enjoyed the boisterous wind on the deck of the packet boat crossing the Channel, Fanny's hat blew away. As soon as they landed Fanny convinced her father that its replacement ought to be an ultra-fashionable 'full-sized Leghorn'* – a sophisticated straw hat with a sweeping brim and trailing ribbons. She sat dwarfed under this preposterous confection for the rest of the journey, mighty pleased with her grown-up dignity, despite the faces pulled by respectable matrons who clearly regarded the hat's extreme proportions as inappropriate for a young girl.

They travelled on from London to Weybridge, where Marie-Thérèse had taken a cottage for the summer. Fanny later recalled that as they jolted nearer to their destination her thoughts were divided between anticipation and anxiety that her mother would be a stranger to her. Dusk fell as they passed the desolate estate of Portmore Park with its ruined mansion. The scattered dwellings of a scanty village appeared in the dim light and the coach drew up at last. Outside, a silvery voice with its French accent rang out in the dark, 'Is there anyone here for Mrs Kemble?' and – hat and all – Fanny returned to her mother's arms.

---

*Leghorn– a type of white straw.

9

The Forging of a Masculine Mind

The fourteen-year-old who returned to her family in her oversized fashionable hat was a sturdy little body well under five feet tall with luxuriant dark hair, clear skin and the melting brown eyes of the Kembles. Her kinship to her mother was by now pronounced in her mobile face and her energetic opinions expressed with that quirk of foreignness that comes from extended periods of thinking and speaking in another language. Mrs Rowden's discipline, however, had equipped Fanny to cope better with the clash of wills that had dominated her childhood, and her mother went so far as to admit that her Paris education had much improved her eldest daughter.

At Weybridge Marie-Thérèse had the rural life she had always craved. Set on the River Wey some twenty miles south-west of London, Weybridge was then a picturesque, rather deserted-looking village standing by the road that ran to Winchester and Southampton. The poverty of the sandy soil had caused the native gentry to move away, deserting the estates that had once supported the village. The neighbouring house at Portmore Park was falling into ruin and even the great estate of Oatlands, famous in the previous generation as the residence of the Duke of York, that summer of 1824 stood mothballed awaiting a new tenant. The wild, neglected solitude of the place, with its lingering traces of aristocracy, suited the Kembles and especially Marie-Thérèse.

Eastlands Cottage was the last respectable dwelling on the outskirts of the village. It was a pretty place except that the front aspect was disfigured by a monstrous heap of sand that the landlord, the village baker, had dumped there. When he refused to remove it Marie-Thérèse cut a path through the mass to the front door, sculpting it into a raised and turfed walkway around a circular planting of shrubs and flowers – an eccentric feature that the family were proud to refer to as 'the mound'.

Fanny's mother was 'infinitely happy' at the cottage. Now fifty, she had grown decidedly stout, which, as she was a small woman, meant she was ill-served by the bulky fashions of the day, the yards of material in skirt and sleeve making her at times seem almost cubic. Her habitual fierce outbursts of emotion were tempered by her delight in her situation. She had at last regained some control over her life. One of her recipe books survives in the hands of a private collector; its pages reflect her enthusiasms and her credulity. Her notes span tips on how to cut glass, instructions on winemaking, the ingredients for a paste to whiten hands roughened by hard outdoor use, and a terrifying potion 'as used by Spanish women to make their hair black' composed of 'lime as prepared for white washing' and white lead (to be left on the hair overnight under a covering of cabbage leaves).

The family convention was that Charles had no taste for the country life apart from the occasional sociable hunt or shooting party. At six foot tall, Charles was 'too high and too wide, too long and too large' for the low-ceilinged rooms of the cottage. During the family's summers there he was an occasional weekend visitor, travelling down by stagecoach on a Saturday and returning to town on Monday morning to a handsome house he had rented at 5 Soho Square.

After three years away, Fanny returned to her household an unfamiliar figure. Her beloved Aunt Dall had not changed much – she was still her pretty, reliable self, with her good humour and dry wit – and yet she was now more particularly Adelaide's Aunt Dall. Adelaide had only been five when Fanny left for Paris. Now, perhaps, Fanny realized that in being sent away to school, she had had the better bargain. In later life Adelaide described her childhood sadly to Annie Thackeray, conveying her sense of having been left behind to run about the country neglected and untaught. At eight years old she had elongated into a slight, shy, bean-pole of a girl used to her own company and grateful for any attention.

Both sisters had, in their separate ways, learned to keep their own counsel to avoid confrontation with their mother. As a result the domestic existence at Weybridge was relatively calm. The family's communal pursuits tended to be silent ones. Marie-Thérèse had a passion for fishing. She would spend days at a time on the wooded bends of the lovely River Wey on the Portmore Park estate. Whether she caught fish or not, she would watch her line through sun and rain, happy to leave her clothes drying on her back after a shower. Many mornings the whole family would set off in the dawn light, a gypsy line of differing heights trooping behind the determined figure of Marie-Thérèse carrying baskets, rods, kettles and folding stools, the family's two dogs – a large Newfoundland with its bear-like head and a boisterous little terrier – scrambling about them. Sometimes even the family cat would follow at a discreet distance in the way of felines. Years afterwards Adelaide would recall the horror of being required to impale the soft, contorting worms on her mother's hook. Fanny's memories were more idyllic. She would lie cradled in the low branches of an ancient cedar tree overhanging the river, reading and writing as she enjoyed the music and movement of the sparkling water that ran beneath her perch. It was only as an adult that Fanny developed her mother's passion for fishing, finding the water and the lights reflected off it hypnotically soothing, a refuge from the many irritations of everyday life.

According to Ann Blainey,[1] who has studied a private collection of Adelaide's letters, the sisters soon grew close, Tottie finding protection behind her sister's new-found confidence in the face of their mother's sharp tongue.

The girls loved Eastlands Cottage as much as their mother did – the garden filled with flowers; the small orchard of greengages, apple trees and a venerable pear tree beyond which the common, dressed in heather, rolled up to a pine wood cresting the ridge. While Adelaide preferred to lie amid the golden gorse cloud dreaming, Fanny walked for miles over the 'beautiful rambling and scrambling ground' of purple heath and fir woods. In her contemplation and enjoyment of the beauties of nature Fanny was free from the strain of countering and accommodating the will and emotions of others. She poured out the passion of her teenage soul in poetry, scribling verses 'without stint or stay', some indeed in very bad Italian. She was establishing a habit that was to remain one of her greatest resources through all the emotional turmoils of her life:

. . . in the inmost chambers of my soul
There is another world, a blessed home,
O'er which no living power holdeth control,
Anigh to which ill things do never come.
There shineth the glad sunlight of clear thought –[2]

Wrapped up in fancy words, and padded into some approximation of metre, she gave order and intellectual expression to things improper for her to articulate in ordinary speech. (She was not alone in this; as Mary Russell Mitford wrote to a friend in 1813 – 'lack-a-day and woe is me! I never can cry except in poetry'.[3]) In later life Fanny specifically referred to the therapeutic element in her poetizing –

> perhaps an eruption of such rubbish was a safer process than keeping it in the mental system might have proved; and in the meantime the intellectual effervescence added immensely to the pleasure of my long rambling walks in that wild, beautiful neighbourhood.[4]

This packaging of her 'intellectual effervescence' was also a way to win her father's attention. On one of her elusive parent's visits she proudly gave him some of her poems to read. Charles Kemble returned them to her 'with his blandest smile', saying, 'Very well, very pretty indeed! My dear, don't you think, before you write poetry, you had better learn grammar?'[5] The reproof sent her scurrying to 'diligent study of Lindley Murray' – the contemporary schoolroom primer.

Fanny's unschooled little sister and resolutely down-to-earth Aunt Dall provided little stimulus to her eager brain. She consumed what books she could lay her hands on. The pleasure of her father's rare visits was enhanced by the books and musical scores he would bring from the outside world. Fanny was captivated by *Oberon* and the other magical German fairy tales she read in translation. She was especially enchanted by de la Motte Fouqué's tale of Undine, the water sprite. Stories of elves and fairies, the Wood-witch and the little dog Stromian enlivened her walks, colouring the Surrey woods with a 'world of supernatural beauty and terror'. Down a tangled path of overgrown shrubs and foxgloves she discovered a circle of huge cedar trees in a secluded part of the Oatlands estate. Its peace underpinned by the sound of a stream running nearby, this place seemed to her romantic imagination to be pervaded by the distilled spirit of all that she found inspiring in nature. The grove became her favourite haunt; her 'Cedar Hall'.

Much as she enjoyed her Weybridge freedom, Fanny was conscious that in leaving Paris her formal education had stopped. She was well aware of the emphasis her father put on the cultivation of the mind. It was their intellect, after all, that made the Kembles genteel. The Parisian holidays they had spent together were fading into the past. She was in danger of losing her special relationship with her elusive father just as her mother had done. His remark about her lack of grammar highlighted the contrast between her situation and that of her brothers. Grammar – that science of language – was 'favourite light reading' for the educated males of her family: her father, her Uncle John Philip and her brother John Mitchell. Grammar symbolized the rigorous honing of the intellect that seemed a masculine prerogative.

Charles Kemble was determined to provide his sons with the best possible education. John Mitchell and Henry were boarders at the Edward VI Grammar School at Bury St Edmunds, then one of the most well-regarded schools in the country. Under an enlightened headmaster, Dr Benjamin Malkin, Fanny's brothers were exposed to a sound classical education and forged life-long friendships with boys who would grow up to become respected intellectuals – William Bodham Donne, Edward Fitzgerald and James Spedding. John Mitchell, who turned eighteen in 1825, was preparing to go up to Trinity College, Cambridge, that autumn.

When their school broke up for the holidays, Fanny's brothers brought an invigorating element of masculinity to the Weybridge household. John Mitchell, known as Jackie to his friends, was an elder brother any sister could be proud of. Flamboyant and opinionated, he had inherited the striking dark looks and height of the Kemble side of the family along with something of his mother's obsessive enthusiasm. One friend described him as 'very clever, very confident, very wayward . . . few . . . had so much of the making of the great man in him'. He was also kind to his younger sisters. Fanny was thrilled to be promoted to the 'nobler companionship' of her brothers. They allowed her to field cricket balls in their games and Jackie even took the time to teach her to shoot. The 'fowling piece' proved too heavy for her small frame but she liked the 'pretty little lady-like pocket pistols', and glowed beneath her brother's approval when she proved to have a steady hand and an accurate eye.

At twelve years old Henry was a beautiful boy – so beautiful indeed that he was encouraged to coast through life on the goodwill engendered by his outward appearance. His sister never remembered him being motivated by anything stronger than his childish ambition to wear leather breeches and be a gentleman. Charles Kemble's sons were the repository of his greatest hopes – a comfort to him through all the vicissitudes of his Covent Garden property.

Charles Kemble made his move into management aged forty-six (in this respect matching his brother who assumed control of the Garden at the same age). In spring 1822, while Fanny was in Paris, he and his fellow proprietors signed Articles of Agreement under which Henry Harris was pushed out of active involvement in the concern, the other proprietors becoming Harris's tenants at the extortionate rent of £12,000 a year. Charles was appointed acting manager with the assistance of the stage manager, Fawcett, the sole remaining member of the board with experience of running a theatre.

Many commentators have judged Charles Kemble's record in management harshly. Alfred Bunn, a manager of the younger generation and a friend of Henry Harris, labelled John Philip's younger brother as being 'taken possession of by . . . a vaulting ambition which o'er leaps itself'. By the end of the century it had become commonplace to dismiss Charles Kemble as a manager who 'spent money like an Irish landlord' – a man whose gentility (or vanity) blinded him to the realities of business. In fact the direction of a London Patent theatre in the first half of the nineteenth century was a corporate affair. The treasurer of the theatre held official overall control of money matters. The mounting of the lavish 'spectacles' so popular with the broader audiences were the responsibility of the theatre's 'purveyor of spectacle'. Charles Kemble's ownership of a sixth share of the Patent gave him insufficient power for the kind of control enjoyed by Garrick. In order to make any serious financial commitments he needed the support of at least two of his fellow proprietors.

Nonetheless, in Charles's mind Covent Garden was still the 'Kemble House'. John Philip Kemble had built himself an influence beyond that owing to his financial stake in the enterprise. Charles drove himself into the ground pursuing the elusive hope of repeating his brother's success. But times had changed. Sarah Siddons, tragedy's greatest draw, had retired. The glittering Devonshire House set that used to fill Black Jack's gilded boxes had faded into anecdotes of a past age. Sheridan was no more. The divine Duchess,

Georgiana, had gone to her grave in 1806 and the once fashionable Prince of Wales had subsided into the stout frame of the petulant and ageing George IV. The new audiences needed to fill the remodelled Covent Garden were an entirely different proposition. Straining their necks to see a distant stage, readers of Pierce Egan rather than Shakespeare, they roared at pantomime and farce. Shakespeare had to be telegraphed and dressed with spectacle if it was to be endured, for subtleties and shading were blotted out by the sheer size of the auditorium. It was Charles's misfortune to be born a generation too late.

With a characteristic combination of optimism and stubborn denial, Charles would not recognize that the Kemble Era had passed. He employed his status as a proprietor to outmanoeuvre both Macready and Harris, thereby alienating both the theatre's biggest draw and its most capable manager. The consensus of contemporary commentators and later historians has been that if Harris had been able to retain sole control he might have steered Covent Garden back to prosperity. As it was, the struggle between the manager and the over-ambitious actor hastened the theatre's decline.

Nevertheless, Charles began his management with the strongest company the theatre had enjoyed for years. Just as it had done when John Philip took over Covent Garden in 1803, the press expressed hopes for an era of 'superior taste', as Kemble was a 'scholar, gentleman and perfect master of his art'. As J. R. Planché recorded, the Kemble presence still made Covent Garden genteel. Despite the fact that the theatre was strong in comedy and spectacle, the leading members of the company were, in general, considered to be 'higher in social status, more refined in manners, more intellectual in conversation' than their Drury Lane rivals.

> It was 'jolly' enough to dine with Kean at the Black Jack Tavern, or sup with him and a few more 'choice spirits' at Offleys; but the retrospection was more gratifying after a quiet little family dinner with Mr and Mrs Charles Kemble.[6]

In his first season as manager Charles Kemble mounted productions of *Macbeth*, *King John*, *Henry IV* and *Julius Caesar*. For a few weeks Charles was in his element. He particularly enjoyed himself rollicking and singing as the merry Friar in Planché's new opera (to music by Bishop), *Maid Marian*. William Robson testified that he played his part with 'such an extraordinary abandonment and gusto . . . that one felt transported back to Sherwood Forest'.[7]

Actors such as Edward Fitzball might appreciate how 'agreeable and intellectual' Charles Kemble made his rehearsals, but sadly gentility did not pay the bills. The proprietors made the fatal mistake of skimping on their actors' fees. Charles did his best to persuade his colleagues that an artist should expect a low salary as the price of belonging to a company committed to the highest standards, but few were convinced. Across at Drury Lane, the rival manager Elliston was paying his stars handsomely on the back of receipts brought in by Kean. The first casualty of the parsimonious policy was Charles Young, the old family friend who had taught the four-year-old Fanny to lisp Lady Macbeth's lines. When Young's contract expired in 1822 the management offered him mean terms that added up to a salary cut. He crossed over to the rival theatre at £20 a night in contrast to the £20 a week he had been paid at Covent Garden.

Now the rival Patent theatre was exhibiting both the great Romantic actor Kean, and on alternate nights, one of the leading exponents of the classical school too:

> Bills were posted all over London, advertising the early appearance on the same boards of the two men who had long been regarded as the rival representatives of the two opposite schools of art. The widespread excitement produced, few but the habitués of the theatre in those times could believe. Places were secured at the box office five and six weeks before hand.[8]

Before 1822 was out, the proprietors of Covent Garden were panicking. They begged Henry Harris to come back. Harris had the satisfaction of turning them down, stating flatly that he could not make bricks without straw.

Charles Kemble fought on bravely under the gathering storm clouds. The solution, he felt, was to return to his brother's policy. In March 1823 he mounted another production of *King John*, hoping that the old war-time favourite would fill the seats once more. It did not. Contemplating the wretched house that attended the second performance, he decided to gamble on an idea floated in a casual conversation with his friend Planché.

Planché was struck by the potential of the stage to bring history to life. It was an affront to the audience's intelligence, he argued, to have actors playing thirteenth-century soldiers at Angiers clothed in costumes men might have worn to fight at Bosworth at the end of the fifteenth century. Planché offered his services for free if Charles would only give him the money to re-dress the production in historically accurate costume.

Like his brother before him Charles cherished his image as a cultured man. Here was a chance to carry forward – and even surpass – John Philip's reputation for scholarship in the Kemble quest for artistic 'truth' on the stage. And best of all, such a production might well prove to be the novelty that would bring in the town once more.

The project highlighted Charles's true weakness as a manager – his lofty disregard for the need to foster consensus. With the patrician arrogance of his brother, he gave Planché a free hand to re-stage the production. In so doing he carelessly overlooked the professional sensitivities of Fawcett, his stage manager, and Farley, the Garden's valuable 'purveyor of spectacle'. In short, he scarcely noticed that he had alienated the two men crucial to the highest earning entertainments at the theatre. In his memoirs, Planché recorded somewhat complacently the disgust of the actors who stigmatized his 'authentic' twelfth-century helmets as stew-pans. 'They had no faith in me, and sulkily assumed their new and strange habiliments.'

Planché could afford to be good-humoured. He was able to look back on this production as the vindication of his theories. At the opening night of the re-launched production in November 1823 the audience were met with the sight of Macready dressed as King John –

> as his effigy appears in Worcester Cathedral, surrounded by his barons sheathed in mail, with cylindrical helmets and correct armorial shields and his courtiers in the long tunics and mantles of the 13th century.[9]

It was the first attempt to create on stage a material vision of the apparent historical realism that had made Scott's novels so popular. The impact on the audience was considerable. The theatre was filled with £400 to £600 worth of business a night. It was Planché's proud boast that 'a complete reformation of dramatic costume became from that moment inevitable upon the English stage' – and Charles shared in the artistic kudos of the innovation.

During those winter evenings in 1823 the actors on the Covent Garden stage became a living embodiment of the past for their late-Georgian audience. The town was charmed. Although the production did not bring about the sudden transformation that he anticipated, during the next generation Planché's notion became a means of reclaiming the stage for respectable purposes (just as recognition of Scott's status as an antiquarian and the way his stories appeared to reanimate the past elevated the reputation of the novel). The 1823 production of *King John* showed the way for the historicism in Shakespearean staging for which the Victorian actor-manager Charles Kean (son of Edmund Kean) was to become famous in the middle of the century. Like John Kemble before him, Charles Kean would augment his stature as a tragic actor through his image as an intellectual. Whereas Kemble cultivated his status as an interpreter of Shakespeare, Kean was to bolster his reputation as a public educator who made history tangible.*

---

*In the words of historian Richard Schoch: 'The theatre of the mid-nineteenth century was thus at last purified and vindicated under the sign and authority of history.' Schoch, p. 64.

With hindsight, his involvement with Planché over *King John* would prove to be Charles Kemble's most significant contribution to the history of the English stage. However, the management's decision to save money by pinching on the performers' salaries was a cancer at the heart of the concern. Covent Garden's best talent drained away to the rival theatre at Drury Lane. By the end of the 1822–23 season, when Macready himself changed theatres, Elliston's liberal salaries had gathered practically all the leading actors of that generation – bar Kemble – into his company. Drury Lane was riding high and Covent Garden was in decline. Then in February 1824 a minor shareholder caused the theatre to be placed under receivership by disputing the terms of the lease. The Kemble House was sinking inexorably into a morass of legal disputes and debts.

Just when it seemed as if the situation was becoming hopeless, salvation appeared in the form of Weber's *Der Freyschütz*. The opera had already charmed audiences across Europe. In the winter season of 1824–25 Weber-mania arrived in London. Barrel organs ground out his best tunes from street corners all over town. Weber's opera filled three theatres simultaneously, running in English, Italian and German versions. The receipts from the Covent Garden production were so encouraging that Charles Kemble was galvanized into visiting Weber in Germany to persuade him to write a new opera for Covent Garden. He returned home with an agreement whereby Weber would conduct the oratorio season at Covent Garden in Lent 1826 and compose the music for a new opera of *Oberon* to a libretto written by J. R. Planché. Weber had managed to extort a much heavier price than Charles Kemble had wished to pay, but Fanny's father was full of optimism.

Fanny, fresh home from school, adopted her father's enthusiasm. She declared herself to be in love with Weber. She and Tottie learned the tunes of *Der Freyschütz* by heart and she sang the opera through as she took her long rambles over the Surrey countryside. In a romantic affectation she folded up a picture of the middle-aged composer and wore it about her neck in a black silk bag.

Weber arrived in spring 1826 and took up residence with Sir

George Smart, Charles Kemble's colleague and friend, and a respected conductor of music at Covent Garden. The rehearsals for *Oberon* were not easy; the actors could not sing and the singers could not act. Charles Kemble also realized something that had not been revealed when he made his bargain with the composer. Weber was dying of a lung complaint. His doctors had told him that if he rested he might have another five years or so. Instead, determined to provide for his family, Weber exchanged his remaining years for the £1,000 Charles Kemble paid him. When Fanny met her idol, he was stooped and yellow with illness. His hooked nose and bony features struck her as 'ugly'. She blushed and told him that she adored him for his music. 'Ah, my music,' he sighed, half-joking. 'It is always my music and never myself!'[10]

Oberon or The Elf-King's Oath had a reasonable success when it opened but the subtleties of Weber's music proved to be too complex for a broad audience. As Planché explained wearily –

> Ballads, duets, choruses, and glees, provided they occupied no more than the fewest number of minutes possible, were all that the playgoing public of that day would endure. A dramatic situation in music was . . . inevitably received with cries of 'Cut it short!' from the gallery.[11]

The artist-aristocrat was out of step with the 'debased taste of the age'.

As Weber lay dying in Sir George Smart's unfamiliar house in Great Portland Street he had the added misery of knowing that Rossini had arrived on the scene and the town was moving on to its next idolatry. Sociable and light-hearted, Rossini made a popular celebrity. As Fanny recorded,

> the brilliant, joyous, sparkling, witty Italian . . . was a far better subject for London lionizing than his sickly, sensitive, shrinking, and rather soured German competitor.[12]

Sixteen-year-old Fanny remained faithful. She kept the black silk bag with its crumbling engraving about her neck for several weeks after Weber died. The man himself was buried at Moorfields. The Covent Garden management put on a dramatic spectacle complete with 'mutes on horseback in silk dresses'[13] and the theatre band playing Mozart's *Requiem* over the grave. Weber's remains lay buried in the alien land that had taken the last three months of his life until 1844 when Richard Wagner instigated their removal and re-interment in Dresden.

Fanny was still visiting her father in town when word arrived from Marie-Thérèse that smallpox had appeared in Weybridge and that Tottie had fallen ill. Marie-Thérèse had had her children inoculated but understanding of the process was so sketchy at the time that it was not realized that the procedure had to be repeated if immunity was to be maintained. Watching her sick little girl, Marie-Thérèse lost her faith in vaccination. She reasoned that as Tottie's case was a mild one, her elder daughter could benefit from a lifetime's immunity from this killer disease at the price of a week or two's discomfort. Marie-Thérèse would brook no argument; she demanded that Fanny return to Weybridge.

Fanny returned and as anticipated fell ill. Unfortunately the effect of the difference in age and constitution between the sisters had not been anticipated. As the vicious pustules gouged into her face and body, Fanny sank under the delirium and pain. She very nearly died. Whereas little Adelaide recovered quickly with only a small blemish on her nose, Fanny crept from her sickbed weeks later badly scarred. The lively teenager who had returned from school with 'a clear, vivid complexion, and rather good features' now saw herself with a 'thick and muddy' complexion, her features 'heavy and coarse'. As she wrote of the incident in later life, she considered herself left with

> so moderate a share of good looks as quite to warrant my mother's satisfaction in saying when I went on the stage, 'Well, my dear, they can't say we have brought you out to exhibit your beauty.'[14]

Given the conventions of the day Fanny could not openly blame her mother – and yet it was Marie-Thérèse's wilful behaviour that had brought this curse upon her. It was not as if her mother had no experience of the fact that siblings could be affected differently by the disease. In her teens Marie-Thérèse had caught smallpox at the same time as her handsome brother Vincent. Vincent recovered with his fine cut features and clear skin intact while his elder sister was badly marked on the cheeks – although the fine outlines of her bone-structure had not been affected. Fanny's account of the episode suggests that at times she wondered whether her mother had taken deliberate revenge on her for being young and for supplanting her in Charles Kemble's affections.

Whatever fragments of motivation might have been drifting about in the depths of Marie-Thérèse's subconscious, once the damage had been done she was desperately repentant.

> Terrified by this result of her unfortunate experiment, my poor mother had my brothers immediately vaccinated, and thus saved them from the infection which they could have hardly escaped, and preserved the beauty of my youngest brother, which then and for several years after was very remarkable.[15]

By the time she wrote her memoirs the passing years had given Fanny the confidence to state that, although she considered herself plain, she by no means always appeared so to others*; even so, the language in which she recounts her story betrays the depth of her trauma. She was 'disfigured for life'. Her mother made her cutting comment with 'satisfaction'. At the age of sixteen her impulsive, wilful, savage mother had robbed her of her true face. For the rest of her life Fanny would have to depend upon her masculine mind as much as other women trusted in their femininity.

---

*In old age she would relate the double-edged compliment of her 'comical old friend' Mrs Fitzhugh against her younger self – 'Fanny Kemble, you are the ugliest and the handsomest woman in London!'

10

'The Glad Sunlight of Clear Thought'

It was not in Marie-Thérèse's nature to dwell on whatever guilt she might have felt over the scarring of her child's face. Her impulse was to action. As soon as Fanny was fit to travel, she packed up her traumatized daughter and set off on a brisk round of visits to friends and relations, ending up with Uncle John's widow, Priscilla.

After burying her husband in Lausanne in 1823, Priscilla Kemble had sold the villa in Switzerland. She returned with a sigh of relief to the Home Counties where she could once more be in regular communication with the genteel society on whose gossip she thrived. Her husband's patron and friend Lord Essex gave her use of Heath Farm on the edge of Cassiobury Park, his Hertfordshire estate just outside Watford. It was an attractive, mellow farmhouse looking over its own lawn and flower-garden to the green slopes and mature trees of Cassiobury's parkland.

The Kembles arrived at Heath Farm that May, just as the first roses were blooming, to find Sarah Siddons a fellow visitor. Having outlived her favourite brother, her husband and her five eldest children, the great actress, now turned seventy, was feeling the burden of her years. She was accompanied by her last surviving daughter, her faithful youngest Cecilia. Cecilia had entered life a sickly child and, as her siblings went to their graves one by one through her youth and teens, Mrs Siddons had kept her close. In 1826 she was in her thirty-first year, a well-meaning woman whose identity was subsumed in her role as her famous mother's dutiful companion.

Maturity and widowhood had smoothed relations between the sisters-in-law. Now Priscilla and Sarah welcomed the entertaining gossip Marie-Thérèse brought from her busy husband and imparted with her Gallic flair. As the three veteran actresses set about dissecting their mutual acquaintance, the scarred young girl might have been forgiven for anticipating a dreary time. Instead, that visit to Heath Farm was to become enshrined as one of her happiest memories, for it saw the beginning of the most important friendship of Fanny's long life.

Priscilla's house party included a genteel Irish spinster who was a year younger than Cecilia. As the daughter of the Honourable Richard St Leger and a granddaughter of Viscount Doneraile of County Cork, Harriet St Leger descended from the aristocracy so beloved by Priscilla. Harriet's elder sister, Marianne, had made the acquaintance of John Philip Kemble and his wife in the early years of the century. Stage-struck, Marianne was pleased to be admitted to the family circle of the Prince of Wales's favourite theatre manager. Marianne eventually married a well-born Church of Ireland cleric, the Reverend Henry Taylor, and went to live in his family home, Ardgillan Castle, a few miles north of Dublin. In 1809, the year Fanny was born in Newman Street, fourteen-year-old Harriet joined her sister's household and Ardgillan Castle became her home for the next fifty years. Introduced to the Kembles by Marianne, Harriet became a devoted admirer of the stately John and after his death, as Fanny put it, she 'retained an enthusiastic love for his memory and an affectionate kindness for his widow'.

Miss St Leger was a striking figure. Tall for a woman at the time, and athletic with a body-type that reminded Fanny of Diana the huntress, her short chestnut hair curled around a pale-skinned, narrow face that tended to melancholy. She was unmistakably genteel and eccentric. She would only wear black, grey and white, disdained all ornament and insisted on having her boots made by a man's boot-maker. (The clumsiness of these boots particularly distressed Fanny as they 'concealed and disfigured' Harriet's 'finely turned ankles and high, arched, Norman instep'.)

The fact that this costume was not merely 'mannish' but an attempt to project an 'other' sort of female persona is indicated by the fact that Harriet was by no means uninterested in her clothes. Miss St Leger was fastidious about the high quality of the fabrics from which her garments were made – 'it was difficult to find cashmere fine enough for her scanty skirts . . . or lawn clear and exquisite enough for her curious collars and cuffs'. Harriet was both a robust, outdoors-type and determinedly intellectual – in recognition of which masculine traits she was known to her family and close friends as 'Hal'. An evocative passage from one of her few surviving letters describes her occupations at home in Ireland to Cecilia Siddons:

> I cut down trees, I play with my dog, I dig, I carry potatoes to the donkeys, I listen to the music of the mind.[1]

Shy in general company, Hal found it easiest to form relationships with women much younger than herself. She displayed intense sympathy for young women eager to stretch their minds. As a younger friend of hers in the next generation, Frances Power Cobbe, explained,

> she was a deep and singularly critical thinker and reader, and had one of the warmest hearts which ever beat under a cold and shy exterior.[2]

Prey to self-doubt and depression herself, the shy spinster immediately recognized the vulnerability of the sixteen-year-old trying to hide her fresh scars. Leaving the rest of the house party to themselves, the pair spent their time at Heath Farm in almost constant companionship. They 'walked and talked together the livelong day', whether striding off into the lovely summer mornings fragrant with lime-blossom or lingering on the lawn of an evening sharing rhapsodies over the song of a nightingale. The time her thirty-something friend was lavishing on her teenage niece offended Priscilla's sensibilities. She tried to curb their endless discussions by sending them up to bed with 'very moderate wax candle ends'. Fanny appealed to Cecilia, who kindly pilfered the full-sized candles unused in her mother's dressing room, and by their light the new fast-friends talked on into the night.

Hal crossed Fanny's path at a crucial time. Not only did the older woman offer Fanny the affection and attention she had always craved, but she also offered understanding. Fanny's leading characteristics, as noted by the majority of her friends – including Henry James – were her energy, courage and 'animal' high spirits. Having first met Fanny when, quite literally, she bore her scars fresh on her face, Hal knew the private self Fanny so successfully disguised to others. With Hal Fanny could air her self-doubt. Unlike Fanny's impatient mother, or even her commonsensical Aunt Dall, Hal never dismissed her insecurities as vanity or silliness. Instead she met those self-doubts with unshakeable affection and practical suggestions, while at the same time bolstering Fanny's confidence.

The visit came to an end and Marie-Thérèse took her daughter back to Weybridge in a happier frame of mind. The summer slipped by and Fanny frequently spoke of the friendship she had formed at Cassiobury Park. As the countryside mellowed into its August glory her parents allowed her to make a second visit to Heath Farm so they might meet again before Hal returned to Ireland. The invitation was a kind gesture on Priscilla's part; the bird-like society woman and her intense niece did not have much comprehension of one another. The old woman who remained faithful to the dialect of the Devonshire House set, pronouncing petticoats as 'pettikits', and oblige as 'obleege', appeared in the teenager's eyes to be an absurd relic of a different age. Unaware of the grand theatrical house parties in the 1800s when the Prince of Wales, Dukes and Duchesses, Lords and Ladies accepted the hospitality of this 'lady of no great advantage to the drama',[3] Fanny was privately scornful of her aunt's 'undue respect for respectablity and reverence for titled folk'. Listening to Priscilla fret about the lack of society at Cassiobury Park and witnessing her excitement whenever someone titled seemed likely to call, Fanny tended to regard her aunt as rather silly and even pathetic.

Looking back on her sixteen-year-old self in her memoirs Fanny noted with admiration Hal's contrasting tolerance towards her wild ways. She described herself as she walked beside Hal that August, marching along talking nineteen-to-the-dozen swinging her bonnet in her hand. All the while the older woman listened 'in affectionate indulgence for my enthusiasm', unruffled even by Fanny's 'frenzied' singing as the teenager attempted to convey the high points of *Oberon*. The thirty-year-old spinster – who was not musical – was utterly captivated by the charisma and energy of this diminutive teenager with her mobile face, and her mother's habit of speaking with her entire body.

On one occasion that summer the pair walked further than they had meant to. The teenager declaring herself to be ravenous, Hal took Fanny into a 'small roadside ale-house' and bought her some bread and cheese – disregarding the conventional rule that unmarried and unattended ladies did not go into public inns.

> . . . while thus vulgarly employed we beheld my aunt's carriage drive past the window. If that worthy lady could have seen us . . . she certainly would have had a stroke of apoplexy . . . for gentility and propriety were the breath of life to her, and of the highest law of both, which can defy conventions, she never dreamed.[4]

The point of the story was to demonstrate that Hal was *noble* and not only in her bloodline. The comparisons the teenager drew between her aunt and Miss St Leger were material in shaping her own particular brand of snobbery. Unlike Priscilla – the outsider who aspired to gentility – Hal was able to rise above the petty considerations of what others might think of her. Aunt Kemble might admire a person merely because they had a title and wealth, but Fanny was drawn to cultivated people with the self-possession to think for themselves.

Hal's nobility was reflected both in the way she met Fanny's youthful exuberance and in the image of the delicate high arched foot she disguised so cavalierly in those ugly boots. Harriet St Leger appeared to enjoy what Fanny desired most – self-determination. The native shrewdness Fanny inherited from her mother, however, led her to identify the material conditions that enabled such nobility: the secure means and social position that Hal, for instance, was born into.

Not that Hal was a confident person. She suffered from constant self-doubts. One of the elements that drew the disparate pair together was their common drive to improve themselves both morally and intellectually. Hal supplied Fanny with the governess-mentor she had lacked since Paris and Mrs Rowden's care. The pair frequently discussed theological matters and although she struggled to keep up with Hal's 'remarkably keen powers of analysis' Fanny much appreciated the exercise of her moral faculties.

For Hal's part, Fanny's essential liveliness, her humour and her youthful propensity to dash up to life, warmed the 'gloomy, neutral tint'[5] of the existence of a shy spinster. During the forty years to come their meetings would be relatively rare. The sinews of their long friendship were formed by correspondence. For Hal, the 'Plato in petticoats'* feeding her donkeys on the high downs overlooking the Bay of Drogheda, Fanny Kemble's letters brought a safe, second-hand encounter with the wider world. Hal's letters in return carried the sustaining assurance of a warm affection and interest in Fanny's moral well-being that remained constant wherever her turbulent life swept her.

Back at Heath Farm that August in 1826 Hal's brother, Francis – a lawyer who had 'made himself favourably known by a good deal of clever periodical writing' – came from Ireland to escort his sister

*As Fanny called her – in reference to a character in *The Inconstant*, a comedy by George Farquahar that had been popular at the turn of the century.

home. Miss St Leger departed, having set Fanny the improving task of transcribing chunks of Greek and Latin texts to send after her. Fanny waved her off, consoling herself with their mutual promises to write to one another, and turned back to life with Aunt Priscilla. They did not have to endure each other's company alone for long. Aunt Whitlock arrived with her baggage.

Initially, the two widows planned to set up home together but the trial was not a success. At close quarters Priscilla found herself appalled by the big-hearted, naive relic of the provincial stage. Smart little Priscilla nearly despaired as she resorted to denying that she was at home rather than have her genteel callers snigger behind their hands at the peculiarities of her well-meaning sister-in-law.

Fanny escaped her elders and spent her days reading, arranged in a romantic picture under a favourite oak tree 'a cabbage-leaf full of fresh-gathered strawberries and a handful of fresh-blown roses' at her side. Now that she was nearly seventeen she considered herself sufficiently responsible to explore Byron's poems at last. She enjoyed the beauty of his verse immensely although she took the precaution of inoculating herself from any possible pernicious effects by interpolating an elevating theological work by the 'wise divine' Jeremy Taylor. She read Wraxall's *Memoirs of the House of Valois*. Her imagination was fired by the story of Françoise de Foix, the 'beautiful Countess de Chateaubriand', and she began work on a dramatic poem.

The shortening days put an end to her summer idyll. Marie-Thérèse gathered up her family for the move back to town, her mood worsening as she faced London. Charles's personal finances were being stretched to breaking point by maintaining his eldest son at Cambridge (some £300 of his £800 annual income). The roomy, elegant residence at 5 Soho Square had to be given up for a house back in the cheaper location of Craven Hill in Bayswater. The landlord was a French diamond trader and his decorations had a certain continental flair that pleased Marie-Thérèse. To Fanny's delight her parents assigned her a room to herself. She spread herself in her new privacy, arranging a table where she could work on her poetry while looking out of the window over 'our suburban bit of garden, and the sloping meadows beyond it'.

Fanny was very much inclined to solitude. The household was not a happy one. As much as he endeavoured to keep up public appearances his family could sense that Charles's buoyant optimism was failing. Professionally, lofty ideals had to be abandoned as increasing financial desperation drove Covent Garden downmarket. The theatre's leading box-office draw was Mme Vestris, a popular singer with very fine legs for breeches parts. The innovation of Planché's *King John* gave way to extracts of Shakespeare's best scenes cobbled together into 'a sort of opera'.[6] Kemble was forever chasing after hits that might save him. But for all his efforts, a succession of great hopes were dashed as the best of them proved to be merely moderate successes. Ill omens were everywhere but no one spoke of them aloud. In the house at Craven Hill Marie-Thérèse swung between dogmatic busy-ness and depression. Aunt Dall went about mending and singing and making sure that the household ran smoothly, while Fanny submerged herself in her imagination, sitting at her bedroom window working on her Françoise de Foix project and writing letters to Hal.

In his popular satire of *The Life of an Actor* published in 1825, Pierce Egan described how his Patent theatre manager Peregrine Proteus would hold monthly suppers for authors, composers and performers. By this means the manager,

> . . . obtained a knowledge of the public taste, and also the opinions of the most clever and intelligent persons who were moving in the polite circles and the beau monde.[7]

Entertaining was part of the business and to the outside world the Kembles carried on as usual. Fanny recorded the joke that her parents' friends often wondered how Charles Kemble could afford the expense of a French chef, when in fact that chef was her mother. The company they gathered in their drawing rooms were not the aristocrats that John Philip and his wife had once entertained. Their guests were literary, musical and a little racy. The Kembles' grandest acquaintance was Mrs Fitzgerald, the flamboyant mother of Edward Fitzgerald, the Kemble boys' shy schoolmate. Mary Frances Fitzgerald belonged to an Anglo-Irish family descended from the Earls of Kildare. She was said to be the richest commoner in England. She was so wealthy in her own right that on the death of her father in 1818 her husband, Mr Purcell, exchanged his name for hers. As John Gay wrote in 1728:

> *A wife's like a guinea in gold,*
> *Stampt with the name of her spouse;*
> *Now here, now there; is bought or is sold;*
> *And is current in every house.*[8]

The sentiment still held in the nineteenth century. That a wife should stamp her name on her husband was unsettling enough; Mrs Fitzgerald was so self-determined that she lived largely separate from her husband (who preferred his country home in Suffolk). Without the presence of a resident husband, she was viewed by many contemporaries as morally suspect.

Mrs Fitzgerald liked to divide her time between London and Brighton, driving from one to the other in a striking yellow carriage drawn by four perfectly matched black horses at the head of a procession of lesser vehicles carrying luggage, footmen and maids. She loved to entertain and threw lavish dinners at her grand London home at 39 Portland Place. As a girl, Fanny was much impressed by Mrs Fitzgerald's gold tableware. She owned 'the first gold dessert service and table ornaments that I ever saw'. There was something not quite genteel about Mrs Fitzgerald. She was not vulgar precisely, for she was elegant, the descendant of earls and her taste was informed by a true love of the arts; but in truth 'polite' society found her too brash in her enjoyment of her wealth. Handsome, magnificent and loud, she was a great trial to her son Edward, who all his life had a morbid distaste of social climbers.

Despite her every effort Mrs Fitzgerald was never invited to the grand houses of London. The Bon Ton kept their distance, barely noting her existence save to remark occasionally on the magnificence of her jewels when she appeared in her box at the Haymarket Opera. Edward Fitzgerald's mother made do, stocking her lavish dinner parties with creative professionals – the best painters, poets, architects, musicians and literary folk. According to her son, she admired Marie-Thérèse more than anyone she had ever known. The two women, unsatisfied and restless within the constrictions of society, had much in common. For all their elegance, wit and charm, their assumption that they were equal to any man was widely judged to be in some way malicious; a corruption of what a woman should be. Even her son judged her harshly. Later in life, he wrote reminiscing about his mother to Fanny Kemble that,

> she was a remarkable woman, as you said . . . and as I constantly believe in outward beauty as an index of a beautiful soul within, I used sometimes to wonder what feature in her fine face betrayed what was not so good in her character; I think (as usual) the lips; there was a twist of mischief about them now and then, like that in – *The Tale of a Cat!* – otherwise so smooth and amiable.[9]

The society drawn to the Kemble home at Craven Hill was unusual for the time in that it valued wit and intelligence in both women and men. A typical regular of the circle was Horace Twiss, the eldest son of Fanny's godmother Frances and her lawyer husband. Trained as a barrister and celebrated for social skills that won him the patronage of Lord Clarendon and thereby the position of MP for the rotten borough of Wootton-Bassett, Horace was renowned for his slightly camp wit. He loved to come and gossip with Marie-Thérèse who more than held her own with him. Listening to the pair talk, Fanny and Adelaide enjoyed an education in the art of conversation that stood them in good stead in later life.

Fanny's mother was a better parent for a teenager than for a child. She focused her attention on equipping her girls as best she could for the world that awaited them. Marie-Thérèse considered it important that her daughters should be competent musicians. Fanny had a melodious contralto voice. The energy her mother now dedicated to her training probably reflected her desire to keep her daughter's professional options open as much as her intention to hone a pleasing drawing-room skill. Despite her recognition of her mother's good intentions, these lessons were a trial to Fanny. Marie-Thérèse had perfect pitch and her habitual impatience was sharpened by her nostalgia for her past professional triumphs. Forced to practise before her irascible parent in her sitting room each day, Fanny 'sang out of tune and played false chords oftener, from sheer apprehension of her agonized exclamations'.[10]

Fortunately her younger sister, Adelaide, rising eleven, was exhibiting the first signs of an exceptional voice. Young Tottie displayed a sensitivity and natural musicality in her singing that drew some of Marie-Thérèse's attention away from berating her elder daughter. Dragged up at her mother's parties to accompany James Smith, the family friend who was famous for his humorous songs, poor Fanny would sit at the keyboard racked with nerves. 'While he sang, everybody laughed, but I perspired coldly and felt ready to cry.' Fanny much preferred to be left alone with her books and diary.

While at school, Fanny had displayed her mother's grace and love of dancing; but since the smallpox she had developed a self-effacing slouch. Marie-Thérèse (who was still complimented on her posture and fluid movements) strapped her daughter into a painful steel back-brace for several hours a day. When that failed to work, she dispatched Fanny to a sergeant in the Royal Foot Guards, who turned Fanny out with a straight back, well-placed shoulders and a resolute step that added inches to her stature.

Rectifying her posture, however, did not solve Fanny's dissatisfaction with herself. She fretted that her erratic education was insufficient grounding for her dreams of literary success. She took physical exercise, practised the piano and singing, but otherwise she was 'left very much to the irregular and unsystematic reading which I selected for myself'. As she turned seventeen that winter unexpected assistance limped into view in the person of Dr Malkin, her brothers' headmaster at Bury St Edmunds, who came to visit the Kembles.

Genial and portly, Malkin was a kind man. He took great pleasure in relating the story of how he got his limp. According to his account, a tendon snapped as he danced with Miss O'Neill (at the time a much-admired leading lady who later snagged a stage-struck baronet and recreated herself as Lady Beecher). The shrewd educator noticed that Fanny was a bright girl and in low spirits. He set her reading lists and suggested that she translate Sismondi's influential romantic history *Histoire des républiques italiennes*. If her translation proved good enough, he hinted, she might even abridge it for publication. This buoyed up Fanny's ego; if she was not pretty, she could at least be clever.

By now Fanny was thinking of a literary career. She did not enjoy society; she did not like to be seen, but she longed for fame. She wanted to be accepted and valued for her intellectual gifts. Unlike most seventeen-year-olds of her day, she dreamed of independence, not marriage.

The financial threats to her family that had been grumbling on for so long now began to tumble into view. After trailing on before a succession of Lord Chancellors, in spring 1827 a judgement was handed down in a long-running legal dispute between the Covent Garden proprietors over the Articles of Agreement signed with Henry Harris in 1822. Charles Kemble was deemed to be personally liable for £27,000 of the theatre's debts. He was not in a position to raise £5,000 let alone five times that much. He and his partners immediately lodged an appeal, their only glimmer of hope being that Harris, the main mover behind the suit, would also be liable for huge sums he could not pay. Nonetheless, the theatre's creditors, sensing a collapse, grew ever more strident. 'That dreary chancery suit seemed to envelop us in an atmosphere of palpitating suspense and stagnant uncertainty.'[11] Charles Kemble now appeared careworn and desperate. One day as he was preparing to leave the house, Aunt Dall pointed out that a button was missing from his coat. Fanny watched her once dapper father shrug as he made a weary joke of it: 'Ah you see, my dear Dall, it is my chancery suit.'

One of the greatest blows to Charles's pride was accepting that he could not afford to keep Henry at Bury St Edmunds. Even his Benefit was poorly attended. The 'palpitating suspense' was too much for Marie-Thérèse. For weeks she was 'alternately deaf and blind, and sometimes both'. She even hallucinated – being tormented by

> whole processions and crowds of visionary figures . . . which she often described as exceedingly annoying by their grotesque and distorted appearance.[12]

Fanny was desperate to help and powerless to do anything. She worked at her poetry, offering it up to her father in an attempt to console him with her budding genius. Charles rewarded her with his fleeting attention, expressing himself 'surprised and pleased at some things I read him lately'. Typically, her intellectual gifts were eclipsed by news from Cambridge that John Mitchell had won a literary prize. She witnessed her father's extreme pleasure at the news: 'He jumped, and clapped his hands, and kissed the letter, like a child; as my mother says, "I am glad he has one gleam of sunshine at least"; he sadly wanted it.'[13] Almost the one thing that kept Charles going was the prospect of his sons joining the class of cultured gentlemen.

Fanny's work on Françoise de Foix progressed very slowly. She tried to be philosophical but she was anxious as she listened to her parents arguing over the need for yet another move. If they could find a cheap house in Westminster, Henry could go to day school there. Fanny would lose her beloved room 'with its cheerful view', but that was not important, she assured Hal:

> I have, luckily, the faculty of easily accommodating myself to circumstances . . . I shall soon take root in the next place. With all my dislike of moving, my great wish is to travel . . . for

> what I wish is never to remain long enough in a place to take root, or, having done so, never to be transplanted.

One book in particular resonated with her sense of unease and unhappiness. *Diary of an Ennuyée* was a fashionable success in 1827. Presented in the form of the diary of a young lady pursuing a Romantic pilgrimage through Italy, the book advertised itself as 'a real picture of natural and feminine feeling'.[14] It purported to be a factual document – a journal found in the effects of a young lady of means who died during her travels of a mysteriously broken heart. Some reviewers were sceptical as to its authenticity, but the diary's claim to be a true record added to the poignancy of the story.

The influence that loomed behind the Ennuyée was that of the godmother of Romanticism, Mme de Staël and in particular her fictional heroine, Corinne. Set in Italy, the foremost Romantic travel destination ever since Mme de Stael set out to promote that country a couple of decades earlier, not only did the *Diary* reflect the detailed travelogue descriptions of Mme de Stael's novel, but the Ennuyée laid her Romantic credentials before the reader by direct reference to it:

> Nov. 28 . . . 'Corinne' I find is a fashionable vade mecum for sentimental travellers in Italy; and that I too might be à la mode, I brought it from Molini's today, with the intention of reading on the spot, those admirable and affecting passages which relate to Florence; but when I began to cut the leaves, a kind of terror seized me, and I threw it down . . . I know myself weak – I feel myself unhappy; and to find my own feelings reflected from the pages of a book, in language too deeply and eloquently true, is not good for me.[15]

The Ennuyée provided a sentimental example of suffering sisterhood for the teenage Fanny. In contrast to the cynicism and defiance with which the Byronic hero endured his fate, here the riot of feeling was met with ladylike resignation. Like Corinne, the Ennuyée dies of her Byronic sufferings, but the way she dies illustrates the transition that was taking place into the Romanticism of the Victorian era. The Ennuyée expires looking piously heavenwards – all traces of atheism have been expunged.

Fanny was much impressed. In particular the Ennuyée gave her a geographical location for her dreams of escape. Ever since Mme de Staël's heroine left England 'where she could not breathe' to reinvent herself as the poetess Corinne (who, it may be noted, deliberately drops her father's surname so that she may be without the stamp of any man), Italy was the destination for a literary woman. At seventeen, sitting in her Bayswater bedroom as her parents argued below, Fanny was

> possessed with a wild desire for an existence of lonely independence, which seemed to my exaggerated notions the only one fitted to the intellectual development in which alone I conceived happiness to consist . . . [the] *Diary of an Ennuyée* . . . added to this desire for isolation and independence such a passionate longing to go to Italy, that my brain was literally filled with chimerical projects of settling in the south of Europe, and there leading a solitary life of literary labour, which, together with the fame I hoped to achieve by it, seemed to me the only worthy purpose of existence.[16]

11

Mothers and Daughters

The theatre managers who cast Marie-Thérèse as a succession of fairies, gamines and soubrettes knew that she was unconvincing as a mother. It was not a role she felt herself suited to, but as Fanny approached adulthood the relationship between Thérèse and her elder daughter changed. It was the temperamental invalid, for all her furious outbursts and episodes of mental instability, who first began to take her daughter's literary ambitions seriously. As a woman who had struggled fiercely to maintain her creative identity, Marie-Thérèse empathized with her daughter's aspirations and an understanding grew between the pair that transcended the verbal wounds she still inflicted on those around her. Her younger daughter Adelaide never entirely forgave her mother for her casual cruelty. In contrast, as the years passed, the irascible Frenchwoman and her equally forceful elder daughter, recognizing reflections of themselves in one another, came to share a bond based on mutual comprehension and respect.

The end of May 1827 brought visitors to the Kemble household. Mrs Harriot Siddons, the widow of Sarah Siddons's eldest child Henry, travelled from her home in Edinburgh to arrive at Bayswater with her 22-year-old daughter, Lizzie. Harriot Siddons was the leading lady of the Theatre Royal Edinburgh, where her husband, Henry

Siddons, had been patentee and manager. Her youngest daughter, Lizzie, all white skin, blue-veined wrists and masses of auburn hair, was delicate and that summer her mother was taking her to Switzerland for her health. Preoccupied with her own concerns, Fanny did not pay her cousins much attention at the time. No doubt echoing her own mother's sharp-tongued assessment, she observed that Mrs Siddons seemed 'all that is excellent, though she does not strike me as particularly clever'. The pair departed and in their place Jackie arrived from Cambridge in a whirl of energy to brighten up the place.

Just turned twenty, Jackie Kemble was a striking young man. With a bold nose and sensual mouth, his features were too strongly marked to suit the contemporary conventions of male beauty but he would never pass unnoticed. Charismatic and exuberant, he relished the opportunities provided by his education. His friends included the well-balanced, much-loved William Bodham Donne, a Quaker from Norfolk, and James Spedding, a gentleman's son from Cumberland, with connections among the Lakeland Poets (he was a friend of Coleridge's son, Hartley). Jackie, the most flamboyant of all the Kemble siblings, blazed a trail as a 'crack speaker' at the Cambridge Union, the famous debating society that at this time met in a back room of the Red Lion Inn. Like many a student before and after him, Jackie celebrated his freedom by getting drunk in the week and flirting with atheism. His reputation was wide among the student body – although those who fancied themselves intellectuals tended to sneer that he was a demagogue[1] rather than a thinking man. Arthur Hallam, a priggish freshman in autumn 1828, described the political fashion among Union men at the time as 'Utilitarian, seasoned with a plentiful sprinkling of heterogeneous Metaphysics.'[2] With his characteristic all-or-nothing enthusiasm Jackie was 'bitten with politics, devoted himself to the Union and the cultivation of oratory, gave up all his time to newspapers and political essayists'.[3]

The French Revolution had dealt a heavy blow to political debate in England. During the war and its aftermath 'radical' was as pejorative an accusation as 'commie' was to be during the Cold War in the next century. After more than twenty years of conflict, the consensus among 'respectable' British subjects was that the need for stability outweighed the injustices of the established system. 'Radicalism' was the province of hot-headed young men and a rumoured underworld of 'low-class' anarchists, symbolized by the luckless Thistlewood and his fellow Cato Street conspirators who were executed in May 1820 as the Regency gave way to the reign of George IV proper. However, the middling classes were increasingly offended by the debauchery of the Regency establishment. Queen Caroline's trial in November 1820 marked a watershed. The unedifying spectacle of the dissolute King (with his fat mistress Lady Conyngham in tow) attempting to shut his legal wife out of her rights as Queen, on the basis of sordid details of sexual antics with an Italian equerry, set the seal on an era. The new King's subjects were increasingly in the mood for a moral backlash, even if that meant taking the risk of reform.

Utilitarianism was an example of the desire to effect reform in a rational manner without the danger of revolution. Bentham and his followers looked past the establishment of aristocracy and Church and, in one logical bound, replaced precedent and privilege with the principle of utility – the Benthamite doctrine that 'the greatest happiness of the greatest number is the foundation of morals and legislation'. Reason, they argued, gave the power of the state to Parliament governing by a law designed for the common good.

Jackie Kemble could not fail to be attracted to this philosophy that envisaged talent and intellectual argument as the arbiters of power. He became 'an adorer of Bentham' and 'a worshipper of Mill'.* His enthusiasm was fuelled by a sequence of events. Lord Liverpool, the leader who had kept the Tories in power for fifteen years, seeing the country through the end of the war and its uneasy aftermath, was struck down by a stroke in February 1827. With his

*That is the economist and Indian administrator James Mill (1773–1836), Bentham's greatest disciple and father of John Stuart Mill, author of the famous *Essay on Liberty*.

removal, the governing party lost its coherence, allowing the calls for reform to come to the fore. King George IV called the Duke of Wellington in to head his government, hoping that the old soldier would restore the status quo. But even the hero of Waterloo could not turn back change. The first wave of pressure for reform built around the campaign to repeal the Test and Corporation Acts (the legislation that placed statutory penalties against Dissenters – that is, dissenters from the Anglican doctrines of the Established Church – and limited their participation in public life).

As she gradually recovered her nerves, reclining on the sofa in her sitting room, Marie-Thérèse fretted that her eldest son might infect his sister with his explosive views. These were pre-democratic times. It is debatable whether Charles Kemble had sufficient property rights to permit him to vote in general elections. In any case, the Kembles, as members of the great Royal Patent Theatre of Covent Garden, were the 'King's Servants', and as public servants had no business proclaiming political opinions. Fanny was unruffled by her mother's concerns. 'I am willing and glad to listen to his opinions and the arguments of his favourite authors,' she remarked as she scratched out her thoughts for Hal at her bedroom window. 'I am never likely to study them myself.'

Her younger brother Henry returned with his box and bags from school, having left Bury St Edmunds. Charles Kemble departed for a summer of provincial engagements 'in very bad spirits. I never saw him so depressed.' Fanny anticipated another relapse in her mother's health, thinking that she would be concerned about Charles's state of mind. She was rather perplexed the next day to find her mother quite cheerful, happily going about the house preparing for the move to Weybridge and talking of the delights of the pike-fishing that awaited her.

Before the family set out, however, Marie-Thérèse sat her daughter down and, as Fanny reported to Hal, had – 'a serious, and to me painful, conversation on the necessity not only of not hating society, but tolerating and mixing in it'. Fanny admitted to her friend that she sometimes felt inclined 'to hide myself', but she could not help fancying . . . that the hours spent in my own room reading and writing are better employed than if devoted to people and things in which I feel no interest whatever, and do not know how to pretend the contrary.[4]

Fanny was at a crucial age. The attractions of youth did not last long in her generation. At seventeen or so a girl had a brief window of opportunity when her fate might be sealed. Whether she was to have marriage, or even a career, a young woman needed to be seen in society. If she hid herself away – tainted, perhaps, by the reputation of being that most unattractive of females, a 'blue stocking' – then, given her parents' lack of wealth, Fanny was very likely condemning herself to a hard existence of poverty and invisibility. Marie-Thérèse was well aware that her intense daughter was not suited to the life of the serving spinster that her sister Dall endured.

Fanny recognized the force of her mother's argument. It was a puzzle how to reconcile her desire for an intellectual life with her duty as a daughter. As was her habit, she took solace in poetry.

When I went to bed last night I sat by my open window, looking at the moon and thinking of my social duties, and then scribbled endless doggerel in a highly Byronic mood to deliver my mind upon the subject, after which, feeling amazingly better, I went to bed and slept profoundly, satisfied that I had given 'society' a death-blow. But really, jesting apart, the companionship of my own family – those I live with, I mean – satisfies me entirely, and I have not the least desire for any other.

Much as she might wish to stop the clock Fanny knew that the demands of 'society' could not be dismissed. She was facing the last Weybridge summer. Charles Kemble's crumbling finances would no longer support their country home. Fanny struggled with a sense of change and unavoidable endings. She was resolutely positive in her letters to Hal, but underneath her words sounded the echo of the determined little girl all those years ago, singing out in the garden shed as footsteps came down the path.

> I care very little where I go; I do not like leaving any place, but the tie of habit, which is quickly formed and strong in me, once broken, I can easily accommodate myself to the next change, which, however, I always pray may be the last.

Just as she had learned from the hard lesson of her first exile to school in Boulogne, she had no choice. She was becoming an adult and the necessity of contributing to the family economy, or at least of ceasing to be a drain on her father's pocket, loomed before her. She decided to make her dreams of literary success a reality.

That summer at Weybridge Fanny worked furiously on her Françoise de Foix project. What had begun as a dramatic poem evolved into a play, *Francis I.* Fanny had once shaken hands with Miss Mary Russell Mitford, one of the foremost female playwrights of her parents' generation, when she had dropped in to discuss the production of her play *Foscari* with Charles Kemble. In the opinion of Charles Kemble – and therefore of Fanny – Miss Mitford had 'achieved the manly triumph of a really successful historical tragedy'. (By the standards of Charles Kemble's generation historical tragedy was the highest dramatic form and therefore the province of men.) Her father's casual comment fired Fanny's ambition. With the rash confidence of youth she decided that what that established authoress with a pile of plays behind her might do, Fanny Kemble could do also.

So she wrote, her mother fished, her younger siblings occupied themselves, Dall took care of them all and the summer weeks passed. A pleasant diversion was provided by the arrival of Jackie. In Weybridge he condescended, cheerfully enough, to walk with Fanny. He gave her a glimpse of his privileged Cambridge world, relating his glittering triumphs at the Union and parading his 'intellectual occupations and interests'. 'He is certainly a very uncommon person, and I admire, perhaps too enthusiastically, his great abilities.' On his part, Jackie was proud of his sister's literary efforts – even going so far as to show some of her verses to his college friends.[5] His approval was a great encouragement to her and by the end of August Fanny had finished the first three acts of her play.

To Fanny's great delight, her parents took her project seriously. Marie-Thérèse even contributed useful advice from her own considerable knowledge of 'producing dramatic effect'. At the end of August Charles Kemble was in Paris presenting a season of English plays to the French. He sent encouragement, even suggesting with exaggerated optimism that the proprietors of Covent Garden might offer her £200 – the same fee paid to Miss Mitford for her *Foscari* – should it succeed.* Fanny's dreams of a literary career seemed to be forming substance. Conscious of the prejudice among the cultured class in favour of published literature over its debased off-shoot, drama as performed for mass entertainment, Fanny was shrewd in her assessment of her father's suggestion as she weighed its merits before Hal:

> By selling my play to the theatre it cannot be read or known as a literary work, and as to make a name for myself as a writer is the aim of my ambition, I think I shall decline this offer.[6]

This piece of mature professionalism out of the way, her excitement broke through: 'I think, irrespective of age or sex, it is not a bad play – perhaps considering both, a tolerably fair one; there is some good writing in it, and good situations,' she told Hal, permitting herself a burst of pride.

As August came to an end the family began to break up. John Mitchell left for London. Fanny revisited her favourite haunts for one last time – the pine woods, the river, the cedar grove at Oatlands. Her childhood summers were over. Even Priscilla had left Heath Farm – moving to fashionable Leamington to join genteel company.

*£200 was an excellent fee at that time, the average payment for a play being nearer £50.

She and Aunt Whitlock had parted ways, the larger-than-life actress happily settling in a quaint, rural cottage in the beautiful neighbourhood of Addlestone near Weybridge.

The Kemble family arrived back in London to settle themselves at 16 St James Street, Buckingham Gate, the tall, narrow house Charles had rented overlooking Green Park. Despite its steep stairs and no more than a couple of rooms on each floor, their new home was well situated within walking distance of Henry's new school and convenient for the theatre. Meanwhile Charles was still in Paris. He opened as Hamlet on 11 September in the company formed by Laurent to present English plays at the Odeon. He sent word to his family that he was a considerable success. One French critic did write of his Romeo that 'we have never perhaps seen a more convincing grief on the stage' – but there was no reality to justify Fanny's comment to Hal that 'the excellent Parisians have not only received him very well, but forthwith threw themselves into a headlong furore for Shakespeare and Charles Kemble'. In truth, it was the high romantic style of Kean and Macready who arrived later in the season that caught the imagination of the young French literati, including that of Victor Hugo. The *Courrier des Théâtres* recorded his farewell performance on 28 September and dismissed him: 'We are far from recognizing in this actor the extraordinary talent so graciously attributed to him.'[7]

Nevertheless, he returned with a managerial coup in his pocket; Edmund Kean had quarrelled with Price, the manager of Drury Lane, and Charles had secured his services for Covent Garden. Prospects were looking up. Charles Young, the old family friend, was also back in the company. The manager celebrated by repeating many of his favourite parts before dropping back into second-rank roles in order to support Kean.

On 15 October 1827, Edmund Kean made his first appearance at Covent Garden as Shylock to 'a crowded and brilliant house'. By now in his late thirties, Edmund Kean was past his prime, an alcoholic dependent on brandy and water to get through a performance; and yet he retained his magic. Fanny too fell under his spell. She was in the family box that first night and returned home a 'violent Keanite':

> While under the influence of his amazing power of passion it is impossible to reason, analyse, or do anything but surrender one's self to his forcible appeals to one's emotion.[8]

She was conscious that her critical faculties might have been suspended and she softened her enthusiasm in her report to Hal. She added that she was to see Kean again as Richard III but expected to be disappointed because (echoing the standard Kemble/classical objection) she was 'afraid Mr Kean will not have the innate majesty which I think belongs to the part'.

The hard truth was that Kean, even raddled with drink and half-seas over, could wipe Charles Kemble from the stage. At his performance as Othello on 21 December, supported by Young as Iago and Kemble as Cassio, too many spectators were allowed into the auditorium and some in the pit were in danger of being crushed. As men clambered up into the lower boxes to escape suffocation, one witness described Charles Kemble 'in his lofty bland way trying to persuade a too-closely packed audience to fancy themselves comfortable, and to be silent'.[9] The audience refused to settle down until Kean appeared. He alone was able to 'subdue them to silence or stir them to ecstasy at his will'. The eighteen-year-old Edward Fitzgerald was in the audience that night. Several decades later, his recollection of the evening was dominated by Kean, 'and how much taller he looked than Kemble when he came in to quell the drunken fray. I think one could see no one but Kean when he was on'.[10]

Edmund Kean kept the rotting concern afloat for a little longer. But Covent Garden audiences continued to decline and financial collapse remained an ever-looming presence. It was in this atmosphere that in October Frances Anne Kemble wrote her fifth act in a day and her tragedy *Francis I* was finished. Her parents' response was all that she could have wished for.

> . . . even if it succeeds and is praised and admired, I shall never feel so happy as when my father greeted my entrance into the drawing room with, 'Is it done, my love? I shall be the happiest man alive if it succeeds!'[11]

Quite apart from his paternal pride, Charles Kemble was well aware that to have a hit play by a seventeen-year-old Kemble (Fanny was a month short of her eighteenth birthday) and a female one at that, was a highly marketable, and therefore a potentially lucrative, asset.

The family critics gathered to hear Fanny read her manuscript through: Marie-Thérèse, stout and determined, her expressive features lit up with interest sitting to one side, and Charles Kemble in his favourite chair, settling into that pose of kindly attention appropriate to the gentlemanly professional. Even John Mitchell was present. In prosecution of his Benthamite enthusiasm, Jackie had enrolled in the Inner Temple with a view to becoming a lawyer – a career choice that pleased his father (the law being a potentially gentlemanly trade). As Fanny read – shyly at first – she gained confidence, speaking out with dramatic emphasis, encouraged by the 'delighted looks' passing between her parents.

> . . . when it was done I was most richly rewarded, for they all seemed so pleased with me, and so proud of me, that the most inordinate author's vanity would have been satisfied. And my dear mother, oh, how she looked at me!

Charles Kemble was immediately full of plans for putting the play into production. Marie-Thérèse and her eldest son, however, argued that the play would benefit more from being published first –

> for they said . . . that the work as a literary production . . . has merit enough to make it desirable that the public should judge of it as a poetical composition before it is submitted to the mangling necessary for the stage.

As befitted a master of theatre, Charles brought out a surprise. While in Paris he had commissioned an expensive costume for himself to wear in the title role. Made of a 'bright amber-coloured velours épinglé, with a border of rich silver embroidery; . . . together with a cloak of violet trimmed with imitation sable', he had designed it himself from old pictures of Francis I. His daughter was utterly captivated by what she took to be a gesture of confidence in her abilities (the play was not even finished when Charles ordered the outfit to be made). She was euphoric, sitting with her big brown eyes shining, drinking up the attention her play had won her at last:

> I sit and hear it discussed, and praised and criticized, only longing (like 'a silly wench', as my mother calls me when I confess as much to her) to see my father in his lovely dress and hear the alarums of my fifth act.

Even allowing for the conventions of the time, *Francis I* demonstrates just how much Shakespeare Fanny had read and how often she had sat in the family box at Covent Garden. The rhythms of Shakespearean speech are in her head. Her heroine, Françoise de Foix, is Juliet crossed with Beatrice, seasoned with the tendency to weep and faint of the sentimental heroine of melodrama. She displays an occasional sense of what the actor needs to make drama. Some parts are clearly directed to the acclaimed strengths of the Kemble clan. Her Queen of Savoy is obviously written with accounts of Aunt Siddons in mind, while her noble soldier, Charles of Bourbon, 'Prince of the Blood', has much of her father's acclaimed portrayal of Falconbridge.

Francis I demonstrates a weakness Fanny was never able to overcome in any of her fiction – a habit of losing her thread between too many characters and too many overlapping plots. It is hard to say whose story is at the centre of the play. Françoise de Foix is the heroine, and yet Louisa, Queen of Savoy, and her daughter Marguerite of Valois, who compete over the romantic attentions of Charles of Bourbon, jostle for space with Françoise and her brother

Lautrec (shades of Ophelia and Laertes) and their triangle with the friend he wishes her to marry, Laval. Then there is the 'hero' of the title, Francis I, whom Françoise secretly loves, although she will not admit it. Hence the star-crossed lovers never have a satisfactory scene together and the consummation of their relationship – being a guilty one – takes place off stage. And finally, there is the Iago clone, Gonzales, the villainous monk, a double agent for Spain, who stirs the whole muddle up into tragedy. As one contemporary reader commented, *Francis I* contained enough material for two or three plays.

Fanny's attempt at a 'really successful historical tragedy' shows her family's theatrical flare rather than literary genius. Her dramatic climaxes are rushed and characters swing from love to violent hate on a pin for no good reason. In truth, she was working an exhausted seam. There would be no more successful tragedies written until opera took over the form as the century progressed. Yet, given this context *Francis I* is an eye-catching first effort for a seventeen-year-old girl.

Francis I was put into the hands of the Covent Garden copyist, its fate as yet undecided between publication or performance. Fanny forged on with her ambitions, splashing about happily in a sea of literary plans. Her favourite project of the moment was a comedy – set in medieval Italy because she found jesters 'bewitching'. The family's excitement over her play hastened her mother's recovery from whatever mysterious illness had been ailing her. (The family seems to have resisted the observation that Marie-Thérèse's ill-health was confined to London; her daughter never records her being anything but happy at Weybridge.) Fanny rejoiced that now Marie-Thérèse was 'less deaf, and rather less blind'. Despite being 'unable to write, read, work, or occupy herself in any manner' she was able to accompany her daughter to the manager's box at Covent Garden twice a week. Fanny's hopes were high that she had made a good start in the direction of her most cherished ambitions.

12

Head, Heart and Literary Talent

Late in October 1827 Harriot Siddons returned from the Continent with Lizzie. Fanny had long wished to see Switzerland, the country her mother claimed as her ancestral home. She pounced on her cousin, eager to cull impressions of this magical land. To her disgust, 'placid' Lizzie could only offer the vague observation that it was a very pretty country. Fanny decided that Lizzie, although perfectly amiable, lacked a romantic soul. Her exasperation did not last long. Lizzie's teenage brother, another Henry, arrived from Portsmouth, where he was studying to be an army engineer at the Indian Military College of Addiscombe. Like Henry Kemble, Harry Siddons was a remarkably good-looking youth. The young Siddonses proved themselves charming house guests and Harriot and Marie-Thérèse hatched a plan whereby Lizzie's elder sister would join her in London to stay with a succession of relatives for the winter months while their mother returned to Edinburgh to perform for the theatrical season.

The Christmas holidays brought Jackie home from Cambridge with a prize for an oration that his tutor praised as the best he had heard for many years. His mother was utterly overcome by the news and the whole family beamed with pride. Fanny's achievements were not forgotten. Charles Kemble had taken over *Francis I* and was attempting to prune it ruthlessly. ('"There is plenty of it, Fan", he said, looking ruefully at it', as the authoress reported to Hal.) The family debate seemed to be resolving in favour of production over publication, although the harassed manager shelved the idea of an actual contract for the time being.

That holiday, Charles Kemble took his children and their cousins on a memorable day out to visit the two most spectacular construction projects of the day – the Thames Tunnel and the East India Dock. Since the turn of the century, expanding trade had outstripped the capacity of the old port of London; the City's merchants had banded together to build gigantic warehouses and quays, beginning with the West India Dock on the Isle of Dogs in 1802. The new docks were a symbol of Britain's seafaring power and the role of the capital in controlling goods brought from every corner of the globe. At the time of the Kemble visit the construction of the tunnel and the last of these docks, carved out by pick and shovel by thousands of Irish navvies, were the foremost tourist sights of London.[1]

Fanny's record of that day in her diary and letters – full of youthful hope in the 'magical' power of machines and glory in 'what men can do when banded together, though the individuals are forgotten and have turned to dust' – is eloquent of the outlook of her generation and the Victorian era to come.

In Fanny's eyes the Thames Tunnel construction site appeared as a scene from one of her favourite German fairytales. The steam engines powering the pumps that kept the water from flooding the tunnel were 'those beautiful, wise, working creatures'. The underground site, its high vault lit by a vista of gas lamps, struck her as 'one of the long avenues of light that lead to the abodes of the genii'.[2] The superintendent of the works was Isambard Kingdom Brunel and, hearing that the famous actor-manager was on site, the great engineer appeared in person to guide the Kemble party. Down at the rock face the workmen 'all begrimed, with their brawny arms and legs bare' stood in water up to their knees within iron cages that were supposed to provide protection from the regular cave-ins. They sang as they shovelled the mud in the 'red murky light of links and lanterns flashing and flickering about them'. Instead of being disturbed by this vision of hell, Fanny was enchanted.

> As we returned I remained at the bottom of the stairs last of all, to look back at the beautiful road to Hades, wishing I might be left behind.

The family party was then rowed down the river to admire the new docks and lunched on board a 'splendid' East Indiaman, one of the great cargo ships anchored in the river. It was a grand day. Fanny's heart swelled with pride:

> I think it is better for me . . . to look at trees, and the sun, moon, and stars, than at tunnels and docks; they make me too humanity proud.

In contrast to such delights her social chores were a bore. Despite a tendency to headaches and moodiness, her mother dragged Fanny out to a number of dinners and parties that winter. Her daughter continued to find her contemporaries insipid, resenting her junior position in society:

> the old people naturally treat me after my years, as a young person, and the young people . . . seem to me stupid and uninteresting, and so, you see, I do not like society.[3]

There was one house, however, that gave her unexpected pleasure. Perhaps coaxed by the suggestion that an aspiring author benefited from being seen in certain circles, Fanny accompanied her parents to a party held by the Montagues in Bedford Square.

Basil Montague was a well-known lawyer and patron of the arts. He was the bastard son of the Earl of Sandwich and his mistress, the actress Martha Ray. Ms Ray became a *cause célèbre* of the late eighteenth century when she was killed by a disappointed lover, a curate, who – it is said – shot her while sitting in her box in a packed theatre and then dispatched himself. Handsome and eccentric (he could hardly avoid being so with such parentage), her son Basil was a minor celebrity in literary London. His house was a meeting place for famous writers and thinkers such as Coleridge, Hazlitt and Charles Lamb. When Fanny first met him, Basil Montague had married, as his third wife, a widow with a daughter from a previous marriage. The third Mrs Montague was a literary version of a drama queen. Her trademark was a self-designed evening dress reminiscent of medieval costume, complete with her own free interpretation of a wimple because it displayed 'the beautiful proportions of her exquisite head' to advantage. Her daughter, Anne, then in her late twenties, was married to Bryan Waller Proctor, a poet and lawyer who, writing under the pen-name Barry Cornwall, had a modest reputation among the English Romantics.*

In Mrs Montague's drawing room an aspiring author could make contact with publishers, editors and other writers. It was a competitive arena, renowned for its brilliant conversation. Both Mrs Montague and her daughter, Anne, had formidable reputations for wit. Indeed, Anne Proctor became a distinguished hostess in her own right and her drawing-room gatherings would remain a literary institution for half a century. (The younger generation of literary men, Thackeray, Browning and Kinglake, christened her – not entirely in jest – 'Our Lady of Bitterness' in recognition of her unusual gift for sarcasm.)

That winter evening Fanny was startled to discover that the Ennuyée had not, after all, expired under southern skies but was resting 'in a very becoming state of blooming plumptitude' on a sofa in Bedford Square. As certain reviewers had suspected when it first appeared, *The Diary of an Ennuyée* was in fact a literary conceit. It was the career-making book of a one-time governess, born Anna Murphy and now Mrs Jameson. Some people never forgave the author for her deception. Henry Crabbe Robinson for one decided

---

*Proctor was the author of *Mirandola*, a passable tragedy in which Charles Kemble had starred.

that, while Mrs Jameson was a 'very clever authoress', he did not like 'the expression of her countenance . . . She has the voice, as well as the fair complexion, of Mrs Godwin, whom Lamb always called the Liar'.[4] Fanny's first impression was more positive. She saw –

> An attractive-looking young woman, with a skin of that dazzling whiteness which generally accompanies reddish hair, such as hers was; her face, which was habitually refined and spirituelle in its expression was capable of a marvellous power of concentrated feeling.[5]

Despite her initial disappointment, young Fanny was eager to meet the author of the book she had so much admired. Mrs Jameson struck her as 'very accomplished', although a touch like a governess in her conversation ('her information, without being profound, was general'). Fanny was moved by the references the authoress dropped into the conversation about the way she looked after her sisters and supported her impoverished parents. Fanny always admired dutiful daughters.

Anna Jameson was at that time thirty-two. In her late twenties she had made an unhappy match with a barrister, Robert Jameson, who if not homosexual certainly found his wife so physically unsuited to him that, within a year of that first meeting with Fanny Kemble, he would take up a post in the colonies to get away from her. In the late 1820s Mrs Jameson was just starting out on a solid career as a writer of travel books and guides to art and culture aimed towards the rapidly expanding market of women readers. The daughter of a charming but inadequate Irish miniature painter, Anna had assumed early in life the burden of caring for her younger sisters and soon her parents as well. She took up her first post as a governess at the age of sixteen. As Mrs Jameson she developed into a fluent jobbing writer with a fine nose for a cultural trend – what certain jealous literary colleagues contemptuously referred to as 'a talent for book-making' (contemporary speak for the gift of writing popular books that sold well).

As her career advanced she collected friendships with outstanding women whom she identified as creatures of genius. The archetypal elder sister, used to taking charge, her 'spirituelle' expression disguised a tenacity in pursuit of her own agenda that was at times quite chilling. She suffered from a tendency to over-familiarity – a desire to insinuate herself into the very core of her friends' lives. In plain terms – her 'dearest friends' were fodder for her 'book-making' or at least added credence to her niche as a popular guide to taste and culture. Although her manner put off many, Anna Jameson was nonetheless a talented woman with wide-ranging interests who could be a good companion in small doses. She was charmed to be introduced to the latest talented representative of the Kemble clan.

For all her youthful enthusiasm, it is clear that Fanny had acquired a measure of her family's professional wariness towards fans. Her summary of her literary encounter to Hal sounded a faint but prophetic note of caution:

> I have made one acquaintance, which might perhaps grow to a friendship were it not that distance and its attendant inconveniences have hitherto prevented my becoming more intimate . . . I like her very much; she is extremely clever; I wish I knew her better.[6]

The new year of 1828 began as Lord John Russell, the leader of the reforming Whigs, prepared to carry his motion to abolish the Test and Corporation Acts. His subsequent parliamentary victory was largely symbolic (the actual penalties against Dissenters had been lifted by an Annual Act of Indemnity for years) but that symbolic significance was great. The resolve of the Tory governing party to resist change had been breached. The reformers, gaining momentum, moved on to the sore question of Catholic Emancipation – that issue so critical to the political headache that was the Irish Question.

The behaviour of Jackie Kemble, home for the holidays, began to worry his family. There were traces of mania in 'the passionate eagerness . . . the sort of frenzy he has about politics'. By now Jackie was a full-blown 'advocate for vote by ballot, an opponent of hereditary aristocracy, the Church establishment, the Army and Navy, which he deems sources of unnecessary national expense'. Both Jeremy Bentham and James Mill lived near the Kembles, and whenever they passed either philosopher's house Fanny complained that Jackie responded as if he were passing 'the shrines of some beneficent powers'.

The pride of the household spent hours in his room scribbling arguments and producing essays he had ambitions of getting published. Charles Kemble was appalled to see his son drifting away from the future he had struggled so hard to provide for him. His political passions engrossed Jackie 'to the detriment . . . of all other studies'. As Fanny echoed her parents' anxiety to Hal:

> the vehemence with which he speaks and writes in support of his peculiar views will perhaps endanger his future prospects.

The young student sensed a momentous change that his elders did not yet perceive. Within a couple of years revolutions would again crack the surface of the establishment all across Europe. At home, the battle for Catholic Emancipation, once won, would lead on within five years to the Parliamentary Reform that would lay the ground for the foundations of the modern democratic state. Jackie Kemble's over-stretched parents, however, belonged to the generation who had lived through the consequences of the French Revolution; to them the possibility of momentous political change promised chaos. As far as the Kembles were concerned, engagement in politics could only be destructive – leading to unhealthy over-stimulation and the frustration of hopes.

Anxiety was closing in around the Kemble household once more. Fanny tried to convince herself that Covent Garden was 'doing very well just now'; but her physical and mental state betrayed a different reality. She suffered from 'the blue devils'; she was always having headaches, side-aches and mood swings. Just as the season started again after Christmas, Charles Kemble went up North to act, which suggests that he was in dire need of cash. Fanny cast about ever more desperately for ways to help her parents. She even wondered whether she might go on stage herself. 'They are in sad want of a woman at both the theatres,' she wrote to Hal that month. 'I've half a mind to give Covent Garden one. Don't be surprised. I have something to say to you on this subject, but have not room for it in this letter.'

Silence followed. Fanny had caught the measles and was very ill for a fortnight. In extreme low spirits she made her will and sent it to Hal along with her copy of *Francis I* and as a keepsake, a sketch a friend had made of her. In a household of drama queens Aunt Dall, who nursed her excitable niece back to health, was the only calm voice of reason. Coming upon Fanny weeping over her miserable sins Dall observed briskly: 'Why, child, there is nothing the matter with you; but you are weak in body and mind' – a statement which struck Fanny as 'the most degraded of all conceivable conditions' and she cried all the harder. The fact that it was not just the virus that ailed her, but that she carried from childhood a shadowy sense that whispered to her in her darker hours that she was cursed for unspecified misdeeds, is suggested by her account of an episode that first took place in the aftermath of this bout of measles but tended to repeat itself throughout her adult life in times of high stress.

In her sickness Fanny became obsessed with a large mirror that overlooked her. Her fear grew that she would see 'apparitions' in it and she struggled up to cover it with a cloth. The fever burnt itself out leaving Fanny listless and weak. One evening she was sitting brushing her hair at her dressing table as she read a book. Happening to glance up she caught sight of herself in the mirror. For a moment she saw herself as a stranger. She described fixing on this other face in 'a sort of trance', watching her own expression change as the horror of the thought registered,

> becoming gradually so dreadful, so much more dreadful in expression than any human face I ever saw . . . while it was next to impossible for me to turn my eyes away from the hideous vision confronting me.[7]

It seemed to her that if she did not break the connection she would go insane in the sight of this face 'suggestive of despair and desperate wickedness'.

She broke the connection and the nightmare faded, leaving her profoundly shaken. It is a measure of the plasticity of her features that Fanny acted well enough to scare herself – but the incident is illuminating. The mirror appeared to show her a revelation of her 'desperate wickedness'; a revelation of possession or a reflection of the sin she felt might be embedded in her. Whether this was a reflection of the sin of possessing the blood of a player, as insinuated by Mrs Rowden's religion; or of a fear that the blood of her mother might carry madness in it; or even whether, being unable to blame her mother or anyone else for the scarring of her face by smallpox, the image was a projection of her own anger – it seems that all her life Fanny was haunted by herself. She lived with a deep-buried sense that she was cursed to be repeatedly punished for some native wickedness.

By the age of eighteen Fanny had a measure of how alike she was to her mother. She looked at Marie-Thérèse, wobbling on the knife-edge between charming genius and miserable insanity, and feared for her own future. Mrs Rowden's Paris schooling had planted a potent seed. The cost of a creative temperament in a woman was high. In Fanny's eyes it cursed her with an 'entire want of self-control and prudence'. She feared that one day the riot of her imagination, her powerful emotions, her wilful temper might tip her over into self-destruction. Security, safety, respectability appeared to reside in the holy grail of Mrs Rowden's self-discipline and moral worth. The tension between the two, between the narrow peace of pious self-denial and the lush sensations of artistic sensitivity, became the matrix of Fanny Kemble's life.

> I have all my life suffered a tendency to imaginary terrors and have always felt sure that a determined exercise of self-control would effectually keep them from having dominion over me.[8]

After the measles had passed, in the sombre mood of recovery and still suffering from a recurring dull ache in her side, Fanny considered her options. Her confidence in *Francis I* had faded. Now she saw her play as 'a clever performance for so young a person, but nothing more'. Inspired by the model of Anna Jameson, Fanny decided it was time she shouldered some of the burden of supporting her family. She needed a profession. Her most likely option appeared to be the stage. She had the background and the connections. Her father had remarked many times that the theatrical world was short of a leading lady for tragedy.

Writing to Hal, Fanny set out her choices as she saw them with the stark, two-dimensional clarity of youthful insight.

> You know that independence of mind and body seems to me the great desideratum of life; I am not patient of restraint or submissive of authority and my head and heart are engrossed with the idea of exercising and developing the literary talent which I think I possess. This is meat, drink and sleep to me; my world in which I live, and have my happiness, and moreover, I hope, my means of fame (the prize for which I pray). To a certain degree it may be my means of procuring benefits of a more substantial nature, which I am by no means inclined to estimate at less than their worth. I do not think I am fit to marry, to make an obedient wife or affectionate mother; my imagination is paramount with me, and would disqualify me, I think for the everyday matter-of-fact cares and duties of the mistress of a household and the head of a family. I think I should be unhappy and the cause of unhappiness to others if I were to marry. I cannot swear I shall never fall in love, but if I do I will fall out of it again, for I do not think I shall ever so far lose sight of my best interest and happiness as to enter into a relation for which I feel so unfit.[9]

Given the stormy nature of her parents' marriage, it is hardly surprising that Fanny did not see herself as suited to the role of wife and mother. Her family history persuaded her that the stage could provide a lucrative career and she tried to convince herself that 'honourable conduct' could make it respectable. Success on the stage would 'place me at once beyond fear of want, and that is closely allied in its nature to my beloved literary pursuits'. It was not a perfect solution but would perhaps offer a compromise while allowing room for the pursuit of her cherished 'glad sunlight of clear thought'.

13

Honourable Conduct and the Acting Profession

At the age of eighteen in spring 1828 Fanny Kemble described herself as 'vehement and excitable, violently impulsive, and with a wild and ill-regulated imagination'. The aches in her side grew acute as her eagerness to do something – to have a purpose and above all to contribute to the family economy – foundered before her father's vacillation. One minute Charles Kemble was dropping heavy hints about the 'fine fortune to be made by any young woman, of even decent talent, on the stage now', the next, when she asked her parents directly whether they thought she might have sufficient dramatic capacity for an acting career, they looked serious and 'with some reluctance' answered that 'they thought, as far as they could judge . . . I might succeed'.

In her own opinion Fanny considered herself adequately equipped to attempt a stage career.

> If the informing spirit be mine, it shall go hard if, with a face and voice as obedient to my emotions as mine are, I do not in some measure make up for the want of good looks.[1]

Her only real concern was whether acting could be an honourable way of life for a young woman of intellect and spirit. She tried to reassure herself that her parents were in the best possible position to protect her reputation in – 'a career . . . where a young girl cannot be too prudent of herself, nor her protectors too careful of her'. By going on the stage Fanny had every hope of nearly doubling the income on which her father was struggling to keep his household (some £500 a year). And yet, despite mounting desperation Charles Kemble still clung to the tatters of gentlemanly appearances. In March, just before he departed for the North to perform in Edinburgh, Fanny pinned her father down to a discussion of the matter.

> . . . he allowed that should our miserably uncertain circumstances finally settle unfavourably, the theatre might be an honourable and advantageous resource for me; but that at present he should be sorry to see me adopt that career. As he is the best and kindest father and friend to us all, such a decision on his part was conclusive . . . and I have forborne all further allusion to the subject, although on some accounts I regret being obliged to do so.

Fanny could have wished for more decisive parents. Her cousins offered her a glimpse of what life might be like in a better regulated family. Sarah, Lizzie and Harry Siddons* presented a picture of the amiable and happy youth that could emerge from a theatrical home. Despite the loss of their father at a young age, they were self-assured, well-mannered and worshipped their mother. Harry, the teenage military cadet, who had inherited the striking good looks of his grandmother Sarah Siddons, had a sweet nature and was mature for his years. His sister Lizzie – the sister nearest to Fanny in age – was slender and tall. With dark blue eyes huge in her pale face and a

*There was another brother, William (1815–37), but Fanny makes no mention of him.

profusion of glossy chestnut curls that made her head seem almost too heavy for her slender neck, Lizzie was a vision of delicate young womanhood.* The *Recollections* that Lizzie published when she was a grandmother provide a striking contrast to Fanny's turbulent origins. Her book is full of affectionate anecdotes of her much loved grandmother Sarah Siddons, and her courtly intellectual great-uncle John Philip and his lively wife. Lizzie was proud of her illustrious relatives.

Something had to be done about Fanny. Blocked in her attempts to find a productive purpose, she fell back into the role in which her family so often cast her – that of being the most disruptive member of the household. When Harriot Siddons arrived in London towards the end of May to collect her daughters, it was decided that Fanny should accompany them on an extended visit to Edinburgh. It is likely that her parents intended to give Fanny a close-up view of the life of a working actress. They could hardly provide their eldest daughter with a finer example of the honorable conduct of the acting profession.

Fanny immediately felt comfortable in the ancient Scottish capital freshened by the air and light of the sea. Mrs Siddons lived in the Georgian New Town on a street that was still under construction. Windsor Street, lying between Leith Walk and the London Road to the north of Calton Hill, at that time broke off 'abruptly above gardens and bits of meadowland'. From her hostess's drawing-room balcony Fanny could see out to the waters of the Forth and the lighthouse at Inchkeith.

Here Fanny had her first experience of a stable household secure

*It was feared at the time that Lizzie might have inherited her father's propensity to 'consumption' (tuberculosis). In the event she lived to become a wife, mother and 'one of the largest women in our family' – it being a general rule that the Siddons/Kemble women began life slender and ended it remarkably rotund.

in its reputation. Much as Fanny loved her own family she was conscious of the uneasy position the Charles Kembles held in society. For all his gentlemanly gloss her father lacked the moral consistency that was the essence of respectability. In the eyes of society her mother's many talents were outweighed by her lack of finish. Harriot Siddons was not only firm and constant at the heart of her family but she was unchanged by wider exposure. As Fanny testified, 'men, women and children not only loved her, but inevitably fell in love with' Cousin Harriot. The sculptor Lawrence Macdonald, then a young man starting out on a career that would take him to Rome, celebrated Mrs Harry in verse that began –

High aims, pure thoughts, deep feelings, and a mind
Bright with intelligence and light divine
Are Heaven's best gift to man, and they are thine.

One cannot imagine anyone saluting Marie-Thérèse in such terms.

In 1828 Harriot was forty-five. She had lived in Edinburgh since her husband purchased the Patent to the Theatre Royal in 1809. Born Harriot Murray, she came from a family of actors. She began her stage career as a child, and by the turn of the century, in her late teens, she had established an excellent reputation for the simplicity of her acting style. Her genius, said the critic Leigh Hunt,[2] was entirely feminine. Her portraits show a pretty, small-boned woman with a pleasing oval face, straight nose, regular features and thick, glossy hair. Her delicate looks veiled a strong character.

When her husband succumbed to tuberculosis in 1815 he left his young widow a property encumbered with debts of over £3,000. For the next fifteen years, with the assistance of her brother, William Murray, who managed the theatre, Harriot sustained a gruelling acting schedule while bringing up four children single-handed. Eventually she was able to clear the debts and build sufficient capital to retire in 1830, two years after Fanny's first visit.

Harriot's reputation despite her public exposure as an actress – in Edinburgh she was known as 'our Mrs Siddons' – was partly due to her own hard work and self-discipline; but it also reflected the different cultural atmosphere in Scotland.

Scotland was a prime illustration of Mme de Staël's theory that a nation without political form could still exist through its art and culture.* After the defeat of the Jacobite Rebellion in 1745 England had emasculated Scotland's political structures. Yet between 1770 and 1830 Scotland experienced a 'golden age' during which its men of science and literature made a formidable contribution to Western civilization. As part of this renaissance, Scottish historians made a determined effort to revive the vanishing Gaelic culture.

The massive popularity of Sir Walter Scott's novels was due to more than just his gift for story-telling. His work coincided with Mme de Staël's notion that the artist, inspired by the 'genius' of the nation, could represent a silenced people by speaking with its voice. Scott's animation of the 'genius' of Scotland – manufactured from his love of its history, people and landscape – resonated with the self-determining Romantic spirit of the age.

By the 1820s Sir Walter Scott was the most famous living Scot and one of the top four Romantic authors read throughout Europe alongside Goethe, Byron and Mme de Staël. He had been a sponsor of Henry Siddons and his wife from the moment they first assumed management of the Theatre Royal† and the status of Harriot Siddons and William Murray was significantly bolstered by his endorsement. They promoted 'Scottish' drama, putting on plays with strong nationalist messages such as *Rob Roy* and *Wallace, Hero of Scotland*. Murray himself added plays to the repertoire based on incidents from Scottish history, while Harriot was much applauded for her stage portrayals of Mary Queen of Scots. Just as John Philip Kemble and Sarah Siddons had built their social status on their ability to personify cultural ideals on stage, so 'our Mrs Siddons' and her brother won recognition among the cultural elite of Scotland.

---

*The French word 'nationalité' first appears in Mme de Staël's *Corinne*.

†Lizzie Siddons told her Cousin Fanny how the famous author loved to hear their mother sing the ballad 'Young Lochinvar', applauding the expression she gave to the 'arch and spirited' words.

Fanny found happiness during the months she spent with her cousins in Edinburgh.

> In the rest and liberty of my life at this time, I think, whatever was best in me had the most favourable chance of growth . . . To the anxious, nervous, exciting, irritating tenor of my London life succeeded the calm, equable, and all but imperceptible control [of Harriot Siddons] whose influence over her children, the result of her wisdom in dealing with them, no less than of their own amiable disposition, was absolute.[3]

Harriot charmed Fanny into 'absolute submission to her will and wishes, and I all but worshipped her'. In fact Fanny demonstrated the fixation of a stalker. When Mrs Harry dropped her sash one day, Fanny refused to give it up and wore it for weeks over every dress she put on. She penned verses saluting her hostess's 'gentle graces that beseem fair woman's best' in a pastiche of a medieval troubadour praising his lady. Each evening, without fail, she would present her idol with a sprig of myrtle to wear – a romantic gesture symbolizing the purity of Harriot's influence.* At the end of the evening the sprig would be given back to Fanny as she kissed her hostess goodnight to be laid up in a 'treasure' drawer in her bedroom. When, after several weeks of this, the drawer became unmanageably full, Fanny burned the sacred sprigs in a little ritual. It must have been tiresome to be the object of such teenage passion, but Mrs Siddons is reported to have enacted her part with her customary grace.

As one obituary writer wrote of Harriot Siddons: 'she was, perhaps, the most perfect example you can conceive, of what Coleridge calls "ladyhood".'[4] Harriot projected an image that was gracious, wise and above all constant.

---

*When put among cut flowers in a vase myrtle leaves were supposed to prevent the water turning foul – 'preserving uncorrupted the water in which it is placed, with other flowers, is a sort of moral attribute'.

> Her manner, which was of the most gentle and winning imaginable, had in it a touch of demure playfulness that was very charming, at the same time that it habitually conveyed the idea of extreme self-control, and a great reserve of moral force and determination underneath this quiet surface.

Marie-Thérèse, who had known Harriot since the time she spent as a member of the Covent Garden company under John Philip's management, described Mrs Harry's manner as 'artificial', forged out of a hard struggle to control a passionate nature and impetuous temper. In short, Harriot's 'ladyhood' was a highly honed performance. As an example of extreme self-control it reinforced Fanny's beliefs about the self-sacrifice and discipline involved in the attainment of proper womanly behaviour.

Mrs Siddons's silken authority did not entirely tame the wilful teenager. The city's intimate proportions allowed Fanny the freedom to explore unchaperoned. She loved to get up early in the morning to run round Calton Hill, 'delighting . . . in the noble panorama on every side'. She would walk the couple of miles to Portobello Sands and bathe in the sea before breakfast. There is no evidence that her cousins Lizzie and Sarah were as adventurous, but it seems that Fanny went about unmolested – in contrast to what might have been expected in London.

Many of her daylight hours were spent exploring miles beyond the limits of the city's new Georgian suburbs. She would watch the boats in the fishing village of Newhaven, or wander further up the coast to Cramond Beach. Rejoicing in the 'wild loneliness' of the vast sky and open sea she would run along the sands, playing tag with the waves, dashing out on to the rocks only to retreat, laughing, drenched in spray.

> *Old paths, whose every winding step was dear, –*
> *Dark, rocky promontories, – echoing caves,*
> *Worn hollow by the white feet of the waves, –*
> *Blue, lake-like waters. – legend-haunted isle.*[5]

The 'legend-haunted isle' filled Fanny's imagination. She became –

> completely enamoured of the wild beauty of the Scotch ballads, the terror and pity of their stories, and the strange, sweet, mournful music to which they were told. I knew every collection of them, that I could get hold of, by heart from Scott's *Border Minstrelsy* to Smith's six volumes of *National Scottish Songs with their Musical Settings*,and I said and sang them over in my lovely walks perpetually; and they still are to me among the deepest and freshest sources of poetical thought and feeling that I know.[6]

Today, phrases such as 'the clarion-hearted Jacobite songs, with the fragrance of purple heather and white rose breathing through their strains of loyal love and death-defying devotion' only serve to highlight the sentimentality of early nineteenth-century versions of these so-called ancient ballads. Fanny's tastes in poetry always leaned towards the conventional – but that is not to belittle the importance that poetry had for her. When she told Hal that her literary imagination was 'meat, drink and sleep' to her and 'the world in which I live', she meant it.

Scott's 'noble stories of virtue conquering fortune and dedicating it to the highest purposes' provided a handbook of personal ethics especially suited to someone aspiring to win status through their talents. The writer's version of the Jacobite story was a restatement of the past that made heroes of ordinary men and women of native courage, wit and charm, who even when they failed against insuperable odds, did so with such integrity that they were judged more noble in defeat than their venal conquerors from the aristocratic establishment. The 'outsiders' win the moral point. It was a story of 'living by the spirit' just as Fanny wished to live by her own 'independence of mind and body'.

Scott fleshed out his fiction in himself. He was the solicitor's son who transformed an old farmhouse by the Tweed called Clarty Hole into 'Abbotsford' – the country seat where he manufactured an 'old world' gentility dressed with suits of armour, roaring fires, bright lights and music. There he embodied his ideal of the hospitable laird, whose simple directness and modesty were balanced by his scholarly library of antiquarian books. (The authentic laird of Jacobite times might well have displayed the simple directness; he was unlikely to own the books or even the armour.) The final triumph of this act of self-creation came in 1820 when George IV made plain Mr Scott a baronet.

Nowadays, when art is largely relegated to the status of entertainment, it is easy to misunderstand the passion with which individuals responded to literature in the Romantic period. Fanny grew up among people to whom politics meant corruption. Politics was an arena where the powerful negotiated their self-interests; it had little connection with the common good. Those who dreamed of bettering themselves and humanity looked to God and Art for inspiration. Through contemplation of the beautiful – in poetry or nature – men and women awakened their finer feelings. It was literature, articulating moral and spiritual ideals, that encouraged people to pursue such things as freedom and justice.

While living under Harriot Siddons's roof, Fanny meditated on the way Byron's poems of *Cain* and *Manfred* aroused 'a tempest of excitement' in her 'that left me in a state of mental perturbation impossible to describe for a long time after reading them'. The Byronic hero is not a cheerful libertine. He recognizes his 'sins'; he details them with a weary detachment, but he does not repent of them. They are a side-product of his heroic destiny to break out beyond the bounds of social conventions and petty morality and live his individuality to the full. Fanny examined the message, weighed the man and diagnosed an immoral refusal to take responsibility for the consequences of personal acts of will. The man who Caroline Lamb famously stigmatized as 'mad, bad and dangerous to know' conducted his life with 'selfish vanity and profligate vice'. Scott, in contrast, lived out his ideals of integrity, generosity and modesty. When, in the pure moral air of Edinburgh, Fanny decided, yet again, that she must wean herself off Byron's verse and stick to

Scott, she was not making a choice of the better poet; she was choosing which literary mentor to follow.

> Doubtless by grace of his free will a man may wring every drop of sap out of his own soul and help his fellows like-minded with himself to do the same; but the everlasting spirit of truth renews the vitality of the world, and while Byron was growling and howling, and Shelley was denying and defying, Scott was telling and Wordsworth singing things beautiful and good, and new and true.[7]

By her own account Fanny took over two years to cure herself of her Byronic addiction. Then, she claimed, she got her 'reward'. She was finally able to appreciate the beauty of Byron's poems without feeling 'the power of wild excitement' that used to possess her.

Marie-Thérèse Decamp was known for her openness and conviviality with all ranks in contrast to the lofty Kembles. Her daughter inherited her lack of concern for the social boundaries that confined most of her contemporaries. Accounts of Fanny at this age suggest an enthusiasm for quaint characters and picturesque situations.*

> I had gone down to the pier at Newhaven, one blowy, blustering day . . . and stood watching the waves taking their mad run and leap over the end of the pier . . . till it suddenly occurred to me that it would be delightful to be out among them . . . and I determined to try and get a boat . . .[8]

(Despite Fanny's repeated self-accusation of cowardice, her impulsive nature seems to have meant she gave little thought to

*One wonders how far she was consciously imitating Scott, who was known for his periodic tours of the countryside to gather material from encounters with authentic Highland folk.

physical danger – it was, after all, a similar recklessness in face of the elements that saw the end of the poet Shelley.*)

> I stopped at a cottage on the outskirts of the fishing town . . . and knocked. Invited to come in . . . there sat a woman, one of the very handsomest I ever saw, in solitary state, leisurely combing a magnificent curtain of fair hair that fell over her ample shoulders and bosom and almost swept the ground.

This statuesque vision, a cross between a Walter Scott walk-on part and Fanny's favourite water-sprite Undine, was a thirty-five-year-old local woman with grey-green eyes and a 'foam-fresh complexion'. Asked whether she knew of anyone who would take Fanny out in a boat, the fishwife, whose name was Mistress Sandie Flockhart: 'Looked steadily at me for a minute, and then answered laconically, "Ay, my man and boy shall gang wi' ye."'

Mistress Flockhart leaned back her head and yelled out for the said man and boy, who did indeed launch their boat and take Fanny out on to the boisterous water. Reality proved uncomfortable and Fanny was soon feeling very sick. So sick, indeed, that she asked to be returned to shore to recover herself, where 'Undine' greeted her with some amusement. Her stomach settled, Fanny set off back to Windsor Street with Mistress Flockhart's cordial invitation to return for another ride when the sea was calmer. On her part, Fanny assured her new friend that her cousin Mrs Siddons would be more than happy to buy her fish next time she came into the town with her wares.

Fanny much admired Mistress Flockhart's Viking beauty. She would watch out for her as she climbed the steep Edinburgh streets on bare white feet, carrying a heavy basket of fish on her back:

> her florid face sheltered and softened in spite of its massiveness into something like delicacy by the transparent shadow of the

*It was Shelley's insistence on sailing despite a rising storm that led to him drowning in July 1822.

> white handkerchief tied hoodwise over her fair hair, and her shrill, sweet voice calling 'Caller haddie!' . . . in [a] . . . melancholy monotone – the only melodious street-cry . . . that I ever heard.

Over the weeks Fanny's close observations of this picturesque character deepened into an acquaintance. The solitary girl who found herself uncomfortable in the company of her peers, visited the fisherwoman's house several times to sit and talk with her and play with her many children.

In Edinburgh Fanny experienced a widening of perspective beyond her childish, fairy-tale impressions of the Thames Tunnel site the year before. She remained 'humanity proud' but she began to awaken to the reality of other lives beyond the protected circle of her environment. In Mrs Harry's house good Christian practice was assumed rather than made an issue of. This habit of demonstration through deeds not words appealed to Fanny. She was much impressed by the 'pure moral atmosphere and kindly affection' shown her by her hostess and her family and friends. She had found the kind of mentors she had always sought – thoughtful and moral individuals who could help her to 'cultivate the best' in herself.

Mrs Harry's close friends included her doctor, Andrew Combe, and his brother George. George Combe was a lawyer who became well-known for his involvement with the new 'science' of phrenology, a system that purported to read a person's personality from the bumps and contours of the head. He had been converted to the theory by one of its inventors (Spurzheim) in 1815, and then dedicated his life to its promotion. Combe was forty when Fanny first met him. A couple of years later he became engaged to her cousin, Cecilia. According to family tradition, George insisted on having Cecilia's cranium examined and took the advice of Spurzheim on his suitability for the match. Reassured that his intended's 'Benevolence, Conscientiousness, Firmness, Self-Esteem, and Love of Approbation' were 'amply developed; whilst her Veneration and Wonder were equally moderate with his own', he married Cecilia in

1833. Their marriage was indeed happy, although Fanny remained sceptical about phrenology. She observed that Cecilia had just as many servant problems as anyone else despite her husband selecting each member of staff on the basis of an examination of their skulls for bumps of practicality, docility and the like.

George Combe was upright, angular, benevolent and humane and he was to remain a respected friend of Fanny's for the rest of his life, but his single-minded passion for phrenology was off-putting. His younger brother, Andrew, was the more lovable of the two. Andrew Combe was in his thirties in 1828 and already showing signs of the tuberculosis that would eventually kill him, but he had a sense of humour combined with a gentle gravity that was most attractive. He was one of those blessed people animated by a genuine interest in his fellow human beings. A reforming doctor, he published pamphlets on such practical matters as promoting health through hygiene and the importance of regular physical exercise during childhood.

One of Fanny's favourite treats while in Edinburgh was to drive out with Andrew Combe to visit some of his patients. Reports of these excursions alarmed Marie-Thérèse.

> She was always in a fever of apprehension about people's falling in love with each other, and begged to know how old a man this delightful doctor, with whom Mrs Harry allowed her own daughters and my mother's daughters to go 'gigging' might be.[9]

Fanny found the idea that the serious-minded, thirty-something doctor might have been interested in courting her absurd. Whether or not Andrew Combe in fact had a deeper interest in her, Fanny's affection for him was firmly as one of her 'elders and betters'.

The Combe brothers shared a house on Northumberland Street to the west of Windsor Street. Fanny visited them there, and her small stature, her youth and her *farouche* enthusiasm caused the Combes and their friends to adopt her as a sort of mascot. The circle included William Murray, Mrs Harry's charming actor-manager brother, and

Robert Chambers, bookseller and antiquarian and later author of *Vestiges of Creation*, a controversial theory of evolution. Fanny was introduced to Duncan McLaren, whose son became an MP and an editor of the *Scotsman*, and William Gregory, the son of an eminent professor of chemistry, who followed his father in the same line.

In the Combes's drawing room Fanny heard debated 'matters of public interest and importance . . . discussed from the most liberal and enlightened point of view'.[10] The atmosphere of these gatherings was more engaged and reflective than the brittle, witty and frequently slightly louche London literary set that paraded through the Montagues' drawing room in Bedford Square. The northern universities, famous for their Common Sense philosophy, turned out independent thinkers with a practical bent. Scotland had a worldwide reputation for producing able lawyers, surgeons, administrators and journalists. It was an intellectual mindset that preferred the useful to the dogmatic – the comprehension of the particular to the speculation of the Grand Idea.

In 1802, one set of ambitious young Scottish lawyers, frustrated by the English Tory control of advancement and appointment in their country's capital, set up the *Edinburgh Review*. On the theory that 'every Tory principle [was] absorbed by the horror of innovation' the young Scottish advocates turned themselves into arbiters of taste across the whole kingdom. By the time Fanny visited in 1828, Edinburgh's title as the 'Athens of the North' owed as much to the power of the *Review* as to its parade of classical Georgian architecture.

All her life Fanny would remember this Edinburgh society as something like her ideal. The diplomacy required of the public servant, reinforced by the timidity engendered by Catholic origins, made Fanny's father shy of 'controversial' topics. The Combe brothers and their friends, in contrast, were much preoccupied with improving society through literary persuasion and practical ideas in education, hygiene, drainage systems and so on. Here Fanny first encountered the confidence of respectable professional classes who, ennobled by their work to bring forward the Kingdom of God through improving the material conditions of the less fortunate in society, were challenging the aristocracy of inherited blood and land for the soul of the new century. The Combes and their circle were confident that it was their kind who would build a better world and not the aristocrats of the decadent Hanoverian establishment.

Winter arrived. Scotland's gentry returned from their country estates to be carried by sedan chair through the steep streets of the old town to evening assemblies, balls and concerts. As the delights of the Season took hold Fanny was no longer plagued by headaches at the prospect of socializing. She enjoyed such treats as being taken to the last public performance of Mme Catalani (the 'Mme Cat' who hid herself from the Old Price Rioters in the year Fanny was born). She was bribed with raspberry tarts to sit for the sculptor Lawrence Macdonald and of course she attended the Theatre Royal to watch her hostess perform.

Her worship of Harriot Siddons did not stop her exercising her critical faculties. Fanny considered that her cousin had no 'power of assumption', judging Harriot's Juliet to be 'comparatively cold . . . [not] the passionate young Italian girl'. Harriot was most convincing in those roles that reflected her personal attributes. Her 'grace and beauty' made her a ladylike Rosalind; she was held to suffer charmingly as the 'enchanting queen' Mary Stuart, while she and her brother were very popular as those on-stage siblings Viola and Sebastian in *Twelfth Night*.

Fanny was much entertained by her hostess's engaging brother, William, who was an 'accomplished' actor. He had a seductive voice and sang sentimentally (he was married to the sister-in-law of Tom Moore the composer of some of the favourite songs of that generation). He suffered badly from mood swings and depression but in public he was witty and charming. And he was a dreadful flirt.

> It was quite out of his power to address any woman (sister or niece or cookmaid) without an air and expression of sentimental courtesy and tender chivalrous devotion, that . . . I am persuaded that until some familiarity bred – if not

> contempt, at least comprehension – every woman of his acquaintance (his cook included) must have felt convinced that he was struggling against a respectful and hopeless passion for her.[11]

Inexperienced as she was, Fanny was quite shrewd enough to notice that Murray's habit of performance was so intermixed with the way that he behaved in real life that neither she nor anyone else could tell where the one began and the other ended. She wrote, 'I do not think William Murray's diamonds were of the finest water, but his paste was.'

Murray's 'powers of assumption' illustrated the aspect of the acting life that most concerned Fanny; the fact that the very qualities that made a successful actor involved being a charming projection around an empty centre.

> It was impossible to determine whether the romance, the sentiment, the pathos, the quaint humour, or any of the curiously capricious varying moods in which these were all blended, displayed real elements of his character or only shifting exhibitions of the peculiar versatility of a nature at once so complex and so superficial.

If her parents had intended, by sending Fanny up to Edinburgh, to convince her of the honourable nature of an acting career, the plan backfired. Harriot and her husband had always been more disciplined than the Kembles about their determination to insulate their offspring from the acting life. As their daughter Lizzie recalled, Henry Siddons senior had not viewed the profession as,

> in any way incompatible with moral or with mental excellence, but he did not consider it healthful to either mind or body to live in the perpetual strain of nervous excitement, and in the constant exercise of imaginative faculties necessary to the attainment of excellence in this art. It interfered, he thought,

> with the calmer, soberer views of life, which he considered . . . to be the most conducive to happiness.[12]

Harriot ran her household on this policy and Fanny liked it much better than the 'anxious, nervous, exciting, irritating tenor' of life among her own family of drama queens. Her year in Edinburgh turned her against the notion of an acting career.

According to her memoirs Fanny's cousin Harry Siddons was twenty and she herself seventeen at the time of her visit to Edinburgh. In fact she was eighteen while the birth dates given by historians suggest that Harry was some three years her junior. In 1828 Cousin Harry was preparing for a military career in the colonies. According to Fanny, they 'walked and talked and danced and were sentimental together after the most approved cousinly fashion'. It certainly seems that Harry Siddons had a crush on his vivacious cousin. When he finally set sail for India in February 1831 he carried the name 'Fanny' engraved on his brand new sword. Harry became a major in the Bengal Engineers and eventually married another cousin, a daughter of Sarah Siddons's second son, George, who made a fortune as Collector of Taxes in Calcutta. It was only many years later that his wife told Fanny of his romantic gesture and the fruitless couple of hours the young pair had spent, oceans away on another continent, trying to rub her name off his sword.

The delights of the winter season melted into spring. Harriot Siddons packed up her household and prepared to escort her young relative back down the country to London. Fanny would always cherish the household at Windsor Street as the –

> *harbour, where my heart*
> *Sometime had found a peaceful resting place.*

She had enjoyed almost a year to cultivate the 'best in her' but she had to plunge back into the turmoil that was destined to be her life. The question was, once separated from Harriot's angelic influence, how far her new confidence in her integrity would hold. In a poem she dedicated to Sarah Siddons, Harriot's eldest daughter, Fanny dramatized herself as a Byronic figure, cursed to roam the world, ever regretful for those benefits of a regular home she had glimpsed all too briefly.

'Tis true, I leave no void; the happy home
To which you welcomed me, will be as gay,
As bright, as cheerful, when I've turned to roam,
Once more, upon life's weary onward way [. . .]
Think of me, then, nor break kind memory's spell,
By reason's censure coldly o'er me cast,
Think only, that I loved ye passing well!
And let my follies slumber with the past.[13]

Perhaps, after all, despite the sincerity of her moral aspirations, Fanny Kemble was a drama queen by birth. Only time would tell.

14

Miranda and Prospero

Fanny returned from Edinburgh to find her home rocking on the brink of disaster. In February the pride of the household, John Mitchell, had fallen from grace. When called before the university authorities for his final examination at Cambridge he had had the temerity to expound his own opinions in response to the formal questions from Locke and Paley.[1] With 'high glee', as a friend put it, the bumptious twenty-one-year-old described Paley, the university's favourite theologian, as a 'miserable sophist' and talked of Locke's 'loathsome infidelity'. His examiners took such offence that they would not confer his degree for two years on account of 'general irregularity of conduct'.

For Charles Kemble the news was the explosion of all his fondest hopes. He had made up his mind that one day John Mitchell would become Lord Chancellor of England. Now his golden boy had carelessly destroyed his own chances for the sake of a knock-about argument.

Fanny was much hurt by the revelation of her favourite brother as a reckless and self-absorbed young man. Given the evident financial distress of their father, she struggled to find extenuating arguments in favour of an eldest son who would not trouble to make the best of his opportunities for the sake of his loved ones. Fanny found her brother much changed. The shock of his disgrace had knocked the desire for a law career out of him. He declared his intention to go into the Church. Although his sister publicly rejoiced at his new choice of career, she was distressed at the way the 'miscarriage' of the brother she admired 'extremely and believed in . . . implicitly' affected her darling father.

The last residue of Charles Kemble's youthful optimism appeared to evaporate before the 'failure of all the brilliant hopes he had formed of the future distinction and fortune of his eldest son'. The handsome hero in his six-foot frame of Fanny's Paris childhood crumpled into self-pitying ill-health. To compound the family's misery – as usual when she felt powerless – his temperamental wife retreated to her bed in sympathy.

That summer was a dismal one – so unseasonably cold that fires had to be lit in August. John Mitchell slid out from under his family's reproaches, taking himself off to Heidelberg to learn German.* Fanny was lonely without him. The weeks dragged by under dirty grey skies and she was 'thrown almost entirely upon myself'. Aunt Dall was fully occupied running the household and supporting the invalids, fourteen-year-old Tottie, a gawky and nervous adolescent, strove to be inconspicuous and Henry, a teenager of sixteen, spent as much time as possible with his schoolfriends. By an unfortunate coincidence, both Fanny's female mentors were also temporarily out of commission. Harriot Siddons was unwell, staying with relatives just out of reach across London. Fanny's correspondence with Hal was interrupted as her Irish confidante nursed her favourite brother Francis, the lawyer, who was seriously ill.

Like the distant rumble of a rising flood, Covent Garden and its financial crises was a constant presence. While Fanny was away the winter season had been a catalogue of disasters. Kean, notoriously touchy, had quarrelled with the management and stormed off to Drury Lane. A gas holder, part of the machinery that manufactured the gas that lit the lobbies, had blown up in the basement, killing two

*Germany, home of Metaphysics, was at the time a mecca for young Romantics.

workmen and causing the theatre to be shut down for two weeks at the height of the season. Mme Vestris, the company's remaining star attraction, grew increasingly skittish. The manager spent many an hour trying to coax her out of her lodgings and into his theatre. Charles Kemble was reduced to 'papering the house with orders' (the Georgian equivalent of complimentary tickets) to fill seats and keep his creditors sweet.*

Fanny grew 'heartsick' at the very name of Covent Garden. She listened to her father as he fantasized about selling his share in the theatre for anything he could get. She lay awake at night contemplating the dissolution of her family as her parents debated below whether Marie-Thérèse and her children would have to be sent away to live cheaply in the South of France.

The storm finally broke in the second half of August, while the head of the household was away performing in Ireland. At the instigation of the parish church of St Paul's, Covent Garden, warrants were issued for overdue taxes and rates against the theatre. With the addition of fines the bill came to over £1,500. The bailiffs took possession of the theatre.

That morning Fanny was sitting alone when her mother came in from a walk. Marie-Thérèse flung herself into a chair and burst into tears. 'Oh, it has come at last. Our property is to be sold. I have seen that fine building all covered with placards and bills of sale; the theatre must be closed, and I know not how many hundred poor people will be turned adrift without employment.' The Charles Kembles were ruined.

'Seized with a sort of terror, like the Lady of Shalot that "the curse had come upon me",' as she later recalled, Fanny did her best to comfort her mother. That evening she poured out her heart to Hal.

---

*According to Alfred Bunn, who was somewhat prejudiced against Kemble, in one three-month period the Covent Garden treasurer issued over 11,000 such orders at the manager's instigation.

> My father's property, and all that we might ever have hoped to derive from it, being utterly destroyed . . . it is right . . . that those of us who have the power to do so should at once lighten his arms of all unnecessary burden, and acquire the habit of independent exertion.[2]

She would write immediately to her father begging that he allow her to find employment as a governess so that at least she should not be 'a useless encumbrance to him'.

When she took the letter in to her mother, Marie-Thérèse's response was subdued. In the event she enclosed her daughter's letter in one of her own, asking her husband to postpone his response until he came back to town. Now that the crisis had at last broken upon her, a purpose began to form in Marie-Thérèse's tenacious brain. She asked Fanny point-blank whether she thought she had any real talent for the stage. Fanny answered truthfully that she had not the slightest idea. Her mother asked her to learn a Shakespearean part by heart and perform it for her so that she might judge for herself. Fanny shut herself in her room and in a few hours had learned the role of Portia from *The Merchant of Venice*, her ideal among Shakespearean woman.

With a typical lack of tact Marie-Thérèse pronounced that there was not enough passion in the part to test any talent for tragedy. She told Fanny to learn Juliet. This time her mother heard her recitation 'without any observation whatever'. She dismissed Fanny back to her daily routine none the wiser as to her parent's conclusions.

Meanwhile, over in Ireland, Charles Kemble was making Herculean efforts to negotiate a way of keeping the theatre in business. At the eleventh hour Charles rediscovered his Kemble fighting spirit. Pursuing his campaign by post, he set a goal of raising £6,000 and organized a subscription inviting Friends of the Theatre to contribute gifts or loans. London began to rediscover its affection for Covent Garden. Principal creditors were charmed into easing their demands for the present. Shareholders agreed to a suspension of dividends for three years. Even rivals rallied to the cause. Day by day, stars of music and drama pledged their services – 'Miss Kelly has consented to perform gratuitously for Ten nights'; 'Mr Kean will act Three nights gratuitously, immediately on his return to London'; 'Mons Drouet has volunteered to perform on the FLUTE for three nights'. The manager of the Opera House even donated the use of his theatre free of charge for a grand fundraising performance.

By the time Charles was free from his Irish commitments at the beginning of September he could be satisfied with the growing momentum of his campaign, but he knew that goodwill and gratuitous performances could not secure Covent Garden's future. He needed a new star – an attraction so novel that audiences would fill his theatre week after week.

At home, Fanny was still awaiting her father's response to her eager offer to throw herself on the job market when he reappeared. Marie-Thérèse summoned her daughter to recite Juliet for her father. In some trepidation, Fanny stood up before her parents and – in her own words – 'repeated my first lesson in tragedy'. When she had finished they responded with, 'Very well, very nice, my dear,' kissed her and sent her off to bed. Fanny got halfway up the stairs before she sat down in a flood of tears.

Her parents appear to have been unaware of the strain they were inflicting by keeping her so little informed of their plans. Fanny was left to stew for another couple of days before, one morning at breakfast, her father announced that he wished her to go with him to the theatre to try her voice.

When Fanny was a little girl her mother used to take her to visit two sisters, the Misses Grimani, who ran a school in Blackheath. Fanny was fascinated by a picture that hung in the drawing room. It depicted a handsome man and a child like herself in a small boat on a perilous, stormy sea. The gracious lady of the house would take her by the hand and tell her the story of the great and noble Prospero who was cast out on a tempestuous sea in a leaky boat with only his precious daughter, Miranda, for his companion and comfort. To Fanny's eyes the handsome Prospero was a portrait of her father.

However daunting the challenge she faced that September in 1829, after all the years of striving for his attention and approval, at last Fanny – like Miranda in that boat – stood side by side with her beloved father in his hour of need. Father and daughter went alone into the theatre that morning. They must have made quite a picture: the tall, distinguished tragedian ushering the small, bonneted figure into the still, expectant, shabby world that is a theatre by day. In the vast sweep of the auditorium the ranks of pit benches stood shrouded in grey holland covers and the circles of boxes rose up to blend into the shadows of the domed ceiling. While her father stayed back in the wings, Fanny walked out on to the boards from which her uncle had struggled to calm the Old Price rioters in the month she was born. To either side of the stage scenery was stacked in racks – pieces of street and forest, banqueting hall and dungeon fashioned from canvas, paint and clever perspective. Fanny felt as if the indistinct recesses of the raked stage behind her stretched into the infinite.

> The great amphitheatre . . . would have been absolutely dark but for a long, sharp, thin shaft of light that darted here and there from some height and distance far above me, and alighted in a sudden, vivid spot of brightness on the stage.[3]

The question was whether the voice of so small a person could possibly reach out and be heard in the vast auditorium that seated 2,800 people – the population of a moderate market town in those days.

> Set down in the midst of twilight . . . with only my father's voice coming to me from where he stood hardly distinguishable in the gloom . . . I was seized with the spirit of the thing; my voice resounded through the great vault above and before me, and, completely carried away by the inspiration of the wonderful play, I acted Juliet as I do not believe I ever acted it again, for I had no visible Romeo, and no audience to thwart my imagination.

In fact, Fanny and her father were not alone. Charles Kemble had planted a friend of his, one Major Dawkins, in the dim recesses of a private box. Unknown to Fanny, the major, a gentleman amateur actor whose critical taste Charles Kemble much respected, watched her solo performance. It was his verdict that sealed the matter. 'Bring her out at once,' he told Kemble; 'it will be a great success.'

By the end of that day Fanny was committed to a very public début as a tragic leading actress. At the age of nineteen the fate of her family rested on her ability to make a hit. Her parents had three weeks in which to prepare her.

15

Selling Juliet

Charles Kemble was gambling his family's financial survival on turning his young daughter into the novelty his theatre needed. A youthful *ingénue* who moved gracefully, spoke confidently and had influential friends could enjoy success for at least a season – but he needed more than a moderately good season. He needed a star.

The difficulty in 1829 was that classic tragedy had gone out of style. The days William Robson and James Boaden wrote about, when men of taste attended tragedy for their moral edification and poetic education, belonged to a passing generation. More evocative of the occupants of the dress boxes in 1829 was Fanny's favourite anecdote of the young guardsman dragged to see his first Shakespeare, turning to his friend with a bewildered: 'I say, George, dooced odd play this; it's all full of quotations.' When Fanny approached her début, the connection between aristocratic culture and the theatre was dissolving before the tastes of middling men.

While Fanny led her dull, lonely existence that July the ancient liberty that English parishes police themselves was being curtailed for the first time. Robert Peel's Bill established a permanent London-wide, uniformed police force. That August, workmen tore down the old royal stables of Henry VIII at Charing Cross to make way for the National Gallery – a place where, in the future, any decently dressed citizen could contemplate cultivation and art. As Fanny and her father made their way to the theatre for her trial that September morning, they would have passed the newly instituted horse omnibus carrying clerks from Islington and Hackney to the commercial houses of 'Change Alley' in the City.*

By the end of the 1820s playgoers were displaying a firm preference for domestic dramas built around sentimentalized family values. A signpost to this shift was Macready's success in *Virginius*, the piece that launched playwright Sheridan Knowles's career. The contemporary critic R.H. Horne commented that Knowles 'personifies our age . . . in his truly domestic feeling'.

> [In *Virginius*] we have Roman tunics, but a modern English heart – the scene is the Forum, but the sentiments those of the Bedford Arms. The affection of the father for his daughter – the pride of the daughter in her father, are the main principles of the play.[1]

At a high point in *Virginius* the free birth of the hero's daughter is challenged and the villain threatens to drag her off as a slave. Macready, as Virginius, would reduce his audience to tears by breaking off in the midst of his heroic rage as if caught by an expression on his daughter's face:

> *I never saw you look so like your mother*
> *In all my life . . .*

Playgoers of the 1820s recognized in such domestic vignettes of familial love 'eternal human truths' while the heroic passions of the Siddonian tragedy queen receded into an alien classical world.

The début of a new Kemble in the celebrated line of Black Jack

---

*In that seemingly insignificant commercial venture lay the germ of the public transport system that would facilitate the spread of the city into the sprawling metropolis of the future.

and the Divine Sarah, made in the cause of saving the great theatre with which they were so closely identified, was a marketable story. But what really caught the imagination of the commentators was how the manager and his daughter duplicated in real life the stage ideals of loving parent and dutiful child.

The first priority was to project Fanny as a pure young *ingénue*. So successful was the Kembles' publicity that their daughter's lack of preparation for the stage has subsequently been picked up as gospel by most biographers. Georgian productions relied on established renditions of parts and stable companies of actors who were used to working together; there were few rehearsals compared to modern times and no formal system of dramatic training. To a degree acting was just like the other trades of the time, when son tended to follow father (with the novel twist that this was a trade open to mothers and daughters as well).

Despite her lack of apprenticeship in minor roles Fanny was reasonably well-equipped as a would-be star. Not only was she a Kemble, having grown up among the leading proponents of tragedy, but she also had the benefit of her mother's experience as a dancer and singer. Years of enduring her mother's singing lessons had given Fanny control over her rich contralto voice and the ability to project it. Her dancing lessons had honed a natural ability and she moved with much of her mother's famed grace. Add to this the expressive, mobile features she inherited along with a measure of her mother's skill as a mime, and the fact that her father's side of the family were the creators of the 'classical' style of declamation, and she was better equipped than most *ingénues*.

Nonetheless, she was being called to rise to an enormous challenge. For all that 'every line of Shakespeare's Juliet was familiar to my mind'[2] she had never attended a professional rehearsal. In three weeks she had to learn how to hold herself with confidence on the stage, how to act in concert with other players and all the basic business of performance.

As news of Fanny's début spread, Mrs Jameson – the *Ennuyée* herself – came calling at Buckingham Gate. The writer's husband had recently sailed for Dominica to take up an appointment as a judge. Although Mr Jameson was difficult to pin down on the subject, it was clear that he was not keen that his wife should follow him. Frustrated and unhappy, Anna Jameson was determined to pursue her literary talent. She had been fascinated by Mrs Siddons ever since she attended one of the actress's readings as a young woman of twenty, when she gazed at the star 'as I should have gazed at one of the pyramids'.[3] Ambitious to make her name as an art critic, Anna leaped at the opportunity to further her acquaintance with the latest representative of the Kemble-Siddons line and witness dramatic history in the making.

Marie-Thérèse was not fond of the white-fleshed, busy redhead, but she sensed that the authoress might be worth cultivating. Fanny was pulled about and discussed over as her sharp-tongued mother put up with Mrs Jameson's uncalled-for advice. Anna Jameson prided herself on her correct artistic taste. She was warm in her arguments that Juliet should be dressed according to contemporary portraits. Marie-Thérèse was adamant that it was more important for her daughter have the freedom of movement to act well rather than appear in historically accurate attire. Mrs Jameson produced picture after picture in vain – engravings from Raphael, Titian or Giorgione. Fanny's mother dismissed them all. 'Remember, this presents but one view of the person, and does not change its position,' she would say. 'How will this dress look when it walks, runs, rushes, kneels, sits down, falls, and turns its back?'[4]

The loquacious Irishwoman threw up her hands at the 'violation of every propriety' in a Juliet attired in a modern ballgown against scenery depicting fourteenth-century Verona, but Marie-Thérèse held her ground. Fanny's small frame was fitted into the simple lines of a plain white satin gown with a long train and short sleeves, cinched at the waist with a 'girdle of fine paste brilliants, and a small comb of the same' to decorate her hair.

The date was fixed, the costume was in the making, but the production still had no Romeo. Now in his mid-fifties, Charles Kemble continued to collect praise as the best Romeo in the business. The management, however, decided that it was more appropriate that he take the part of Mercutio. Given his dramatic countenance and charisma, John Mitchell might have been the ideal pairing for Fanny. (What a *coup* it would have been to recreate for a new generation the partnership between John Philip Kemble and Mrs Siddons!) But John Mitchell was in Germany and unavailable. (It is a measure of the rushed nature of the début that John Mitchell learned of Fanny going on the stage from reading a newspaper in Munich.[5]) In his absence the family turned to that clear-skinned, handsome youth, Henry. He was a little young (three years Fanny's junior) but at a glance he looked the part.

The family assembled in the drawing room at Buckingham Gate to hear the sixteen-year-old try the balcony scene. Henry (who evidently hated the idea of a stage career) stumbled through his lines with such a combination of awkwardness and giggles that his father at last threw down his prompt copy of the play and roared with laughter along with the rest of the family. Henry expressed his relief by clapping his elbows to his sides and giving voice to a series of triumphant cock-crows.

Fanny was left with Mr Abbott, a worthy leading man of forty with a glossy pair of whiskers. He had a pleasant reputation as a 'gentlemanly' man in private life but the role was not suited to his style. 'Must we speak of Mr Abbott's Romeo?' sighed Leigh Hunt in the *Tatler*. 'Mr Abbott has taken it into his head that noise is tragedy, and a tremendous noise he accordingly makes.'

One day shortly before the opening of the season, the neat figure of a well-preserved sixty-year-old accosted Charles Kemble in the street. It was Sir Thomas Lawrence – a man he had avoided for thirty years. Speaking with 'great feeling', the celebrated artist said that he had heard of Miss Kemble's forthcoming 'trial' and, Fanny reports, 'begged permission to come and see my mother and become acquainted with me'.[6]

When he was in his early twenties, Charles Kemble and his friend Charles Moore had been the 'two Charleses', the handsome young men who with Thomas Lawrence had been the favourite beaux of Mrs Siddons's two eldest daughters. In those giddy, exhilarating days when Lawrence seemed destined to rival the fame of Reynolds, he had fallen in love with Sally Siddons. She was the elder of the sisters and the good, gentle one. They became engaged. But then Lawrence became captivated by her younger sister, Maria, a pretty, fiery, selfish minx of a girl. He threw himself on Mrs Siddons's mercy and declared his mistake. Sally concealed her broken heart and graciously gave way for what she hoped would be her sister's happiness.

Soon it transpired that Maria, elfin and big-eyed, was being eaten away by consumption. As the weeks of visiting his invalid fiancée went by, Lawrence's attention wavered again. Sally made such a gentle nurse and considerate sister. He recognized his mistake and hoped to revert to his original choice. Maria would have none of it. On her deathbed she employed her remaining energy to elicit a promise from Sally that she would never marry the faithless artist. Devastated, Lawrence was cast out from Mrs Siddons's presence, and was expelled from the tribe he had so long looked to as his spiritual home. The breach became irrevocable when Sally too died five years after her sister.

Now, thirty years on, Charles stood in the street face to face with the man who had betrayed Mrs Siddons's trust and embittered (or, in the romantic version, hastened) the death of his two nieces. In loyalty to his sister, Charles had cut the connection with Lawrence along with the rest of the Kemble clan. Over the years the artist had tried to make overtures to heal the breach. Priscilla's polite response to the letter of condolence Lawrence wrote to her on her husband's death in 1823, paying the portrait painter the compliment that John Philip had taken pride in the fact that 'by your aid he would be remembered', indicated how awkward the Kembles found the conflict between personal and professional relationships. Charles had always got on well with Lawrence personally, and the artist had played an important part in fixing the Kemble image of gentility before public and posterity.

By 1829 Lawrence was the last representative of the great generation of British portrait painters still living – Reynolds, Gainsborough, Hoppner and Raeburn were all dead. In the intervening years since his disastrous relations with the Siddons sisters his career had soared. At the end of the war with Napoleon, he became the first English painter to gain a truly international reputation with his series of portraits of the victorious Allied monarchs and their commanders.

Lawrence was President of the Royal Academy and renowned across Europe and yet his day had passed. He was a lonely man, rattling about in his big house at 65 Russell Square where he lived in one bedroom and a parlour, the rest of the house being given up to the ghosts of his imagination – the host of canvases that bore half-finished portraits of sitters, many of whom had by now grown old and even died. He never got over the break with Mrs Siddons and so the acting début of her dark-haired niece was bound to draw his attention. For Charles's part, at this time of trial, he was happy to gloss over the past and the celebrated artist became a welcome visitor at Buckingham Gate.

The publicity around Fanny's début gathered pace. Journalists were much taken by the crowning touch to the family theme: Marie-Thérèse was coming out of retirement to play Lady Capulet 'for one night only' in order to support her daughter on stage.

The season was launched on Friday 2 October with a star-studded fund-raising gala at the Royal Opera House for the benefit of the Covent Garden fund – a successful night that netted £750 and cranked up the public enthusiasm.

> To Covent-garden, which commences its season to-morrow, the public eye is turned with an unusual degree of interest, the family of the manager, united in the common cause, come forward in hopes of aiding the fortunes of the theatre. MRS. CHARLES KEMBLE, who had retired from the worries of

> public life, and her amiable and highly *gifted* daughter, whom it was never intended should endure them, both make their appearance in the play, MRS. CHARLES KEMBLE as *Lady Capulet*, and the accomplished MISS KEMBLE as *Juliet*. Her father plays *Mercutio*, and ABBOTT, returned, is to be the *Romeo*.[7]

In no time at all Fanny was waking up on the morning of Monday, 5 October 1829. She faced a blank day. There was no rehearsal on the principle that she needed to conserve her strength for the evening. With considerable self-discipline, Fanny determined that she could best control her nerves by following her normal routine: a morning of piano practice, a walk in St James's Park just across the way from the house, and an edifying couple of hours reading chapters on St Peter and Jacob in *Blunt's Scripture Characters*. Mid-afternoon a carriage drew up at the gate. In she climbed with her mother and Aunt Dall and they were off to the theatre.

The mellow autumn sunlight glanced into the carriage. 'Heaven smiles on you, my child,' remarked her mother, perhaps more in hope than with conviction. As soon as they arrived, Marie-Thérèse darted off to her own dressing-room for fear that her nervousness would be contagious. Fanny was left in the hands of neat, capable Dall. It was she who directed Fanny's maid and the theatre's dresser as they decked her niece out in her white gown, the glittering belt, the white satin shoes and the comb in her hair. Once she was ready Fanny sat in a chair pressing her gloved hands together, tears running down her cheeks from sheer nerves. Dall divided her time between patiently reapplying the streaking make-up and going to reassure Fanny's father who, in full costume as Mercutio, kept tapping on the door and hissing anxiously, 'How is she?'

It was seven o'clock and time for the curtain to go up. Mrs Siddons was ensconced in the little box overlooking the stage that Charles Kemble had fitted up for her special convenience opposite the prompter's station. In the auditorium, the atmosphere was thick with the smell of humanity warmed by the flickering gas-chandeliers, the taint of the gas mixing with the softer odour of the oil-lamps and candles that illuminated the stage. On the pit benches, critics and reviewers jostled with the young gentlemen clutching their playbills reeking of cheap ink overlaid with a whiff of oranges. The dress-boxes were full and the galleries packed to the ceiling. In the aisles the unfamiliar uniforms of Sir Robert Peel's Bobbies* moved among the strident orange-sellers offering the programme sheets for the night along with their pieces of fruit.†

At last the boy's knock on the dressing-room door brought Fanny to her feet: 'Miss Kemble called for the stage, ma'am!' Surrounded by her dressers and held up by Aunt Dall, Fanny was led into the wings in sight of her mother who, dressed as Lady Capulet, stood at the edge of the green baize that covered the stage to signify tragedy.

> I saw my mother advance on the stage: and while the uproar of her reception filled me with terror, dear old Mrs Davenport, my nurse, and dear Mr Keeley, her Peter, and half the dramatis personae of the play (but not my father, who had retreated, quite unable to endure the scene) stood round me.[8]

Mrs Davenport, a fair-skinned, motherly woman of sixty-four who had played the Nurse in *Romeo and Juliet* since before the Kembles first came to Covent Garden, clucked at the sight of Fanny white and shaking in her aunt's arms. 'Courage, courage, dear child!' she whispered, punctuating the remark with an audible refrain of 'Poor thing! Poor thing!'

'Never mind 'em, Miss Kemble! Never mind 'em!' offered the comedian Keeley in his trademark lachrymose voice. 'Don't think of 'em any more than if they were so many rows of cabbages!'

'Nurse!' called Lady Capulet and Mrs Davenport limped into the

---

*Charles Kemble was taking no chances of disturbance: 'for the better preservation of decorum and security of the Public, the arrangements before the curtain' were 'under the direction of the new Metropolitan police'.

†To avoid stamp duty on printed paper the orange-sellers gave away the programme sheets for the night along with the fruit they sold.

light of the stage lamps, turning back to call in her turn: 'Juliet!' Aunt Dall gave Fanny a tremendous shove and she ran straight across the stage.

> . . . stunned with the tremendous shout that greeted me, my eyes covered with mist, and the green baize flooring of the stage feeling as if it rose up against my feet; . . . I got hold of my mother, and stood like a terrified creature at bay, confronting the huge theatre full of gazing human beings. I do not think a word I uttered during this scene could have been audible; in the next, the ball-room, I began to forget myself; in the following one, the balcony scene, I had done so, and, for aught I knew I was Juliet; the passion I was uttering sending hot waves of blushes all over my neck and shoulders, while the poetry sounded like music to me as I spoke it, with no consciousness of anything before me, utterly transported into the imaginary existence of the play.

In the event Fanny's initial nervousness only added an extra *frisson* to the general sympathy among the spectators. According to *The Times* reviewer she 'almost immediately recovered her composure'. By the balcony scene all eyes were fixed on the brilliant white figure of the girl who moved with such grace.

Fanny demonstrated that she shared her family's dramatic gift to the extent that there was some dispute as to her actual physical appearance. Observers were enchanted by the expression of her splendid dark eyes defined under their symmetrical eyebrows,* while the intensity of her passion made up for her lack of height – *The Times* reviewer being sufficiently misled to describe her as tall. She is 'of graceful and well proportioned figure', he wrote. 'Her voice is flexible and of considerable volume, and her utterance so perfectly distinct

---

*Recalling what James Boaden said of her mother – that her 'expression in look and gesture was even more intelligent than Speech'. Boaden, *Memoir of Mrs Inchbald*, vol. II, p. 50.

that her lower tones are always audible and effective.'[9] Another critic, sitting a few seats away, judged her slightly differently:

> . . . if her figure is spare, and her voice rather thinner than we could wish, there is about her that quality which made 'Pritchard genteel, and Garrick six feet high' – a mind to conceive and skill to execute her conceptions.[10]

The impression that comes down through the years of Fanny's performance that night is one of vitality. Accounts report how light she was on her feet and the grace with which she moved. One family friend, Lady Dacre, told her afterwards that as soon as her troubles as Juliet began she had unconsciously caught up her flowing train and carried it over her arm. Fanny herself only dimly remembered dealing with some encumbrance that got in the way of Juliet's feet.

The conditions of the theatre at that time required a form of acting that we would probably find over-stylized and histrionic in the extreme. The expansion of the Covent Garden auditorium to accommodate those 2,800 seats had spoiled the acoustics. By 1829 only the critics in the pit and the occupants of the boxes closest to the stage went to the theatre expecting to enjoy every nuance of speech and facial expression from the actors, even in tragedy. Modern acting has been transformed by the intimacy of the camera; in the early nineteenth century successful performances had to be choreographed to catch the attention of a distant, restless audience. As Fanny once explained to Hal, 'our immense houses . . . require acting almost as <u>splashy</u> and coarse in colour and outline as the scene-painting of the stage is obliged to be'.[11] Performances proceeded before an auditorium fully lit by the jets of gas chandeliers.* The occupants of the galleries were notorious for their tendency to chat when bored, contributing their voices to the atmosphere along with the orange peel they dropped on to the stage and the spectators below them. As

*The notion of darkening the auditorium during the performance was an innovation of the second half of the nineteenth century.

Kean had demonstrated, successful acting in such conditions depended on telegraphing emotion through physicality – body-line, vigorous movement and mime – as much as words.

This convention explains the apparent self-contradiction of the reviewer who remarked that Fanny's acting was 'unembarrassed and natural' while at the same time noting that 'her conduct in what is called the business of the stage [is] evidently regulated . . . by the skilful tuition she may have received'. 'Natural' is not perhaps the word that springs to mind today when reading of how, before drinking the Friar's potion, Fanny's Juliet would make 'a desperate rush' down the stage, ending with a sort of slide on to one knee.*

'I have often been accused of studying my attitudes', Fanny wrote a couple of years after her début,

> but the truth is that most things that are presented to my imagination, instead of being mere abstractions, immediately assume form and colour, and become pictures; these I constantly execute on the stage as I had previously seen them in my imagination.[12]

'Attitudes' were an element of mime or ballet in late Georgian acting that would seem odd today. An attitude was a trademark pose (or a movement ending in a pose) that was supposed to highlight the character's emotion at that moment. If it approved the 'conception' the audience would applaud, giving the actor time to catch his or her breath. The success of a new interpretation of a role required a series of such highlights that became the distinguishing marks of a performance and that actor's claim to particular genius.

As Juliet, Fanny displayed an ability to take and hold an eloquent position. For instance, on the line: 'Come, what says Romeo' in Act II, scene V she would kneel on one knee before Nurse, with her back to the audience and her arms held out, the fluid line of her body extended by the flowing curl of her satin train.

---

*That particular effect did not please everyone, one critic condemning this 'novelty' as 'exaggerated, and the celebrated slide altogether pantomimic'.

However mannered her performance might seem today, it gathered her Georgian audience that night up into the fantasy. 'She seemed too good for Romeo,' wrote the twenty-year-old Richard Milnes enthusiastically to his mother:

> her execution of the last scene was as original as simple & sublime – no tossing about & dragging and convulsions. She came forward on one knee, drove the dagger into her heart with the calmest look of desperation – gave a look of deep agony, turned her head round with a smile of triumphant defiance, bounded up as with a tremendous convulsion and fell flat on her back – the impression was quite awful.[13]

The curtain fell to ecstatic applause. Charles Kemble, with tears in his eyes, came forward to announce that 'he was induced, by the indulgence which the audience had shown to his daughter, to give the tragedy out for repetition on Wednesday, Friday and Monday next'. The house received the announcement with cheers of approval. 'The public has stamped, with their approbation,' wrote one journalist portentously, 'the merits of another of a family to whom the British stage owes more than to any individuals who ever made the drama their profession.'[14]

At the end of the evening the Kembles returned home for a quiet family supper at Buckingham Gate. It was a happy gathering. Charles exultant; Marie-Thérèse, Dall and Fanny all glowing with the proof that, after all the hopes Charles had placed in his sons over the years, in his hour of need it was his womenfolk he could rely on. Fanny's night crystallized into perfection when her father laid a Geneva watch worked with gold and jewels beside her plate. It was the first watch she had ever owned. She christened it Romeo and went 'a blissful girl, to sleep with it under my pillow'.

The next day visitors began calling. Among the first to congratulate the Kembles was Washington Irving. Irving first came to know the Kembles around 1817 when, as the 34-year-old representative of his family's New York hardware business, he was introduced to

Marie-Thérèse. Fanny's mother took the then unknown American under her wing and he never forgot her kindness. Within a couple of years of their acquaintance Irving would gain international recognition with the publication of his vastly popular *Sketch Book of Geoffrey Crayon, gent.*, his collection of short stories that included the famous tales of Rip van Winkle and the 'Legend of Sleepy Hollow'. Sweet-natured and unaffected, Irving remained a favourite of the Kemble household.

Fanny scampered off to fetch her new watch. Irving examined it with care, offering suitable comments on its fine workmanship. Finally, holding it up to his ear with an exaggerated look of comic surprise he exclaimed, as if to a child: 'Why it goes, I declare!' His humour at her enthusiasm was appropriate. After all her years on the periphery of her parents' attention, Fanny was revelling in the role of the petted child.

The newspapers arrived, confirming her success. 'That highly gifted and accomplished young lady' was 'by general consent . . . placed in the high road to fame'.[15] Fanny's acting was 'of the Siddons school', they said. Her parents were not forgotten. Marie-Thérèse's performance as Lady Capulet convinced the gushing reviewers that she ought not to have left the stage, while Charles Kemble's Mercutio was deemed to be 'admirable'.

> We have often thought that KEMBLE was the only man on the stage capable of playing 'Mercutio' and now we are sure of it.[16]

Charles Kemble's gamble had paid off. He put his daughter to work and almost immediately the material benefits began to flow. Within a year Fanny Kemble, as the star attraction of Covent Garden, would be credited with paying off £13,000 of the theatre's debts.

She was no longer an obscure teenager, contriving to squeeze the price of necessary gloves and shoes out of an annual allowance of £20. As Covent Garden's leading lady she was earning 30 guineas a week. There was no more trudging through muddy London streets because the hire of a hackney cab would be prohibitive. The Kembles acquired a carriage of their own. Fanny shed her faded, turned and re-dyed frocks and emerged 'transfigured' in the latest fashions.

Fanny was euphoric. 'I hail my success as a source of great happiness to my dear father and mother,' she wrote to Hal that December.[17] At last her family was pulling together and she herself was at the centre of attention. Her star status was confirmed when Sir Thomas Lawrence begged her mother's permission to sketch her. The resulting picture, simply dedicated to 'Mrs Charles Kemble/Sir Thomas Lawrence', became the defining image of Fanny's new public self.

The pretty pencil sketch was finished in the first week of November. Within days it was with Mr Lane the engraver being prepared for public use.* 'I was at Charles Kemble's a few evenings ago,' reported John Sterling, a college friend of John Mitchell's, to his brother in Ireland on 10 November:

> A drawing of Miss Kemble by Sir Thomas Lawrence was brought out, and I have no doubt you will shortly see, even in Dublin, an engraving of her from it, very unlike the caricatures that have hitherto appeared.[18]

The shopkeepers, artisans and clerks, along with their wives and daughters, who filled the expanding suburbs of London and the blossoming provincial cities, were forming an ever-broadening market for celebrity merchandise. In her day Mrs Siddons had spawned a host of commemorative items. Her image adorned jugs, snuff-boxes, brooches and bowls. Wedgwood sold plaques of her

---

*This was an example of Lawrence's gallant generosity. Having given the sketch to Fanny's mother the artist waved aside the question of any payment for the copyright of it. Mr Lane, Fanny heard, made £300 from the first impression taken from it. Such gestures no doubt partly explain why Lawrence, who worked unceasingly at a lucrative career throughout his life, left very little when he died.

profile and hand-tinted prints depicting her in theatrical character were to be found in private collections up and down the country.

By the time of her niece's début refinements in copper-plate printing made it possible for manufacturers to turn out quantities of cheap scarves bearing a celebrated face within days. Transfer printing and hardier, more malleable mixes of clay meant that potters could produce a hundred decorated plates in the time it would have taken to produce half a dozen a generation before. Improvements in the transport system had matched the progress of mechanization. By 1829 goods could be distributed in days through the 4000 miles of navigable canals and rivers or over the newly macadamized highways.

Within weeks of Fanny's début plates bearing dramatic scenes from her Juliet were leaving the potteries of Staffordshire by canal barge, hardly days behind the tinsel pictures* and copies of the Lawrence print carried to booksellers in places as far apart as Dublin and Edinburgh.

> When I saw the shop-windows full of Lawrence's sketch of me, and knew myself the subject of almost daily newspaper notices; when plates and saucers were brought to me with small figures of me as Juliet and Belvidera on them; and finally, when gentlemen showed me lovely buff-coloured neck-handkerchiefs which they had bought, and which had, as I thought, pretty lilac-coloured flowers all over them, which proved on nearer inspection to be minute copies of Lawrence's head of me, I not unnaturally, in the fullness of my inexperience, believed in my own success.[19]

*'Tinsel pictures' were popular in the 1820s and 30s. A tinsel picture, in this context, was a regular monochrome print of an actor dressed in one of his or her famous roles, hand tinted with the armour, crown, jewels and the like picked out with pieces of metal foil or enamel paint to represent the paste and French coloured glass of stage finery.

PART III

A QUEST FOR SUBSTANCE –

The Making of Mrs Frances Anne Kemble

16

Artists and Lay-Figures

'I have become convinced that fame and gratified ambition are not the worthiest aims for one's exertions,' Fanny Kemble wrote to Harriet St Leger in December 1829. She intended to dedicate herself to the role of Miranda, the fond and dutiful daughter. Fame pursued for itself was a corrupting ambition. 'I have not embraced this course without due dread of its dangers,'[1] the twenty-year-old solemnly assured her Irish friend. But so long as her public exposure was out of duty to her family, that duty would be her *raison d'être* and her salvation.

Fanny relished her transformation from 'useless encumbrance' into her beloved father's professional partner. The Saturday following her début she took great delight in presenting herself at the Covent Garden treasury to collect thirty guineas for her week's work – the first money she had ever earned. She carried the heavy coins home in triumph to pour them into her mother's lap.

Her enormous energy at last had a focus and occupation. Her life was no longer solitary. In her first season Fanny appeared as Juliet on thirty-one occasions, performing three times a week. It became her aunt's role to accompany her to the theatre. Dall would supervise the dressers and walk her niece into the wings, carrying her train to keep it from the dirt. The instant Fanny stepped out of the limelight

Dall would be there ready to wrap her in a shawl and escort her back to her dressing-room; her comforting presence ever in the background as Fanny occupied herself sewing tapestry between scenes.

Marie-Thérèse had found her own brief reappearance on the boards reinvigorating. She shed her hauntings and bouts of hysterical illness to emerge as her daughter's acting coach. Fanny, who had a constitutional distrust of fair words and flattery, depended heavily on her mother's habit of brutal directness. During Fanny's first season her mother's sharp eyes followed every move and gesture. Fanny's elation or despair depended less on her audience's applause than on the pithy critique from her mother's lips.

'Beautiful, my dear,' sent her happy to bed. But quite as often she would reel under her mother's disdain:

> 'My dear, your performance was not fit to be seen! I don't know how you ever contrived to do the part decently; it must have been by some knack or trick which you appear to have entirely lost the secret of; you had better give the whole thing up at once than go on doing it so disgracefully ill.'[2]

Fanny became increasingly conscious of how ill-prepared she was to sustain the burden thrust upon her. She found it difficult to sleep and regularly suffered from sharp pains in her side. London's newest star would sit up into the early hours of the morning confiding her fears to Hal. 'I am totally inexperienced in all the minor technical processes most necessary for the due execution of any dramatic conception,' she fretted.[3]

Fanny was proving so valuable to Covent Garden treasury that it was inevitable that the management would expand her repertoire. From December 1829 to the end of her first season in May 1830 she was brought out in a new role every month. In November she followed up her Juliet with Belvidera, the heroine on whom Otway hung his lurid tragedy of *Venice Preserved*. The role played on the popular father/daughter theme (Belvidera is torn between duty to her father and love of her husband, the two men being enemies), but it was also one of Mrs Siddons's parts. Mrs Siddons had never been known for her Juliet* but her Belvidera was renowned.

Belvidera struck Fanny as 'a sort of lay figure in a tragic attitude, a mere "female in general"'. The inevitable comparisons with her celebrated aunt appalled short, sturdy, pock-marked Fanny. 'Look at her, Harriet,' she wrote to her friend,

> look at her fine person, her beautiful face; listen to her magnificent voice; and supposing that I were as highly endowed with poetical dramatic imagination as she was (which I certainly am not), is it likely that there can ever be a shadow of comparison between her and myself, even when years may have corrected all that is at present crude and imperfect in my efforts?[4]

Her parents and even Aunt Dall had little time to spare for her self-doubts. The money was coming in at last and the Decamp sisters belonged to the 'just get on with it' school of life. As for her father – Fanny, acutely conscious of the brittle nature of Charles Kemble's desperate optimism, was determined not to express any doubts that might erode his confidence. As she struggled to master her new career in those first busy weeks, help came from an unexpected quarter – the one outsider whose eminence allowed him to breach the protective circle of her family: Sir Thomas Lawrence.

Lawrence was infatuated with her. 'That girl makes me ashamed of myself for having tolerated Miss O'Neill,'† the venerable artist declared to his friends. 'Indeed, with the single exception of Mrs Siddons, I look upon her as by far the greatest dramatic genius that our times have produced.'

Whenever he was in town the carefully groomed figure of Lawrence could be seen at Fanny's performances, sitting in the box at the side of the stage Charles Kemble had fitted up for Mrs Siddons.

---

*Sarah Siddons's first recorded appearance as Juliet was at the age of thirty-five, after she had been in the profession for over fifteen years.

†Miss O'Neill had been the reigning Juliet of the previous generation.

Invariably Lawrence would follow up his attendance by sending Fanny 'a letter full of the most detailed and delicate criticism'.

In his youth Lawrence had had ambitions to go on the stage. His father – his eyes firmly fixed on the money his son made with his pencil and chalks – ensured that he was discouraged, but Lawrence had always kept up his interest in the mechanics of dramatic performance.

> A little – a *wee* – bit too much of varied inflection in the following passage 'and therefore both the wind-swift Cupid wing' etc.

he writes in one of these notes.

> *Doves draw Love* for 'Doves draw Love'. All is but one stream of impetuous thought.

Fanny, in general so impatient of the unsolicited advice of strangers, lapped it up. She made a point of reading each letter through to prepare herself for her next performance. For years afterwards she would insist that Lawrence was the 'only unprofessional person I ever heard speak upon [acting] whose critical opinion and judgement seemed to me worth anything'.[5] With his own early experience as a childhood celebrity, she trusted Lawrence's comprehension of her situation.

> Sometimes when I have been thinking I was acting well and carefully, that severe judge, my mother, has destroyed all my flattering self-approbation with a word, and at others when I have been labouring under depression and want of animal spirits, rowing against wind and tide with the dreadful consciousness of heaviness and want of life in everything I did, I find that I have been distressing myself very unreasonably and have acted very fairly.
>
> So much of what is casual and often totally unconnected with what one is about, influence both the feeling and the execution of it, and this inequality of course is more glaring in so

> unartist-like a person as myself, who really and truly have as yet not one principle of my profession . . . when I am what I ought to be as a professional person, I shall be less at the mercy of circumstances, and shall have art to assist me when my own spirits and feelings are not up to the mark.[6]

Lawrence was a contrived man,* in many ways reminiscent of Charles Kemble's famous stage lovers, and as such was both charming and, one suspects, unthreatening, to immature Fanny. When Lawrence was young he had been considered one of the most handsome men in London. Now sixty and balding, he still retained the magnetism of an attractive man. Fanny was drawn to 'the elegant distinction of his person, and the exquisite refined gentleness of his voice and manner'. There was much of the actor about Lawrence; like Harriot Siddons's charming brother William Murray he had conspicuous 'powers of assumption'. Indeed he was proud of the empathy by which he tuned himself to his sitters, enabling him to fix their likenesses on canvas.

With head-turning flattery the eminent painter assured Fanny that he and she were fellow artists who could learn from one another:

> In every future work of mine that may at all address itself to the imagination – the heart – or the reasoning faculty, you shall be the monitor to whom I shall refer it, if you choose to bestow the time.

As autumn sank into winter he wove his 'dangerous fascination' about Fanny while she sat for him at his house in Russell Square. His studio bore more than a passing resemblance to an empty stage – its lofty ceiling and barrack-like space lit from tall window panes

---

*Charles Greville, that practised man about town, described Lawrence as 'remarkably gentleman-like, with very mild manners' but detecting a certain sterility in the painter's admiration for feminine beauty, Greville added that he found the artist 'rather too doucereux'. (Reeve, vol. I, p. 220).

running along one wall, the canvas portraits of all sizes stacked about like so many pieces of scenery. The experience of being sketched by him had an almost erotic intensity – the intimate attentiveness of his eyes, the deftness of his hands, the faint scratch of pencil on paper. Lawrence never talked much as he worked. The silence was only broken by the occasional personal comment – delivered as artistic observation rather than flattery – such as the fact that Fanny had a double row of eyelashes giving definition to her expressive eyes.

Marie-Thérèse was, of course, present throughout these sessions. Like her husband, Fanny's mother was perfectly conscious that the attentions of the President of the Royal Academy gave her daughter considerable cachet. Old hand that she was, Marie-Thérèse was also aware of Lawrence's penchant for mixing sentimental seduction into his sittings when working with attractive women.

Lawrence's art was an extension of himself – just as his portraits aimed to give every sitter (as Fanny put it) the 'best look they ever wore' so his sentiments were equally contrived. It is perhaps significant that he had such difficulty finishing so many of the portraits he started. Like many bachelors who cannot commit, he appears to have enjoyed the exquisite stimulation of being tangled up in impossible love.

Marie-Thérèse was a careful chaperone but it is likely she judged Lawrence no physical threat to her daughter's virtue. Fanny found herself drawn into a bewildering, hot-house relationship with this sixty-something man of genius. Her scenes with Lawrence began to be almost as theatrical as those she performed in costume on stage.

When a sitting was finished, Lawrence would encourage Marie-Thérèse and Fanny to linger while he opened the long drawers of the cabinets running under the studio windows to show them rare prints, or took them into his drawing room to admire his collection of original Old Master drawings.* In return, Sir Thomas would spend cosy evenings with the family at Buckingham Gate.

---

*According to Charles Greville, Lawrence owned the most magnificent collection of original Old Master drawings in the world.

One day, after a sitting had ended, Lawrence, 'in a strange, hesitating, broken manner', said to Fanny: 'I have a great favour to beg of you; the next time I have the honour and pleasure of spending an evening with you, will you, if Mrs Kemble does not disapprove of it, sing this song for me?'[7] With that he thrust a furled songsheet into Fanny's hand, turned on his heel and left the room without a word.

On the way home Fanny unrolled the sheet. Against the creak and jolt of the carriage she read out loud: 'These few pale Autumn Flowers.' Her mother greeted the recitation of the plaintive words with a knowing snort but did not offer to elaborate.

The next time Lawrence turned up at Buckingham Gate Fanny fulfilled his request. While she sang the artist stood by the piano in a thoughtful pose, the dome of his handsome skull focusing attention on his melancholy eyes, the line of his straight nose, his sensitive mouth. As the last chord lingered he recovered himself, 'as if coming back from very far away . . . with an expression of acute pain on his countenance', to thank her profusely for the great favour she had done him. Being, as she later described herself, 'a very romantic girl, with a most excitable imagination' Fanny was suitably intrigued.

At her next sitting, when she and her mother had risen to leave, Lawrence detained them: 'No, don't go yet. Stay a moment – I want to show you something – if I can.' He fussed about, opening drawers, moving pencils and chalks, 'standing, and sitting down again, as if unable to make up his mind to do what he wished'. Finally he removed some sketches from an easel to reveal the portrait of a silvery lady in a turban who leaned her elegant head in profile on her hand over a huge book.

'Oh, how beautiful!' exclaimed Fanny, just as she should. 'Who is she?'

'A – a lady,' stammered Lawrence, blushing furiously, 'toward whom – for whom – I entertained the profoundest regard.' At which pronouncement he fled the room, leaving Fanny amazed.

It was a portrait of Mrs Wolff who had died earlier that year, explained her mother. 'She was an exceedingly beautiful and accomplished woman, the authoress of the words and music of the song Sir Thomas asked you to learn for him.'

The English wife of a Danish consul in London, Mrs Wolff and her husband had been friends of the artist before the couple separated in 1810. Through the next twenty years Lawrence convinced himself that his feelings for Mrs Wolff were something more. Typically he flooded his sentiment on to his canvas. When his portrait of Mrs Wolff was exhibited at the Royal Academy summer exhibition in 1815 reviewers saluted its 'delicacy and feeling'.*

Early in November 1829 Lawrence finished his sketch of Fanny. Her mother was the first to be shown the drawing. (Showman that he was, the artist did not allow glimpses of work in progress.) As she stood in silence contemplating it Lawrence prompted her:

'What strikes you?'

'It is very like Maria,' commented Marie-Thérèse matter-of-factly. The mention of Mrs Siddons's dead daughter, his one-time fiancée, brought on one of Lawrence's surges of emotion. 'Oh, she is very like her; she is very like them all!' he forced out at last. After thirty years of separation he was bringing the central relationship of his life full circle.

As it happened, a few days before, Mrs Siddons had dined with the Kembles. The great actress had enquired after the progress of her niece's portrait. The conversation stalled. Then Mrs Siddons – reaching across to lay her hand on her brother's arm to emphasize her point – pronounced: 'Charles, when I die, I wish to be carried to my grave by you and Lawrence.'

Marie-Thérèse dropped her sister-in-law's visit into the conversation. Lawrence asked eagerly after Mrs Siddons's health, her looks, what she had said. When Marie-Thérèse repeated the aging legend's wish, Lawrence 'threw down his pencil, clasped his hands, and, with

---

*Knowing both subject and painter, William Hazlitt remarked slyly that Lawrence's style was 'enough to make the ladies vow that they will never again look at themselves in their glasses, but only in his canvases'. Hazlitt, review in the *Champion*, 7 May 1815.

his eyes full of tears and his face convulsed, exclaimed: 'Good God! Did she say that?'

A few days later, on 27 November – Fanny's twentieth birthday – a beautifully framed proof-plate of Reynolds's portrait of Sarah Siddons as the *Tragic Muse* arrived at Buckingham Gate with Lawrence's compliments. It was inscribed: 'This portrait, by England's greatest painter, of the noblest subject of his pencil, is presented to her niece and worthy successor by her most faithful and humble friend and servant, Lawrence.'

'I am surprised he ever brought himself to write those words – her worthy successor,' remarked Fanny's mother tartly as she examined it. She was quite right. Within days Lawrence had made an excuse to reclaim the gift for a minor alteration and when it was returned the inscription no longer made any reference to Mrs Siddons's worthy successor.

Fanny did not miss the significance of Lawrence's withdrawal of his inscription. For all his sentimental effusions Sir Thomas was using her as a coda to the chivalric romance he had constructed throughout his life around his adored lady-love Mrs Siddons – and Fanny did not like it. Her own identity was being suffocated in a web of nostalgia. It seemed as if – off stage as well as on it – she could not escape being used as a lay-figure on which others felt free to project their fantasies.

As the year turned, Lawrence – the dissembler who liked to be thought in love – was writing unctuously of Fanny to his old friend, Mrs Hayman, the widow of another artist –

> Let me give you Washington Irving's opinion of her to me the other night at Mr Peel's. 'She is much more beautiful in private than she is on the stage, and the nearer one gets to her face and to her mind, the more beautiful they both are.' Now *I* have never ventured to say half as much, for why, my Dear Friend? Why, because be it known to you, I have the shackles of 'sixty' upon me, and therefore these Love-chains would turn into skeletons of Roses, did any one attempt to throw them around

me. But tho' I seldom see her, I have almost a Father's interest for her, and a Father's resentment towards those who will not see the promise of almost all that Genius can do.[8]

Three days after his pen scratched these words, Fanny was sitting at home reading through the artist's latest letter of advice about her performance as Belvidera, when her father entered the room and announced: 'Lawrence is dead.' The artist had not lived to be a pall-bearer for his Muse.

Naturally, Fanny was shocked. Only days before, she and her mother had been discussing with the artist the date for Fanny's first sitting for a life-sized portrait of her as Juliet. No one had realized that he was ill (indeed a rumour circulated that he might have committed suicide). As she performed Belvidera that night and spoke the lines Lawrence had discussed in his last letter, the poignancy of the moment caused her some distress. She cried when she sat down to write to her Cousin Cecilia to warn her that her mother, Mrs Siddons, would need to be prepared for the news of the artist's death. But the truth was that she had been ready to break free of the relationship.

As with William Murray's disorientating charm, Lawrence's diamonds had proved to be paste. Some ten days after the artist's death, Fanny admitted to Hal that she had thrown away many of Lawrence's letters of criticism because – apart from those technical details that helped her to improve her performance – they seemed 'such mere specimens of refined flattery'.

As Fanny once declared with such force, she had never liked dolls: 'they always affected me with a grim sense of being a mockery of the humanity they were supposed to represent'.[9] She was quite prepared to dedicate her life to duty and her family but she was constitutionally unable to efface herself beneath a compliant mask. As a new year dawned, her determination to take control of her own destiny was reviving. In her own mind the only way for a woman to keep her dignity and self-respect in a business that made her a 'public woman' (with its taint of prostitution) was to become a professional whose public exposure was justified by her Art.

Unfortunately, Fanny's scope for self-determination was limited. Her career was in the hands of the Covent Garden management. They thrust her into what appeared to her to be a sequence of roles of declining quality. Belvidera, whose 'coarsely agonizing' situations she judged inferior to the poetic passions of Juliet, was followed by Euphrasia, the pious heroine of *The Grecian Daughter* by Arthur Murphy, who takes filial duty to the unsettling extreme of suckling her starving father (mercifully off stage). After Euphrasia came Mrs Beverley, the tiresomely admirable heroine of that long-established favourite *The Gamester*. These were all her aunt's roles. Despite Fanny's protestations that 'to be compared with . . . Mrs Siddons . . . is above my expectation', her stage career unfolded in the shadow of her aunt's awesome reputation.

Fanny found this both frustrating and unfair. Sarah Siddons's triumphant success at Drury Lane in 1782 had come on the back of long years served in provincial companies. (Indeed, Mrs Siddons's first attempt to conquer the West End sent her back to Bath for a full five seasons to improve her technique.) Fanny was too young and too inexperienced to impose her will against the pressures ranked against her. However conscious she might be of her need to cultivate her 'art', her early roles were not selected with her particular talents in mind and the management allowed her no time to polish her technique. Covent Garden needed cash and Mrs Siddons's niece was a means of milking the legendary Sarah's past glory. So Fanny Kemble was tumbled into her aunt's mature roles and expected to make the best of it.

Fanny needed to learn her art for personal as well as professional reasons. Her lack of technique left her at the mercy of stormy emotions. The first night she played Belvidera, Fanny became so carried away by the last scene – where the heroine, mad with guilt at causing her husband's death, imagines herself scrabbling in the earth for his bloody corpse – that she worked herself into real hysterics.

The screams with which she made her final dramatic exit carried on as she ran about backstage pursued by Aunt Dall and various attendants. According to Fanny's own account, they chased her right into the street before they caught her and carried her back to her dressing-room to recover.

The Kemble creed was that the art of tragedy 'renders necessary a degree of . . . elevation in the mind of the spectator . . . at variance with the critical spirit of prosaic reality'.[10] From this classicist perspective tragedies were supposed to be 'comparatively unnatural' because they aimed to communicate grand, universal human truths. 'To represent . . . the dwellings of the kings of the earth,' as Fanny once put it, 'there must be a certain distance observed.' The measured delivery of John Philip Kemble served precisely to mark out this distance. According to the Kemble definition, Drama was a synthesis of reason, intellect and imagination; too much reality debased that art into vulgar exhibition. As Fanny commented on her role as Mrs Beverley* – that loving wife who suffers poverty and humiliation at the hands of her noble (if misled) gambler of a husband:

> It is a most touching story, and Mrs Beverley is a most admirable creature, but the story is such as might be read in a newspaper, and her character has its like in many an English home. I think the author should have idealized both his incidents and his heroine a little, to produce a really fine play.[11]

---

*A popular favourite from the late eighteenth century, *The Gamester* is a moralistic piece set around the destructive fashion for high stakes gambling. The foolish husband Beverley is drawn into a life of gambling by his pseudo-friend Stukely who is systematically plotting his ruin because he, Stukely, had wished to marry Mrs Beverley. Both husband and wife persist in believing in Stukely's good intentions, despite mounting evidence to the contrary, until Beverley ends up in prison for debt and under accusation of attempted murder, having ruined his family. In despair, Beverley takes poison – a sufficiently slow-acting one to enable him to take part in the discovery scene where his true friend, Lewson, arrives with Mrs Beverley to reveal Stukely the villain and tell him the good news that his uncle has died leaving him rich. Stukely gets his come-uppance, at which Beverley dies in an affecting manner.

The king and queen of tragedy: Fanny's uncle, John Philip Kemble, and her celebrated aunt, Sarah Siddons, as Macbeth and Lady Macbeth, painted by Sir Thomas Beech in 1786.

The Kemble house: Covent Garden Theatre as rebuilt after the devastating fire of 1808.

Fanny's mother, Marie Thérèse Decamp, at the height of her career as Patie in *The Gentle Shepherd* – one of her famous 'breeches parts'. One of her sons' friends remarked, 'Mrs C. Kemble [performs] in *very tight men's clothes* . . . don't suppose it's absolutely indecent: but only so as one certainly would not wish one's Mother to be represented.'

Charles Kemble, Fanny's father – 'the best Romeo in the business'.

Fanny's parents on stage at the time of their engagement. Charles Kemble as the rebel West Indian slave, Three-Fingered Jack, and Marie Thérèse as Rosa, in the hit pantomime of 1800 – *Obi*.

Fanny Kemble sketched backstage at Covent Garden by a friend, waiting to go on as Juliet in autumn 1829.

Fanny Kemble's brothers sketched by Richard Lane. John Mitchell, the adored elder brother of Fanny's girlhood: 'He is certainly a very uncommon person, and I admire, perhaps too enthusiastically, his great abilities.' And Henry, three years her junior: 'the beauty of my youngest brother . . . [was] for several years . . . very remarkable.'

Fanny Kemble in her dressing room at Covent Garden watched by (from left to right) Charles Kemble, in costume as Mercutio, her mother, with Aunt Dall just visible behind her, and Mrs Davenport, dressed as Juliet's nurse and standing by the window.

The attitudes of a tragedy queen: prints of Fanny in three of her most popular tragic roles – Belvidera in *Venice Preserved*, Euphrasia in *The Grecian Daughter* and Mrs Beverly in *The Gamester.*

Fanny's favourite cousin and mentor, Mrs Harriot Siddons, the leading lady of the Edinburgh Theatre Royal: 'men, women and children not only loved her, but inevitably fell *in* love with [her]'.

The new and the old: Fanny as a young girl painted with her famous aunt, Sarah Siddons.

Fanny depicted with her major rival in the West End during her first season: Mademoiselle D'Gelk, the celebrated acting elephant.

Pierce Butler, 'pretty-spoken' and 'genteel' – Fanny's husband for seventeen dramatic years: 'Myself and my husband act as mental moderators to each other. He is nothing if not mathematical, and in every subject whatsoever that comes under his contemplation . . . truth, reality, *fact* is the end upon which he fastens.'

The overseer's house on Butler Plantation in Georgia where Fanny, her husband and her two small daughters spent the winter of 1838–9. 'Society, or the shadow of it, is not to be dreamed of . . . our residence [is] a half-furnished house in the midst of rice-swamps.'

Divorced and magnificent, the substantial figure of Mrs Fanny Kemble,
the renowned reader of Shakespeare.

Fanny's dislike of the 'realism' gaining ground in the theatre was not merely an artistic judgement. On top of wrestling with a demanding new career, she struggled with a professional relationship with her father that paralleled and confused their private one.

'My father not acting Romeo with me deprived me of the most poetical and graceful stage lover of his day,' she once wrote of her début.[12] The classicist view that permitted father and daughter to play lovers on stage was premised on the idea that acting was artificial and intellectual. No cultured person would make the vulgar mistake of drawing parallels between roles and the real-life relationships of the actors. Fanny was proud to perform as daughter, lover, wife (and even later an older woman when she played Queen Constance to his Falconbridge) opposite her father. Intellectually she considered their private relationship immaterial – just as she would not expect an educated playgoer to snigger at the contrast in their heights (at six foot Charles Kemble must have loomed over Fanny who was well under five foot) or their ages (a Romeo of fifty-four playing to a Juliet of twenty). It was precisely the distance that some critics complained of in Charles Kemble's stage lovers that made his performances 'poetic' to his daughter. His 'gentlemanly' portrayals, perfumed with art and ideality, had no flesh or sex about them.

That was the theory. But when theory gave way to performance, Fanny found her emotions muddled and bruised by the blurring of her private and professional personas. The family relationship 'added infinitely to my distress in all tragedies in which we acted together; the sense of his displeasure or the sight of his anguish invariably bringing him, my father, and not the part he was acting, before me'.[13]

If a woman was to be exhibited on the stage, then to perform with family members offered some mitigation with respect to her reputation. But the theatre management wanted to engage the increasingly voyeuristic appetites of the new consumers of celebrity. The management's choices pandered to a popularization of Charles and Fanny Kemble as a contemporary Virginius and his daughter – caricatures of domestic feeling with a modern English heart. To her broader audience the raw, unpolished quality of her performances was a principal feature of her drawing power. The galleries relished those moments when real emotion or confusion broke through the protective mask of make-up and fiction; they were part of the alchemy that lifted her performance to the extraordinary. And yet for Fanny, personally, to break down in real sobs over the fictional corpse of her husband/father was genuinely traumatic – and for a mass of strangers to witness that experience carried an additional element of humiliation. Despite all her family's professionalism and experience, to her dying day Fanny was adamant that she had never presented herself 'before an audience without a shrinking feeling of reluctance, or withdrawn from their presence without thinking the excitement I had undergone unhealthy, and the personal exhibition odious'.[14]

Fanny's feelings of discomfort coalesced around the third part assigned to her – that of Euphrasia in *The Grecian Daughter*. Euphrasia saves her dethroned, ageing father Evander from Dionysius (the son of the Tyrant he, Evander, had once deposed) by stabbing that tyrant to death. The play held mixed associations for the Kembles. Charles Kemble had the memory of the Old Price rioters cheering as he died on stage as Dionysius in the year Fanny was born. (Now he took the role of Evander.) On the other hand, the play owed its place in the repertoire largely due to Mrs Siddons whose Euphrasia had been one of her classical creations – an embodiment of heroic grandeur and grace. A new generation, however, was beginning to find the play's language stilted and some of its heroine's most 'heroic' gestures offensive.

The Grecian Daughter, Fanny wrote, with thinly veiled disgust:

> has . . . the sort of parental and conjugal interest that infallibly strikes sympathetic chords in the *pater familias* bosom of an English audience . . . I mean the constant reference to Euphrasia's filial devotion, and her heroic and pious efforts on behalf of her old father – incidents in the piece which were seized upon and applied to my father and myself by the public,

> and which may have perhaps added to the feeling of the audience, as they certainly increased my dislike for the play.[15]

She tried to do her best with the part.* She designed a new attitude for Euphrasia at the climax of the play when she has stabbed Dionysius. Mrs Siddons used to fall to her knees as if imploring heaven's mercy, struck down by the awful realization of having committed the mortal sin of murder. Her niece's reassessment of Euphrasia's emotions was typical of her (and, her contemporaries might have argued, of her 'masculine mind'):

> Euphrasia had just preserved her father's life by a deed which, in her own estimation and that of her whole nation, entitled her to an immortal dwelling in the Elysian Fields. The only feeling, therefore, that I can conceive as checking for a moment her exultation would be the natural womanly horror at the sight of blood and physical suffering, the expression of which seems to me . . . to reconcile an English audience to so *unfeminine* a proceeding as stabbing a man.[16]

Fanny's attitude had Euphrasia stand over the body with her face turned away, one arm veiling her eyes with her drapery, the other hand brandishing the knife heavenwards in triumph. The sculptor Lawrence Macdonald found this 'picture' so striking that he talked of making a statue of it. Fanny regarded her costume as her one consolation in having to play such a 'flat, poor and trashy' role.† To her mind, the management's choice of her starring vehicles was not only frustrating her efforts to develop her art, but revealed a vulgar tendency to appropriate her private relationship with her father as a commercial device.

---

*'Nothing better proves her great dramatic genius,' she commented sourly of the role, than Mrs Siddons's ability to clothe 'so meagre a part in such magnificent proportions as she gave to it.'

†She was dressed in merino wool draped in Grecian fashion, cinched by a bright scarlet sash embroidered with gilt acorns – an outfit that she thought made her look taller.

In January 1830 – as Lawrence, the creator of Fanny's most ladylike image died – a new caricature appeared in the print-shop windows. After suffering depressed receipts over Christmas, the management of the Adelphi, one of the leading minor theatres, came to the conclusion that the draw of Miss Kemble at Covent Garden was sufficiently threatening to warrant the engagement of a rival novelty. That novelty, depicted in her full magnificence in the print of *The Rival Actresses* beside Fanny (dressed in her costume as Belvidera complete with a large picture hat) was Mlle d'Gelk, the celebrated acting elephant.*

The Kemble princess had grabbed her share of the limelight, but she divided the talk of the town with a circus attraction. It was hardly an image appropriate to an Aristocracy of the Word.

*It was reported that this elephant was 'so far instructed . . . that she was nearly able to perform the parts of all the comic actors of the Adelphi Theatre', Matthews, vol. IV, pp. 35–7. The comedian Mathews was managing the Adelphi at this time with a partner.

17

'One of Shakespeare's Women'

While passers-by were smirking at the picture of the Actress and the Elephant in print-shop windows that January, John Blakesley, a Cambridge student, sat trying to convey his impression of Fanny Kemble's performance as Belvidera to his friend Richard Trench. Her acting, he said, differed 'not in degree but in *kind*, from . . . every actress I have seen. She seems like one of Shakespeare's women rather than anything else'.[1]

As her first season slipped by, Fanny could no longer pass for a sweet young *ingénue*. Whatever reasons had brought her to the stage, repetition and practice – even her very success – reduced her to an actress plain and simple. It was becoming clear that, in real life, Miranda could not remain on her father's island. Duty might be sufficient for a dramatic heroine but Fanny needed something more to sustain her self-esteem.

Although she remained stoutly loyal to him, Fanny was aware that her father's obsession with the receding mirage of the 'Kemble Era' was doomed to failure. For while on the boards she was pressed into her magnificent aunt's stage shoes in plays that had once entertained the grandparents of her peers, Buckingham Gate was filling with the aspirations of a new generation.

During the winter of her first season John Mitchell was away in

Germany, but Fanny's début had drawn several of his friends to London. William Bodham Donne,* a gentle, decent twenty-two-year-old from Norfolk with an interest in the theatre, who had been Jackie's boyhood friend, attended her opening night. He was soon joined by another Cambridge student, the cosmopolitan Richard Monckton Milnes (he who had been so impressed by Fanny's death scene as Juliet†). The Cambridge connection also introduced William Makepeace Thackeray to the Kemble circle. This tall, sardonic nineteen-year-old who, at the time, displayed more interest in sketching satirical cartoons than literature, attended a couple of Fanny's performances. He discussed the benefits of potatoes to the human race with her and put up her picture in his rooms, but on the whole the future author of *Pendennis* and *Vanity Fair* preferred attending Covent Garden rehearsals with her younger brother Henry with whom he shared a mutual enthusiasm for pantomimes.

As the winter wore on, growing numbers of college men competed for invitations to the manager's Sunday suppers at Buckingham Gate. Bumptious and witty Monckton Milnes, the offspring of a minor diplomat, could be observed swapping literary allusions with James Spedding, the scholarly gentleman's son from Cumbria who claimed acquaintance with various Lakeland poets, and at twenty-three was already distinguished by his mature manner and fast receding hairline. Then there was the brilliant John Sterling with his quick eyes and vigorous views, whose determination to right the wrongs of the world convinced all his friends – and Fanny too – that he was destined to do something great.

Word spread and other interesting young men followed. Two poets from Trinity College, Arthur Hallam and his good friend Alfred Tennyson, first saw Fanny as Belvidera in December, at

---

*W. B. Donne had poetic connections – his mother being a cousin of the poet Cowper.

†'The thing I was intended for by nature is a German woman,' Milnes once declared whimsically. 'I have just that mixture of häusliche Thätigkeit [domesticity] and Sentimentalität [sentimentality] that categorizes that category of Nature. I think Goethe would have fallen in love with me; and I am not sure that Platen didn't.' – quoted Brookfield, p. 234.

which Arthur claimed to fall in love. 'Hallam had an opera glass,' recorded Doyle, a friend, 'which whenever I asked for it he presented to me with a damn . . . and went raving home to write two sonnets about her. When I go back to town I expect to see about a dozen more. As for me I was exceedingly moderate and tranquil as I merely wished to shoot Mr Ward, who was acting Jaffier, upon the spot.'*

John Mitchell had bonded with a particularly fascinating crowd at Cambridge. It was John Sterling, a leading figure of the year above him, who introduced him into the student society that changed his life.

'To my *education* given in that society,' Jackie Kemble wrote years later, 'I feel that I owe every power I possess, and the rescuing of myself from a ridiculous state of prejudice . . . From [them] I, at least, learned to think as a *free man*.' That 'society' was the Cambridge Conversazione Society. It was founded in St John's College in 1820 by a group who felt that the post-war times called for more intellectual exploration and debate than the narrow university curriculum then afforded. They would meet every Saturday night after hall in the rooms of each member in turn. There the host of the meeting would present an essay on a topic of his choice for general debate. The great principle of the society was absolute freedom of thought, in defence of which it was agreed that meetings would be held in secret. At a time when an accusation of atheism could blight a man's career for life, the society's members were determined that every man should be free to speculate as widely as he wished without fear of condemnation.

It soon became apparent to others that a new clique had formed. Every Saturday night the same students could be spotted filing into a set of rooms. (It was even reported that they locked the inner door to be perfectly sure of privacy.) Other students, resenting such elitism, nicknamed the band the 'Apostles' – a teasing play on both their official number (twelve) and contemporary slang for the dozen

*Jaffier is Belvidera's husband in *Venice Preserved*. Kolb, p. 350 n5.

students who received the lowest marks in the examination for Bachelor of Arts. Being supremely self-confident, the members of the society embraced the name and the Apostles they became.*

At Buckingham Gate, Marie-Thérèse – delighting in a house filled with youth – was at her most charming, providing delicious suppers and enjoying motherly tête à têtes with adoring young men. 'What an enchanting family is Kemble's!' enthused William Donne.

> I left Mrs Kemble with no common feelings of regret. I never met with any one whose education and circumstances have been necessarily artificial with so young a heart, and such birth-freshness of feeling and thought.[2]

For Fanny, to be drawn into such company was to glimpse an intellectual home, a society in which she was stimulated and sheltered. 'My own home spoils me for society,' she wrote to Hal; 'perhaps I ought not to say it, but after the sort of conversation I am used to, the usual jargon of society seems poor stuff.'[3] Fanny was so happy that she even began to be more vocal in her appreciation of her younger sister. Adelaide, soon to turn fifteen, was still coltish and gawky, but she was emerging from her shell. Her voice and musicianship had by now developed to the point where her family began to recognize that they had another budding artist in their midst. Fanny, at first, was somewhat taken aback as her little sister demonstrated a surprising inclination for radical views and a quick wit; but with Totty's unshakeable loyalty to her celebrated sibling the two sisters were closer than they had ever been. Adelaide 'is almost more of a woman than I am' Fanny declared with proprietary pride to Hal.

Meanwhile, aloof from the stream of youthful consciousness

---

*The Apostles had gained such a reputation as 'leading men' in the university that Thackeray said that it was supposed to confirm status on a man simply to be seen in the company of Brookfield who was not even an Apostle himself, but merely friends with several of them. Among Jack Kemble's circle, Sterling, Maurice, Donne, Spedding, Trench, Hallam, Tennyson, Blakesley and Milnes were Apostles, but William Thackeray and Edward Fitzgerald were not.

bubbling around him, Charles Kemble pursued the habits of the old world. After considerable lobbying, he extracted the half-promise of a curacy for his eldest son from some noble patron, and in February he summoned John Mitchell home from Germany.* The father hoped to see his son return a well-rounded gentleman. He overlooked the fact that the German universities, home of continental Romanticism, were then among the most exciting places to be for a young idealist. Jackie returned from Heidelberg having acquired some unsettling new enthusiasms along with his continental polish.

The results of this infection were not immediately apparent to his family. The pride of the Kemble household returned claiming that he had resolved his doubts and was committed to ordination in the Church. Fanny's initial response reflected her allegiance to her father's world. She was thankful for the influence of John Mitchell's friends in leading him to his decision. The Apostles, like Charles Kemble, expected great things of Jack, but unlike his father (who saw the Church as a safe route to gentrification) they saw him as a radical reformer destined to shake the Church of England out of its complacency. 'He will be a bright and burning light in God's church,' declared William Donne; 'a resting place and beacon for the many, who, [have] no delight in the slumber of orthodoxy.'[4] Tennyson was more lyrical, addressing his friend in a sonnet:

> *My hope and heart is with thee . . . thou wilt be*
> *A latter Luther, and a soldier-priest*

Jackie returned to the convivial atmosphere of Cambridge to take his degree but between divinity lectures he entertained his friends singing rousing German songs of liberty† (inspiring Arthur Hallam with a fierce desire to visit 'Bonn, Heidelberg, or such-like fine place', where his friend assured him he could provide introductions

*In those days, young men without private means looking to the Church for a career did not embark upon the process of ordination without the promise of a place from some patron.
†Although Jackie was dismissive of the Germans themselves who, he claimed, 'while singing the Glory of freedom are content to know themselves slaves'.

to 'the principal Burschen Clubs, in which I will drink beer and clash swords for the fatherland').[5]

That year of 1830 the Apostles were fired by the notion of becoming agents of change. John Sterling declared that they were the salt of the earth and that their purpose – through poetry, intellect and questioning – was to add savour to the bulk of their fellow men. Inspired by the poetry of Wordsworth and Shelley, and with 'the vague idea that it should be our function to interpret the oracles of transcendental wisdom to the world of Philistines or Stumpfs, as we designated them'[6] they set out to be intellectual missionaries and literary reformers.

Of all her brother's friends, Fanny was most taken with John Sterling, at twenty-four the oldest of the bunch. In many ways the most like her elder brother, his was a charismatic personality – 'the extreme vividness of his look, manner and speech, gave a wonderful impression of latent vitality and power'.* After graduating from Cambridge in 1828, Sterling moved to London where his father's wealth enabled him to take on the publication of the *Athenaeum* with another Apostle, his friend Frederick Maurice. Sterling threw himself into the role of the 'one-voiced Reviewer', whose championing of sincerity and right thinking would mend the wrongs of the world. The *Athenaeum* promoted the modern poets – Keats and Shelley – and Sterling took up with fellow Scotsman Thomas Carlyle, a determined popularizer of the ideas of the German Romantics.

At that time Carlyle was a not particularly successful essayist for the *Edinburgh Review*, but he was engaged on the work that would make his name. *Sartor Resartus*†, a spiritual autobiography presented in the form of a philosophical novel, charted Carlyle's struggles with the intellectual scepticism spawned by the Enlightenment. Working through 'the Everlasting No' and the 'Centre of Indifference' Carlyle emerged with his memorable cry to arms

---

*Fanny Kemble as an old woman recalling her youthful impressions of John Sterling, *Records of a Girlhood*, vol. II, p. 3.

†First serialized in *Fraser's Magazine* in 1833.

addressed to the new generation: 'Close thy Byron, open thy Goethe! Love not Pleasure; Love God. This is the Everlasting Yea, wherein all contradiction is solved.'

John Sterling was no mere theorist. He was determined to put his fine ideas to practical use. That winter of 1829–30 he was much preoccupied with the cause of the Spanish constitutionalists driven out by the French in league with Ferdinand VII in 1823. These exiles, with their long Spanish cloaks, had become a feature of the area around Euston Square and the new church of St Pancras, where they used to congregate, sometimes as many as a hundred at a time, to walk up and down the broad pavements meditating their sad fate. Sterling had met their leader, General Torrijos, while he was still a student. Not content with publishing rousing articles arguing their cause, he organized fund-raising events for their support and enlisted his friends to contribute by taking Spanish lessons. Jack Kemble, Richard Trench, Arthur Hallam and Alfred Tennyson would gather in Sterling's rooms to sing Spanish songs with the exiled 'patriots', talking late into the night, weaving fantastic plans for the restoration of liberty to a Spain in the grip of the tyrant Ferdinand VII. There was a comic opera aspect to the whole affair, and Fanny, for one, did not take it very seriously. She was inclined to leave politics to the men. She was more interested in the Apostles' poetic mission.

While several of Sterling's friends were dubious about his political radicalism, they all agreed on the importance of poetry. Poetry, with its blend of the particular and philosophy, art and the imagination, was the transcendent medium through which to engage the great questions of human existence and 'speak unto the general mind'.[7] The Apostles – like Fanny – were all amateur poets to one degree or another*, but among them the two figures around whom this intellectual mission coalesced were Arthur Hallam and Alfred Tennyson.

Fanny was fond of Arthur Hallam, a bright, intense young man

*Five members of the society in that generation were to win the Chancellor's Medal for English Verse at Cambridge.

with grey eyes 'lit up with summer lightnings of a soul/so full of summer warmth'[8]. The son of a respected historian, Arthur had demonstrated a precocious intellect from childhood. At nineteen he had the charming tact to speak to everyone as if he thought them as intelligent as himself. He knew most of Shakespeare by heart; he was passionate about Wordsworth and Shelley and shared Fanny's love of Dante (he composed elegant sonnets in Italian). Fanny enjoyed their literary discussions and Arthur fancied himself in love – after a suitably poetic fashion. 'I mean to live in her idea,' he announced to his friends. Fanny had the sense not to take his admiration as a fleshly one, commenting later that 'there was a gentleness and a purity almost virginal in his voice, manner and countenance'. Elected to the Apostles in May 1829, Hallam had the endearing quality of being ambitious for his friends rather than himself. It was as if, accustomed to mastering intellectual challenges so easily from childhood, he had no need to prove himself. Young Arthur disarmed his friends with his sincerity and affection, and they in turn cherished him as almost other-worldly – a grace-filled being in whom 'the God within him [lit] his face'*.

The year before he met Fanny, Arthur Hallam befriended the freshman with whom he formed the relationship that would dominate the rest of his short life. Thomas Carlyle once described Alfred Tennyson as a 'life-guardsman spoilt by making poetry'.[9] Having grown up in a secluded Lincolnshire vicarage among a large and eccentric family, Tennyson went to Cambridge as one of three handsome poetry-writing brothers. He was tall and strong with a leonine head, but despite his physical presence he was shy. Extremely short-sighted, he tended to hide behind a cloud of evil-smelling tobacco, a small, old, blackened pipe never far from his lips. In his first few months at Cambridge, Alfred Tennyson won the Chancellor's Medal

*Verse by Alfred Tennyson, quoted Brookfield, p. 131. Fanny herself wrote of Arthur: 'Some time or other, at some rare moments of the divine spirit's supremacy in our souls, we all put on the heavenly face that will be ours hereafter . . . On Arthur Hallam's brow and face this heavenly light, so fugitive in other human faces, rested habitually, as if he was thinking and seeing in heaven.'

for English Verse with his poem 'Timbuctoo'. Many tried to form an acquaintance with him but were repelled by his moods and tendency to wear the same shirt unwashed for a week. Arthur Hallam, however, discerned genius and a warm heart and Tennyson repaid him ten-fold in affection. Hallam became: 'My Arthur! . . . Dear as the Mother to the son,/More than my brothers are to me.'

All his friends worried about Arthur's poor health. He suffered from high blood pressure that made him prone to dizzy turns and he was often oppressed by an obscure sense of doom. He died suddenly of a stroke at the age of twenty-two on a visit to Vienna in 1833. The shattering loss of Arthur encapsulated a sense of the glory of youth that can never be recaptured and many of the circle never ceased looking back to the 'early perfection' of that Cambridge companionship they had lost*.

Out of the shock and grief he experienced at Arthur's death, Tennyson created his ground-breaking poem *In Memoriam*, the poetic monument he raised to 'his dear and cherished friend'. Tennyson's pilgrimage through the despair and doubts stemming from his loss became an exploration of where humanity stood in the middle of the nineteenth century. He created a new poetic form out of his pain. Abandoning the regular progression of traditional forms of narrative or elegy, because they failed to convey the rawness of his feelings, he charted the conflicting waves of emotion in a necklace of fragments, leading the reader alongside him through a poetic expression of the stages of his grief. (Thus advancing the 'modern' notion that a collection of fragments reflects human experiences of spiritual truth more faithfully than the coherence of narrative.) In the end Tennyson worked his way through his despair to embrace Carlyle's 'Everlasting Yea'. And when *In Memoriam* was published in 1850, the poem's ultimate optimism in the progress of mankind

*'One feeling that remains with me is a longing to preserve all those friends whom I know Hallam loved and whom I learnt to love through him. He was so much a centre round which we moved that . . . since Hallam's death I almost feel like an old man looking back on many friendships as something bygone.' Monteith to Tennyson, quoted Brookfield, p. 320.

and confidence in God's eternal plan came to epitomize the assurance of his generation, establishing Tennyson as *The* Victorian poet.

When Fanny was an old woman, Tennyson's widow responded to her son's news that he had met the extraordinary Mrs Kemble. Fanny Kemble and her brother, Lady Tennyson wrote, 'were the first to discover that Papa was one of the greatest English poets'.[10] Fanny Kemble came to know the Apostles just as the group adopted Tennyson as 'their' genius. He was elected around the time of Fanny's début, but resigned after five weeks, finding the stress of presenting a paper and hosting a meeting too much for him. Nonetheless, the friends set about incubating his poetic talents. Tennyson was to be the new Milton* – a poet to justify God's ways to man.

Tennyson was disinclined to the effort of committing his verse to paper. So when the young giant stood over the fire with one foot on the fender reciting his verses from memory, Hallam would slip round to a desk out of his eye-line to copy down the lines and preserve them for posterity. Listening to Alfred's verses became a regular Apostolic event. When his father's death forced Tennyson to leave Cambridge without a degree in summer 1830, he remained prominent in the minds of the group. They wrote to him constantly, toasted him at their dinners and continued to meet up to discuss the developing fragments of his work and sustain him in his task.

As Fanny was mastering her first roles, the Apostles were busy helping Tennyson prepare his first solo collection – *Poems, Chiefly Lyrical* – for publication. She was thus one of the first witnesses to the emergence of the artist of the future. And the young literary reformers had a grand vision of the role of the artist.

---

*Monckton Milnes was confident that *Timbuctoo* was 'certainly equal to most parts of Milton', and organized a debate at the Cambridge Union: 'Tennyson or Milton – which is the greater poet?' to promote that opinion.

Art had shifted from a reflection of man's civilization to a central expression of man's moral being. Hallam and his friends believed that the artist was called to aspire to heroic sincerity. The artist was a higher being who had the potential to serve as a prophet or everyman to his generation. For these Romantics intuition was the mysterious connection between man and the divine immanent in life and nature. The truer the artist was to his intuition, the deeper his sincerity; and the true artistic nature dedicated itself to holding to that sincerity, whatever the personal cost. The poet no longer merely contributed his skill and vision for the edification of his fellow man; his mission was to make his most intimate emotions, his vulnerability, his very humanity, materials of his art – what Keats called the 'egotistical sublime'. If the classical outlook of the end of the eighteenth century could be characterized as the grand, authoritative 'coup d'oeil', then Romantic theory brought in the intimacy of the close-up. The poet drew the reader in to share his insights with a new vividness of colour, sound and sensation (Arthur Hallam characterized Tennyson as a 'poet of sensation', while John Mitchell wrote to his sister, 'There is no man who has done so much as Tennyson to express poetical feeling by <u>sound</u>. Titian has done as much with colours.')

Fanny was caught up in the exhilaration of being in at the birth of a cultural revolution. For the rest of her life she would cherish the copy of *Poems, Chiefly Lyrical* that her brother gave her fresh from the press with 'a prophecy of [the poet's] future fame and excellence written on the fly-leaf'.

> 'those poems . . . became the songs of our every day and every hour, almost; we delighted in them and knew them by heart, and read and said them over and over again incessantly; they were our pictures, our music.'[11]

Like all revolutionaries, these enthusiastic young literary pioneers enjoyed the spice of being misunderstood, for naturally their elders did not appreciate their vision. The Kembles' adult social circle still revolved around the literary and musical set of the Montague-Proctor crowd. In that company of established authors, would-be playwrights, critics, musicians, newspaper editors and the occasional publisher, Tennyson was yet to be appreciated. Fanny was pugnacious in her favourite's defence. When Mrs Milman, a friend of her parents, teased her about a poor review of Tennyson's work in the influential *Quarterly Review* (known satirically as the 'hang, drawn and Quarterly' for its tendency to savage non-establishment writers) she was distinctly pert.

'It is so amusing! Shall I send it to you?' offered Mrs Milman.

'No, thank you,' riposted young Fanny, severely. 'Have you read the poems, may I ask?'

'I cannot say that I have,' admitted Mrs Milman, smiling.

'Oh then, perhaps it would be better that I should send *them* to *you*.'[12]

The reform of art and the future development of poetry was a serious business and not to be laughed at.

In the company of the Apostles Fanny developed a new sense of the calling of an artist. She discussed poetry as 'the natural and necessary language of general emotion' with Hallam and listened respectfully to Tennyson whenever he plucked up the courage to hold forth from behind his pipe smoke. With James Spedding she deplored the 'stage pageantry' that disfigured modern representations of Shakespeare, such as the 'dreadful' funeral procession with which managers liked to dress up the last act of *Romeo and Juliet*. John Sterling read her *Francis I* and proved a sympathetic critic. (Sterling adopted the Romantic theory of literary criticism, as established by the Schlegel brothers, holding that the first function of the critic was not to pass superior judgements – in the authoritative manner of Lord Jeffrey in the *Edinburgh Review* – but to 'characterize' a work; to seek to interpret it in light of a respect for the higher claims of creative genius.)

The fine-minded principles of her brother's friends heightened Fanny's distaste for her theatrical work. The Apostles admired the Kembles for their record as interpreters of Shakespeare, but they were forthright about the degradation of the dramatic stage. James Spedding declared that whenever he attended the theatre in London he invariably came away with a headache – 'an infallible sign of badness in a work of art'.* While poetry communicated directly, forging an intimate connection between reader and poet, the actor semaphored promiscuously to a vulgar mass of strangers; it was the difference between a whispered confidence and a billboard by the highway. Just as Charles Lamb had declared a generation before, the young literary reformers claimed that no theatrical performance could do justice to the intellectual pleasure of Shakespeare. While she held that the 'mere embodying of the exquisite ideals of poetry' gave her great enjoyment, Fanny was forced to deplore 'the immeasurable distance between a fine conception and the best execution of it'. Her new friends tried to reassure her that it was not her acting, but her *sincerity*, both off stage and on, that provided ample evidence of her artistic intuition. With time and practice, her native artistry would prevail over the smell of the thunderflashes and greasepaint. 'She was never taught to act at all,' reported John Sterling enthusiastically to his brother –

> . . . and although there are many faults in her performance of Juliet, there is more power than in any female playing I ever saw, except Pasta's *Medea* . . . She has far more ability than she ever can display on the stage; but I have no doubt that by practice and self-culture she will be a far finer actress at least than anyone since Mrs Siddons.[13]

Fanny could not avoid drawing comparisons between her young friends' fervour and her father's indifference. With the cultivated detachment of the classical era, Charles Kemble simply could not appreciate what all the fuss was about. 'How hard it is to do right and be good!' cried Fanny, in her private correspondence with Hal.

---

*The degradation of drama so offended him that he eventually published a substantial article on 'Romeo in Covent Garden *versus* Romeo in Shakespeare'.

Her generation valued women for their private virtues. Womanhood was enshrined in the figure of the wife and mother, the 'holy depository' of a man's higher affections. A true woman aspired to be a 'steady and a shining light to guide and direct' her husband's course in life. It was clear that the celebrated Fanny Kemble could never fit such a model of women as passive, unworldly creatures, whose sole object was to nurture their men.

As the faithful daughter, Fanny had dedicated herself to helping her father support their family – and she was proud to do so, but the personal cost was climbing. She had expected to gain confidence with experience; instead she found her fear of failure mounting. 'So much of the most serious interests and so much of the feelings of those most dear to me, is involved in the continuance of my good fortune,' she wrote to Hal. On her first night as Mrs Beverley in *The Gamester*, she was in such a state of nerves that she was almost crippled by crying and the stitch in her side. But when she appeared before the audience in 'silver-grey silk and a white crêpe hat with drooping feathers' to impersonate her father's wife they seemed to relish the performance. She managed well enough until the last act when her strung-out nerves and her father's acting combined to make her sob so hard she could hardly form the words and she collapsed on the corpse of Beverley 'with a hysterical cry that had all the merit of pure nature, if none other, to recommend it'.[14] Fortunately, that was the point when the closing curtain fell and Fanny could be carried off to finish her hysterics in her dressing-room in private.

In her correspondence with Hal the thoughtful young star pondered the oddity of the acting process and the 'perfectly prosaic and commonplace' watchfulness required in the performance of 'sincere' feeling –

> . . . in that very last scene of Mrs Beverley, while I was half dead with crying in the midst of the *real* grief, created by an entirely *unreal* cause, I perceived that my tears were falling like rain all over my silk dress, and spoiling it; and I calcu-

> lated and measured most accurately the space that my father would require to fall in, and moved myself and my train accordingly in the midst of the anguish I was to feign, and absolutely did endure.

To project sincerity over the footlights involved artifice, while the business of reproducing the same effect night after night was inevitably manipulation, the very opposite of sincerity. The stage made Fanny too knowing – whatever her sincerity, she had also acquired the art to be aware of the effect she was producing.

> . . . while I am uttering all that exquisite poetry in Juliet's balcony scene, while I feel as if my own soul was on my lips . . . [that watchful faculty] prevents me from falling over my train, from setting fire to myself with the lamps placed close to me, from leaning upon my canvas balcony when I seem to throw myself all but over it.

Her very professionalism made her untrustworthy in a domestic context. Hallam might hail Fanny as 'An Admired Lady' in verse, but when he thought of a wife he engaged himself to Tennyson's sister Emily, chief among the 'household deities' residing in rural seclusion at Somersby. Even John Sterling, whom Fanny probably liked best, later in that year of 1830, chose instead to marry the nurturing Miss Barton, the anonymous sister of a minor Apostle rather than the talented Miss Kemble. As a celebrity, actress – and even as an artist – Fanny was 'too costly to wear everyday'.[15] Being polite youths, the Apostles disguised the problem by hailing Miss Kemble as sister to Imogen and Juliet[16] – elevating her into a category of her own, an artistic nature above the humdrum existence of everyday life, but in truth her profession de-sexed her.

Fanny was powerfully drawn to the 'beauty and truth' of those ideals celebrated in fiction where women sacrificed all to their men, but at the same time she could not help observing her own experience was somewhat at odds with the respect society demanded for men as the protectors and governors of their womenfolk. Her high-minded brother, for example, was wont to recall how, when in far-off Munich he read of her going on the stage, the news struck him 'with the sensation of a cold sword through the heart'[17] – and yet he was content to have her earnings support the family so that he might enjoy the life of a gentleman at Cambridge.

The fate of the tragedy queens Fanny played night after night provided a mocking counterpoint to the contrast between what she was brought up to admire in men and the actual function of the menfolk in her family. As Mrs Beverley she embraced angelic resignation, powerless to do anything but wring her hands and voice 'womanly' fears – even when it was plain that she had more wit, virtue and capability than her hero. When, in contrast, Belvidera acts – persuading her husband, Jaffier, to give up the conspirators who have drawn him, without any good reason, into their plots against the state – her man chooses to preserve his honour by dying with his friend rather than fulfil his responsibilities as a husband, leaving his 'beloved' Belvidera alone to go mad with guilt.

The message of this dramatic education in love and gender roles was that the 'beauty' of femininity was to serve with 'meekness and over-during patience'[18] whatever indignities the follies of men heaped upon a woman. Given the wretched illogicality and injustice of it all, the nightly stabbings and mad screaming fits that brought down the final curtain must have been somewhat cathartic.

Fanny had become the family work-horse. The Apostles drifted back to their idyllic Cambridge life and Buckingham Gate fell silent. 'The house is in mourning for its liveliest inmates,' sighed Fanny to Hal. Even brother Henry had departed, slipping over to Paris to enjoy the sights in company with Edward Fitzgerald, whose private means and admiration for beautiful youths such as Fanny's younger brother made him a useful host. Fanny was back to her father's world – a stage life of hard work with occasional moments of humiliating farce. Her leading man Mr Abbott – her portly whiskered Romeo – was a positive menace as her husband in *The Grecian Daughter*. Whenever they were on stage together she was distracted by her nervous anticipation of his tendency to rush at her when seeking to express violent emotion. One night he clasped her to his bosom 'so energetically' that they fell down together in a heap mid-stage. At such moments Fanny could not more heartily agree with James Spedding's low opinion of the theatre.

John Mitchell's sister might be forgiven for wondering about the price she paid so that her elder brother might enjoy a genteel life. She dodged Mr Abbott on the boards of Covent Garden, while her brother sent home happy accounts of his success as Dogberry in a student production of *Much Ado about Nothing*. Jack Kemble sketched a rollicking picture of the portly Richard Milnes playing the cultured Beatrice as a 'languishing trull', and capping his performance on the line 'He is a stuffed man, but for the stuffing – well, we are all mortal' by falling through his couch on to the stage where he lay issuing distinctly unladylike curses from beneath a flurry of petticoats. It was not all horse-play, however. Arthur Hallam had won the university declamation prize with the great poet Wordsworth himself sitting in the audience. James Spedding approached the celebrated poet as a fellow Lakelander and invited him to tea. To the Apostles' pride and satisfaction, the sixty-year-old poet condescended to be lionized and they spent several happy hours sitting at the master's feet.

Privately, Fanny could relish 'the *happiness* of reading Shakespeare's heavenly imaginations' as much and more than the average cultured lady. She could declare with complete sincerity to Hal that all she required to be content was to

> sit obliviously curled up in an armchair, and read what he [Shakespeare] says till my eyes are full of delicious, quiet tears, and my heart of blessed, good, quiet thoughts and feelings –[19]

but her exhibition on the public stage tainted her. She would always be regarded as coarsened and less of a woman for it.

She rarely slept a night through, even when her performances left her so tired that she ached all over. The best Charles Kemble could think of as remedy was to give her permission to take riding lessons. From childhood the sight of a woman galloping across the countryside on horseback had always struck Fanny as a vision of liberation. 'I shall be in right earnest "an angel on horseback",' she rejoiced to Hal.

Marie-Thérèse, who had been a fine horsewoman in her youth, took her daughters, looking like 'two nice brown robin-redbreasts' in their new riding habits, to her old teacher, Captain Fozzard – the instructor of the 'best lady riders' in London. Adelaide remained nervous of quadrupeds, but Fanny became Fozzard's star pupil, mastering all his most rigorous exercises. Sitting side-saddle, without stirrups and with her arms behind her back, she delighted in 'violent plunging, rearing and kicking lessons', even managing to take her horse over the bar in that condition without losing her seat. Fanny was fearless. She took great pride in the fact that when the future Queen Victoria, a silent girl with her chaperone, was brought to inspect the academy she, Fanny Kemble, was the one Fozzard used to demonstrate his techniques. Riding – along with dancing – became her substitute for sleep and her remedy for the nervous stitches in her side. For years she was convinced that an hour's gallop in the fresh air restored her energy levels better than rest.

There was no other relief in sight. Fanny's fate as a woman was to serve men. 'The talent which I possess . . . was, I suppose, given to me for some good purpose, and to be used.' She was concerned that her profession put her at risk of becoming addicted to false things –

> that admiration and applause, and the excitement springing there from, may become *necessary* to me, I resolve not only to watch but to pray against such a result. I have no desire to sell my soul for anything, least of all for sham fame, mere notoriety.

Like her famous uncle before her, Fanny clung to Shakespeare as the standard by which she would maintain her respectability and foster the noble within herself. She reassured Hal and herself too that –

> the *happiness* of reading Shakespeare's heavenly imaginations is so far beyond all the excitements of acting them (white satin, gas lights, applause and all), that I cannot conceive a time when having him in my hand will not compensate for the absence of any amount of public popularity.

So when Charles Kemble announced that she should study Portia in *The Merchant of Venice* for her spring Benefit on 25 March 1830 Fanny greeted the opportunity like a well in the desert. Here was a part she could put her heart into, a part for a proper artist. Portia, her ideal model of womanhood, was a perfect subject for a Romantic essay in characterization: 'my heart goes with every sentiment Portia utters . . . Juliet, with the exception of the balcony scene, I act; but I feel as if I were Portia'.[20]

Portia was not a popular role among actresses of Fanny's day. The part lacked those 'violent situations with which to (what is called) "bring the house down"', but none of these considerations dampened Fanny's enthusiasm.

Marie-Thérèse excelled herself, costuming her daughter in a flattering dress inspired by portraits by Titian and Veronese, 'a gown . . . of strawberries and cream' made of a fabric that shifted with rainbow hues where the light caught it. Fanny could not decide which she liked better – the dress or the matching shoes decorated with jewelled roses. But when it came to the night of her Benefit she was 'frightened FLAT to a degree I could hardly have believed possible after my previous experience'.

The subtleties of her performance failed to carry beyond the first few rows. Despite all her efforts it was the 'curious little authentic black velvet hat' she put on as the lawyer in the trial scene that received the most applause. 'Covent Garden is too large a frame for that exquisite, harmonious piece of portrait painting,' she admitted sadly. Her public did not appreciate the celebrated Miss Kemble as the noble, independent-minded Portia. If she was to be one of Shakespeare's women, they preferred her to be that loving child-woman, Juliet.

18

Revolution and Railways

That Easter Marie-Thérèse and her daughters took a short holiday while theatrical performances were suspended during Passion Week. After the effort of rising to the challenges of Fanny's début Marie-Thérèse's spirits were faltering. She was drawn to revisit Blackheath where as a young mother she used to take Fanny to stay with her friends, the sisters Grimani, at the school they ran in Lea.

The school had closed years before. Fanny was upset to find that she could not even identify the building with its elegant lawn and cedar trees, where the gentle Miss Bella had stood in front of that picture of the storm-tossed boat and enthralled her with the story of Prospero and the baby Miranda. The rural character of Blackheath was dissipating into suburbia, a 'little town of new, white citizen-retreat-like villas' crowding in around the picturesque church.

Charles came to join them. For a few hours on the common Adelaide and Fanny revelled in a rare glimpse of their family at its best, content and relaxed in one another's company. Being Kembles the day had to have its dramatic highlight. They came across a pair of gypsies and the girls rushed up to have their fortunes told. Fanny was promised two lovers, good luck and that she would marry blue eyes. Then the gypsy turned to Charles Kemble.

'Pray sir, let me tell your fortune; you have been much wronged, sir, kept out of your rights, sir, and what belonged to you, sir – and that by them as you thought was your friends, sir.'[1] It was as if the family could never escape the shadow of Covent Garden and its persistent woes. Fanny's father laughed it off, but the reminder took the edge off her pleasure.

On returning to London Charles Kemble decided to bring his daughter out as Isabella in *The Fatal Marriage* for his spring Benefit. Isabella was one of Sarah Siddons's iconic roles.* Perhaps the most popular print of Fanny's aunt depicted her as that grieving widow, her elegant figure bending tenderly towards her son (played in the early years, for added effect, by her own young son Henry). Fanny disliked 'both play and part extremely'[2] and she was exceedingly glad when the whole thing was over. Her public's response to Isabella was muted. The management counted the receipts and moved on.

In the enclosed garden behind the house at Buckingham Gate sooty trees were unfurling fresh leaves under a blue sky. Spring had come and Fanny's spirits rose with the good weather.

As her first London season drew to a close Fanny was caught up in a frenzy of costume fittings, rehearsals and travel plans for provincial engagements that Charles had arranged for the summer. He needed a repertoire of plays that could be sustained by two stars so that he and his daughter could satisfy audiences whatever the quality of the local company around them.† With this in mind, he set his wife to training Fanny up in her first true comic role, Lady Townly, the disruptive wife of *The Provoked Husband*, a comedy of manners by Sir John Vanbrugh and Colley Cibber. It was a part Marie-Thérèse had made her own playing opposite her husband back in the days when they were the leading young couple of the stage. Now she came to the conclusion that neither nature nor nurture was able to

*Sarah Siddons initiated her reigns at both Drury Lane (in 1782) and Covent Garden (in 1803) in the part.

†London stars touring during the summer would dictate to the provincial managers which plays they would appear in.

transmit her comic knack to her daughter. Later in life Fanny explained her failure in the role in terms of social change – the Restoration creation falling flat in an age that interpreted that vivid noblewoman in the pastel shades of a Jane Austen belle with pert manners. The inevitable friction involved in a jealous wife training up her twenty-year-old daughter to replace her as play-wife to her increasingly neglectful husband was never explored.

Fanny soldiered on to give Covent Garden her Lady Townly on 28 May. It was her farewell for the summer. The management marked the triumph of her first season by making the performance her second Benefit – a signal honour reserved for the top flight of stars. The packed house enjoyed the occasion as much as the play and Fanny left the stage in a glow of fond feelings for 'her' London audience.

The next day the Kembles set off for the first engagement of their summer tour – Bath. The mood in the carriage was buoyant. It was a moment for Charles Kemble to savour the dramatic partnership that promised to revive his career for many profitable years. As for Fanny – she had not revisited Bath since her mother had exiled her there at the age of five to be 'bettered' by her Aunt Twiss. And here she was, all grown up, rolling into the elegant, broad-paved streets a star, with her mother at her side her attentive drama coach and costume designer.

Bath was home to the most established Theatre Royal outside London. The company was proud of its reputation.* Fanny inspected the theatre's smaller dimensions with unwitting condescension; Marie-Thérèse and her daughter were much amused by the local niceties. Sitting in on a rehearsal of *Romeo and Juliet*, the French comedienne commented loudly on the fumbling of a line, curious as to why a competent actor should forget 'the shirt and smock'. She was informed stiffly that in Bath one did not offend the audience with references to 'body linen', even if the words came from the pen of Shakespeare.

*It was the Bath company that had fostered Sarah Siddons, making her a provincial star and preparing her for her London triumph, after the failure of her first attempt at the West End.

The engagement went well enough. Free of the restraint of his fellow Covent Garden proprietors, Charles Kemble was enjoying himself in the role of the affable senior thespian. The local press was by no means effusive about the Kembles' performances, but Charles brushed off the reviews, putting them down to provincial independence. They had full houses and that was what mattered.

For her part, Fanny was content to have a half-decent Romeo for once. The 'walking gentleman' of the Bath company was a cousin, the son of Charles's older sister, Jane. John Mason was a strapping youth with the family good looks, little imagination and an even temper. Fanny's father declared an interest in the young actor and invited him to cosy family dinners where he dispensed useful advice and half-promises of a London engagement.

The young people worked comfortably together. Fanny was much happier acting with family. She liked to tell the story of the performance when – while the audience watched Romeo pluck his lifeless Juliet from her bier – she heard her cousin murmur in her ear, in the midst of his frenzied grief, 'Jove, Fanny! You are a lift!' Fanny cheerfully admitted that she was solidly built. Her brothers had long called her 'the Shetland Pony' and she seems to have accepted Cousin John's comment in the same sisterly spirit.

When the Bath engagement ended, Marie-Thérèse returned to London to supervise another move. Charles had taken the lease on his elder brother's old home at 79 Great Russell Street, the substantial house next to the British Museum where Priscilla Kemble had once kept the ladder outside her bedroom window during the Old Price Riots. Charles was putting the gloom of his dark days behind him and laying the ghost of his brother to rest.

Fanny waved her mother off without much regret. For all Marie-Thérèse's importance in dressing her daughter for the stage, it was Aunt Dall who was most material to Fanny's equilibrium. As she described her aunt to Hal, 'she is in some sense my all the world . . .

the kindest soul and cheerfulest good human being that ever dedicated her life to the comfort and happiness of those around her.'[3]

Both aunt and niece were looking forward to the next stop on the tour – Edinburgh. Fanny was eager to see her old friends, while Dall had happy memories of the city as a young actress with Stephen Kemble's company.

Once again there were good houses and indifferent reviews. With a conspicuous lack of gallantry, the Scottish critics passed over Fanny's acting to focus on her small stature and unconventional looks. One night she was introduced to the Lord Advocate, Jeffrey, the renowned and recently retired editor of the *Edinburgh Review*. Their conversation was brief. After they parted, the reviewer, whose judgement was much respected, was heard to complain that she was not prettier. Fanny tried to make light of the insult, but it could not fail to revive her old insecurities. 'I am very sorry for it; and I heartily wish I were; but I did not think him handsome either . . . though I don't care so much about his want of beauty as he seems to do about mine.'[4]

Fortunately, old friends gathered round to support her. Her dear doctor, Andrew Combe, who turned up to her first night looking more skeletal than ever, assured her that he found her performance 'transcendently beautiful'.[5] And her angelic Cousin Harriot was at hand with her soothing charm and good sense. When Fanny complained that she found the 'death-like stillness' of the Edinburgh audiences 'paralysing', Mrs Harry described how Mrs Siddons used to despair at the 'coldness' of the Edinburgh audiences. When her mother-in-law played there, her colleagues would hear her muttering under her breath as she panted from the exertion of her dramatic efforts, 'Stupid people! Stupid people!' Apparently it was against Edinburgh good manners to be considered effusive.

One morning, while riding sedately down Princes Street beside her father, Fanny spied Sir Walter Scott walking towards them. The fifty-nine-year-old novelist stopped by the shoulder of Charles Kemble's horse and asked to be introduced to Charles's daughter.

Sir Walter made the effort to attend a performance of the niece of his old friend John Philip Kemble. The next night he had a headache and decided not to see her as Mrs Beverley (the truth was that he 'hated to be made miserable about domestic distress') but the story of Fanny's self-sacrifice for her father and Covent Garden disposed him to like Miss Kemble. Offended by the tone of the Scottish reviewers, he wrote to his friend Ballantyne, the influential editor of one of the city's newspapers, to state that he had seen nothing so good since Sarah Siddons.

To Fanny's great regret, her father was only able to accept one of Scott's many invitations. They breakfasted with him at his town house among a small party of his close friends. Fanny relished her few hours with Scott and thought he looked just like the familiar busts and portraits, his sandy-haired, unremarkable head enlivened by shrewd eyes and an affable Borderer's burr. He put her at her ease at once, despite his 'awful celebrity', and she listened, tears brimming, to his account of an old Jacobite noblewoman weeping over the recently rediscovered regalia of the Scottish kingdom 'as if it had been the dead body of her child'.

Fanny struck Scott as 'merry, unaffected and good humoured'* and both were disappointed when Charles decided that commitments prevented him from accepting Scott's invitation to stay at Abbotsford. Fanny always regretted the missed opportunity. By the time she visited Abbotsford she was a middle-aged woman, Scott was long dead and his beloved home had become a hollowed-out curiosity, the haunt of literary tourists and picnicking strangers.

There was one other meeting Fanny was determined to fit in before she left her favourite city. One morning she set off for Newhaven, driving in a carriage down the familiar roads she used to walk only two years before. Dressed in all the 'star-like splendour of a lilac silk dress and French crape bonnet' she created quite a stir

* 'Miss Fanny Kemble has very expressive though not regular features,' Scott recorded in his diary on 17 June; 'and, what is worth it all, great energy mingled with and chastened by correct taste.'

among the fishing community. Undine had moved from her cottage by the sea. Fanny was directed to the slums that had grown up since her last visit. Climbing three storeys of a filthy tenement, she finally knocked on the right door. It took her 'dear fish-wife', Sandie Flockhart, a moment before recognition dawned, then, with a cry of 'Ech, sirs! But it's yer ain sel' come back again at last!' she dragged Fanny across a room running over with lively children to introduce her to her latest and eleventh baby, a sturdy boy peacefully asleep in his cradle.

Fanny left Edinburgh in a melancholy mood. The happiness and refuge that city represented in her imagination had been undermined by the reality of going back. That summer Mrs Harriot Siddons sold her interest in the Theatre Royal and retired. She planned to move to England and soon the house in Windsor Street would be inhabited by strangers. With her departure, the circle that had welcomed Fanny, the society in which she first found a place, vanished.

They moved on to Glasgow. News of King George IV's death on 26 June shut the theatre for a period of mourning and the Kemble party grabbed the opportunity for a brief holiday. Fanny returned to Glasgow bearing 'a white rose from Dumbarton, in memory of Mary Stuart, an oak branch from Loch Lomond, and a handful of heather . . . from the rocky shore of Loch Long'.[6] All of which put her in a good humour with her Glasgow audiences whom she declared 'warmer' than their Edinburgh counterparts. In no time at all the party was preparing to board the boat for Dublin where Harriet St Ledger waited to greet them.

Hal and Fanny had not met for four years. Hal, who had tracked Fanny's evolution from traumatized sixteen-year-old to star of the stage by letter, now saw the result in all its vivid reality. Fanny introduced her retiring friend to Aunt Dall; to her delight the three of them quickly settled into easy familiarity. For all her intellectual pursuits and hermit-like tendencies Hal was fascinated by the glamour of the stage. She kept Dall company at the theatre night after night, happy to observe the colourful audiences and listen to theatrical gossip.

If Fanny was sentenced to a nomadic life, then this was her ideal of domesticity – both intellectual companionship and hearth and heart in one dressing-room. In Dublin, when she came off stage between scenes escorted by Dall, she had the pleasure of the sight of Hal's neat angular figure waiting for her, her curly chestnut head bent over a book, ready to raise those serious grey eyes to enter into any topic if required and happy to be quiet if not. Fanny was so content in their company that she was reluctant to be drawn out into wider society. The energetic feminist and socialite Lady Sydney Morgan – that reputed coiner of the word 'celebrity' – introduced herself, eager to show Miss Kemble off to Dublin society. Fanny attended the parties she could not avoid but she preferred reading *The Tempest* and catching up on her correspondence.

Although the Kembles were not regular letter writers between themselves, Fanny was scrupulous about returning an answer to those who wrote to her. Mrs Jameson pursued her from London, where she was gathering material for a book on Shakespeare's heroines. Lonely and depressed, Anna Jameson sought to attach herself to the Kembles, calling regularly at 79 Great Russell Street.

> 'I am glad you see my mother often, and very glad that to assist your recollection of me you find interest and amusement in discussing the fitting-up of my room with her.'

If the Glasgow audiences were warmer than the Edinburgh ones, the Irish spectators were positively effusive. One night after the play Fanny was escorted back to her hotel by a crowd of nearly two hundred male admirers – 'shouting and hurrahing like mad'. They surged about the carriage, taking it upon themselves to let down the steps and hand out Fanny and her aunt (Charles Kemble was not with them at the time). As she ran to the hotel, young men fell to their knees to snatch a glimpse of the face beneath the star's overshadowing bonnet. After the unflattering Scottish reviewers, the vociferous admiration and cries of 'Bedad, she looks well by gaslight!' and 'Och, and bedad, she looks well by daylight too!' were disorientating. For all the reflections of Fanny's cooler moments, at the time the adulation *felt* sincere.

Towards the end of July real-life drama broke in. News came from France that barricades had been thrown up in Paris. On 28 July rebels captured the Town Hall and within hours the Bourbon King Charles X had abdicated. While the news raised the spectre of the two decades of war that had followed the French Revolution, reassured by the lack of bloodshed, many English commentators were prepared to acknowledge the event as an uprising against royal despotism. There was relief when the Duke of Orléans, a crafty and wealthy exile of fifty-seven, was swiftly installed as King Louis-Philip. The means of the 'Citizen King's' accession, however, presented an unsettling precedent for the British Establishment, whose own monarch of barely a month was the little known and unremarkable sixty-four-year-old 'Bluff Billy', William IV. The new French King acquired his throne by a pledge of moderate democratic reforms – a widening of the electorate to include more of the expanding middle classes, the abolition of censorship of the press and the abandonment of Catholicism as the established state religion. As Tory ministers went about their business on their country estates, a brooding question hung in the summer air – might the British Isles too see revolution before the year was out?

In Dublin there were plenty of enthusiasts for the French action. Lady Morgan was in ecstasies. 'I never witnessed anything so like tipsiness as Lady Morgan's delight at it,' remarked Fanny, amused.[7] On the whole she was glad that her sex excused her from having to think too deeply about politics. She was looking forward to a quiet holiday far from the noise and trouble of the world – she and Dall were going to stay at Hal's home by the sea.

Ardgillan Castle still stands on the high coastline between Balbriggan and Skerries, twenty miles north of Dublin. When Fanny first set eyes on Ardgillan the substantial two-storey country house with its tall windows had recently been remodelled with castellated decorations. Looking out over pasture and woodland to sweeping views of the Bay, Ardgillan was an old-fashioned country household that ate fresh produce from its own kitchen garden, drank milk from its own cows and slept on cotton sheets made in the cottage industries of nearby Balbriggan. To Fanny it was a living picture of Scott's ideal of chivalrous patriarchy. She described her hostess, Hal's sister, Mrs Marianne Taylor, as a charming example of 'real antique toryism'. Each day family and staff met for prayers; Fanny was especially taken with the sight of rosy-cheeked servants filing past their mistress as she acknowledged each bow or curtsy with a gracious smile and stately nod of the head.

Fanny and Hal spent those sunny days taking long walks along the coast or sitting under a tree in the Dell, Hal's favourite spot sheltered from the winds off the sea. They read Milton and Shakespeare together and discussed theology and philosophy and moral duty.

> *Beneath the shadowy tree, where thou and I*
> *Were wont to sit, studying the harmony*
> *Of gentle Shakespeare and of Milton high*[8]

Fanny was enchanted by the sea, the company and the life-style. At Ardgillan she felt free to be her true self. 'I am sure I have felt taller by three inches, as well as three times more vigorous in body and mind, than I really am, when running by the sea.'[9]

Fanny and her aunt rejoined her father in Liverpool in early August. The contrast between the bustling, grubby port and the Arcadian delights of Ardgillan was almost too much to bear. Eager to make money, Charles Kemble had set up a gruelling sequence of dates across the North-West and the Midlands. 'I would rather make shoes,' Fanny sighed.

She was trying to pull herself together for her Liverpool audience when a letter arrived from John Mitchell. His family was under the impression that he was in Norfolk, studying for his exams. Now Fanny read that he had sailed for Gibraltar to help 'revolutionize' the kingdom of Spain. All those late-night drinking sessions with Torrijos and his followers in John Sterling's rooms had led to something altogether more dangerous.

John Sterling and General Torrijos were persuaded that Spain was ripe for a French-style revolution. They imagined that a small band of patriots could prompt a people's uprising that would force the King to submit to constitutional monarchy. To his everlasting regret, John Sterling's health collapsed, forcing him to stay at home groping after the progress of the others by letter. A young cousin of Richard Trench's, Robert Boyd, a red-blooded ex-army officer who had recently come into a small inheritance, was persuaded to invest in a boat. While this was being fitted up, John Mitchell slipped out of the country heading for Gibraltar where he was to prepare for the arrival of the main party.

John Mitchell's letter swore his sister to secrecy but as it arrived under the noses of her father and aunt she was forced to tell them of its contents. The three agreed that it was best not to inform Marie-Thérèse; they considered her incapable of dealing with the worry. The British government got wind of the expedition and Robert Boyd's boat was seized in the Thames estuary. Richard Trench, Torrijos and the others on board only avoided arrest by jumping over the side and escaping in a rowing boat. But they were not to be put off. The group split up to make their way to Gibraltar by other means. Meanwhile, Arthur Hallam and Alfred Tennyson boarded a packet boat for France heading for a walking holiday in the Pyrenees, carrying letters in their packs from Sterling and Torrijos to Spanish patriots on the frontier.

Ignorant of these details, in Liverpool, Charles Kemble and his daughter were left to hope that John Mitchell would come to his senses and return home. Throughout August the Kembles acted in Liverpool, Birmingham and Manchester, taking in the sights of England's booming industrial heartland. They inspected button-making in Birmingham, docks in Liverpool and power-looms in Manchester. Fanny was awed by man's abilities to shape the elements, the new methods and machines appearing to her eyes like a benign version of sorcery. 'Did you know that the solid masses of iron-work which we see in powerful engines were many of them cast in moulds of sand? – inconstant, shifting, restless sand!'[10]

That summer it seemed as if the whole of Europe was shifting sand in which a new world was being forged. The July revolution in France inspired liberal and nationalist uprisings across Europe. The day revolution broke out in Belgium, on Wednesday 25 August, the Kembles were in Liverpool.

Charles Kemble had made the acquaintance of some of the backers of the scheme to build the first passenger railway between Liverpool and Manchester. After four years and some £830,000 the project was just coming to fruition. The engineer, George Stephenson, had completed his railroad and it was to be opened to the public the following month.

That August no one was entirely sure that the project would pay off but everybody knew it was a ground-breaking achievement. Stephenson had had to overcome a multitude of engineering challenges in the hills, valleys and swamp that nature had placed in the path of his railroad. When he suggested a trial run on the new railway for his directors, some of his backers invited Charles Kemble and his daughter to join them.

On a fine summer's day sixteen people gathered in a large covered yard where they were seated on six benches back to back in an open carriage set on iron rails. The carriage was given a push and it trundled down an incline into a dark tunnel. Emerging into the sunlight, it rolled to a stop as the ground levelled out and here, with a natural showmanship, George Stephenson, a sturdy, 'rather stern-featured man' in his middle fifties 'with a dark and deeply marked countenance' brought up his engine. The *Rocket*, constructed in Stephenson's Forth Street works in Newcastle, comprised of a boiler, a stove, a bench, and behind the bench a barrel of water, all mounted on a platform on wheels. Fanny was delighted with the huffing machine; it was a 'snorting little animal, which I felt rather inclined to pat'. Stephenson invited the young actress to sit beside him on the engineer's bench. She accepted, full of pride at the honour, and they set off at ten miles an hour.

No fairy-tale was half as wonderful as the sights Fanny saw that day. As his 'tame dragon flew panting along his iron pathway' the

Northumbrian engineer regaled her with the story of his grand project – a tale that 'passed the first reading of the Arabian Nights'. Although his Northern accent and expressions seemed 'peculiar' to her, Fanny found him a natural gentleman ('his language has not the slightest touch of vulgarity or coarseness'). With Fanny's caramel eyes riveted on his craggy face, Stephenson recounted how a 'common coal-digger' had made himself into an engineer from dismantling a watch as a boy and teaching himself to reassemble it. He told her of his vision of passenger railways transforming the land as they travelled between the soaring stone sides of embankments he had designed and under bridges he had engineered – bridges from which people looking down seemed 'like pigmies standing in the sky'. In his evocative, simple way 'the master of all these marvels' painted for her the frustration of an inarticulate, self-taught engineer, utterly convinced of the truth of his vision being 'badgered and baffled' by the 'Parliament men', who sneered at him and, superior in their 'book-knowledge', dismissed his plans as fantasies. A major objection raised to Stephenson's projected railway line had been the impossibility of laying a sound road across the Chatmoss swamp. 'Did ye ever see a boat float on water?' demanded Stephenson. 'I will make my road float upon Chatmoss!' But the Parliament men (some of whom, no doubt, as Fanny remarked, did not want railways cutting into their parks) did not believe him.

Stephenson had his proposal turned down. However, the authority of Parliament itself was insufficient to 'smother the irrepressible prophecy' of this natural genius. He went to Liverpool, where some shrewd merchants – 'men, of less intellectual culture than the Parliament members, had the adventurous imagination proper to great speculators, which is the poetry of the counting house and wharf', as Fanny put it.

Fanny was thrilled by this romantic tale of sincerity and industry triumphing over the stagnant indifference of the old order. Stephenson was a hero for a new age – an industrial celebrity (who before long would have his biography written by that Victorian apostle of self-help, Samuel Smiles). And here were these two celebrities of the new age – the actress and the engineer – side by side, chugging over the very Chatmoss swamp where 'no human foot could tread without sinking, and yet it bore the road which bore us . . . and the road does float, for we passed over it at the rate of five and twenty miles an hour, and saw the stagnant swamp water trembling on the surface of the soil on either side of us'.

They travelled for fifteen miles and stopped to admire the nine-arched viaduct Stephenson had built to carry his railroad, the vast structure framing the beauty of the valley within its central arch. Helping her down, Stephenson took his new acolyte for a walk. She hung on his arm Miranda-like with wonder as he entertained her with interesting facts – how he believed that the Mersey had once flowed through this valley; how tides and floods were caused and how, when digging the foundations for the massive pillars of his viaduct, his men had uncovered a whole tree buried fourteen feet below the surface of the earth. Fanny found herself 'most horribly in love' with this Northumbrian Prospero. 'He has certainly turned my head.'

On the way back from the viaduct, Stephenson gave them a run at top speed – thirty-five miles an hour – 'swifter than a bird flies (for they tried the experiment with a snipe)', a pace none of the passengers had ever experienced before. Fanny loved it.

> You cannot conceive what that sensation of cutting the air was; the motion is as smooth as possible . . . I stood up, with my bonnet off and 'drank the air before me' . . . When I closed my eyes this sensation of flying was quite delightful, and strange beyond description; yet, strange as it was, I had a perfect sense of security, and not the slightest fear.[11]

The excursion ended in an exhilaration of bonhomie, the directors offering the Kembles three places for the grand opening of the railway, to be attended by the Prime Minister, the Duke of Wellington, on the fifteenth of the following month. Charles Kemble, with the affable detachment typical of him, immediately undercut his daughter's high-flown enthusiasm by suggesting that he probably would not be able to accept this honour, as he was hoping to take his younger son, Henry, over to Heidelberg before the opening of the Covent Garden season. Charles Kemble was interested to see the wonders of science and industry, but his attention was fixed on his own affairs. The Kembles were moving on to Manchester where a chance invitation was to introduce Fanny into the world of the aristocracy.

19

An Introduction to Silver Forks

In Liverpool Charles Kemble received an invitation from the daughter of an old acting colleague to come and stay at her home outside Manchester. Lady Wilton was the one surviving child of the twelfth Earl of Derby and his second wife, Elizabeth Farren,* the elegant actress whose portrait helped launch Sir Thomas Lawrence's career. Elizabeth Farren's daughter had married well. Her husband was the second Earl of Wilton, a younger son of the Marquis of Westminster who had inherited a fortune in land and mineral rights from his grandfather, the first Earl.

Although she had never been introduced to him, the Earl had caught Fanny's attention backstage at Covent Garden. Recently turned thirty-one, Lord Wilton was the picture of a lady novelist's dream. 'With his slender, perfectly dressed figure, his pale complexion, his regular features, fine eyes and dark, glossy waves of hair' Fanny thought he looked so precisely like 'the Earl of So-and-So' in the fashionable novel of the day that she was always tempted to ask him 'what he did at the end of the "third volume", and whether he or Sir Reginald married Lady Geraldine'.[1]

---

*Elizabeth Farren had died and been buried as the Countess of Derby the previous year, 1829.

The Earl was to live a long life (he died in 1882 at the age of eighty-three). Urbane, as suited his ultra-smooth good looks, he was also an energetic man. On the one hand, he studied anatomy, on the other, he was a daring horseman who liked to don the silks and ride as his own jockey. He was a competent musician, fond of playing the chamber organ that his grandfather had installed in one of the drawing rooms of his country seat, Heaton Hall. He was an enthusiastic yachtsman and in 1851 would become one of the founders of the America's Cup race. Fanny's admiration for the breadth of Lord Wilton's interests was tinged with reservation. She was not blind to his reputation; it seems that the Earl had a roving eye. A piece of contemporary doggerel is double-edged.

Next upon a switch-tailed bay with wandering eye
Attenuated William canters by
His character how difficult to know
A compound of psalm tunes and tally-ho,
A forward rider half inclined to teach
Though less disposed to practise than preach
An amorous lover with a saintly twist
And now a jockey, now an organist.

It was 'in spite of his character of a mere dissipated man of fashion' that, in later life, Fanny emphasized the Earl's many talents and interests. It was Lady Wilton who won Fanny's trust and affection; she was a sweet-natured woman of twenty-nine, whose somewhat horse-like features were lightened by a winsome smile.

As September passed the Kembles fell into an easy intimacy with the young couple at their neo-classical house set among the hills east of Manchester. They would travel out to Heaton Hall after morning rehearsals to spend the day there until early evening when their hosts would accompany them back to the theatre. After all the Kemble obsession with the gentlemanly life over the years, Fanny was sampling the real thing – if only in half-days and at weekends. Lady Wilton made a pet of the diminutive actress, pinning her into her own luxurious riding habit and giving her her favourite horse to ride. It was all very pleasant. One weekend, in keeping with the fashionable interest in folk traditions, there were pastoral festivities to mark the changing season. In a 'curious little bit of *ancientry*' described as a 'Lancashire Rush Bearing', a procession of Lord Wilton's tenants, decked out with ribbons and nose-gays, performed Morris dances on the front lawn with handkerchiefs flying.

> The contrast between this pretty picture of a bygone time and the modern by no means unpicturesque group assembled under the portico, filled my mind with the pleasantest ideas, and I was quite sorry when the rural pageant wound up the woody heights again, and the last shout and peal of music came back across the sunny lawn.[2]

Fanny bridled a little when the Wiltons began introducing them to their neighbours and friends, holding dinner parties where the actors were forced (being pressed for time) to sit at table in all the tinsel magnificence of their pseudo-medieval stage costumes. But Fanny's concerns that she and her father were being served up as a novelty to entertain the Wiltons' aristocratic guests soon faded. 'The persons I was surrounded by were all singularly kind and amiable to me, and my appearing among them in these picturesque fancy dresses was rather a source of amusement to us all.'

It was at Heaton Hall that Fanny first encountered the upper classes on their own ground. If Fanny and her father had entered the house as performers, they left as friends.

Fanny's contemporary, the French author Pauline de la Ferronnays, once observed that in the great country houses of England, 'the official, political, and literary element mixed with what is called "the world" as in no other country'.[3] At Heaton Fanny made connections that would transform her access to London society. She met the amiable Mr Baring of the famous banking family and his wife, Lady Harriet, who was 'much cleverer than he'. Then there were the two sisters, both celebrated society beauties, Anne and Isabella Forrester and their brother Cecil. For a splash of cosmopolitan colour, there was the Hungarian Count Betthyany and his countess, who was the widow of a celebrated Austrian general. Perhaps the most significant introduction was to Henry Greville.

Greville came from a prominent political family. His mother was Lady Charlotte Bentinck, daughter of the one-time Prime Minister, the Duke of Portland, a close friend of the Duke of Wellington (one of Henry's brothers was the Duke's private secretary). His elder brother was Charles Greville, that Clerk to the Privy Council who was to become the most famous society diarist of his age (and whose impressions of Fanny were typically merciless*). Opinionated, witty, cultured, considered an authority on fashion, Henry Greville was welcomed by society hostesses from London to Paris. Although nominally attached to the Embassy at Paris for several years, and rejoicing in the appropriately camp sinecure of 'Gold-Stick in waiting' to the royal household, Henry Greville was the epitome of the 'exquisite' man of leisure. He was reputedly one of the best society singers of his day. He also had a passion for acting. He was rather bad at it, but made up for a lack of talent by being on terms of 'friendly intimacy' with several of the leading musical performers and actors of that generation. He and Fanny got on like a house on fire and he was to remain her 'kind and constant friend' until he died.

As Fanny played battledore and shuttlecock on the lawn under bright autumn skies, wrote letters on Heaton stationery in the new library and sang catches with Henry Greville, she was almost able to forget the drudgery of the stage. Greville's brother-in-law arrived late. He was Francis Leveson Gower, a younger son of the Marquis

*'I saw Miss Fanny Kemble for the first time on Friday, and was disappointed. She is short, ill made, with large hands and feet, an expressive countenance, though not handsome, fine eyes, teeth and hair, not devoid of grace, and with great energy and spirit, her voice good, though she has a little of the drawl of her family.' Charles Greville, diary entry for 9 November 1829, quoted Reeve, vol. I, p. 246.

of Stafford.* At thirty he had already been an MP of the liberal–conservative persuasion for eight years. He was delighted to meet the talented Miss Kemble. A follower of the Romantics, he was a scribbler, having published a rather bad translation of *Faust*, a drama by Goethe, and Schiller's *Song of the Bell* in 1823. Fanny was much taken with him. 'I have met . . . Lord Francis Leveson Gower, the translator of *Faust*. I like him very much; he is a young man of a great deal of talent, with a charming, gentle manner, and a very handsome, sweet face.' She had resolved to learn German, she informed Hal.

The summer tour was over. Charles Kemble returned to London to prepare for the winter season. As Dall set off for a holiday with friends in Buckinghamshire, Fanny's mother arrived in Manchester to take over as her chaperone. In reward for all her daughter's hard work, Marie-Thérèse had torn herself away from some good fishing so that Fanny might take advantage of the places they had been offered to attend the opening ceremonies of the Manchester–Liverpool railway. Being reunited with her mother introduced a certain tension. Marie-Thérèse remained ignorant of her eldest son's whereabouts. Fanny was forced to listen to her chatter about John Mitchell's prospects and studies, acutely aware of the guilty secret she was keeping. She had had no news from Gibraltar. It was a relief to join the party that gathered at Heaton Hall on Tuesday, 14 September to make the journey down to Liverpool so that they could participate in 'one of the most striking events in the scientific annals of our country' the following day.

The Wiltons were playing host to the MP for Liverpool, Mr Huskisson, and his wife. Huskisson was something of a maverick among the Tories, being an advocate of free trade and broader representation in a party dominated by protectionist land-owners. He had built a reputation as that rare thing, a minister who understood

---

*The 2nd Marquis of Stafford was created Duke of Sutherland in 1833, the year of his death and three years after Fanny first met his son. Hence, some biographers refer to Francis Leveson Gower as a younger son of the Duke of Sutherland.

enterprise and the economy. Huskisson was a Canningite, and since the death of his leader, George Canning, in 1827, he had been the head of that faction. The patricians of the governing party could not deny his ability, but they did not take to him personally (as indicated by Charles Greville's description of the MP as 'tall, slovenly and ignoble-looking'.)

There was a political undercurrent to the house party that gathered at Heaton that day. Huskisson had recently resigned from the government over a dispute about two disenfranchised Parliamentary seats. He had argued that the spare seats should be transferred to the industrial cities of Birmingham and Manchester. When Tory peers blocked the proposal with respect to Manchester, Huskisson resigned, taking his Canningite associates with him and leaving Wellington's government seriously weakened.

When the Kembles reached Liverpool there was not a hotel room or lodging-house bed to be had in the city. Marie-Thérèse drew on her professional connections and Mr Radley, of the Adelphi Theatre, put mother and daughter up overnight in a tiny garret under the eaves.

The next day opened in a burst of sunshine. The streets were thronged with sight-seers. Fanny reckoned that they were among eight hundred people assigned places in the various carriages of the train. In the press Fanny and her mother were unable to find seats together. The weather began to look uncertain but the rain held off as the train ground into motion. Dense crowds lined the route, waving and shouting as they passed. Fanny's mood rose 'to the true champagne height' as she revelled in the speed and atmosphere.

After about an hour the train stopped to pick up water. Marie-Thérèse took the opportunity to swap seats and rejoin her daughter, at which point Fanny discovered that her mother was frantic to escape, convinced that they were all about to be killed by the unnatural speeds at which they had been travelling. Fanny was doing her best to calm her mother's fears when there was a commotion outside. A man ran past calling out for a surgeon; somebody in the director's carriage had been hurt. Then word spread that Mr Huskisson had been killed.

After a sickening wait, seeded with rumours and half-truths, during which Fanny tried to keep her mother from leaving the carriage, the train started again. It drew into Manchester as the sky turned stormy and it began to rain. The crowds that met them were not the holiday-makers of Liverpool. A 'grim and grimy' collection of working men lined the streets, hissing and groaning as the directors' carriage passed carrying the Duke of Wellington. The Prime Minister sat stiff and expressionless pretending not to see the ragged and starved-looking weaver who had been set up at his loom high above the crowd 'as a representative man, to protest against this triumph of machinery, and the gain and glory which the wealthy Liverpool and Manchester men were likely to derive from it'.

The contrast between the beginning and end of that day could not have been more striking. Clutching her semi-hysterical mother in the midst of the seething confusion Fanny was relieved to be found by a shaken Lady Wilton who persuaded the Kembles to change their plans and return with her to Heaton.

Lady Wilton had been hardly three yards from the scene of the accident. She described how, when the engine had stopped to take water, several of the gentlemen had disembarked to stretch their legs. They had been blithely unaware of the danger of standing so close to the second line on which, further up, another engine was parading back and forth to show off its speed. Alerted by frantic cries of 'Clear the track!' and 'Stop the engine!' the younger men sprang into the safety of the carriages just in time, but Mr Huskisson, who was older and moved stiffly, stood bewildered in the path of the engine. Lady Wilton said she distinctly heard the crushing of the bone as his leg was severed.

In the dreadful silence that followed, Lord Wilton went to the victim's aid. Calling on his knowledge of anatomy, he tied up the pumping femoral artery and prevented the MP from bleeding to death on the spot, but it was clear that the injury was likely to be fatal. The Earl accompanied the devastated Mrs Huskisson and her dying husband as they were bundled on to the second engine and rushed to Manchester. The Duke of Wellington was all for turning back but his advisers persuaded him to complete the ceremony. They knew of the protests that awaited them in Manchester. The government could not afford to look weak for fear of riots and worse.

It was a subdued group that returned to Heaton Hall that evening. After ten o'clock at night the Earl returned with the news that Mr Huskisson had died.

Fanny looked back on that day in terms of Greek tragedy. A 'terrible cloud' had darkened an outstanding national achievement. The heavy price paid by artisans and manual workers for the progress of mechanization had been 'atoned for to the Nemesis of good fortune by the sacrifice of the first financial statesman of the country'. More prosaically, the death of Huskisson proved a further blow to Wellington's already shaky administration. Other witnesses related that the reason Huskisson had left his carriage was because Holmes, a government whip, had fetched the Canningite leader to come and talk to Wellington. The two men had shaken hands and were beginning to converse when Huskisson was caught by the passing locomotive.

Fanny's mood of solemnity did not last long. By the following Sunday she was watching Lord Wilton read evening prayers to the assembled household and meditating on how pleasant it was to see that privileged people did not forget a proper piety amid the pomp and vanity of their world. She made a note to pursue a programme of self-improvement and returned to enjoying herself – 'I mean to make studying German and drawing (and endeavouring to abate my self-esteem) my principal occupations this winter.'

She and her mother said their farewells to the Wiltons and departed with Fanny throwing many a wistful glance back to Heaton Hall, glowing amid the rich autumnal foliage. They were on their way to rejoin Aunt Dall, Henry and Adelaide for a short family holiday in Buckinghamshire.

The revolutions breaking out across Europe (and the mischief his elder son had got into) had persuaded Charles Kemble to cancel his plans to take his younger son to Heidelberg. Fanny was glad. In her opinion, to leave her younger brother unsupervised in a foreign land would only risk his falling in love and being pursued home by some unsuitable Fraulein he had 'got into trouble' (a prophetic assessment, considering Henry's later career.)

In Buckinghamshire Fanny found her younger brother in his element: 'Henry is the perfect picture of happiness when in his shooting jacket and gaiters, with his gun on his shoulder and a bright day before him.'

In contrast, she found little to delight her. Was the country not pretty? She had seen much better on her summer tour. 'I have no fancy for gypsying,' she informed Hal. Miss Kemble had acquired 'the greatest taste for all the formal proprieties of life, and what I should call "silver fork existence" in general'. Fanny decided that there was a lot to be said for 'fine people' –

> . . . they do not often say very wise or very witty things . . . but neither do they tread on one's feet or poke their elbows into one's side (figuratively speaking) in their conversation, or commit the numerous solecisms of manner of less well-bred people.[4]

She was looking forward to returning home. London promised to be 'particularly gay this winter'. The new King and his Queen were said to be very fond of dramatic entertainments. 'I think there is every probability of our having a very prosperous season.'

20

Living on the Highway

On 30 September 1830 Fanny arrived back in London to spend her first night at 79 Great Russell Street. Marie-Thérèse had refitted the rooms where John Philip Kemble had once displayed his library of early English plays and entertained the great of his day, and she had made them her own. Fanny was delighted with the neat eyrie her mother had decorated for her on the fourth floor overlooking the chimney-pots and roofs of the West End. The omens seemed good for her second season.

Sticking to his tried and tested formula, on 4 October Charles Kemble reopened Covent Garden with *Romeo and Juliet*. Fanny had a new nurse. Mrs Davenport, that last remnant of the company John Philip had known, had finally retired. Fanny rolled up her sleeves and set to work.

The audiences were good but there was a new restlessness among the critics. Miss Kemble began her first scene, 'her manner and tones . . . natural, her smile equally so' reported Leigh Hunt, the doyen of the breed, but then:

> the moment she gave us the first burst of feeling, our expectations fell many degrees, and they never rose again . . . the regular theatrical start and vehemence were substituted for

> the natural emotion of the artless girl we had been contemplating.[1]

Charles Kemble had discovered a young playwright called Wade who was hoping to make his name with a brand new tragedy. In *The Jew of Aragon* Charles Kemble looked magnificent in the heavy brocade vestments of an authentic medieval rabbi. Fanny played his daughter and, like that seasoned success *Virginius*, the plot made much of the domestic affection between the pair. The piece seemed to have all the right elements for a hit. And yet, on the opening night Fanny experienced her first hisses on stage. She realized that it was the play that was being damned and not herself, but she found the experience no less shocking. 'I think if they had been the whistling of bullets . . . I could not have felt more frightened and furious.' There was worse to come.[2]

A hack journalist named Charles Molloy Westmacott, the disreputable owner and editor of a paper entitled the *Age*,was known for the robust tone of the personal abuse he printed. There were persistent rumours that he supplemented his income with blackmail, offering victims the chance to prevent the publication of his calumnies if they paid him enough. Westmacott was particularly sensitive about those he deemed to be getting above themselves – and Charles Kemble and his much-praised daughter were just the kind of people he loved to hate.

The *Age* had been sniping at Covent Garden for some time. Now it claimed Charles Kemble was insulting the patrons of his theatre by repeating the popular comedy *Black Eye'd Susan* in alternation with his daughter night after night. And as for the daughter:

> Miss Fanny Kemble is unquestionably a child of genius, but nature has been very sparing of those requisites which ought, in our estimation, to grace the tragic muse. The figure, from the waist downwards, is distinctly bad . . . Her bust is, perhaps, not sufficiently formed to criticize; but the face has probably quite as much expression as it will ever possess, and that is as deficient in

dignity as it is unconscious of the highest and sweetest expression of sentiment . . . her squat figure, we suspect, judging from her mama's, will rather grow worse with years.

Westmacott went on to offer some 'advice' to the Covent Garden manager to put aside his vanity and self-interest and buy in some new talent:

If you don't, you well may tremble
Soon you'll find your two pet doxies
Will leave you nought but empty boxes.

The choice of 'doxy' was no doubt dictated by the need for a rhyme for boxes, but the word was commonly understood to mean a criminal's whore and Charles Kemble decided that this was an insult too far. He cancelled Westmacott's free press pass to Covent Garden.

Westmacott was livid. On the evening of the second Saturday in October, while Fanny stayed at home writing, Charles Kemble was making one of his periodic tours of the building when he noticed Westmacott watching the play from a box. The manager paused to collect a bamboo stick, called the journalist out into the corridor and proceeded to give him a beating.

Members of the audience sitting nearby left their seats, summoned by Westmacott's cries for help. Charles Kemble was a good deal taller than his slight opponent who was struggling to shield himself, but once word spread as to the identity of the victim, the general opinion in the gathering crowd was in favour of the outraged father defending his daughter's honour. Mr Thomas, a superintendent of police attached to the theatre, hurried up. Westmacott howled out to him that he should do his duty and arrest the theatre manager for assault, but the policeman turned his attention to keeping the crowd from joining in the mêlée. The more Westmacott called out for justice, demanding that spectators stand witness for the suit of damages he would be bringing, the uglier the crowd got, hissing and threatening the journalist.

Charles Kemble slipped away to restore order to the Green Room while the policeman summoned a sleepy doctor from nearby Brydges Street to give the irate victim first aid. The gesture did nothing to soothe Westmacott's fury.

Charles Kemble – who had the advantage of many years playing the noble fellow confronted by the insane and vulgar opponent – stepped out of the Green Room the very picture of the gentleman straightening his cuffs. He declared that he was happy to accompany the policeman to the magistrate's office to await Westmacott and whatever charges he might wish to make. True to his word, Charles Kemble repaired to Bow Street accompanied by Thomas, but Westmacott never came. The editor had gone home to nurse his bruises and dreams of revenge.

When Charles Kemble appeared in the auditorium the following Monday night he was met with a spontaneous round of applause. He had played the melodramatic role of the protective father well and the galleries had enjoyed the show. But that was not to be the end of the matter.

A new publication had recently been launched in the capital. Placing itself in opposition to the Whig-tending *Edinburgh Review*, *Fraser's Magazine* was looking to establish itself as the influential journal for literate gentlemen of Tory leanings. In the autumn of 1830 the incident at Covent Garden gave the editor just the opening he was looking for. He represented Charles Kemble's assault of Westmacott as an illustration of the depths to which English drama had sunk:

> There was a time when . . . the first night of a piece drew the whole London world to the house . . . What a change has come over us! We are now actually obliged to apologize for intruding into a Magazine, having any literary pretensions, even the casual notice of the existence of any such things as theatres . . . The newspapers themselves, which are their last hold, huddle them into a corner.[3]

The theatre had lost its connection with literature. Good authors no longer wrote for the stage; they chose novels as their medium, and the actor, 'having lost the main link which bound him to the living intellect of the country, becomes a mere mechanic'.

'Actors,' the reviewer stated baldly, 'though in general respectable men, are no longer companions of the upper classes either of rank, fashion, or literature; . . . they are no more than tradesmen.'

This was the dashing of all John Philip Kemble's ambitions to raise his tribe above the status of mere players to the acknowledged virtue of artists and professional gentry. While the pretext of Charles Kemble's thrashing of Westmacott had been Fanny's honour, it was also symbolic of his frustration at the turn the times had taken.

The *Fraser's Magazine* article was casually dismissive of the actor-manager's contribution to the drama he had served all his life. John Philip Kemble's little brother 'was never able of himself to support a theatre in his best days' and now he was too old to play his best parts:

> His Mercutio, as he played it last year, was exquisite and original. We are sorry to learn (we have not seen him in it this season) that he is now overdoing it. The deuce is in these players, they cannot get a good thing but they spoil it . . . His Douglas, his Romeo, his Benedick – many more – are or were excellent; but the rude hand of Chronos, we are afraid, has interfered to take away the bloom of his acting in such characters . . .

It was the self-obsessed Macready, that old thorn in the Kemble side, who was singled out as 'a scholar and a gentleman, and, if we except Kean, the only man at present upon the stage who has *inspirations*'.

Charles Kemble was even denied his 'taste'. For all the pains Fanny's father had taken over the years to study the Bard's meaning, the reviewer gave him no credit as a thoughtful interpreter of Shakespeare. Instead he was portrayed as a vain man, with a bloated sense of his own talents that led him to hog all the best roles for himself and his daughter – a strategy that forced him to make up the commercial deficiency with vulgar, gallery-pleasing entertainments.

> Conscious it would seem of being ill provided, the manager has called in T.P. Cooke from the minor theatres, to display his talents in various 'tales of the sea'. In nautical characters Cooke is excellent; but is not *Black Eye'd Susan* a most nauseating piece of blubbering sentiment? . . . we submit that its popularity is a strong proof of the decided cockneyism of the London audiences.[4]

Charles Kemble's world had fragmented around him. The window in time when talent as a dramatic artist had been a means to reach the heart of the aristocracy had closed. Even while Fanny's father poured his energies into keeping the Patent Theatre alive, the upper-classes were abandoning the theatres for the more exclusive entertainment of the Opera.

Fanny only knew what her parents told her of the Westmacott incident, supplemented by a glance at reports in the more respectable newspapers. She claimed to be indifferent 'to everything that is said about me', although when her father told her of the 'doxy' reference she 'could not help blushing with indignation to my fingers' ends'.

Her father was bullish about the action he had taken. 'The law affords no redress against such attacks as this paper makes on people, and I thought it time to take justice in my own hands when my daughter is insulted.'

Fanny was more cautious.

> Perhaps . . . it is not surprising that my father has done what he has, but I think I should have admired him more if he had not. Mr Westmacott means to bring an action against him, and I am afraid he will have to pay dearly for his momentary indulgence of temper.[5]

The last thing Charles Kemble needed was to be embroiled in another law suit. Fanny's response to the incident was to redouble her determination to find a publisher for her play and poems so that she might create a fund against any possible damages. There was a new note of exasperation in her exclamation to Hal over the whole affair: 'What does my poor, dear father expect, but that I shall be bespattered if I am to live upon the highway?'[6]

Fanny's love for her father had shifted from the unquestioning adoration of a child to settle around the conviction that he was an other-worldly being, dependent on her support and protection. Her experiences as an actress – the encounters with Lawrence, the uses the management put her to, the Westmacott episode – unquestionably left Fanny resentful, a resentment that manifested itself in her view of her Aunt Siddons.

Mrs Siddons was now seventy-five and in poor health. Fanny was haunted by her aunt's shrunken state. The legendary actress was still greeted with a wave of applause whenever she appeared in her box at Covent Garden. And yet –

> What a price has she paid for her great celebrity! – weariness, vacuity, and utter deadness of spirit. The cup has been so highly flavoured that life is absolutely without savour or sweetness to her now, nothing but tasteless insipidity. She has stood on a pinnacle till all things have come to look flat and dreary . . . Poor woman! What a fate to be condemned to, and yet how she had been envied as well as admired![7]

Here was a warning of the consequences of becoming the creature of that whimsical entity 'the public': their favour robbed the performer of privacy, trivialized their individuality and in the end rendered them a desiccated and ridiculous husk of what the human being should have been.

When Mrs Siddons, dressed in hoop and feathers, had made her audience believe that the trials of Belvidera or the passions of Lady Macbeth spoke to them of the human condition, she stood on a relatively bare stage against stylized sets, often out on the apron stage that literally brought her into the very midst of her spectators –

some of whom could be sitting to either side of her on the boards. Cocooned in the soft light of candles diffused by the mirror-backs of crystal chandeliers, these conditions served to wrap up the acting experience in a mystery that fostered a respect, and even awe, of the charismatic performer as a communicator of humanity touched by the gods.

In contrast, by her niece's day, the dramatic action had receded behind and within the picture frame of the proscenium arch. There, Fanny (with the added disadvantage of her short stature) worked as a small figure – a cartoon almost – set amongst increasingly busy sets, her features impersonalized by the Grand Guignol shadows thrown by the harsh up-lighting of gas- and oil-lamps. It was a distance that cut the magnetic connection between living beings, and detached the audience from the performer. The player became a commodity whose value was created by public admiration and was stripped of that value as the admiration waned. Thus the actor was reduced to a public lay-figure, a skilled tradesman at best, rather than an artist.

The *Fraser's Magazine* article presented Fanny with some harsh personal criticisms. The over-blown praises with which the critics had greeted Miss Kemble's début had 'done her mischief in more ways than one' and the provincial audiences of Fanny's recent summer tour had been the first to recognize the imposition.[8] Fanny stood accused of arrogance and her Kemble diction was mocked.

> Her odd and affected pronunciation has daily become more odd and more affected: – 'whole' was originally 'hull' – now 'soul' is 'sull' – 'roll', 'rull' etc . . . The capricious up and down intonations of her voice have become more capricious . . . She has no new conceptions of any importance, and her general style is manneristical . . . she may believe, when we tell her, that she is not a first-rate actress.[9]

The Westmacott incident brought home to Fanny all that she hated about her profession – the public exposure, the greasepaint, the sickly smell of the gas and making sham love to a portly, whiskered Romeo in the harsh light of the stage-lamps. The sting of the specific slights would soon fade. Fanny would go on to many more successes as an actress but the incident marked a sea-change. From that point she was convinced that she would never be free to live as herself unless she could free herself from the stage.

The year 1830 was a watershed. Old certainties crumbled and shifted. The image of the Duke of Wellington sitting stiff-backed and grim in face of hostile crowds in Manchester at the opening of Stephenson's railway proved prophetic. That autumn a disastrous harvest ignited rumbling discontent. There were incidents of machine-breaking in the Midlands and the North, while in the South letters circulated threatening the well-to-do with violence and arson in the name of 'Captain Swing'.*

The Covent Garden management responded to the uncertainty by resorting to more Siddonian revivals. There was one success among them – the German melodrama *The Stranger* in which Fanny appeared, dressed in grey silk, as the reformed sinner Mrs Haller playing opposite her father in the title role as her husband. Fanny had toothache, which may have coloured her sour commentary that *The Stranger* 'is the quintessence of trashy sentimentalism; but our audiences cry and sob at it till we can hardly hear ourselves speak on the stage, and the public in general rejoices in what the servant-maids call "something deep"'.† In a time of public crisis audiences were finding the familiar reassuring.

At the West End parties Fanny attended several nights a week the talk was all of social chaos:

---

*'Captain Swing' was the mythical leader of the agricultural riots in Southern England in 1830.

†Thackeray in Chapter IV of his satirical novel *Pendennis* neatly sums up the way in which *The Stranger* is also the quintessence of melodrama: 'If a man were to say it is a stupid play, he would not be far wrong. Nobody ever talked so. If we meet idiots in real life, as will happen, it is a great mercy that they do not use such absurdly fine words. *The Stranger*'s talk is sham, like the book he reads, and the hair he wears, and the bank he sits on, and the diamond ring he makes play with. But, in the midst of all the balderdash, there runs that reality of love, children and forgiveness, which sets all the world sympathizing.'

> The alarm and anxiety of the aristocracy is extreme, and exhibits itself . . . in the half-angry, half-frightened tone of their comments on public events. If one did not sympathize with their apprehensions, their mode of expressing them would sometimes be amusing.

Fanny shared the conviction about the importance of social discipline, that preservative against 'the recklessness bred of insecure means and obscure position'. After all their heroic efforts and hard work, insecurity was threatening to engulf the Kembles once more.

While Westmacott's threat of a costly action for damages hung over the household, the absence of news about John Mitchell was a constant anxiety. Charles Kemble finally recognized that the whereabouts of his eldest son could no longer be kept secret from his wife and Fanny had to break the news. Her mother's reaction was hysterical, as anticipated. The newspapers reported that the Constitutionalists had found the Spanish King prepared and his coasts guarded. There was a price on the head of Torrijos and of any man who followed him. John Mitchell's family could only hope that the conspirators would stay out of harm's way in Gibraltar. Marie-Thérèse's seething anxiety affected her health and a miasma of depression filled the household once more.

With her confidence in her father's omnipotence gone, and left to cope with both stage work and her ailing mother, Fanny's frustration with her errant sibling grew. While she – a girl who might have expected the protection of her menfolk – had been out at work in the world for over a year to support their family, the eldest son, two years her senior, had cast himself into danger without a thought to his responsibilities. 'Heaven only knows what plans he has formed for the future! . . . It is . . . melancholy . . . that such abilities should be wasted and misapplied.'[11] Yet another of the men she had so admired in her girlhood was failing to live up to her trust in him. A side-effect of her disillusionment was a growth in her own self-confidence. As the Reform agitation overflowed into the very streets where she lived, Fanny was no longer in the mood to leave politics to men. 'These troubled times make politicians of us all,' she told her Irish friend.

On 16 November the Duke of Wellington was forced to resign, leaving his reluctant King, William IV, with no choice but to invite Lord Grey* to form a Whig ministry with the declared purpose of piloting a Reform Bill through Parliament. In the midst of this turbulence Hal arrived in London on a much anticipated visit. She knew the house at Great Russell Street almost better than its present occupants, for she and her brother had passed many happy days there as guests of John Philip and his wife Priscilla. The contrast between the life she had witnessed then and the tensions of the present household was unspoken confirmation of all that had slipped away.

Her philosophical friend bolstered Fanny's growing confidence in her own opinions on public matters. Hal had a firm belief in the importance to a rational female of being well informed about public events and she tried to get Fanny to read the newspapers every day. Fanny never took to the habit but there was plenty to discuss; almost every morning brought fresh reports of some new riot or outrage.

'The country is in a more awful state than you can well conceive,' wrote Arthur Hallam dramatically from Cambridge on 2 December. 'While I write, Maddingly, or some adjoining village is in a state of conflagration and the sky above is coloured flame red. This is one of a thousand such actions committed daily throughout England. The laws are almost suspended; the money of foreign factions is at work with a population exasperated to reckless fury.'[12] Merivale, another member of the Apostolic circle, pointed out that the fire proved to be 'some twenty-three ricks . . . set alight (no houses)'.[13] But whatever

---

*The 66-year-old Lord Grey was a veteran of the Whig moves towards reform, having been Charles James Fox's lieutenant in the campaign for parliamentary reform that was cut off by the French Revolution.

the reality, the panic at Cambridge was indicative of the rumours and fear circulating among the prosperous that winter.*

Hal's visit was all too short. In the third week of December, accompanied by Fanny's younger sister, she departed all bundled up for the rigours of a winter journey to Ardgillan where Adelaide was invited to spend Christmas. 'I stood in the dining room listening to your carriage wheels until I believe they were only rolling in my imagination. You cannot fancy how doleful our breakfast was.' Wandering through Hal's vacated room, Fanny pounced on two essays by the American Unitarian preacher William Ellery Channing that her friend had overlooked in her packing, and set to reading them by way of intellectual connection with her lost company. She struggled against the resurfacing of her childish sense of abandonment, filling the lonely hours left over from her theatrical work with her latest literary project – a tragedy called *The Star of Seville*.

There was one highlight amid the gloom. On Christmas Eve all available members of the extended family gathered at Mrs Siddons's home in Baker Street. That night all Fanny's images of her aunt's decay faded before the sight of her venerable predecessor surrounded by more than three dozen of her children, grandchildren, nephews and nieces, 'some of them so handsome, and many with a striking likeness to herself'. Edinburgh Harriot was there, as elegant as ever, accompanied by her two lady-like daughters and two gentlemanly sons. Fanny was able to revisit her girlish romance with her Cousin Henry – she now the celebrated star of the stage and he a young ensign handsome in his uniform as he enjoyed his last

*'It was imagined that there was a plan for a general strike for wages, throughout the country,' recorded Merivale, 'but I believe that there is only one place . . . at which anything of the kind has taken place.' Nonetheless, the Mayor of Cambridge swore in 'an amazing number of special constables' and the students of Trinity prepared to defend their college, organizing themselves into six troops under elected captains. 'I look on with exceeding amusement at the alarms of my neighbours,' observed the sanguine Merivale. 'Some of my friends could not go to bed last night without looking into their beds, and overhauling their trunks for fireballs and other dreadful engines which Swing (the alleged leader) is supposed to be in the habit of placing there by means of air-guns.'

Christmas at home before sailing to make his career in India. Horace Twiss, MP, was also there with his handsome young wife. Cousin Horace was not quite his usual witty self, having just lost 'a very good place owing to the unexpected going out of the Tory Ministry', but he still managed to gossip entertainingly with Marie-Thérèse who was on form that night – her 'voice like a silver trumpet ringing through the house'.[14]

For all the jibes of Westmacott and his like, the clan had come a long way since Sarah Siddons and John Philip Kemble's early days as strolling players. And yet, the vignette of Edinburgh Cousin Harriot presiding serene among her upper-middle-class brood was symbolic. Whatever cachet the Drama had bestowed on the family in the past, respectability in the future hung on an ability to move off the stage and into the drawing room.

21

Looking for Bassanio

In the unseasonably spring-like weather of January 1831, Fanny Kemble carried her first play as sole star. She appeared as Bianca, the heroine of Fazio,* a new tragedy by the Reverend Henry Hart Milman,† without her father in the cast. She made light of this emancipation – 'I hear, people object to my father's constant support, and wish to see me act alone; what geese, to be sure! I wonder whether they think my father has hold of strings by the means of which he moves my arms and legs.'[1] Nonetheless, at twenty-one, she had outgrown the role of Miranda. Her recognition of her own economic power and professional identity caught

*Although *Fazio* was a new play, its form and content were strictly traditional. The theme is jealousy. Set in some suitably historic Italian past, the heroine, Bianca, finds her husband, Fazio, has been tempted by Aldabella, the local scarlet woman. In a jealous rage, Bianca denounces her faithless spouse on a trumped-up charge of theft complicated by suspicion of murder. Once he is condemned to death, she repents and appeals to Aldabella who can exonerate him. Proving that all sirens are bad to the bone, her rival refuses and Fazio is executed. Bianca denounces Aldabella as the origin of all her misfortunes, gets her locked up in a nunnery and then, her work done, dies of a broken heart on the line: 'It breaks, it breaks – it is not iron.'

†Milman, a family friend of the Charles Kembles, was a literary cleric and Professor of Poetry at Oxford who ended up as Dean of St Paul's Cathedral in London.

her in a dilemma. Fanny Kemble was not a natural rebel. She wrestled to square her sense of self with conventional expectations of womanhood.

That winter Fanny's acquaintance with Anna Jameson took on a new dimension. It had been several years since the Irish author's first success with her *Diary of an Ennuyée*. Now thirty-seven, her virtual abandonment by her husband had left her with no option but to make her own living. Since the previous year, she had been eager to draw Fanny into discussions about Shakespeare's heroines, to help with her book *Shakespeare's Heroines: Characteristics of Women, Moral, Poetical and Historical*, which would be published in 1832.

Anna Jameson began to call regularly at Great Russell Street, climbing the three flights of stairs up to Fanny's apartments to pursue conversations in which the pair explored models of womanhood within the authenticating context of Shakespeare.* Neither of them questioned the traditional assumption that God had created man to be the master and protector of woman. Anna was careful to state that 'the intellect of woman bears the same relation to that of a man as her physical organization; – it is inferior in power, and different in kind'.[2] But she argued that while a woman's intellect was inferior in *power* to a man's, it had *moral* qualities that made it valuable in its own right. While Anna Jameson accepted that it was in the female nature to owe authority to the male, she pointed to Shakespeare's Portia as the image of the true nature of woman.

Portia's story addressed the dilemma preoccupying both Anna and Fanny: how could a self-sufficient female come to terms with surrendering her identity to the role of wife, when convention and law treated the wife as a mere dependent of her husband? And if she

---

*As Anna would later explain in her preface – 'These studies were [not] written . . . to present a complete commentary on Shakespeare's women . . . but . . . merely to throw into a pleasing and intelligible form some observations of the natural workings of the mind and feeling in my own sex which might lead to good.'

was to resist such effacement, did that make her an 'unnatural' woman?

Neither Anna nor Fanny could quite face up to the implications of their own sense of self. On the one hand they knew their own worth; on the other they were profoundly uncomfortable with the notion of social rebellion. The love story of Portia and Bassanio offered a comforting fiction that appeared to square the circle.

Portia's father is dead, leaving her in sole control of his fortune (although she is bound by his will in her choice of suitor, so patriarchal authority is not denied). Portia's wealth gives material substance to the theoretical worth of a virtuous woman and, because of it, Portia is able to act. She might have to cross-dress as a young lawyer to do so, it is true, but she still saves the day and gets to marry the man she loves – and through it all she remains 'a true lady'.*

For both Fanny and Anna the casket scene (Act III, Scene I) was the fulcrum of the story. Bassanio, the suitor that Portia favours – rejecting outward appearances for the worth concealed within[3] – selects the right casket and wins Portia's hand in marriage. She then gives herself to him in a speech[4] that both author and actress highlighted as certifying Portia's femininity – proving her 'not less loveable as a woman, than admirable for her mental endowments'.

The picture is of a woman who surrenders herself entirely to her lover in 'generous self-denial'. Anna Jameson had a vivid sense of the enormity of that self-denial –

> [Portia's] subsequent surrender of herself in heart and soul, of her maiden freedom, and her vast possessions, can never be read without deep emotions . . . It is, in truth, an awful moment, that in which a gifted woman first discovers, that besides talents and powers, she has also passion and affections; . . . when she first confesses that her happiness . . . is

*Other critics disputed this reading – Hazlitt for one thought Portia unattractive and pedantic.

> surrendered for ever and for ever into the dominion of another! The possession of uncommon powers of mind is so far from affording relief or resource in the first intoxicating surprise – I had almost said terror – of such a revolution, that they render it more intense.[5]

Fanny was younger then and refused to be quite so despondent,* although her reading of the play was not entirely complimentary to Bassanio:

> . . . chance . . . gives [Portia] to the man she loves, a handsome, extravagant young gentleman, who would certainly have been pronounced by all of us quite unworthy of her, until she proved him worthy by the very fact of her preference for him; [6]

Fanny set great store by the fact that Bassanio was a gentleman[7] (on the principle that a gentleman treated a lady with respect). Apart from that bare security, the seductive fiction was that Portia's leap of faith was a self-fulfilling gesture of romantic heroism: since Portia's love was true then her virtue and wisdom would *make* the man she loved worthy – her love would redeem him.

Fanny was able to report to Hal that *Fazio* had 'made a great hit'. The success was entirely hers, for her Fazio was Mr Warde, an actor known for little save his remarkable resemblance to Napoleon.† She was touched and pleased that her mother (who, it might be argued,

*Their disagreement on such points may have been behind Fanny's judgement that 'Mrs Jameson's . . . work on Shakespeare's female characters . . . are very pleasing sketches – outlines – but her criticism and analysis are rather graceful than profound or powerful.' Letter to Hal, Sunday, 13 March 1831, *Records of a Girlhood* vol. II, p. 287.

†He had had some success in the title role of a sensational melodrama called *Bonaparte*. Fanny's rather brutal dismissal of her co-star was that Mr Warde was 'a very respectable actor' with 'no genius whatever' who 'never rose above irreproachable mediocrity'.

had extensive experience of the emotion of jealousy) praised her interpretation of the self-tortured heroine.

Her mother had been cheered by news from her eldest son. John Mitchell was alive and well in Gibraltar.* In his letter he admitted that 'all hope of rousing the Spaniards [was] over'. Lost without a cause, he sat in Gibraltar vacillating towards a law career one moment and dreams of a life of foreign adventuring the next. Richard Trench, the last of the Apostles to accompany him to Spain, called at Great Russell Street to tell the Kembles that he had tried his best to make Jack board the boat with him, but he had declared that he could not abandon Torrijos.

There were other worries. Covent Garden Theatre had become embroiled in a vital lawsuit. Mr Arnold of the English Opera House had initiated an action claiming that 'the right to act the legitimate drama . . . should be extended to all British subjects desirous to open play-houses and perform plays'.[8] A Parliamentary committee was set up to investigate the desirability of deregulation. The challenge to the validity of the Patents struck at the heart of Charles Kemble's sole financial asset. If Arnold was successful then it would be the final end of the Kemble House.† The tension was palpable as Fanny rehearsed Beatrice in *Much Ado about Nothing* with Marie-Thérèse, her sharp-tongued coach claiming that her eldest daughter played the mischievous Beatrice 'like the head mourner at a funeral'.‡

---

*It seems likely that the lack of communication had been sheer carelessness on John's part. Fanny later discovered that, finding the Spanish King alerted and the element of surprise denied them, the young English adventurers had rented a comfortable house, christened it 'Constitution Hall' and settled down to a pleasant winter of 'smoking and drinking ale' while her brother held 'forth upon German metaphysics, which grew dense in proportion as the tobacco fumes grew thick and his glass grew empty'.

†A new Lord Chamberlain had begun to liberalize the licensing system. For instance, the Haymarket season had been extended from the summer alone to ten months of the year. Already performers were leaving Covent Garden and Drury Lane to play other venues at higher salaries. As Alfred Bunn explained – 'The public not being a dramatic public, not caring a fig how the piece was sustained throughout so long as they could see a leading actor in a principal part, would naturally rather pay 4 shillings to see Mr Kean in a theatre nearer their own homes than 7 shillings to see him in Drury Lane Theatre.' (Bunn, vol. I, pp. 48–9.)

‡Despite which, Fanny liked her role. She boasted that she learned her lines in an hour – 'it will be the second part which I shall have acted with real pleasure' (Portia being the other).

In the House of Commons Lord John Russell introduced the First Reform Bill against a background of freakish natural phenomena.* 'I saw by the paper today that an earthquake had been felt along the coast near Dover. Adelaide says the world is coming to an end,' wrote Fanny in her weekly letter to Hal.[9]

The management and her own father continued to push Fanny into roles at random, rarely even giving her the courtesy of early warning of the next part. 'Heaven knows . . . I never even object to anything I am bidden to do; that is, never visibly or audibly,' she complained to Hal. She had taken to visiting the Zoological Gardens with her brother Henry to watch a handsome tigress who paced her cage there. 'I admire and envy the wild beast's swiftness and strength,' she explained wistfully to her friend; 'but if I had them I don't think I would tear human beings to bits unless I were she; do you see?'[10]

As usual, in her frustration, Fanny took refuge in her literary pursuits. She made a fresh start on her second tragedy, *The Star of Seville* – 'I wish I could make anything like an acting play of it; we want one or two new ones so very much.' At the same time she revised her first play, *Francis I*, slipping next door to the British Museum to check historical details.

Her efforts were rewarded when John Murray, the well-known publisher of Byron, paid her the princely sum of £450 for the copyright of *Francis I*. 'I am so happy, so thankful for this prosperous result of my work, so delighted at earning so much . . . it is too good almost to be true, and yet it is true.'† She rushed out and bought her sister a guitar and a new dress in heavenly blue velvet for herself.

That weekend, storms struck the South of England. Young Adelaide was quite terrified; even Fanny was 'awed'. She got down the encyclopaedia to try to explain the causes behind equinoctial gales to her sister, but found herself none the wiser. The weather

*1 March 1831.

†In the late eighteenth century prints of popular plays had been money earners for the publishers, but by 1831 the market had fallen off. That Murray paid £450 for *Francis I* testified to his high estimate of the selling power of Fanny's celebrity.

seemed to have caught the general unease. The true thunder-clap for Fanny, however, was the information that she was to attempt the part of Queen Constance in Shakespeare's *King John* so that her father could play his ageing Falconbridge for her Benefit.

'Shut your eyes while you read this, because if you don't, they'll never shut again,' she wrote in terror to Hal. 'I am horribly frightened; it is a cruel weight to lay upon my shoulders . . . I almost think now I could do Lady Macbeth better. I am like poor little Arthur, who begged to have his tongue cut off rather than have his eyes put out . . . Pray for me.'[11]

Weighed down under a massive cloak and an exact copy of the head-dress her Aunt Siddons used to wear in the part, she did her duty. She was deaf throughout the play* and afterwards 'lay . . . for an hour on my dressing-room floor, with only strength enough left to cry'. Fortunately, the performance passed off almost unnoticed before a thin house. It had coincided with the Second Reading of the Reform Bill.

Fanny was now preoccupied with a more congenial challenge. Perhaps in reward for her Queen Constance, for the first time the theatre management mounted a play of her choosing. She had been lobbying for Massinger's *The Maid of Honour* – as edited and 'purified' of its lewdness by the Reverend Alexander Dyce – ever since she first came across Dyce's edition of the text some months earlier. She was struck by the power of the play's forceful heroine Camiola.

> . . . there was at once a resemblance to and a difference from my favourite character, Portia, that made it a study of much interest to me. Both the women, young, beautiful, and of unusual intellectual and moral excellence, are left heiresses to

*'My Constance [is] . . . over,' she wrote to Hal a couple of days later, 'but I am at this moment still so deaf with nervousness as not to hear the ticking of my watch when held to one of my ears; the other side of my head is not deaf any longer now; but on Monday night I hardly heard one word I uttered through the whole play.'

enormous wealth, and are in exceptional positions of power and freedom in the disposal of it.[12]

Comparisons between the two characters prompted more meditations on how intelligence and economic independence affected a woman's femininity.

In her journal Fanny noted a conversation around the Kemble dinner-table about *The Maid of Honour*.* Female love, she stated, 'is characterized generally by self-devotion and self-denial . . . as women are by nature dependent on and inferior to men.'[13] Camiola is dependent on no one. A merchant's daughter who is wealthy in her own right, Camiola falls in love with a noble warrior-hero. He is captured and she uses her fortune to buy his liberty on the understanding that he will marry her. When he jilts her in favour of a duchess, she denounces his caddish behaviour. He repents and comes back to her – whereupon she informs him that she has decided to become a nun instead.

Camiola highlighted the difficulty of how a capable maiden was to assert her virtue and value without seeming strident and unwomanly. 'What in Portia is the gentle wisdom of a noble nature appears, in Camiola, too much a spirit of calculation . . . Camiola is sensible and sententious: she asserts her dignity very successfully; but we cannot for a moment imagine that Portia is reduced to the necessity of asserting hers.'

Fanny's reflections led her to the conclusion that a woman with her own means was most likely to retain her due respect if she married a richer gentleman (or like Mrs Fitzgerald, Edward's bold mother, she would be tempted to dominate her husband in an 'unwomanly' way). A rich Bassanio would be her template – a 'scholar and a soldier',[14] a well-mannered gentleman who combined intellect with authority.

Fanny's Camiola,† dressed in 'amber-coloured cashmere and

---

*April 1831.

†On 25 April 1831.

white satin', enhanced her reputation as an actress but her public did not warm to that managing, unbending vision of womanhood. Reluctantly she admitted that it was 'a cold play, according to the present taste of audiences'.* After this Covent Garden gave tragedy a rest for a while.

The struggle over Reform was dominating public affairs. The Tories defeated Charles Grey's Whig government in a committee stage of the Bill's progress. The King dissolved Parliament and called a General Election, at which the Reformers were returned with a majority. The Lord Mayor of London ordered a general illumination to celebrate.

> The streets are thronged with people and choked up with carriages, and the air is flashing and crashing with rockets and squibs and crackers, to the great discomfort of the horses. So many R's everywhere that they may stand for reform, revolution, ruin . . . according to the interpretation of every individual's politics.[15]

At Great Russell Street the gloomy talk among the adults was on how the family was to survive the likely eventual collapse of the theatre.

> Dall was saying that she thought in two years of hard work we might – that is, my father and myself – earn enough to enable us to live in the South of France. This monstrous theatre and its monstrous liabilities will banish us all as it did my Uncle Kemble.

For a moment Fanny revisited her old dreams of a life of literary seclusion in southern climes.

> But that I should be sorry to live so far out of the reach of Hal, I think the South of France would be a pleasant abode: a delicious climate, a quiet existence, a less artificial state of

---

*Fanny's own verdict was that the role was the 'best thing I have acted.'

> society, . . . a picturesque nature round me, and my own dear ones and my scribbling with me – I think . . . I could be happy enough in the South of France or anywhere.

On the other hand, perhaps marriage would not be so terrible an alternative after all.

In the previous generation, Fanny's mother had known more than one actress who had married well. There was her witty colleague Louisa Brunton who had become the Countess of Craven, and Miss O'Neill – Charles Kemble's sometime Juliet – who was now the respectable Lady Beecher. Marie-Thérèse believed her talented daughter had a chance of making a brilliant marriage. Rallying her failing energy, Fanny's mother looked up an old friend, the ancient and redoubtable Lady Cork.

A couple of generations before – when George III still had his wits – Lady Cork, then Mary Monckton, had been a maid of honour to the wife of one of the royal princes. By 1831 she was a spirited nonagenarian who made liberal use of her age to win the indulgence of genteel society.* Lady Cork was an original. She had a habit of carrying off pieces of other people's property whenever they caught her fancy,† despite which the best people attended the assemblies she held in her lofty rooms where she presided dressed in white like a little witch bride or a more cheerful version of Charles Dickens's Miss Havisham. Her eccentricities made her just the person to give Fanny a chance of presenting herself as marriageable material to the right sort of man. She was wise in the ways of society and Fanny records a telling vignette of her mother trying to make a social date with her:

> 'Wednesday – no, Wednesday won't do,' says Lady Cork as she goes through her appointment book. 'Lady Holland dines with

*Such as the note she once sent to draw Samuel Rogers away from a concert of early music – 'Dear Rogers, leave the ancient music and come to ancient Cork, 93.'

†Including, on one occasion, a door-porter's pet hedgehog which, at her next stop, Lady Cork exchanged for a sponge-cake with a baker, assuring him that it would eat the black beetles that she knew on good authority always infested bakeries.

me – naughty lady! – won't do, my dear. Thursday?'

'Very sorry, Lady Cork, we are engaged.'

'Ah yes, so am I; let's see – Friday; no, Friday I have the Duchess of C——, another naughty lady; mustn't come then, my dear. Saturday?'

'No, Lady Cork, I am very sorry – Saturday, we are engaged to Lady D[acre?].'

'Oh dear, oh dear! Improper lady too! But a long time ago, everybody's forgotten all about it – very proper now! Quite proper now!'[16]

Marie-Thérèse made every effort to guard her daughter's reputation. Her mother's caution, however, could not guard Fanny from Covent Garden. As his response to Westmacott indicated, Charles Kemble meant to be a careful father. He banned his daughter from the Green Room, that delightful parade ground of wit and charm, in case she should encounter 'undesirable associates'. But some 'undesirable associates' did not confine themselves to the Green Room.

A prime example of a prowling male was Francis Henry Fitzhardinge Berkeley, the youngest of seven bastards of the 5th Earl of Berkeley and his mistress.* In the early 1830s Henry Berkeley was killing time while he waited for his legitimate brother Thomas, the 6th Earl, to find him something from family holdings. His elder (illegitimate) brother, an enthusiastic amateur actor, had been a good friend of Sarah Siddons and John Kemble in the early years of the century, and young Berkeley was excellent company, so Charles Kemble did not think twice about welcoming him at his theatre. In his thirties, a proficient musician, an excellent – if reckless – sportsman,† a charming and successful womanizer, Henry Berkeley was a cautious mother's nightmare. He enjoyed lounging backstage (he found more than one mistress there). If Fanny came across him

*Henry Berkeley's parents did eventually marry and produced another six legitimate offspring.

†He was said to be one of the best amateur boxers of his generation.

occasionally talking to her father at the theatre, shrewd Aunt Dall would always be at her elbow ensuring that she was not *too* well entertained. It was probably fortunate for Marie-Thérèse's nerves that neither sister had an inkling of the role Berkeley was later to play in Fanny's future fate.

Another noble bastard was more persistent. A stout, earnest young man emerged as a faithful occupant of one of the stage boxes in the autumn of Fanny's second season. Soon he had advanced closer to the acting area, occupying one of the reserved orchestra seats, then one night Fanny was startled to see him standing in the wings. Throughout the performance she kept being distracted by glimpses of the light kid gloves he clutched in one hand 'waving and gesticulating about' as he echoed her dramatic distress in reverential dumb show. Her father admitted, slightly shamefaced, that the young man was the Reverend Augustus Fitz-Clarence, the natural son of the much-loved comedienne Dorothy Jordan and her royal lover, now King William IV. He explained that the young man had accosted him, pleading for his dead mother's sake* to be allowed to watch the play from backstage. The manager murmured his opinion that backstage was hardly a suitable environment for a clergyman, but he did not know how to refuse such a heartfelt request.

Fitz-Clarence became a bit of a pest. He insisted on being presented to Fanny, but as she never lingered backstage, she was able to limit her acknowledgement of his attentions to abstracted nods and little bows as she passed on her way to and from the stage. Finally, he tracked her down at a society ball and rushed up, exclaiming, 'Oh, do come and dance with me, that's a dear good girl.' He had a charming voice (inherited, it was said, from his mother) and as she liked to dance Fanny did so, but she found her partner's conversation so unseemly that she would remember their brief encounter for the rest of her life.[17]

---

*At the height of her fame Dorothy Jordan generously lent the weight of her popularity to the first play Marie-Thérèse ever wrote, playing the heroine of *First Faults* opposite Charles Kemble at Drury Lane in May 1799.

Seeing her face light up as they performed the movements of a quadrille, her partner demanded, 'Who are you nodding and smiling to? Oh, your father. You are very fond of him, ain't you?

'Ah yes, just so. I dare say you are,' continued Fitz-Clarence at Fanny's enthusiastic nod, going on to express his dislike of his own father so aggressively that the Royalist Fanny was shocked. At first she thought he was drunk. She told him firmly that if he did not behave himself she would leave him alone on the dance floor. He immediately apologized, submitting a potted history of his life in his own defence.

He had good reason to dislike his father. His mother (Dorothy Jordan) had been the then Duke of Clarence's faithful mistress for many years. She bore him ten children and frequently contributed her earnings to her royal lover's upkeep. Nonetheless, when he realized that he was to become King, Augustus's father shed his mother unceremoniously, ultimately allowing her to die neglected after several years spent in poverty in France. 'Tuss', as he was known to his family, was not so indiscreet as to bring this story up in a ballroom, but he told Fanny how he had been destined for the Navy (his father's chosen career) from the age of three. The sea life had suited him and he had been happy. But then an elder brother died, leaving the lucrative family living of Maple Durham free. Without warning Tuss was plucked from his ship and forced to become a clergyman, a life that made him miserable. As he explained loudly to Fanny as they met and parted in the dance, 'Some people have a natural turn for religion; you have, for instance, I'm sure; but you see I have not.'

Embarrassed to be the recipient of such unwelcome revelations, Fanny suggested primly that since he found himself in that 'sacred calling' perhaps he should attempt to conform to it 'at least by outward decency of language and decorum of demeanour'. That silenced him for a moment but he soon rallied, asking her brightly if she could help him out by writing a sermon for him. Fanny, who recognized that she had been preaching, could not help laughing out loud at the idea. She told him that it was an improper suggestion and that he ought to write his own. 'Yes,' the sailor cleric replied with touching humility, 'but you see I can't – not good ones, at least. I'm sure you could; I wish you would write one for me. Mrs Norton has.'

At which point the dance ended and Fanny was able to escape. Her admirer never caught a moment with her again. The encounter led her to question the legitimacy of the Church of England as a propagator of God's truth more than all the free-thinking arguments of her brother's friend, John Sterling.

Had Fanny been a different woman, it is conceivable that she might have snagged the Reverend Fitz-Clarence as a husband.* However, the harsh truth was that he might only have seen her as mistress material. Given her morals and her respect for her own intellect, only a Bassanio would tempt Fanny from the single state – and she was about to meet him.

*Although she was by no means naive; in referring to the marriage of Georgiana Sheridan who wed a Duke in 1830, she commented to Hal, 'Matrimony in that world is not always the securest haven for a woman's virtue or happiness; it is sometimes in that society the reverse of an honourable estate.'

22

Augustus

All that April, the capital was on edge. At the theatre rowdy audiences applauded any speech in the drama that could be construed as loyal to the King. When driving at night, houses the Kembles passed were frequently lit up, their householders fearing that dark windows might be smashed by 'Reformers'.

'One hopes and prays that the "Old Heart of Oak" will weather these evil days,' Fanny wrote, 'but sometimes the straining of the tackle and the creaking of the timbers are suggestive of foundering, even to the most hopeful.'[1] The General Election had stalled an appeal that the Patent Theatre Proprietors had before the House of Lords. Charles Kemble's prospects hung in agonizing limbo. 'Oh, what weary work this is for those who are tremblingly waiting for a result of vital importance to their whole fate and fortune!'[2]

It was in this atmosphere that Miss Kemble received an invitation from Lord Francis Leveson-Gower,* the young MP she had met at Heaton the previous summer, to take part in some private theatricals. Leveson-Gower had written a verse translation of Victor Hugo's

*Francis Leveson-Gower was one of those tiresome English aristocrats who kept changing his name. On his father's death in 1833 he became Lord Egerton. In 1846 he was elevated to the dignity of the Earl of Ellesmere. In her memoirs Fanny tends to refer to the couple as Lord and Lady Francis Egerton.

Hernani. When he failed to persuade a theatre manager to take on his play, he hit on the idea of mounting an amateur production to be performed before a select audience at his family's London mansion, Bridgewater House. It occurred to him that the lively Miss Kemble was just the person to give his heroine, Dona Sol, that professional touch.

Lord Francis and his wife, Harriet, would grow into Fanny's 'kind and constant friends' – the wife becoming 'a sort of idol of my girlhood'. Fanny much admired the couple's mutual devotion* despite marked differences of taste. Harriet had no sense of humour and very little imagination (she once informed Fanny solemnly that she was sure she would like poetry if only it could be written in prose) but with the profile of a goddess struck on a Greek coin she was a pattern of integrity – 'excellently conscientious, true and upright'. Mrs Leveson-Gower did not act and her presence through the whole affair gave Fanny the reassurance of respectability.

Lord Francis assured her that she would be performing opposite the most talented amateur actor among his wide acquaintance. The part of her hero, Hernani, was to be filled by Mr Augustus Craven.

It is not clear whether Fanny immediately recognized Augustus Craven as the handsome young ensign she had met all those years ago at that school dance in Paris when she wore her first ballgown with its bright red sash. In later life she dropped a tantalizing suggestion that he had been pursuing her for several months.† However,

---

*According to *The Dictionary of National Biography*, Lord Francis and Harriet were both born on the very first day of the new century, 1 January 1800, an act of togetherness they seem to have sustained throughout their married life.

†When she first began publishing reminiscences in the *Atlantic Monthly* in the late 1870s, Fanny inserted an anecdote beside letters she wrote in May 1830. She said that as her first season drew to a close her father had made last-minute alterations to the start of their summer tour.

> There had been some talk of my beginning with Brighton, but for some reason or other this fell through. I do not suppose the fact of my father's hearing that Captain C—— had made interest with the manager to be allowed to act with me had anything to do with his decision not to go there, as of course no such arrangement could have been fulfilled without our agreement to it, which was impossible; so I am afraid the gentleman amateur was disappointed and annoyed. 'Old Woman's Gossip' XIV, *Atlantic Monthly*, September 1876, p. 333.

the general impression she decided to leave to posterity was that his reappearance was a complete surprise.

On 1 May, a grey, wet Sunday, Fanny sat at home receiving visitors after church. She had just had an hour of Lord and Lady Wilton all in a dither with dark prophesies of revolution and nightmares of their beloved Heaton being burned to the ground, when Craven reentered her life with prints of the costumes for *Hernani* under his arm.

Augustus was perfect casting for the archetypal romantic hero. Described as 'melodramatically' handsome, he was slim and straight with an aquiline nose, 'fine eyes and marked and mobile eyebrows', and he came complete with an aura of mystery. Craven was clearly a gentleman but his family history was a puzzle. It was generally believed that he was the natural son of Keppel Craven, who was the youngest child of Elizabeth, the irrepressible wife of Lord Craven. However, no one knew who his mother was. There are many people who have spent their life in ignorance of their fathers, but very few are kept ignorant of their maternal origins; those who knew Augustus well, said that the secret blighted his whole life. That sections of high society were prepared to overlook such a blank in his family tree was largely due to the fact that Augustus grew up as the pet of his paternal grandmother, Elizabeth.

Elizabeth was born a Berkeley* and at an early age was married off to the 6th Baron Craven. Eventually tiring of her lord and their mutual infidelities, Lady Craven left England in a flurry of scandal taking with her the youngest of her seven children, Keppel (who was generally assumed to have been fathered by someone other than Lord Craven). Lady Craven spent several years enjoying the Continent and its wealthier men before she settled down with the

---

Clues in subsequent paragraphs of the article support the idea that Captain C—— was Augustus Craven. By the time she published her reminiscences in book form, however, Fanny had cut the reference.

*Part of the same rambling aristocratic clan as that Backstage Johnny, Henry Berkeley – although Elizabeth's parents were married.

Margrave of Anspach, a nephew of Frederick the Great. When Lord Craven died in 1791, Lady Craven married her margrave and persuaded him to sell his entire country to Prussia in return for an annuity that made the couple fabulously rich. They moved to England where they lived in luxury in various houses including Brandenburg House in Hammersmith. There the margravine built a theatre (alongside her aviary and ballroom) where she and her friends performed plays she frequently wrote herself.

This was where Augustus was said to have been born in 1804 and grew up to acquire his grandmother's passion for amateur theatricals. The household was racy, colourful and cosmopolitan – during her trial, Queen Caroline made Brandenburg House her headquarters.* Augustus's grandmother had high social ambitions but the English aristocracy smirked at her pride in the many titles she had collected in Europe and refused to address her as 'Elizabeth, Margravine of Brandenburg, Anspach and Bayreuth, and Princess Berkeley of the Holy Roman Empire'. Her beloved son Keppel was passionately devoted to art and travel, writing several books on these subjects. Augustus emerged from this extraordinary household with excellent manners, fluent in several languages and with a refined 'artistic sense'.

When the margravine died, a wrinkled old widow confident to the last that she was 'not only . . . a genius and a beauty, but . . . a pattern for wives, mothers, daughters, sisters and friends',[3] she left a considerable fortune to her son, including three palaces in Italy. Keppel Craven immediately removed to Naples where he set up house with his 'intimate friend and inseparable companion', the distinguished antiquary and archaeologist Sir William Gell, in the Villa Anspach, a palace on the Chiatamone overlooking the bay. Soon the couple were joined by Sir William Drummond, a diplomat and scholar, and the three lived 'in the closest bonds of friendship', as *The Dictionary of National Biography* put it. When their ends came, one after the

*She bestowed the honorary title of 'Chamberlain to the Princess of Wales' on Keppel Craven in thanks for the hospitality.

other, all three were laid to rest in a single tomb in the Protestant cemetery in Naples. As one biographer remarked, Keppel Craven was 'an exquisite of the first water', a hint that only adds to the mystery surrounding his so-called son. 'Not of woman born', Augustus could hardly have had a more appropriately Byronic secret and silent sorrow.

When Augustus entered the drawing room at 79 Great Russell Street that rainy Sunday afternoon he had recently left the Army and was dawdling on his way towards a post as attaché to the British Legation at Naples. He carried the assurance of wealth and the prospect of a substantial inheritance. With his excellent manners and cosmopolitan polish, enough of a gentleman to pass and yet not so noble as to be beyond her reach, fiction could hardly have fashioned Fanny a more appropriate Bassanio.

Fanny drove with her mother to the first rehearsal of *Hernani* at Bridgewater House in an atmosphere of 'nervous excitement'. She found several acquaintances gathered in the cast. 'The acting, which, allowing for a little want of technical experience, was, in Mr Craven's instance, really very good . . . The whole play, I think, will be fairly acted for an amateur performance.'[4] Fanny had the support of one other professional: Mrs Bradshaw, who took the part of Donna Sol's duenna. Everyone was very welcoming and easy. When Lord Francis announced that the next rehearsal would be at his country house, Harriet insisted that Marie-Thérèse and her daughter stay for a couple of days. This invitation was all the more poignant because the country place, it transpired, was Oatlands, the old house with rambling grounds near Eastlands Cottage. 'I should like of all things to see Weybridge once more; there's many a nook and path in those woods that I know better than their owners.' And now the little nobody of her childhood was to be an honoured guest at the big house.

Fanny and her mother left the chatter of the drawing-room

rehearsal for the sobering reality of Aunt Siddons's sickbed. The great actress's body was slowing to a halt. Her legs were swollen and she complained of intense headaches. She was cared for by her ever-faithful daughter, Cecilia. Fanny sat through the visit with her mind as much on Portia, her role that night, as her aunt: 'Poor woman! She suffers dreadfully . . . Cecilia's life has been one of enduring devotion and self-sacrifice. I cannot help wishing, for both their sakes, that the period of her mother's infirmity and physical decay may be shortened,' she noted in her diary before hurrying back to her own life – 'My dear, delightful Portia! The house was good, but the audience dull . . . what with sham business and real business, I have had a busy day.'[5]

A week later, in an afternoon bright with May sunshine, Fanny and her mother set off in an open carriage to retrace the familiar twenty-one-mile journey to Oatlands. The 'hawthorn lay thick and fragrant on every hedge, like snow that winter had forgotten to melt'. They reminisced about old times, pointing out familiar landmarks to one another – the old Walton Bridge and the fine chestnut trees on the banks of the broad, bright Thames. They arrived at their destination to meet the rest of the house-party returning from a ride. Fanny was introduced to Hal's idol, Lord John Russell, the Whig manager of the Reform Bill. His hosts, being of the opposing party, pressed him hard on Reform. He remained good-humoured. Fanny reported to Hal that he responded with 'the well-satisfied smile of a man who thinks himself on the right, and knows himself on the safe side'.

The next day she rose early and set off through 'a bright, sunny morning, the trees all bowing and bending', to trace her way across the park to Weybridge. Eastlands Cottage stood derelict, the vine torn down from its walls, the grass knee-deep and the gate to the wood gone. She ran up the mound 'where John used to stand challenging the echo with his bugle' barely five years before and surveyed the past that had well and truly gone. Gathering a rose and a piece of honeysuckle as a souvenir for her mother, she ran back to breakfast.

If Fanny was interested in Augustus, she knew just how to behave.

In the conversation after dinner – 'sauntering on the lawn' and enjoying 'pleasant, bright talk indoors' – Fanny concentrated on Lord John Russell, who she reported to Hal 'would be quite charming if he wasn't so afraid of the rain'. When it finally came time to rehearse her scenes with Augustus, she flirted with the handsome Captain Shelley,* who took the role of Charles V, *Hernani*'s opponent in the drama. The result was satisfactory. There was 'much pleasant sparring' between the two heroes, and their brief visit ended with the pair driving back to London together 'cheek by jowl, in a pretty equipage of Mr Craven's, in the most amicable mood imaginable'.

Fanny and her mother's visit was cut short by news that John Mitchell was back from Spain. The Kembles packed up and rushed back to welcome the wanderer, Marie-Thérèse overwhelmed with joy to have her lamb back at last.

John Mitchell was subdued. He was no clearer as to what he should do with his future and reluctant to take his place in facing the family's financial problems. Meanwhile Lord Francis's theatricals drew his sister 'daily "deeper and deeper still" in incessant occupations of one sort and another that crowd upon and almost overwhelm me'.[6] There were sittings with the artist John Hayter who was drawing a series of Fanny's attitudes as Juliet;† there were parties and balls and exchanges of visits – and all alongside her 'real work' in the 'real theatre' three times a week.

Fanny was quite candid with herself about her penchant for the high life. 'I pick up and treasure like a baby all the little broken bits of splendour and sumptuousness.' Her sense of 'ideality', she told

---

*Captain Shelley was the son of Sir John Shelley, a 'handsome, good-humoured, pleasant young gentleman'. Fanny wrote of Captain Shelley that he was 'a nice lad, and, considering his beauty, and the admiration bestowed on him by all the fine ladies in London, remarkably unaffected'.

†Mrs Jameson would write a tasteful essay to accompany them and the prints sold well, although Hayter was unable to find a buyer for the originals until some months later when – at a time when the artist was in dire need of cash – Lord Francis stepped in and bought the collection.

Hal wryly, much appreciated 'all the refinements of luxurious civilization'. How could she not delight in 'the music, the lights, the wreaths, and mirrors of a splendid ballroom, and . . . the smooth lawns, bright waters, and lordly oaks of a fine domain'? But she remained aware of the gulf between her situation and that of her new aristocratic friends.

Even in their best intentions, she noted, fine people were insulated in the unconscious arrogance of their wealth. Some charitable ladies told Fanny about Elizabeth Fry, the prison reformer. Fanny was much impressed: 'What a blessed, happy woman to do so much good; to be the means of comfort and consolation, perhaps of salvation, to such desolate souls!' Fanny joined one of Mrs Fry's visits to Newgate Prison but she found the experience an uncomfortable one.

> [Mrs Fry's] divine labour of love had become *famous*, and fine ladies of fashion pressed eagerly to accompany her . . . The unfortunate women she addressed were ranged opposite their less excusable sister sinners of the better class, and I hardly dared to look at them, so entirely did I feel out of my place by the side of Mrs Fry, and so sick for their degraded attitude and position . . . Altogether I felt broken-hearted for *them* and ashamed for us.[7]

Fanny was never wholly at ease among people who lived entirely luxurious lives. At the dress rehearsal of *Hernani*, standing amid the chaos, a glimpse of the room that served as the men's dressing-room – 'rouge, swords, wine, moustaches, soda water and cloaks strewed in every direction' – prompted an acute moment of alienation. 'All those foolish lads, taking such immense delight in that which gives me so very little, dressing themselves up and acting.'[8]

The first performance of *Hernani* took place in the long gallery at Bridgewater House. As 'the finest folk in England' filed in to take their seats, Fanny was in her dressing-room 'literally crying with fright'. The amateurs did well in the glare of their brilliant stage* – although Augustus 'got out' in his first speech. Fanny suspected that a society beauty in the front row might have distracted him, but he recovered and everyone assured one another that it all went off admirably. When the play was repeated a couple of days later, the audience had grown and Fanny had found her confidence.

> At the end of the play, as I lay dead on the stage, the King (Captain Shelley) was cutting three great capers . . . for joy his work was done, when his pretty dancing shoes attracted, in despite of my decease, my attention, and I asked, with rapidly reviving interest in existence, what they meant, on which I was informed that the supper at Mrs Cunliffe's was indeed a ball. I jumped up from the dead, hurried off my stage robes, and hurried on my private apparel.[9]

When a production is the success of the season, it is only natural that one should dance with one's co-star – particularly when both hero and heroine are such graceful dancers. It is no surprise that the relationship with Craven blossomed.

> 'Oh pleasure is a very pleasant thing,' as Byron sings and Henry for ever says . . . Such shoals of partners! Such nice people! Such perfect music! Such a delightful floor! Danced till the day had one eye wide open . . . I hope I have not been very tipsy tonight, but it is difficult with so many stimulants to keep *quite* sober.[10]

Everyone was so very kind. Fanny was the centre of attention and in particular of the attention of her romantic lead. They talked of Dante, and Italy and Shakespeare. Augustus was well read and the

*In an innovation, in contrast to the practice at Covent Garden at the time, the Bridgewater House audience watched the play in darkness while the stage was lit. The first professional theatre in London to darken the auditorium 'to give dignity to the stage' was the Lyceum under the management of Irving during the second half of the nineteenth century. Rowell, p. 92.

melancholy tinge to his charm pleased her, hinting at emotional depths unusual among fine young men.*

Charles Kemble returned to town from acting engagements in the provinces and, to Fanny's pleasure, took over chaperoning duties from his wife, who was finding the pace killing. Her father was indulgent of the enjoyments of the young and at fifty-six still had the stamina to stay flirting with 'all the pretty, pleasant women he meets' until the early hours of the morning. One ball given by a countess at which Fanny danced with Augustus in a magnificent room hung with tapestry deserved special mention in her journal.

> At half-past two, though the carriage had been ordered at two, my father told me he would not 'spoil sport', and so angelically stayed till past four. He is the best of fathers, the most affectionate of parents, the most benevolent of men! There is a great difference between being chaperoned by one's father instead of one's mother: the latter, poor dear! Never flirts, gets very sleepy and tired, and wants to go home before she comes.[11]

In the midst of all this enchantment, Aunt Siddons died. Fanny was more distracted by the personal inconvenience than grief.[12] While her father hurried off to see if he could do anything for Cecilia she sat down to write a note to Lady Francis; she would no longer be able to attend a delightful house-party planned for the coming weekend. Her time with Augustus was running out and in a couple of weeks she and her father would be touring.

Her father was aware of her disappointment. That evening at dinner, talking of the engagements he had arranged through the West Country ending up at Southampton, he said: '"Suppose we take the

---

*As one biographer wrote of Craven: 'At best his humour was rooted in serious thought. The mystery which attached to his birth affected him painfully throughout life. But if he had the trials which belong to emotional though reserved natures, he had the compensations of deep and earnest feeling.' – Bishop vol. II, p. 194.

steamer thence to Marseilles, and so on to Naples?" My heart jumped into my mouth at the thought; but how should I come back again?'

Naples, of course, was where Augustus would be. That Charles Kemble raised the possibility suggests that he perceived his daughter was serious about Augustus and he was prepared to encourage the relationship.

The implications of her aunt's death began to dawn on Fanny. News came from the management that now she would be expected to play Lady Macbeth. 'I feel as if I were standing up by the great pyramid of Egypt to see how tall I am! . . . the Lady Macbeth will never be seen again! I wish just now that in honour of my aunt the play might be forbidden to be performed for the next ten years.'[13] Her family inheritance had never seemed more suffocating.

Belatedly, the management decided that, out of respect for Mrs Siddons, their two Kemble stars should be given a week's holiday from the theatre. Fanny could go down to Oatlands after all. Lady Francis insisted that there would be nobody there 'but ourselves' but when Fanny arrived, accompanied by her mother and John Mitchell, she discovered that Augustus had been made an exception to the 'positive no one'. It would seem that family and friends were conspiring to give Fanny's prospect an opportunity to declare himself.

The Surrey countryside was at its most lush. While her mother visited Aunt Whitlock at Addlestone, Fanny sat cosily with Lady Francis in her private sitting room sharing confidences and reading sections of their diaries to one another. When the gentlemen returned from their shooting there were sunny afternoon rides and 'long, delightful strolls'.

> We walked on through a part of the park called America, because of the magnificent rhododendrons and azaleas and the general wildness of the whole. The mass was so deep one's feet sank into it; the sun, setting, threw low, slanting rays along the earth and among the old tree trunks.[14]

Fanny woke on Sunday to a letter from her father telling her that the theatre could spare her a little longer. There was a warm afternoon spent gliding on the lake in a boat – Lord Francis rowing and Lady Francis, Fanny and her mother murmuring 'half-voice, all sorts of musical memories' in counterpoint to the rhythm of the oars.

In the drawing room, after dinner, Fanny and Augustus entertained with extracts from *Andromache* (her old hit from her school days) and sentimental scenes from a French play called First Loves.* Fanny had found a man to whom her character, bisected between France and England, was nothing strange; a man who saw past her pock-marked face to the worth concealed within and could win her heart with French puns:

> 'Que font les Vaches à Paris?'
> 'Des Vaudevilles' (des Veaux de Ville).
> 'Quelle est la sainte qui n'a pas besoin de jarretières?'
> 'Ste Sébastienne' (ses bas se tiennent).†
> What absurd, funny stuff!

Conversations began to skirt around marriage. One morning while the ladies gardened on the lawn, Augustus amused them with town gossip. At one sad tale of a troubled aristocratic marriage Fanny exclaimed –

> What might, could, would, or *should* a woman do in such a case? Endure and endure till her heart broke, I suppose. Somehow I don't think a man would have the heart to *break* one's heart; but, to be sure, I don't know.

Her imagination was filled with the sight of Lord and Lady Francis bathed in summer morning light:

---

*Scribe's *Les premiers amours*.
†'What do the cows do in Paris?'
'Vaudeville' (they're calves about town).
'Which female saint does not need garters?'
'St Sébastienne' (her stockings stay up by themselves).

I wish I could have painted my host and hostess this morning as they stood together on the lawn; she with her beautiful baby in her arms, her bright, fair forehead and eyes contrasting so strikingly with his fine, dark head. I never saw a more charming picture . . . They looked to me holy as well as handsome and happy.

Meanwhile, Sarah Siddons was buried in Paddington churchyard among the very headstones where Fanny and her brother used to picnic as children. On the day of her aunt's funeral, there were races held in Oatlands Park, and to avoid being seen in public in their mourning Fanny and her mother slipped off to see Aunt Whitlock. They returned in the evening to meet Charles Kemble who came up from London. The great Tragedy Queen had been laid to rest and Fanny was ensconced in aristocratic domesticity, watching her beloved father talk to Augustus, the two men mirroring each other's easy manners and charm. The refuge of a private life seemed at hand.

In the morning Fanny and her mother walked with her father to meet the London coach and, having waved him off, returned to enjoy their last day at Oatlands. The party drove out to a local beauty spot, while Augustus and Fanny followed on horseback.

On our way home much talk of Naples. I might like to go there, no doubt; the question is how I should like to come back to London after Naples, and I think not at all.[15]

The evening's pleasures were subdued, Fanny reading 'a pretty French piece', the romance of *Michel et Christine*, that her father had given her. The next day the Kembles drove Augustus back to town in their carriage.

According to Ann Blainey, a recent discovery among the letters of Fanny's sister indicates that Augustus had asked Fanny to marry him.*

---

*In a 'letter just discovered', says Blainey, Adelaide writes that Fanny is 'in love with Augustus Craven, and they were engaged to be married', Blainey, p. 63. The fact that there were rumours of an engagement circulating among close friends is

No engagement, however, was made public. Fanny went back to the theatre, rehearsing Juliet with her cousin John Mason who was to make his London début as her Romeo. Mason had a cold but her mother told Fanny that she played 'beautifully', a special pleasure since the Leveson-Gowers and Augustus Craven were watching from a box. Also, the Bridgewater theatricals had been given an unexpected extension; Lord Francis had received a flattering request for a third, royal performance.

Fanny drove to Bridgewater House for more rehearsals through Westminster streets bustling with preparations for the state opening of the new Reform Parliament. The cast gathered at a window to watch the royal carriages drawn by cream-coloured horses in rich silver trappings and coal-black ones in coral-coloured harness. London society was beginning to pack its bags for the summer exodus.

When she arrived for the royal performance Fanny felt so unwell she could hardly stand. Once she was dressed, she had to lie down until called to go on. The audience was their most magnificent of all – the Queen and various princes, princesses, dukes and duchesses graced the front rows. Unfortunately etiquette prevented applause in the presence of royalty and Fanny did not play well. Her voice broke at least twice. 'The fact is, I am fagged half to death; but as I cannot give up my work and cannot <u>bear</u> to give up my play, the only wonder is that I am not fagged <u>whole</u> to death.'[16]

She was in no mood for the celebrations after the play. Lady Francis presented her to the Queen, who was most gracious. Then everyone moved on to a magnificent formal supper at Lady Gower's. Lady Francis snagged a table in an alcove out of plain sight where she and her brother Henry Greville, Fanny, her mother and Augustus ate quietly while looking out on the grandees. Fanny and her mother took Augustus home in their carriage, dropping him off just before dawn.

---

suggested by a surviving fragment of a letter between Arthur Hallam and Richard Milnes written the following spring – 'Kemble, whatever the world may say, is not going to be married, nor am I clear that his sister is, although the case is . . . [cut out]' – Letter 8 May 1832, Kolb, p. 572.

The next day she stayed in bed feeling unwell. Mrs Jameson came to keep her company. Their talk turned to marriage and a woman's chance of happiness in giving her life into another's keeping. 'I said I thought if one did not expect too much one might secure a reasonably fair amount of happiness, though of course the risk one ran was immense,' Fanny recorded in her diary. 'I shall never forget the expression of her face; it was momentary, and passed away almost immediately, but it has haunted me ever since.'

All at once references to Mr C— disappear from Fanny's journal. She and her father, accompanied by Aunt Dall, set off on their summer tour opening at Bristol with *Romeo and Juliet* on 4 July. She jotted down days of sightseeing – the picturesque market, the Abbey Church. In her letters to Hal, Fanny made a point of reporting how happy she was in her father's company but her accounts of pleasant weather and pretty sights could not conceal a dramatic change. The mirage of Italy and marriage had dissolved.

A fortnight after leaving London Fanny wrote crossly to the meddling Anna – 'I can neither bid you confirm nor deny any "reports" you may hear for I am in utter ignorance, I am happy to say, of the world's surmisings on my behalf, and had indeed supposed that my time for being honoured by its notice in any way was pretty well past and over.'[17]

A few days later she broke a mirror and in a fit of weeping confessed to Dall how much she disliked her profession. That led to a long talk with her aunt 'upon my prospects in marrying'. Aunt Dall was perfectly direct.

> 'While you remain single, and choose to work, your fortune is an independent and ample one; as soon as you marry, there's no such thing. Your position in society is both a pleasanter and more distinguished one than your birth or real station entitles you to; but that also is the result of your professional exertions, and might, and probably would, alter for the worse if you left the stage.'[18]

Unlike the noble Portia, the actress's fortune lacked bankable substance.

> It seems that I have fortune and fame (such as it is) – positive real advantages, which I cannot give with myself, and which I cease to own when I give myself away, which certainly makes marrying any one or any one marrying me rather a solemn consideration; for I lose everything, and my marryee gains nothing in a worldly point of view.

Two days later, in answering Hal's weekly letter, Fanny flinched at her friend calling her 'Juliet'. 'There is but one sentiment of hers that I can quote with entire self-application . . . this contract . . . is too rash, too unadvised.'[19]

Love could not overcome questions of money and status. Fanny discovered that she could not risk imitating Portia's act of 'generous self-denial', and her perceived worth, in the end, proved insufficient to secure the commitment of her Bassanio.

Some biographers have argued that Craven thought Fanny richer than she was; others that he had no intention of marrying her but was temporarily carried away by their summer romance. It has been speculated that he dropped Fanny when his father threatened to disinherit him. His salary as attaché would never keep him in the style he was accustomed to.

The evidence is that the love between Augustus and Fanny was mutual and sincere. Descriptions of the woman Craven eventually married carry many echoes of Fanny – 'her decisive judgement in every moral question, her energy of enthusiasm for all noble thought and action, her instant appreciation of social circumstance'.[20] The two women even seem to have been similar physically. Augustus's bride was a small woman with large dark eyes, perfect teeth and a 'golden voice' (so perfect in its expressiveness, one friend recalled, that it was a model of what actresses could only aspire to).

However, Craven needed the right kind of wife. In 1834 he married Pauline de la Ferronnays, the daughter of a Breton aristocrat who had served the French King Charles X as Ambassador to St Petersburgh*. Equally at ease in French, Italian and English, Pauline was described as a 'perfectly accomplished woman of the world', a woman of 'shrewd political instincts', but perhaps her most significant attraction for Augustus was her coherent family.

Perhaps Augustus was looking for the harmonious family missing from his own background. Pauline was part of a cohesive and pious Catholic family. She had a distinct sense of purpose that unified her life; she existed to glorify God, or more particularly, to convince others of the desirability of becoming a Catholic. (She became well-known as the author of a proselytizing novel, her *Le Récit d'une Soeur*.)[21] The de la Ferronnays clan embraced Augustus as 'a brother, not only in law but in faith and sentiment' and he converted to Catholicism to join them, despite the damage to his diplomatic career.[22] Augustus's father was violently anti-Catholic; when he learned of his engagement, Keppel Craven partially disinherited him. Nonetheless Augustus married Pauline.†

Many years later, talking over old days, a friend recorded Pauline Craven commenting to her husband: 'That was when you were so much in love with Fanny Kemble.'[23] Perhaps the failure of the romance between Fanny and Augustus was a mere matter of timing. Once the Kembles left on their summer tour, Craven talked himself out of such an inconvenient passion in light of the social difficulties and the likelihood of his father's displeasure. A sincere romantic, after all, knows that true love is always doomed love and from that fact draws its intensity. Then again, perhaps Augustus's wife had the greatest insight when she remarked to her husband after many years of marriage – 'if you have not had in me so clever a wife, I

---

*When Augustus spent time with Fanny that summer of 1831, it is entirely possible that he had already met his future wife in Naples where she and her family were living in exile after the French July Revolution of the year before.

†Keppel Craven relented and settled some £17,000 on the young couple, giving them a moderate yearly income of £530 or so, and in the end he made his son his principal heir, but for many years Augustus Craven and his wife did without the wealth he felt himself entitled to.

think at least you have had a more amiable one'.[24] In truth Fanny was more Camiola than Portia, and her Bassanio, another 'handsome, extravagant young gentleman', chose the easier road.

In retrospect, after many years had dulled the pain, Fanny recognized Craven's luxurious and lazy nature. One of the few comments she left behind betrays a twinge of contempt. 'I used to think that my friend C[raven] had occasionally the tone of a disappointed man, who attributed his want of success to want of zeal on the part of his friends, or active disservice on that of his enemies.'[25] For all his charm, Augustus certainly lacked the industry that Fanny, in the end, most admired. His fine potential petered out in his thirties and his diplomatic career never amounted to much. He and his wife had no children and they lived a nomadic life, restlessly moving between Naples, London, Paris and Rome. When Keppel Craven died, leaving his son a shrunken remnant of his grandmother's great wealth, Augustus lost a good deal of money in an attempt to become a member of the House of Commons. After that he led the purposeless life of a dilettante always living beyond his income. It was his wife who defined him and eventually supported them both with her writing.[26]

To the end Augustus retained his theatrical interests. When he was in his sixties, living in 'reduced circumstances' in Rome, a friend pictured him 'always ready to speak of Dante, of whose work and life he was an accomplished student, or to read Shakespeare according to the Kemble traditions.'[27] He kept his good looks and Pauline's devotion to the last. And when he finally died at the age of eighty, the bastard who did not know his mother was given a place among his wife's people in the ancient de la Ferronnays mausoleum in Normandy.

Whatever we may speculate about that summer romance in 1831, one fact is clear; the intensity of that short experience had significance for Fanny Kemble out of all proportion to the time it lasted. It was the logic of Romanticism that fictional models represented intellectual realities – things that could be realized in a life pursued with sufficient sincerity and a little luck. During that brief summer idyll she experienced the materialization of a fiction, and to have fallen from that Eden represented more than a simple disappointment in love. It was a touchstone experience that affected the rest of her life.

'The first serious experiences of our youth seem to me like the breaking asunder of some curious, beautiful and mystical pattern,' she wrote eighteen months later. 'All our lives long we are more or less intent on replacing the bright scattered fragments in their original shape: most of us die with the bits still scattered round us – that is to say, such of the bits as have not been ground into powder, or soiled and defaced beyond recognition in the life process. The few very wise find and place them in a coherent form at last, but it is quite another curious, beautiful, and mystical device or pattern from the original one.'[28]

23

Exile

Fanny was Undine, the water nymph who belonged to another element; the changeling whose mortal love destroyed her just as she killed her knight with a kiss.* She felt doomed. On a glorious August day on the road from Exeter to Plymouth, driving through a picturesque landscape, the purple heather by the roadside reminded her of Weybridge 'and the hours I had lately spent there so happily'.

---

*The German Friedrich, baron de la Motte Fouqué (1777–1843) published the fairy romance of *Undine* in 1811. Undine is a nymph, the personification of the watery element. She is brought up by a mortal fisherman and his wife who have lost their own child in a drowning. She falls in love with the knight Huldbrand and agrees to marry him, despite the fact she is not mortal and has no soul. After they are married Huldbrand begins to neglect his wife – having an affair with the haughty Bertalda. Undine warns her husband that if he is unkind to her she must leave him. One day as they are sailing on the Danube, Huldbrand, taunted by his wife's fairy kindred, speaks angrily to Undine – at which she is forced to slip away into the water. As Huldbrand is about to marry Bertalda, betraying his fairy lady love, Undine reappears and kills him with a kiss.

The tale of Undine struck a chord with many of Fanny's generation. William Thackeray, Edward Fitzgerald and Arthur Hallam – all men who, it could be said, had problems with strong women – were passionate fans of the watery fairy tale. It seems to have articulated a barely conscious sense that women were emerging as more threatening creatures just as they developed their admirable moral and poetic qualities.

> It seems to me that memory is the special organ of pain, for even when it recalls our pleasures, it recalls only the past, and half their sweetness becomes bitter in the process. I have a tenacious and acute memory, and . . . no hope.[1]

A fortnight into the summer tour, her father raised the spectre of America. 'If my cause (our Chancery suit) goes ill before the Lords, I think the best thing I can do will be to take ship from Liverpool and sail for the United States'.[2] Mr Price, the English manager of the Park Theatre in New York,* had offered Charles Kemble a lucrative contract. Several English stars – including Aunt Whitlock – had amassed respectable capital working in the US. But it was not a venture to be taken lightly. Crossing the Atlantic was a dangerous business in wooden sailing ships. Even in good weather the journey took a month. An American tour would mean exile from family and friends for two years.

At first, Charles declared that he would make the sacrifice alone. Fanny could not permit that and yet it was her nightmare to be severed so completely from the world she knew.

> I remember my Aunt Whitlock saying that when she went to America she left my father a toddling thing that she used to dandle and carry about; and the first time she saw him after her return, he had a baby of his own in his arms. That sort of thing makes one's heart jump into one's mouth with dismay; it seems as if all the time one had been living away, unconsciously, was thrown in a lump at one's head.[3]

After only two summer tours, she was already weary of 'living half in one's trunks and travelling-bags'. Now she faced the prospect of two entire years of it. 'I think a blight of uncertainty must have pervaded the atmosphere when I was born, and penetrated . . . my whole earthly destiny.'[4]

---

*Mr Price had succeeded Mr Elliston as Manager of Drury Lane in London before crossing the Atlantic to try his fortunes as manager-proprietor of New York's Park Theatre.

'My work tires me,' the twenty-one-year-old scribbled in her journal. 'I am growing old.'

Back in London, Hal came to stay for most of the month of September, lightening some of the gloom, but the theatre continued its downward slide. Public affairs were as turbulent as ever. In early October Tory Lords managed to scupper the second Reform Bill after an intense five days of debate. London papers were published with black bands of mourning in protest. As news spread across England muffled bells were tolled in Birmingham, riots broke out in Nottingham and Derby, and in Bristol a mob sacked the Mansion House and set fire to the Bishop's Palace.

'The shops are all shut. The windows of Apsley House [the residence of Lord Wellington] have been smashed . . . They say that Nottingham and Belvoir castles are burnt down.'[5]

As if to underline the sense of insecurity, cholera was reported in the north-eastern ports.*

The management informed Fanny that she was to act Queen Katherine in Shakespeare's *Henry VIII*. 'You will easily conceive my distress at having such a task assigned me,' she reported wearily to Hal as she prepared to repeat the role associated with her aunt's mature powers.

> Dall . . . wishes me to remonstrate upon the subject, but that I will not do. I am in that theatre to earn my living by serving its interests, and if I was desired to act Harlequin, for those two purposes, I should feel bound to do so.[6]

They made Fanny a pint-sized copy of her aunt's costume and she went through her part with the embarrassment of a schoolgirl playing dress-up before strangers.†

---

*France had been suffering a fearful epidemic, but now it crossed the Channel.

†'Mr Harness said that seeing me in that dress was like looking at Mrs Siddons through the diminishing end of an opera-glass . . . In truth, I could hardly sustain the weight of velvet and ermine in which I was robed, and to which my small girlish figure was as little adapted as my dramatic powers were to the matronly dignity of the character.' *Records of a Girlhood*, vol. III, pp. 111–12.

In late autumn her mother took Adelaide to Paris to begin training as an opera singer. Fanny would miss her little sister. Nearly seventeen, Adelaide had developed a teasing charm resting on a 'quick, observant mind and a tendency to wit and sarcasm' that her more intense elder sibling much appreciated. Marie-Thérèse had barely returned from France when the head of the household collapsed.

Fanny had never known her father to take to his bed before. She was panic-stricken. 'All my plays require him, except Isabella and Fazio, and these are worn threadbare.' The nights she did act, she could hardly remember her lines she was so terrified that she would return home to find her father dead. Her mother moved furniture and 'the boys' were no help at all. Ignoring the financial crisis, John Mitchell and Henry continued to lounge about with their friends, taking fencing lessons at Angelo's* and practising their riding skills at Fozzard's.[7] If it had not been for Dall, the family would have fallen apart. 'Anything like Dall's incessant and unwearied care and tenderness you cannot imagine . . . every day adds to her claims upon our love and gratitude.'[8]

Expensive doctors were called and pronounced a case of inflammation of the lungs. One Saturday afternoon, as the invalid lay near death, coughing blood, and Fanny huddled crying with her brother Henry on the sofa, a letter arrived from Lady Francis inviting them all to Oatlands. It was a cruel time to remind Fanny of what she had lost.

> Everything is winter now, within and without me; and when I was last there it was summer, in my heart and all over the earth . . . Poor Undine! How often I think of that true story.[9]

The Kembles declined the invitation. 'I am hardly sorry for it,' Fanny confessed to her journal. 'How many things one ought to die of and doesn't!'

---

*Angelo's Fencing and Boxing Academy was the leading gym of the day and a fashionable haunt of gentlemen of means.

The pantomime season was in sight. At morning rehearsals the stage was filled with 'the whole corps de ballet attitudinizing in muddy shoes and poke-bonnets, and the columbine, in dirty stockings and a mob cap, ogling the harlequin in a striped shirt and dusty trousers'.[10] All those high ideals Fanny once discussed so bravely with James Spedding and Arthur Hallam never seemed more distant.

As Christmas approached the shocking news reached London that Torrijos and fifty-five of his remaining followers had been enticed on to Spanish soil, taken prisoner and every one summarily shot – including Richard Trench's young cousin, Robert Boyd. 'Poor John. You may imagine how grateful we are that he is now among us, instead of having fallen a victim to his chimerical enthusiasm.'[11] Fanny had become accustomed to referring to her brothers in this way – 'poor Henry'; 'poor John'. Henry (who turned nineteen that December) she still considered a child to be cared for, but Fanny's resentment of her elder brother's abdication of his duty would last a lifetime.

One night at Covent Garden, attending the first performance of a promising young opera singer of nineteen (the same age she had been when she made her own début) Fanny was struck by a vision of sacrifice –

> When I saw the thousands of eyes of that crowded pitful of men, and heard their stormy acclamations, and then looked at the fragile, helpless, pretty young creature standing before them trembling with terror, and all woman's fear and shame in such an unnatural position . . . It seemed to me as if the mere gaze of all that multitude must melt the slight figure . . . shrivel it up like a scrap of silver paper before a blazing fire.[12]

Fanny Kemble resolved that she would not shrivel up and burn away. The American scheme became 'her' scheme.[13] She decided that in two years abroad she might reasonably expect to make £10,000. She would then return to England for a farewell round of performances and, having amassed sufficient capital, she would retire to live as she pleased. She had given up on marriage, quoting a derisive vaudeville rhyme to Hal –

> *'Ji! Ji! Mariez-vous,*
> *Mettez-vous dans la misère!*
> *Ji! Ji! Mariez-vous*
> *Mettez-vous la corde au cou.'**

She was going to work for her independence.

First, there were family affairs to arrange. Henry must go into the army. He was 'too young and too handsome to be doing nothing but lounging about the streets of London . . . a mere squanderer of time, without interest, stake, or duty, in this existence'.[14] With the help of a dining acquaintance, Sir John Macdonald, the adjutant general of the forces, Fanny bought Henry a commission in an Irish regiment with the remainder of the fee Murray had paid her for *Francis I.*†

John Mitchell was not so easy to manage. Her elder brother had just discovered his life's purpose in the library of the British Museum preparing an edition of the earliest and most complete Anglo-Saxon text then known, *Beowulf.*[15] His diligent work would eventually win him recognition as one of the founding scholars of English Anglo-Saxon studies, but it widened the rift between him and his family. As far as Fanny was concerned he chose a new hobby above his family in desperate need.[16]

By the time a haggard Charles returned to rehearse Mercutio in *Romeo and Juliet* in the second week in January, Fanny had grown in assurance. For the first time she had designed her own costumes, dressing her Juliet after a sketch by Mrs Jameson.

---

*Roughly translated as: 'Marry/& put yourself in misery;/Marry/& put the rope around your neck.' FK, *Records of a Girlhood*, vol. III, p.150.

†At that time officers' commissions were bought, although they were brokered through military commanders. Fanny purchased her brother a commission as ensign (the starting rank for officers) in a regiment then serving in Ireland, but which was soon sent out to the West Indies.

> I sat on the cold stage, that I might hear them mumble over their parts as they do. My father seemed to me very weak, and not by any means fit for his work tonight.[17]

The role reversal was complete. Fanny was now the star of the family and Charles the supporting player. Her father, 'horribly thin and pale', was drained of that virile male charm that had formed the core of his attraction as an actor. Analysing his performance with her new-found detachment, Fanny saw her father as a fine performer rather than a great actor. 'My father, whose fulfilling of a particular range of characters is as nearly as possible perfect, wants depth and power, and power seems to me the core, the very marrow, so to speak, of genius.'[18]

Given the problems it was a triumph of will that Charles returned to work at all. He had to testify in front of the House of Commons Committee enquiring into the validity of the Theatre Patents. He argued passionately that: 'the great companies of good sterling actors would be broken up . . . the school of fine and careful acting would be lost, no play of Shakespeare's could be decorously put on the stage'.[19]

His daughter was convinced that the Committee intended to rule for the abolition of the Patents.* At the same time as he was pressing his case before the Committee, Charles and Fanny were playing in Francis Leveson-Gower's translation from a French drama, *Katherine of Cleves*. As Fanny remarked, the piece was 'nothing more than an interesting melodrama, with the advantage of being written in gentlemanly blank verse instead of turgid prose'. But the play was not staged for its merits; the hope was that the author would attract his West End friends to the theatre.

Katherine of Cleves filled the boxes for a couple of weeks and then

*In fact the Patent Theatres' monopoly survived until it was abolished by Act of Parliament in 1843. 'We then had a stage, now we have not,' wrote Edward Fitzball in his memoirs. 'The reason is obvious – there were then certain people for certain things, and certain theatres for certain performances: everyone had a chance. Now they seem always on the look-out to snap up each other's ideas, to eat up each other's thoughts.' – Fitzball, vol. I, p. 856.

was quietly laid to rest. The theatre management, casting about ever more desperately, judged the time ripe to bring out Fanny's *Francis I*. Fanny herself had entirely lost confidence in her first work.

> It is of an *unendurable* length . . . did I not feel bound to comply with my father's wishes I would have no hand in this experiment. . . . it is a mere snatch at a bit of profit by a way of catchpenny venture, to secure which they are running the risk of injuring me in more ways than one.[20]

The disagreement brought her the closest she had ever been to open confrontation with her father. As 'the management' cut her text and changed the cast without consulting her, Fanny assured Hal with a tight-lipped sense of grievance that she would make the best of what she could not help. She would play the wicked queen mother, Louise of Savoy. Her near contemporary, the long-legged Miss Ellen Tree (who was rumoured to be a romantic pursuit of Charles Kemble's) would be the heroine, Françoise de Foix. Fanny's costume was hideous, Cousin John Mason played the King like a vulgar apprentice, and the whole project was doomed.

That winter Charles joined the comedian Charles Mathews, and others of the old guard, to found the Garrick Club* in an attempt to assert the gentility of the best of the profession. Fanny could scarcely conceal her frustration.

> Covent Garden is going to the dogs faster and faster every day; and, in spite of the Garrick Club and all its noble regenerators of the drama, I think the end of it, and that no distant one, will be utter ruin.[21]

She took refuge where she could. One Saturday Fanny lost herself in a new novel, *The Borderers*, by the American author Fenimore

*The opening dinner was held on 15 February 1832.

Cooper. 'The soft sobriety' of the tale about simple, pious pioneering folk carving a new world out of savage territory caught her imagination. 'I cannot help sometimes wishing I had lived in those days, and been one of that little colony of sternly simple and fervently devout Christian souls. But I should have been a furious fanatic; I should have "seen visions and dreamed dreams", and fancied myself a prophetess to a certainty.'

She was enjoying a sentimental cry, having just finished the story, when her mother interrupted her with the news that her father had been forced to declare himself bankrupt. The theatre would be closed at Easter and 'we must go different ways'.

> It is astonishing what a different effect real and fictitious distress has upon one. I could not answer my mother, but I went to the window and looked up and down the streets that were getting empty and dark and silent, and my heart sank as I thought of leaving my home, my England.

Covent Garden was to be let to the French entrepreneur Laporte, who planned to use it for concerts. Abandoning her previous fortitude, Fanny snatched at the hope that the Kembles might still avoid America. They could easily find engagements; the provinces would be kind to them, she assured her father. The house would be given up; the carriage and the horses sold, but they had lived happily enough without luxuries before. 'Nothing need signify, provided we are not obliged to separate and go off to that dreadful America.'[22]

She was more than half glad to see Covent Garden go. She could not understand her father's shock and mourning – although she echoed it with an unconscious lilt of her Uncle John Philip's 'eagle in the marketplace' oratory after the burning of the old Covent Garden in 1808.

> It is pitiful to see how my father still clings to that theatre. Is it because the art he loves, once had its noblest dwelling there? Is

> it because his own name and the names of his brother and sister are graven, as it were, on its very stones? . . . What can . . . make him so loth to leave that ponderous ruin? Even today, after summing up all . . . the waste of life and fortune which that concern has cost his brother, himself and all of us, he exclaimed, 'Oh, if I had £10,000, I could set it all right again . . .' My mother and I . . . stared at this infatuation. If I had . . . a hundred thousand pounds, not one farthing would I give to the redeeming of that fatal millstone . . . The past is past, and for the future we must think and act as speedily as we may.

Charles was not ready to accept the full reality of the collapse. The playwright Sheridan Knowles was in negotiation with Covent Garden about his new play.* If *The Hunchback* could be as successful as Knowles's *Virginius*, perhaps it could still rescue Covent Garden.

The rehearsals for *The Hunchback* went ahead and for the moment the theatre's creditors dropped into the background. *Francis I* was published to coincide with a 'handsome' review in the *Quarterly Review*. Fanny was much happier and life seemed deceptively normal.

One morning a rehearsal ended early, and Fanny went to sit in her father's office. Charles was having a meeting with the stage manager. She noticed that her father 'seemed too bewildered to give any answer, or even heed, to anything'.[23] Afterwards Charles Kemble paced the room before flinging himself into a chair and burying his head in his arms.

> I was horribly frightened, and turned as cold as stone, and for some minutes could not muster up courage enough to speak to

**The Hunchback* had been around for over a year. Knowles had read the play to the Kembles back in spring 1831. But as he had written the title role for Kean he had spent the intervening months trying – and failing – to come to an agreement with that mercurial genius and Drury Lane.

him. At last I got up and went to him, and, on my touching his arm, he started up and exclaimed: 'Good God, what will become of us all!' I tried to comfort him, and spoke for a long time, but much, I fear, as a blind man speaks of colours. I do not know, and I do not believe any one knows, the real state of terrible involvement in which this miserable concern is wrapped.

She knew then that exile to America was inevitable.

Hal dropped everything and rushed over from Ireland to give what support she could. On Wednesday 15 March Fanny donned her 'hideous' costume and suffered the opening night of *Francis I.* The curiosity value of a historical tragedy written by a girl of seventeen, in which the twenty-two-year-old author appeared as the wicked queen mother, gave the production a short but honourable run. 'Its entire want of real merit,' its authoress pointed out, 'made it impossible that it should do anything more.'

Four years after she finished the work, Fanny had grown uncomfortable with more than just its language. Though she dies for it – plunging a dagger into her own breast – there is no avoiding the fact that her heroine, Françoise de Foix, has carnal knowledge of King Francis out of wedlock.* That she submits herself to save her brother had been considered a possible dramatic excuse (although even Shakespeare lets Isabella get away with her virtue in *Measure for Measure*), but in Fanny's play there is the improper twist that Françoise is in love with her King – leaving the shocking suggestion that her heroine might have secretly enjoyed her sexual bargain. James Spedding's careful comment was that he liked the rhetoric and pacing of her play but mistrusted those 'darker passions . . . reflected from Shakespeare – I do not believe that she is a whit more familiar with them than you and I, who know them out of the Bard of

*On stage, the villain of the piece, the monk Gonzales, is specifically gleeful that his planned murder of Françoise is commuted to her defiling.

Avon, and Walter Scott, and Don Juan.'[24] Nevertheless, *Francis I* displayed its author as an uncomfortably knowing Juliet. As Charles Greville commented wryly, it was a 'very strange play for a girl to write'.*

Fortunately a true hit was waiting in the wings. *The Hunchback* was an immediate and solid success from its first performance on Thursday 5 April 1832. It was 'a real play, with real characters . . . full of life and originality' and the female lead was a gift to an actress.† Her role as Julia became Fanny's greatest part‡ and the play went on to become a staple of the theatrical repertoire on both sides of the Atlantic for the rest of the century.

The basic story is melodramatic. Master Walter, the Hunchback, is agent to the Earl of Rochdale. His daughter Julia is loved by Sir Thomas Clifford. She gets silly ideas and assumes the giddy fashionable airs of town life causing Clifford to reject her. Eventually she learns her lesson and Walter reveals himself as the real Earl. Despite its confused plot, the play was full of 'powerfully dramatic situations'. Knowles was an actor himself and he knew what devices worked with an audience. He had an ear for the rhythms of colloquial speech, bringing a touch of realism to his dialogue that led him to be hailed in his own day as 'near to Shakespeare'.[25]

Charles Kemble took the second male lead of 'the insignificant lover' Clifford, while Knowles played the key role of the Hunchback. Fanny had her work cut out controlling the volatile Irishman, 'endeavouring to keep him in his right mind with regard to his exits and his entrances, and receiving from him explosive Irish benedictions in return'.[26]

---

*'Fanny Kemble's new tragedy came out last night with complete success, written when she was seventeen, an odd play for a girl to write. The heroine is tempted like Beatrice in *Measure for Measure*' [he means Isabella], 'but with a different result, which result is supposed to take place between the acts.' – Reeve, 16 March 1832.

†Saturday 23 April 1831. Fanny described the role as a part 'in which it would be almost impossible to fail . . . every Julia may reckon upon the sympathy of her audience'.

‡Although she played Juliet more times, her original creation of the heroine of *The Hunchback* led her to be more exclusively identified with the part.

The reviews were good. Even Charles Greville thought Fanny acted well.[27] *The Hunchback* revived all Arthur Hallam's enthusiasm for 'La Kemble'.

> The scene in the 2nd act where she plays the fine lady was excellent, but the tragic parts yet finer . . . Her 'Clifford, why don't you speak to me?' and 'Clifford, is it you?' . . . and her 'Do it' with all the accompanying speech . . . I shall never forget.[28]

In the suburbs beyond the dingy streets of the capital signs of spring stirred. John Mitchell was sent over to Paris to fetch Adelaide home. He came back full of lurid stories of the cholera epidemic and 'hearses . . . going about like omnibuses & dead carts in black because there are not enough of other conveyances to meet the increasing demand'.[29] Henry looked very handsome in his new uniform; when he was not ordering clothes, he spent his time at the theatre with William Thackeray watching the rehearsals for the Easter pantomime.* At the end of April he left to join his regiment in Ireland.

On 9 May Grey's ministry was forced to resign when Tory peers yet again blocked the Reform Bill. News of the resignation, after months of unrest and with death tolls rising as cholera advanced down the country, galvanized dissatisfaction with the reactionary position embodied in the Duke of Wellington. Petitions in favour of Reform issued from across the land. Radical leaders such as Francis Place urged a run on the banks. Placards and graffiti appeared, urging: 'To stop the Duke, go for gold.' The Tory Party examined its soul (and interests) and decided to back the compromising Robert Peel and abandon the Duke of Wellington. The Whigs returned to office and William IV promised to create as many peers as necessary

*Thackeray much enjoyed these expeditions, such entertainments being much more to his taste than tragedy. One morning he records Henry Kemble giving him a tour backstage during which the theatre 'Tailor asked Henry to pay him a bill for clothes . . .' Thackeray to Edward Fitzgerald, Ray, p. 241.

to force the Bill through. In June 1832 the Bill passed its third reading and became law. The old world was gone for good.

The Covent Garden management announced Fanny Kemble's Lady Macbeth.* 'Surely it is too great an undertaking for so young a person as myself,' anguished Fanny. 'That towering, tremendous woman! What a trial of courage and composure for me!' *The Times*[30] compared her performance favourably with that of Sarah Siddons, but the reviewer was being kind. 'It was not very successful,' admitted the staunchly loyal Arthur Hallam to his fiancée, Emily Tennyson; 'she seemed to sink under her consciousness of the grandeur of the character, and the remembrance of Mrs Siddons, still vivid in the minds of many.'[31]

Arthur was in town to promote Tennyson's second collection of poetry, and he was busy handing round snatches of manuscript among 'true believers'.

> Foremost of these last may be reckoned Miss Kemble, who the other night astounded the weak faculties of old Sotheby by shouting out at one of his crowded parties: 'I am glad! I am glad!' 'Of what, Miss Kemble?' 'Glad that there is yet a man in England capable of performing such glorious things.' She added, 'He is the greatest painter in poetry that I know.'†

Visitors to Great Russell Street found Adelaide copying out *The Lady of Shallot* and 'raving at intervals in the most Siddonian tone', while Fanny set *Sisters* to music ('she inclines however to think it too painful, & to wish such things should not be written'.[32]) The

---

*The idea of Fanny appearing in her aunt's great part had been shelved since it was first mooted at the time of Sarah Siddons's death – a sign that even the over-optimistic Charles Kemble was doubtful about Fanny's ability to carry the part off.

†Hallam to Emily Tennyson from London, Saturday 19 May 1832. Ever the promoter, Arthur Hallam adds, 'Bid Alfred make haste to idealize her somehow; she deserves some gratitude; & as for paying her in the simple old-fashioned way, by plain verses about herself in her natural capacity, I am sure he will not condescend to anything so unartistical. Tell him that she gives her vote for the "Palace" as his greatest effort; her brother differs, saying, "Women always want a moral: give me the Lotus-eaters".'

Apostles returned in force to enjoy Marie-Thérèse's 'splendid spreads'. The Great Alfred himself came to dine, unsettling Fanny with his 'massive' presence and a shadow of sarcasm about his mouth.[33] In contrast, Arthur took Alfred to see *The Hunchback* and reported that the poet was 'in great delight at it'.*

Fanny's family was fragmenting. After Henry, Hal was the next to leave – her long visit ended on 14 June. As they said their goodbyes, America was all anyone could think of. Dall cried bitterly – she would be sailing from Liverpool with Charles and Fanny on 1 August and did not expect to see Hal again for two years or more.

There were farewell visits, presents exchanged, solemn moments – and comical ones such as the 'bawling conversation' with the rather deaf Lady Cork through her carriage window – 'which ended by her ladyship shrieking out to me that I was a "supernatural creature" in a tone which must have made the mummies . . . in the adjacent British Museum jump'.[34]

On Friday, 22 June 1832 Fanny and Charles Kemble gave their final performance together at Covent Garden in *The Hunchback*.† When it was over, the audience rose in their seats, shouting and waving farewell with handkerchiefs and hats – 'my friends, as I feel them to be; my countrymen, my English folk'.[35] Blinded with tears, Fanny took the flowers from her sash and threw them into the pit with 'handfuls of kisses' as she was led off by her weeping father. Backstage was a blur of fond farewells – to the actors, the scene-shifters, the prop-man and his boy, the maid sobbing by the dressing-room door and amid it all an inarticulate exchange with Laporte, the new lessee of the theatre, who declared with a flourish that he ought to cry more than anyone at losing such stars. It was the end of the Kemble House.

Great Russell Street hosted one last manager's Sunday Supper. A select group of Apostles – Edward and James Spedding, Arthur Hallam

* 'Fanny Kemble acted better than ever, &, I think, because she knew Alfred was there. She has lent him her unpublished play, *The Star of Seville*, which he admires extremely; & so do I. It is far above *Francis*.' Hallam to Emily Tennyson 23 June, Kolb p. 601.

† 'I only played pretty well, except the last scene, which was better than the rest.'

and Alfred Tennyson – came to say farewell. The evening degenerated into youthful silliness with 'French and German oaths and curses set to music' and 'Fanny Kemble's self singing the two Sisters who dwelt in a bower – Edinbroo, Edinbrooooe, which was not a little edifying'.[36]

The day before their departure, two arrests were served upon Charles Kemble in the street by creditors of the theatre. For a moment Fanny indulged the faint hope that they would be prevented from leaving England but, somehow, her father made arrangements. Early the next morning Fanny left Great Russell Street for the last time. It was bitter parting with Adelaide. Fanny's younger sister was left behind in the echoing house with Dall, who was to meet up with father and elder daughter later at Liverpool. Marie-Thérèse travelled to Edinburgh to spend a last few days with them. John Mitchell escorted his parents and Fanny as far as Greenwich where they embarked on the steamboat to Scotland. He lingered on the shore until Marie-Thérèse could bear it no longer.

> My poor mother stood crying by my side, and bade me send him away. I gave him one signal, which he returned, and then ran up the beach, and was gone.[37]

It seemed fitting that Edinburgh, the place where Fanny gained her first sure sense of self, should be the staging post where she was to be separated from the life she had known. She was surrounded by dear friends – Mrs Harry Siddons, the Combe brothers and Lawrence MacDonald, the sculptor; even Cousin John Mason was there to play her Romeo.

On the fifth day of their engagement, Marie-Thérèse announced abruptly that she had decided to leave early to travel south with Sally Siddons.* Fanny always remembered that Saturday morning,

*That is, Mrs Harry Siddons's eldest daughter, Fanny's Cousin Sarah.

returning from rehearsal to find her mother packing. 'Miserable day of parting! Of tearing away and wrenching asunder!'

After her mother had gone, Fanny and her father sat by a window framing her mother's steamboat rocking on the Forth. She held a book in her lap and pretended to read, listening to her father's stifled sobs.

> I had resolved not to raise my eyes again from my book, when a sudden exclamation from my father made me spring up, and I saw the steamer had left the shore, and was moving fast toward Inchkeith, the dark smoky wake that lingered behind it showing how far it had already gone from us.[38]

At least there was still work to be done. Rehearsing every morning and acting every night kept her occupied. In between there were long farewell rides with three middle-aged cavaliers, who formed themselves into an Order of Knighthood, pledging themselves to drink her health on her birthday every year until she returned.

Fanny heard that Sir Walter Scott, suffering his final illness, had reached the city on his way to Abbotsford. 'I am glad he has come back to die in his own country, in his own home, surrounded by the familiar objects his eyes have loved to look upon.'[39] She spent a suitably melancholy afternoon sitting on the floor of the Phrenological Museum with a lap full of skulls. George Combe told her she was wearing herself out in body and mind. After a final performance of *The Provoked Husband*, it was over. She came off stage to find Mrs Harry Siddons and Cousin Lizzie waiting to say goodbye.

In Liverpool cholera was raging. The Kembles found Dall waiting for them at Radley's Hotel along with a parcel from Anna Jameson. Inside was a copy of Mrs Jameson's freshly published *Characteristics of Woman*. The book was dedicated to Miss Kemble and, in a further touch, the frontispiece (designed by Anna) depicted a mournful female figure looking out to sea at a receding ship.[40]

The Kembles played *Romeo and Juliet*, *Francis I* and *School for Scandal* in one exhausting night after the other. There was even a brief dash for a night at Manchester. The Chatmoss swamp was in the process of being drained and the spot where Huskisson had been struck down was now marked by a neat marble tablet.

Fanny carefully excised most references from her published record, but it would seem that when she returned to Liverpool, on a day so cold that the fires had to be lit at the height of summer, she received a letter of farewell from Augustus. 'I did not think there was such another day in store for me as this. I thought all was past and over, and had forgotten the last drop in the bitter cup.'[41] She spent the wretched day reading *The Merchant of Venice* and writing to Anna Jameson.

As the month ended *The Pacific*, a square-rigged sailing ship of the Black Ball Line, tied up at Liverpool. The Kembles' host of trunks were stowed aboard. Hal suddenly turned up to say goodbye in person, carrying a picture of herself so that Fanny might not forget her face. On 1 August her constant friend was standing on the dock to watch them sail. As the coastline sank into the horizon behind them, Fanny sat with her journal on her knee and wrote: 'Here I am on board *The Pacific*, bound for America, having left home, and all the world behind.'[42]

Her life-long fears of exile from her family and, worse still, of her family's dissolution, had come to pass. Her childhood love of the picture that once hung in Miss Grimani's drawing room had proved prophetic. At twenty-two, her heart broken with a love gone wrong, Fanny found herself back in the role of Miranda accompanying a broken Prospero into exile. Her one consolation was that dear, sensible Aunt Dall was making the journey with her.

24

That 'Big Bragging Baby'

As *The Pacific* bobbed just off Holyhead in the drizzle, waiting for a good wind, Fanny's resentment overflowed. While she mourned her separation from home and friends, Charles Kemble was rediscovering something of that youthful excitement with which he had once boarded a ship to St Petersburg on a whim to escape the burdens of family and duty. The upper cabins housed some twenty first-class passengers. They elected Charles their chairman and he rapidly settled into the shipboard conviviality, presiding genially over the evening entertainments and round-table dinners. Apart from Aunt Dall, who was a wretched sailor and spent most of the time in her berth, Fanny seemed to be the only one whose thoughts lingered on the old world dropping behind them.

In crossing the Atlantic in 1832, the Kembles were in the forefront of a budding fashion. By the end of the 1820s, as revolutions bubbled up across Europe, commentators awoke to the fact that the political models being worked out in America were likely to have profound implications for the old world of Europe. In 1832 it was still an open question whether the Union would survive. The very political existence of America, therefore, was 'a momentous experiment, upon which many eyes are fixed, in anxious watching of the result'.[1]

Anglo–American relations remained in a delicate condition. That

March, Mrs Trollope had published her *Domestic Manners of the Americans*, an acerbic account of her recent residence in the United States. Other English travellers had published their impressions of the new nation before, and many more would follow Mrs Trollope to press that decade, but *Domestic Manners* made a particular splash. Rarely has a piece of light reading caused such offence. Mrs Trollope became a by-word for ill-natured English snobbery across the United States, fuelling the suspicion that persisted for decades that every second English visitor only crossed the Atlantic so that they could profit back home by publishing abuse about the new nation.

The tenor of the debate between rival national commentators was infused with that outrage peculiar between parties who had assumed that they knew one another. The one thing that was for certain was that, even if they were 'two nations sprung from the one family',[2] American society was not English; a fact that many British observers, remembering a revolution begun over an English gentleman's right not to be taxed without representation, found hard to accept.

For generations it had been the Englishman's proud boast that his nation with its Mother of all Parliaments led the world as a model of a just and civilized society. Then in 1776 Jefferson wrote his preamble to the Declaration of Independence:

> We hold these truths to be self-evident, that all men are created equal, that they are endowed by their Creator with certain unalienable Rights, that among these are Life, Liberty and the pursuit of Happiness. That to secure these rights, Governments are instituted among Men, deriving their just powers from the consent of the governed.

In that Declaration the proposition was put that a just, progressive and civilized society rested not on culture but on a political theory.

As the Kembles sailed across the Atlantic that summer, the Republic founded in 1776 was in the process of transformation. By 1832 the original thirteen states had become twenty-four. The United

States did not yet stretch from coast to coast and expansion would continue. The theory of democracy – the incorporation of the masses – was evolving in application and under pressure. As the Reform agitation in Britain and the revolutions of 1830 indicated, democratic aspirations were a preoccupation of the old world as much as the new, but European reformers continued to wrestle with the notion that to safeguard civilized standards, the right to vote needed to be tied to certain levels of property or education. Indeed, this was the tradition to which the Founding Fathers had belonged. When Jefferson wrote his preamble he believed that every man could be educated to wield his democratic rights in theory, but as a rational gentleman of the late eighteenth century he feared the mob. The commonwealth required reasonable and informed citizens and it was reason, rather than a blind political belief in the liberty of the individual, that would produce a just society.

However, that preamble – written in an afternoon – was taken up by others who did not share the Founding Fathers' assumptions. In 1828* the Democrats won the presidency for the first time on the principle that a man's right to vote was his birth-right. An aspiration had become a universal truth. Democracy was emerging as a concept of sovereignty residing in a politicized citizenry expressing its will by vote – a ground-breaking idea insofar as it was intended to apply to diverse populations across a continent rather than within the intimate boundaries of an ancient Greek city. With the election of Andrew Jackson, Old Hickory, the sparsely educated,† Indian-fighting general and self-proclaimed man of the people, the Founding Fathers' Federalist model of the American citizen as the self-respecting artisan faded before the Westerner, the self-made man of action forged on the frontier.

---

*Andrew Jackson won his first presidential election in December 1828; he was inaugurated as President in March 1829.

† In 1833 the President of Harvard refused to countenance awarding Andrew Jackson an honorary degree, fuming that the Democrat President was 'a barbarian who cannot write a sentence of grammar and can hardly spell his own name'.

In autumn 1832 Jackson was in the race for a second presidential term and his rule and the manner of it was in hot dispute. The divisions over the benefits of democracy made themselves felt in the first-class stateroom of *The Pacific* as the Whig* majority among the American passengers fell into furious debates with the lone Jacksonian Democrat. Listening to them, Fanny rather doubted that the fledgling Union could survive, although her interest was fleeting. When Charles entertained his fellow passengers, declaiming a speech by the Whig senator Daniel Webster, expounding the particular virtues of the Founding Fathers, his daughter's comments to her journal betrayed her turbulent feelings about her parent† as much as her response to the American orator:

> My reason for objecting to Webster's style – though the tears were in my eyes several times while my father read – is precisely the same as my reason for not altogether liking my father's reading; 'tis slightly theatrical – something too much of passion, something too much of effect – but perhaps I am mistaken; for I do so abhor the slightest approach to the lamps and orange peel.[3]

Fanny succumbed to sea-sickness and for the first fortnight of the crossing hardly left her berth. The enforced inactivity uncurled some of the resentment that had wound up within her over the preceding months. One other female passenger shared the first-class cabin with Fanny and her aunt. Harriet Hodgkinson was a diffident, pretty young Englishwoman travelling to Boston with her brother, William. Harriet provided the young star with an appealing substitute sister and companion. It was an added bonus that Harriet's

---

*By 1832 the Federalist Party was no more. Patrician opponents to the Democrats called themselves Whigs, an allusion to the English opposition party and their own portrayal of Jackson as 'King Andrew'.

†She later admitted to Hal that she had been 'profoundly affected' by that speech 'when my father read it to us on board ship' – to Hal, New York, 30 September 1832, *Records of a Girlhood*, p. 547.

brother was 'intelligent, tolerably well informed and extremely handsome'. He, along with the willowy Mr Staley of Philadelphia, supplied a couple of attentive cavaliers.

Whenever the weather permitted, an awning was unfurled on deck to provide the first-class passengers with an outdoor lounge. There were dances on deck and intimate readings under the stars by lantern light, Fanny's resonant voice carrying 'that glorious hymn to the sea' from Byron's *Childe Harold* up into the night. Regrets for Augustus Craven still pursued her – a glorious sunset gave rise to melancholy verses on the passing of youth, followed by a graveyard number about lost loved ones (Why art thou weeping/ Over the happy, happy dead etc.) but she was sufficiently recovered to be writing again. The weird beauty of the ocean prompted some evocative prose:

> Evening came down; the sea, from brilliant azure grew black as unknown things, the wind freshened . . . the stars . . . lit their lamps in heaven: their wondrous brilliancy, together with the Aurora Borealis, which rushed like sheeted ghosts along the sky, and the stream of fire that shone round the ship's way, made heaven and earth appear like one vast world of flame, as though the thin blue veil of air and the dark curtain of the waters were but drawn across a universe of light. Mercy, how strange it was![4]

As they neared the American continent, head-winds battered *The Pacific*. While Aunt Dall cowered, the miserable embodiment of seasickness in her berth, Fanny cradled herself in the rigging and 'enjoyed it all amazingly . . . it stirred my spirits to ride over these huge sea-horses, that came bounding and bellowing round us'.[5] As ever, sensation proved an effective anodyne.

Four weeks after leaving Liverpool, standing on deck, the sun beating down out of a cloudless sky, Fanny looked through a telescope and made out trees on the shoreline of Long Island. On 3 September, as the first-class passengers danced an interminable country dance on deck, *The Pacific* cast anchor. The ship swung round 'and there lay New York before us, with its clustered lights shining like a distant constellation against the dark outline of land'[6].

The next morning a thick fog obscured the shore and the rain poured down. A steamboat came and took the passengers off, leaving *The Pacific* rocking forlorn with her reefed sails. 'I feel like a wretch swept down a river to the open sea and catch at the last boughs that hang over the banks to stay me from that wide loneliness.'[7]

America in the 1830s was marked by speculation and enterprise, and New York was the embodiment of that energy. Fortunes were being made from land deals, from speculations in railways and canals, and all sorts of innovations from mass-produced biscuits to steel pens. Immigration from Europe was beginning to overwhelm the original seventeenth-century Dutch settlement on the southern tip of Manhattan Island.* The novelist Catharine Maria Sedgwick wrote that the population was 'so multifarious and changing that compared with other cities it is somewhat like the ocean – constant in nothing but change.'[8] Before long, old New York – the painted houses with their green shutters interspersed with trees – would be swallowed up by the host of new structures that left Fanny with the impression 'of an irregular collection of temporary buildings, erected for some casual purpose, full of life, animation and variety, but not meant to endure for any length of time'.

Cholera was in the city – 4000 people were said to have died that June. The epidemic was still taking victims in the heat of the Indian summer. In their handsome rooms in the American Hotel, the new arrivals were perpetually flushed and uncomfortable in the unaccustomed temperatures. At that time, pigs still scavenged the New York

*The population of New York grew from 60,500 in 1800 to half a million by 1850.

streets, contributing to a plague of insects during the hot months. 'Mosquitoes, ants, and flies, by day; and flies, fleas, and worse, by night . . . We spend our lives in murdering . . . creeping and jumping things.'[9] Fortifying herself with quantities of iced lemonade and sliced peaches Fanny took a lively interest in her new surroundings. She wrote her first letter to Hal late at night in the midst of a sudden storm, thunder concussing the air and the lightning darting over the city illuminating her page with flashes of 'livid violet-coloured flame'. She commented on the comfortable, commercial bathhouses and the drinking water supplied in daily deliveries by huge water-butts mounted on carts.* She enthused about a market piled with 'heaps of melons, apples, pears and wild grapes in the greatest profusion', and a walk by the wooded shores of the Atlantic where each step in the warm grass started up clouds of grasshoppers with scarlet wings.

The weather was 'intolerable'. Fanny described herself as in a 'state of perpetual fusion'. The Park Theatre was the coolest place to be. Days were spent rehearsing on the dark stage by candlelight with the street doors standing open to the baking boardwalks. Mr Price, the manager, had bills up promising New Yorkers that never before had they had the chance to see such an elite pair of actors perform. And Charles Kemble was so relieved to have put the Atlantic between him and his disastrous financial affairs that he was looking ten years younger.

Harriet Hodgkinson and her brother said their farewells and left for Boston. They all planned to meet up again as that city was to be a stop on the theatrical tour. Fellow passengers who remained in New York called daily at the American Hotel, making every effort to ensure that the visitors felt welcome. There was a cautious family reunion when Dall's rakish brother Vincent Decamp appeared. He had an engagement at the Chestnut Street Theatre in Philadelphia. Since his emigration to America he had acquired a reputation for

*New York – like Paris at that time – did not yet have a piped water supply. Drinking water was brought in daily from natural springs outside the city. American hotels did not expect to provide baths, directing their visitors to commercial bathhouses.

playing comic eccentrics*. One contemporary thought Vincent's charms were best restricted to the stage – 'as eccentricity was his forte . . . so were his personal traits . . . they rendered his social intercourse at times obnoxious. He was captious and fretful . . . a child of larger growth'.[10] Fanny rather warmed to her uncle but her father was eager to keep the connection private.

Charles Kemble had a letter of introduction to Philip Hone, a prominent Whig and a former Mayor of the city. Hone was a New Yorker who had made his fortune as an auctioneer of ship cargoes; at that time he was remarkable for his informed interest in Europe and the arts.† He made a habit of gathering notable foreigners at his handsome house at 235 Broadway overlooking City Hall Park.

As luck would have it, when the ex-Mayor called to invite the Kembles to dinner, he found Charles Kemble out. Fanny received the tall, spare, fifty-one-year-old with a grudging sense of duty. 'Mr Philip Hone is one of the men of New York in point of wealth, influence and consideration,' ran the pert note in her journal that night. 'His is one of the first houses here, so I conclude that I am to consider what I see as a tolerable sample of the ways and manners of the best society in New York.'[11]

Fanny assumed that she and her father would be welcomed in America in their private character as visitors of distinction. In his diary Hone noted drily after that first encounter: 'Miss Kemble, like all young persons who have become celebrated, has many and strong admirers. But many dislike her on first acquaintance. Her manners are somewhat singular . . . Allowance should be made for the peculiarity of her situation, just arrived among strangers, with a consciousness that she is viewed as one of the lions of the day, and as such the object more of curiosity than of affection.'[12]

---

*He was later rumoured to have married a wife with a little money. He tried his hand at dairy farming in Mobile, Alabama, although according to his obituary, Mr De Camp 'of the Mobile theatre' died a resident of Houston, Texas.

†A keen self-improver, once he had established his fortune in his forties, Hone visited England and Europe determined to make up for a lack of formal education.

At the Hones' dinner party Fanny refused to make idle conversation and was brusque in the face of compliments, while her critical appraisal of the table settings and food was transparent to her hostess. Her host fared better once he got her talking about horses, whereupon she charmed him with a display of the conversational vivacity of her mother at her best. Turning the evening over with his son afterwards, Philip Hone decided that Miss Kemble preferred married men.

> She has certainly an air of indifference and nonchalance not at all calculated to make her a favourite with the beaux . . . Her fault appears to be an ungracious manner of receiving the advances of those who desire to pay her attention. This may proceed from the novelty of her situation and may soon be removed. But now is her time to make friends if she wants them . . . I am of the opinion that she does not like her profession. It is not her favourite theme of conversation; necessity, rather than choice, has led her to adopt it.[13]

Many English actors had performed on the New York stage and the city's elite did not necessarily turn out to see them. Hone noted in his diary the significant absence of ladies in the audience that gathered to watch Charles Kemble's opening night as Hamlet on Monday, 17 September. Fanny sensed enough to be anxious as she watched her father's performance. She reported stoutly in letters home that her father 'acted admirably, and looked wonderfully young and handsome', but she judged the applause inadequate.

The New York critics thought her father – now in his late fifties* – too old for his part.† His muted reception made it clear that the suc-

---

*He would turn fifty-seven that November.

†Henry Wikoff of Philadelphia wrote slyly that Charles Kemble's 'physique was somewhat too portly for the philosophic Dane', while Philip Hone admitted that his 'pauses are too long and too frequent, so much so as to make the representation fatiguing' – although he concluded that Kemble was 'a good study for the younger men, and his visit to this country ought to improve the American stage'. Wikoff, p. 37 and Tuckerman, Sunday, 16 September 1832.

cess of the tour rested on Fanny's début the following night as Bianca in *Fazio*.

The performance had the makings of a disaster. The theatre management had engaged an English actor, Mr Keppel, to play Bianca's husband, Fazio. The choice was unfortunate for he had had an ignominious trial as Fanny's Romeo in London (she referred to him as that 'washout man'). So on her opening night Fanny found herself burdened with a wretchedly nervous co-star whose principal means of conveying the emotion of the part was to fall to his knees and grapple her unwilling hands. She was near to despair by the time Fazio died at the end of the second act, but once free of him, she triumphed.* The reviewer for the *New York Mirror* was enchanted:

> The curtain rose and discovered two characters, the one a man, the other a young female, slight but gracefully formed, seated at a table, drawing, with her back partly towards the audience, so as to preclude any immediate recognition. Her companion had proceeded some time in his opening speech before she turned and discovered a sweet new face, glowing with soul and feeling, and the large, dark eyes of Miss Fanny Kemble, half lifted to the audience who returned their glances with long, hearty, and reiterated thunders of applause. The deafening peals at length died away into a hushed and pervading silence, and the low tones of a silvery voice rose in the silence, tremulously sweet, and at once seducing every heart. We were surprised, delighted. She was different from our anticipations and much beyond them.[14]

---

*Mr Keppel managed to create a brief local scandal. He had been engaged to play Fanny's Romeo a couple of nights later but, despite concerns about his age and relation to his Juliet, Charles Kemble stepped into the role at the last minute. No one was happy with the result. The New Yorkers did not get to see Charles Kemble's popular Mercutio and both the Kembles were uncomfortable. Mr Keppel resorted to the newspapers, complaining that he was the victim of snobbery and English high-handedness. A surge of democratic outrage bought him one more chance to play opposite a furious Fanny in *Venice Preserved*, but he did not last.

Any man who witnessed her performance that night without emotion, declared his fellow critic at the *New York American*, deserved to be 'compelled to pass his days among such barbarous peoples as Mrs Trollope describes, and be embalmed in her immortal pages'.[15]

At the end of their twelve-night engagement father and daughter were said to have earned the Park Theatre nearly $17,000.[16] The *New York Mirror* concluded that the Kembles' visit had initiated a new era in American stage history, attracting people 'who had been strangers to the theatre, the serious and the gay, the aged and the young'.*

Still smarting from Mrs Trollope's strictures about their nation's lack of cultivation, the New York critics might be at pains to demonstrate their appreciation of the English performers, but for the most part New York audiences found the Kemble style of declamation too slow and their acting overly restrained.† The classical idea of legitimate drama as a stimulus to the cultivation of the mind, on which the Kembles had built their name, had never taken root across the Atlantic.

The American theatrical system was focused around stars.[17] The language of the reviews was significant. Fanny seduced her audience with her half-lifted eyes, tremulous voice and face glowing with soul. It was her person rather than her parts that made her popular.

This focus on personality was illustrated night after night as Fanny was expected to linger after the curtain fell, bowing to her cheering audiences as vast baskets of hothouse flowers were handed

---

*_New York Mirror_, 13 October 1832, quoted Gibbs, p. 122. The poet Walt Whitman, then a teenager from Brooklyn, was one of her ardent fans. As an old man he recalled saving his money to travel into town to see 'that young maturity and roseate power in all their noon, or rather forenoon, flush . . . Nothing finer did any stage ever exhibit – the veterans of all nations said so, and my boyish heart and head felt it in every minute cell'.

†Fanny was told of the complaint of one spectator overheard after watching her father in *Venice Preserved*: 'Lord bless you! It's nothing to Cooper's acting – nothing! Why, I've seen the perspiration roll down his face like water when he played Pierre! You didn't see Mr Kemble put himself to half such pains!' 'The stamp-and-stare-and-start-and-scream school,' she admitted, 'has had its admirers all the world over since the days of Hamlet the Dane.'

to her. She found these ceremonies 'embarrassing and almost ridiculous for the object of the demonstration'.[18] She resented the implication that she owed this mass of strangers her grateful thanks for their applause, as if she had not already provided the entertainment they bought with their tickets. She and her father were expected to sustain their celebrity performance off stage as well as on.

'You have no idea how they are beset by troops of vulgar well-meaning blackguards,' reported an English acquaintance, 'who cut off all retreat by standing outside the door and sending their cards in by a waiter . . . they hem her in, and talk of Cotton and Muscovado, and the price of land at Texas . . . and they try to get him [Charles Kemble] to give praise to the City and Country and to cry up democracy, all of which he praises as well as he may.'[19] In such conditions, the ostentatious bouquets – those 'perishable tokens of anonymous public and private favour'[20] – seemed in fee for something Fanny had no wish to sell.

Apart from Philip Hone's hospitality, the Kembles were ignored by New York society – and they were expected to understand why. When Dr Wainright, an eminent Episcopalian preacher, asked to meet father and daughter at a privately arranged dinner party in their hotel, it was explained to them that the rector's 'congregation are so strait-laced that he can neither call upon us nor invite us to his house, much less set his foot in the theatre. The probable consequence of any of these enormities, it seems, would be deserted pews next Sunday, and perhaps eventually the forced resignation of his cure of souls.' Fanny got on well with the good doctor face to face but she still felt the snub. 'This is rather narrow-minded, I think, for this free and enlightened country.'[21]

Whereas back in England Fanny had been moved by Fenimore Cooper's picture of the Republican spirit as a story of simple, pious, pioneering folk carving a new world out of the wilderness, here in New York, America seemed a 'big, bragging baby'. The lack of respect accorded to poetic imagination and the artists who served it could only indicate a raw and immature society.

They have no legendary lore
No knightly marvel-haunted years,
The nursery tales of adult ears,
The busy present, the bright to come,
Of all their thoughts make up the sum.[22]

The intrusive nature of 'democratic' manners became a regular theme in her journal. She was offended by New York shop assistants who addressed her by name and attempted to strike up conversations ('I have no idea of holding parley with clerks behind a counter, still less of their doing so with me'). From the casual manners of callers who presumed on the slightest of introductions to unco-operative servants – the hotel cooks who went home at their own convenience and refused to provide a hot dinner for actors returning hungry after the play; the washerwomen who sat down before her while Fanny stood giving instructions, and the delivery boy who kept his hat on in her drawing room – this sovereign people appeared to suffer from 'a vulgar misapprehension which confounds ill-breeding with independence and leads people to fancy that they elevate themselves above their condition by discharging their duties and obligations discourteously'.[23]

When an edited version of Fanny's *Journal* was published a couple of years later, these opinions were taken as a betrayal of the hospitality of a generous people who had made an actress rich. The offence ran so deep that decades after her death Fanny Kemble's American biographers continued to express bewilderment at the 'contradiction' between this celebrity's snobbish outbursts and her proven affinity with the outsider and the oppressed in society.

Much of what she wrote was heavily tinted by the emotional self-defence of a twenty-two-year-old exposed far from home, but the question of manners was central to the cultural debate between the English and Americans. The debate was taken very personally because what was at issue was the very definition of a civilized human being. From the English perspective the concept of 'knowing your place' was not necessarily about being *kept* in that place but rather about showing respect for civilized values. Hence, Fanny's life-long impatience with what she considered bad manners did not prevent warm fellow feeling towards anyone of any condition who displayed courtesy and a desire to improve themselves.

At that time, what were characterized as national attitudes towards servants provided one of the most frequent grounds of cultural misunderstanding between the Americans and the English. Typically Americans accused their English visitors of snobbery and a determination, in the name of privilege, to stifle the initiative of free men and women, while the English countered that it was hypocrisy to make such an issue of the independence of the individual while countenancing slavery.*

During her first crossing of the Atlantic, Fanny recorded an incident concerning the black steward Essex, 'a very intelligent, obliging, respectable servant' who served them on board *The Pacific*:

> . . . after giving that same man some trouble, Dall poured him out a glass of wine, when we were having our dinner, whereupon the captain looked at her with utter amazement, and I thought some little contempt, and said, 'Ah! One can tell by that you are not an American'; which sort of thing makes one feel rather glad that one is not.[24]

Fanny and her aunt saw an intelligent and respectable servant; the democratic captain saw a freed slave. When, after they had landed in New York, Essex asked Charles Kemble for a pass to the play, adding that it had to be for the gallery as people of colour were not allowed in any other part of the theatre, Fanny was outraged. 'I believe I turned black myself I was so indignant. Here's aristocracy with a vengeance!'[25]

---

*Slavery had been declared unlawful in the United Kingdom in 1772 – Fanny wrote indignantly to Hal, 'the prejudice against these unfortunate people is, of course, incomprehensible to us'; a statement she assumed to be shared by all educated English folk, despite the fact that Parliament only finally abolished slavery in all British colonies in 1834.

The outlook Fanny acquired from her family upbringing and developed in the pages of Mme de Staël, Scott and Goethe, adopted and transformed notions of aristocracy into a 'nobility of mind' that was not tied to class or race or material wealth; it was a human quality that could be cultivated in anyone with the will to pursue it.

As the bitter disputes Fanny overheard in the stateroom of *The Pacific* illustrated, in 1832 Americans continued to be deeply divided over the interpretation of the compact made in the Declaration of Independence. With the arrogance of youth, her experience of American society in those first few weeks led her to observe that the result of the American democratic experiment was not to do away with aristocracy but rather to degrade the concept to purely material terms:

> The aristocracy here is one of wealth which I hold to be nearly as contemptible as that of nobility of mere birth . . . the man who has made his fortune by trade looks down with infinite disdain upon the man who is building his upon the same foundation. Wholesale turns up his nose at Retail. I have heard such expressions as 'the lower orders finding their level – exclusive – select' – all the jargon in fact of our high English circle . . . They are as tenacious of a Judgeship or a Militia military title as ever German Baron was of his countless quarterings. In short the very essence of aristocratic feeling prevails here, and 'tis my own belief that this country will soon lose the form as it certainly has the spirit of a Republic.[26]

Fanny Kemble had many points of sympathy with Republican values: her admiration for hard work; her distrust of idle luxury; her belief in the genius of the ordinary man as embodied in George Stephenson's triumph over the pompous Parliament men. But as an actor, fully aware of the ease with which a crowd could be manipulated, she had no faith in the voice of the people expressed en masse. A political dogma that every man's vote was presumed to carry equal weight, whatever his education, wisdom or stake in society, discounted the value of cultivation in a way that was bound to be anathema to a Kemble, for whom deference to education and gentility was the framework that preserved society from the 'recklessness bred of obscure means'. In New York she saw a society where the power and influence of American Whigs, such as Philip Hone, who balanced a respect for old world culture with their Republican independence, was waning. The new leadership of America was headed by the first President to master working a crowd;* a general who drove savage Indians from the frontier lands so that they could be safely annexed by the waves of pioneers moving West. Andrew Jackson's second presidential term would confirm a new era. The future of Western Democracy was set to become fixed around its populist definition.

Just as Fanny was feeling so alienated and alone, a familiar face appeared. Francis Henry Fitzhardinge Berkeley was idling about New York writing the occasional review for the city's newspapers while entertaining unrealistic ambitions that he might be in line for a consular post. It was natural that he should come to call on his good friend Charles Kemble to congratulate him on his success at the Park.

Back in England, Marie-Thérèse would have made sure that such a man was kept at a distance from her daughter. But whatever Aunt Dall's reservations, the loneliness of exile overcame all objections. How could Fanny resist the company of such a pleasing representative of that world of gentlemanly manners where people did not 'tread on one's feet or poke their elbows into one's side (figuratively speaking) in their conversation'. Besides, Henry was her dear, lost Augustus's cousin. No matter that the forty-year-old was known to be travelling with his mistress, Mrs Austin, an English singer,

---

*As the Whig Philip Hone bitterly summed up the general's popularity in contrast to his more intellectual predecessor, President John Adams: 'Adams is the wisest man, the best scholar, the most accomplished statesman; but Jackson has the most tact. So huzza for Jackson!'

who was appearing in New York at the time. So long as he left Mrs Austin at home, chaperoned as she was by Aunt Dall, there seemed no harm in enjoying Berkeley's amusing company and musical evenings at the piano singing through his manuscript copies of Rossini's operas.

Mrs Austin's schedule not permitting him to travel on with the Kembles, Berkeley offered to write to Pierce Butler, the heir to one of the leading families of Philadelphia. Butler was a talented amateur musician with taste and a proper appreciation of the drama; he would be enchanted to meet the celebrated actors. Charles Kemble accepted this kindness. Pierce Butler might be just the kind of connection to introduce a distinguished tragedian into the society that had so far eluded him in New York.

25

Enter Pierce Butler – American Gentleman

Pierce Butler was eighteen years old when he first became acquainted with Henry Berkeley. One might speculate on the motives of a man of Berkeley's reputation befriending an heir to wealth, a lad twenty years younger than himself. Apparently the engaging wastrel forged an 'intimate' friendship with Butler, introducing him to the pleasures of a gentleman in the dance halls and theatres of New York.*

'Why don't you come here and see the Kembles?' Berkeley wrote to 'my dear Pierce' who was at home in Philadelphia.

> Charles is the best and most finished Actor you have ever seen, and Fanny is . . . superior to anything that can be imagined. When you see her, if we are not together, remember to observe her when jealous of Fazio she says, 'You have seen Aldebella.'

---

*With the benefit of hindsight Fanny would write that it was to Berkeley's 'example & precepts I attribute much of Mr Butler's subsequent profligacy & want of principle'. In the long run she was more forgiving of Berkeley than she was of Pierce. As an old woman she would describe Henry as 'one of the most profligate and unprincipled men I have ever known' adding that he was 'also one of the most agreeable and accomplished'. Addition to *Journal*, vol. 1, p. 124, Wister, pp. 98–99.

The workings of her fine face and the subdued and smothered voice of intense passion which she brings forth with the eye of Fire is only met with once in a man's life. In person she is pretty, rather taller and more round than Miss George, large legs and feet, large hands, large arms: never mind, you will fall in love with her . . . for she is right lovely to look upon . . . Her eyes when flashing with spirit vividly beautiful, when half closed with a sorrowful expression, tenderness itself; when playful they are archness itself . . . her mouth large with teeth of Ivory, her nose straight occasionally (and too often) with a curl of contempt rather inclined upwards . . . her voice soft and beautiful. Off the Stage, rather swarthy, with her face all expression, a pleasant agreeable well-bred Girl . . . worthy of the Family, a French woman able to act in the French Drama, an Italian Scholar and a fine Musician.'[1]

Henry Berkeley was a generous fellow; he was reputed to have found several mistresses for his male friends from among his wide female acquaintance. His letter was not an innocent one. The physical details in his description of Fanny – and indeed his familiarity in referring to her by her first name to a stranger – throw a particular cast on the phrase 'a pleasant, agreeable, well-bred girl'. He was suggesting to his young friend that the latest star of the American stage might be an entertaining affair for a gentleman of taste.

Just before five o'clock on a damp, dreary October morning, Colonel Sibell, an acquaintance from *The Pacific*, came to collect the Kembles from their New York hotel and escort them to the Philadelphia steamboat tied up at the bottom of Barclay Street. Mid-morning the ship touched the New Jersey shore. The Kemble party disembarked to be crammed, along with six other passengers, into a leather-sided and unsprung coach that proceeded to jolt and bounce over deeply rutted roads littered with fallen timber. Pressed hard against the open window, Fanny watched the passing countryside with a jaundiced eye. The farms reminded her of the dilapidated homes of French or Irish peasantry – windows stuffed with rags, 'the gates broken, fences carelessly put up'. The glorious autumn crimsons and coppers of the trees struck her as morbid: 'The brilliancy of this decay strikes one . . . with a sudden sadness, as if the whole world were dying of consumption.'[2] The party transferred with relief to carriages drawn by horses down the track of a half-finished railway* that crossed to the steamboat landing on the Delaware River. In the late afternoon – ten hours after leaving New York – weary and nursing a cold, Fanny Kemble disembarked in Philadelphia.

From the very first, Philadelphia presented itself as a place of civilized comforts. The host of the Kembles' hotel, the Mansion House, was on the dock to greet them. By the time he had arranged for a piano to be installed in Fanny's rooms, he had become 'the enchanting Mr Head'.

> The town is perfect silence and solitude compared with New York. There is a greater air of age about it too, which pleases me. The red houses are not so fiercely red, nor the white facings so glaringly white.[3]

The decorous atmosphere of the city was ascribed to the influence of the wealthy descendants of the Quakers who settled it. In 1832 the Philadelphian social elite was composed of a number of families who had 'held the same station for several generations'.[4] Lingering anglophile affections had survived the Revolution. The leading families prided themselves on their old world sensibilities. 'The public,' Fanny noted, 'has high pretensions to considerable critical judgement and literary and dramatic taste.'[5] The Chestnut Street Theatre was

---

*The journey between the two cities had taken two days' ride in Jefferson's time. When finished, the railway would transform the journey, traversing the fourteen miles between the steamboat stages in 'in comfort and decency in half the time'.

'literally crammed from floor to ceiling' when she opened on Friday 12 October.

The following afternoon she came down from her hotel room to find a well-groomed young man chatting with her father. Charles Kemble introduced Mr Pierce Butler.

Pierce Butler was short – noticeably so at a time when average heights were much lower than today. Accounts differ, but it is likely that he was barely taller than Fanny, who herself was well under five foot. At the time of their first meeting he was twenty-two years old. A wealthy young man with expectations, Philadelphians regarded him as someone with genuine 'old blood' in his pedigree (his grandfather, the younger son of a Baronet, claimed descent from Irish Earls). The few photographs that remain of Pierce, taken in middle age, are not flattering, but contemporary descriptions of him in his youth recall accounts of Fanny's younger brother Henry. He had a smooth, boyish beauty combined with an air of composure beyond his years.

'He was a pretty-spoken, <u>genteel</u> youth enough,' recorded Fanny that night. 'He drank tea with us and offered to ride with me. He is, it seems, a great fortune. Consequently, I suppose (in spite of his inches), a great man. Now I'll go to bed. My cough's enough to kill a horse.'[6]

Mr Butler had come prepared for a challenge. Fanny, Henry Berkeley had informed him, was:

> . . . dogged and obstinate, will call a male fowl a Cock and her ambulatory pedestals legs, and thighs . . . in conversation she is very free but highly educated and accomplished, rather too much so for my way of thinking . . . because she puts you out of countenance by cursed apt quotations . . . from horrible old Writers, and if you shew any French, kills you with Racine, if Italian, knocks you down with Dante . . . Rather blue!! But not obtrusively so![7]

Pierce Butler had a pattern of being attracted to women who did not at once melt before his 'perfect amiability'. The 'curl of contempt', as

Berkeley put it, with which Fanny sometimes looked down her nose was just the sort of thing to spark his interest.[8]

Miss Kemble, it seems, did not dwell on Mr Butler. She lost no time inspecting the local stables and soon she was taking frequent rides into the countryside along the banks of the Schuylkill River, composing rhapsodic verse about the glory of the autumn woods. The presidential contest was in full swing. In the late afternoon the Kembles would drive to the theatre through crowded streets hung with 'star-spangled banners, and villainous transparencies of Old Hickory'.[9] The electors of Philadelphia were treated to the sight of Fanny hanging out of the carriage window brandishing her father's play sword 'by way of striking salutary awe in the hearts of all rioters who might come across our path'.

They were doing good business at Chestnut Street. *The Hunchback* in particular was a tremendous hit. 'The affecting phrases of the idolized Julia were repeated at every corner' as Philadelphia went wild for Miss Kemble. 'I did nothing,' recalled Henry Wikoff, a young law student at the time, 'but frequent the theatre and abandon myself to the fascinations of this bewitching actress.*

Many gentlemen came to call on the Kembles at the Mansion House.

> I am infinitely amused at the extreme curiosity which appears to me to be the besetting sin of the people here. A gentleman whom you know very slightly will sit down by your table during a morning visit, turn over every article upon it, look at the cards of the various people who have called upon you, ask half a dozen questions about each of them, as many about your own private concerns, and all this as though it were a matter of course that you should answer him, which I feel greatly inclined occasionally not to do.[10]

---

*Wikoff pictures his younger self going about 'like one possessed' muttering snatches of his favourite passages from Miss Kemble's plays until his friends doubted his sanity.

Fanny often came down to tea to find Pierce Butler ensconced with her father – 'they talked politics, abused Republicanism, lauded aristocracy, drank tea, took snuff, ate cakes, and pottered a good deal'.[11] Other regular visitors included the physician Dr Charles Mifflin, a relative of the Governor, and young Edward Biddle, the son and heir of Nicholas Biddle, the all-powerful director of the Second Bank of the United States and a prominent opponent of General Jackson.*

> . . . in walked that interesting youth Mr Biddle with a nosegay as big as himself in his hand . . . He sat some time, making the most excessively fine speeches.[12]

Young Mr Biddle was easily upstaged by a mystery admirer who, identifying himself only as 'a Philadelphia friend', wooed at a distance with a parade of enchanting nosegays.† When she came in from her ride Fanny would find flowers waiting for her. When she came home from the play, there would be another bouquet – 'so sweet, so brilliant, so fragrant, and fresh', flowers that in England would only be seen in midsummer.

'Found another beautiful nosegay waiting for me, from my unknown furnisher of sweets. This is almost as tantalizing as it is civil; and I would give half my lovely flowers to find out who sends them to me.'[13]

---

*The Bank of the United States was a private speculation set up a couple of decades earlier with a charter to act as the Federal bank. President Andrew Jackson regarded the institution as a bastion of East Coast opposition to himself and his policies and in 1832 was determined to veto the renewal of the Bank's Charter (due in 1836). After a protracted contest, Biddle and his Bank lost their Charter. The Federal Funds were distributed to a network of 'pet' banks about the United States and the consequent disruption contributed to the repeated currency crises that dogged the American economy into the 1840s.

†Fanny took this to mean a Quaker, but in truth it might just as well have been a hint to a prospective mistress. 'This place, as you know, is the headquarters of Quakerdom, and all the enchanting nosegays come from "a Philadelphia friend", the latter word dashed under, as if to indicate a member of the religious fraternity always called by that kindly title here.' Letter to Hal, from Philadelphia, 22 October 1832, vol. III, p. 264.

Fanny was in need of her mother. Charles Kemble's casual worldliness, along with his dislike of confrontation, made him an ineffective chaperone. Fanny's admirers soon worked out that the riding stables provided the best chance of proximity to the busy actress. Many gentlemen offered her their escort as she took her exercise.* Marie-Thérèse would have met such suggestions as opening gambits in a less than innocent negotiation, assuming that an actress's well-heeled admirers were likely to be in pursuit of all that feminine passion she displayed on stage. The annoyance Fanny expressed to her journal at the impertinence of some of these approaches recognized that such 'liberties' might indicate a lack of respect, but she was not prepared to tailor her behaviour to conform to the conventions. She liked to ride, and since she knew no Philadelphian ladies in the habit of taking that exercise, and Aunt Dall's pace being too slow for her liking, if a gentlemanly acquaintance offered her his escort, she would take it and very likely out-ride him into the bargain. Her journal is peppered with images of her portly aunt, red faced, and wind-blown, struggling to catch up and interpose herself between her niece and the pursuant male of the moment.

Fanny was in no mood to mind her elders. She had been particularly looking forward to visiting Boston, the acknowledged literary capital of America – 'whence look to receive volumes from me about Webster and Channing',[14] as she wrote to Hal. But, finding the manager of the Boston Tremont Theatre better at haggling than he liked, Charles Kemble abruptly broke off negotiations.[15] The trip to Boston was replaced by return engagements at New York and Philadelphia.

The incident added to Fanny's simmering despair over the reliability of her father's judgement. The post had brought Charles Kemble a letter from Mr Bartley, their erstwhile stage manager at Covent Garden, proposing a new partnership to take back the management of the old Patent Theatre. Charles Kemble was full of the

---

*She had a firm belief that happiness was rooted in fitness, arguing that 'violent bodily exercise' was the one sure remedy for low spirits.

idea. After all Fanny's sacrifices, he seemed in danger of falling back into his destructive obsession.

> My father has hitherto been able to lay by nothing, and my assistance is absolutely necessary to him . . . now, when his remaining health and strength will no more than serve to lay up the means of subsistence when health and strength are gone, the idea of his loading himself with such a burden of bitterness as the proprietorship of a new theatre makes me perfectly miserable.[16]

'I do not think that during my father's life, I shall ever leave the stage,' she wrote wretchedly to Hal. In his hunger for cash Charles Kemble was over-packing the schedules and Fanny was exhausted – 'money brought with health is bought too dear, I think'.[17]

At a time when the security of a private life seemed so distant, it was doubly distressing to realize that while she found the civilized standards of Philadelphia's upper classes so familiar, Philadelphian society was not so accepting of her. For all the attentions of the city's gentlemen, their wives were reluctant to invite the actors into their homes. Fanny professed herself furious on her father's behalf: 'It gave me something like a feeling of contempt, not only for the charities, but for the good taste of the Philadelphians when I found them careless and indifferent towards one whose name alone is a passport into every refined and cultivated society in Europe.'[18] In reality much of the disapproval was directed at her: 'The fact is, I am not "genteel" enough,' she scoffed on hearing that her portrayal of Lady Teazle in *School for Scandal* had been criticized as insufficiently ladylike. 'I, unfortunately for myself,' she fumed to her journal, 'have seen ladies "ripe and real", who, from all I can see, hear, and understand, differ widely from the good manners of their "beau ideal".

'To an Englishman,' she pronounced, 'this fashionable society presents, indeed, a pitiful sample of lofty pretensions without adequate foundation.'[19]

Fanny's exclusion from the city's drawing rooms underlined the importance of the domestic context in securing the status of a woman. A girl could not guarantee her own purity. Miss Kemble's unconventional behaviour was interpreted as unfeminine worldliness. If she was knowing, then she was not innocent; if she was not innocent, then she could not be respectable. The sight of the diminutive hard-riding actress pursued along the banks of the Schuylkill River by a pack of virile young men encapsulated the distinction between public and private womanhood. That sort of unruly, public chase implied only one end and that was not the marriage bed.

In their last week in Philadelphia the besotted Edward Biddle at last convinced his fond parents to call on the Kembles and invite them to dinner. That dinner improved Fanny's impressions of the place.

> I should say that not only the style of living but the society is superior to that which I saw in New York. Certainly, both the entertainment itself and the guests were irreproachable; the first in very good taste, the latter appeared to me well informed and very agreeable.[20]

As she stood on the steamer dock with her father and aunt in the rosy dawn light on the day of their departure, Fanny was sorry to leave that glimpse of private life: 'I like the town, and the little I have seen of its inhabitants, very much; I mean in private, for they are intolerable audiences.* There is an air of stability, of well to do, and occasionally of age, in the town, that reminds me of England.'[21]

Back in New York, social life improved further when Gouverneur Kemble, a wealthy arms manufacturer and a friend of Washington Irving, decided to claim father and daughter as distant relatives.

---

*She had been unsettled by the polite silence of the stiff-backed audiences that filled the uncushioned benches of the Chestnut Street Theatre: ''Tis amazing how much an audience loses by this species of hanging back, even where the silence proceeds from unwillingness to interrupt a good performance . . . an actor . . . is deprived by that very stillness of half his power . . . it is chilling and uncomfortable to go toiling on, without knowing whether, as the maid-servants say, "one gives satisfaction or no".' *Journal*, 12 October 1832.

As soon as the Kembles returned to Philadelphia Pierce Butler was on hand to welcome them back – paying his first call at their hotel on the very evening of their arrival. News of the Biddles' hospitality had spread, and, grudgingly, one or two hostesses sent cards of invitation.

One well-connected visitor to Philadelphia that winter, a young woman called Julia Kean, wrote an account of the ball the Kembles attended at the home of Mr and Mrs Willings on their second night back in the city. Her sketch of the scene vividly recalls Philip Hone's comment that the Kembles were objects more of curiosity than affection. Julia Kean was a friend of Emily Chapman, one of the reigning belles of the social elite. Arrayed in her pink crêpe and emeralds, she arrived with the Chapman party: 'We of course carried a great many beaux in our train and I had plenty of partners.' Julia had never seen so many beautiful women, 'and just enough men to fill up the corners and to screen us from the heat of the fire . . . Everyone is so hospitable and attentive to strangers here, that I feel quite at my ease and as if I had known all the young ladies for years.'

In contrast, Fanny's brief comment to her journal about the occasion was redolent of the outsider – 'I have beheld Miss Emily Chapman and should doubtless now depart in peace.'* It was clear that the Philadelphian belles regarded Miss Kemble as an interloper.

'Among the lions of the evening were Mr and Miss Kemble,' young Julia recorded spitefully:

> 'everyone crowded in the room where they were and everyone expressed their disappointment when instead of the graceful and elegant female they had seen on the stage they beheld a dark-complexioned, unhappy, diminutive little person, who looked as if she had been studying for some time the character of a witch. Mr Kemble is a finer looking man in a room, I think,

---

*After another large party, Fanny noted acidly: 'Saw and spoke to all Philadelphia. [Emily Chapman] was there and actually sitting still.' *Journal*, vol. II, p. 64.

than on the stage; his daughter dances well but in rather an affected style.'[22]

What Fanny – 'a stranger among strangers'[23] – did not realize, and would not learn until many years later, was that Mr Pierce Butler was widely regarded as Miss Chapman's special property. Emily Chapman was the daughter of Philadelphia's leading fashionable physician. The Butler and Chapman families had grown up together and the appropriateness of a match between the pair had been the favourite gossip of Philadelphia's inner circle for months. Indeed, young Butler and Miss Emily were even whispered to be engaged already.

Fanny may not yet have discovered that Pierce Butler had only lived under that name for six years. He was born Pierce Mease (pronounced 'Maize') in Philadelphia in 1810, one of six children of Sarah (née Butler) and Dr James Mease. His family was dominated by the shadow of its founder, Pierce's maternal grandfather, Major Pierce Butler, a younger son of an Irish Baronet who came to America in his late teens as a British officer during the French and Indian Wars.* The Major laid the foundations of his fortune by carrying off an heiress from Charleston, South Carolina.† It is said that his wife lived to regret her choice. Major Butler was not a kind man. He was, however, energetic in his own interests, amassing considerable property and wealth.

A tyrannical egotist, the ageing Major made a point of quarrelling with his heirs. He largely disinherited his own son Thomas and he had a virulent dislike of Pierce's father, Dr James Mease. Pierce's elder brother had been his grandfather's favoured heir. When that

---

*It was the Major's proud boast that his family connections could be traced back (probably through an illegitimate branch) to the Earls of Ormonde.

†Major Butler married Mary ('Polly') Middleton, the daughter of Thomas Middleton of Prince William's Parish, South Carolina, in 1771. His father-in-law was a wealthy merchant and slave trader and the Major's new wife came with an impressive fortune. According to Philadelphian gossip he had 'tried several heiresses' before he 'finally ran off with Mary . . . Middleton'. Fisher, p. 262.

brother died tragically young, the Major restructured his legacies, stipulating that those of his grandsons who took the Butler name would be eligible to be co-heirs to the bulk of his fortune. Pierce was the only one to take up this offer before his grandfather's death; at sixteen he traded his father's name for inheritance.

With his wealthy 'expectations',* Pierce became a catch and by the age of twenty-two he had become practised in the gentlemanly art of running parallel lives. Hints dropped in the papers of male contemporaries suggest that he was known as a regular patron of brothels in both New York and Philadelphia. His erotic tastes inclined to older women and actresses. The archives of the Historical Society of Pennsylvania contain letters, legacy of an 'intimacy' with a certain Mary Griffith. In a letter apparently written a couple of months before he met Fanny, Mary, an older woman, exhorts Pierce to give up immoral companions:

> Dearest Butler, *instantly and courageously* break off all connexions with the stage . . . I *entreat* you to break off *suddenly* and *for ever* all intercourse with a set of people so far beneath you.[24]

Pierce was not inclined to take this advice. During that winter he successfully preserved his 'official' relationship with Emily Chapman while pursuing a private flirtation with Fanny.

He would turn up unexpectedly at the riding school Fanny attended every morning. Walking in on her while she waited for her lesson, he would make her laugh with satirical accounts of the trials of a gentleman in a democratic society: 'He told me sundry steamboat stories that made my blood curdle, such as a public brush, a public comb, and a public <u>toothbrush</u>.'[25] Pierce prided himself on his horsemanship – that mark of the finished gentleman. And whereas her hard riding left many of Fanny's would-be attendants behind her

---

*Although, since his majority in 1831, Pierce had been in receipt of one quarter of the revenues of his grandfather's estate, the bulk of the fortune was still held by his maiden aunts, the Major's two surviving daughters.

in the dust,* he rode well enough to win himself the position of her prime escort. He put himself out to charm Aunt Dall, making her the gift of an expensive riding whip. Then, just as Fanny came to rely on his company every day, he would unaccountably be absent for a spell, only to reappear without comment.

Pierce Butler was an attractive flirt. He dressed elegantly and carried himself well. He had taken courses in law at the University of Pennsylvania and he could converse like a rational man – although he did not like to talk too much. He never seemed put out by anything Fanny might do. Fanny was by no means an easy pursuit. She turned one Sunday ride in the woods into an endurance test by insisting on taking a particular turn, with the result that they got thoroughly lost and Pierce, Fanny and the long-suffering Dall finally trailed back into town in the dark, exhausted and dishevelled.

Fanny professed herself amused by the rivalry that sprang up between Pierce and Edward Biddle for her attention. Young Ned marked Christmas with the offering of a workbox so elegant and sumptuous that Charles Kemble directed his daughter to return it as too expensive.† Pierce countered by revealing himself as the 'Philadelphia friend', the supplier of all those wonderful flowers. There were hardly a couple of years between the two young men, but the over-enthusiastic Ned Biddle could not but show up Pierce's greater experience of women to advantage. While Fanny's references to Butler in her journal remained teasing – 'that bright youth', or 'that interesting youth' – when the Kembles left for Baltimore on the last day of the year, she would miss his attentions.

In Baltimore the weather was so warm, windows stood open and the camellias were in bloom. Fanny found the raw, red-brick city

---

*Fanny was not flattering about her hosts' horsemanship. Americans, she wrote, 'never use a curb, but ride their horses upon the snaffle entirely, dragging it as tight as they can, and having the appearance of holding on for dear life by it; so that the horse, in addition to the awkward gait . . . throws his head up, and pokes his nose out, and with open jaws "devours the road" before him'. (Letter to Hal, from Philadelphia, 10 October 1832, *Records of a Girlhood*, vol. III, p. 257.

†Fanny finally persuaded him to let her keep it to save the boy's feelings.

straggling between parcels of waste-ground depressing.[26] They found that the theatre Charles had contracted to appear in was too ramshackle to serve and there was a flurry of alarm while he rapidly transferred their performances to a rival concern. In a poignant moment, Fanny and her father came across prints of her Uncle John Philip in his role as Hamlet and Mrs Siddons as Reynold's Tragic Muse forelorn in a print-shop window. 'It was a sort of sad surprise to meet them in this other world where we are wandering, aliens and strangers.'[27]

They moved on to Washington. The American capital was still a construction site. Fanny surveyed the marshy ground and the half-finished government buildings and pronounced it as 'where everything is to be, and where nothing is' – a common enough perception among visitors at the time.[28] The welcome was warm, however, in the person of Washington Irving. Fanny thought the popular writer was looking older and more careworn since the year of her début, but their reunion was affectionate. Well-established in Washington circles, Irving's sponsorship ensured that the Kembles were received in style. They were taken to see the Declaration of Independence, the paintings of red-skinned Indians hanging in the War Office and the Senate. Fanny was eager to hear the Senator from Massachusetts, Daniel Webster, speak. She was rather shocked by the informality of America's government. The Senators sat in comfortable armchairs drawn up in 'two semi-circular rows, turned towards the President'. The public gallery that ran round the chamber was only separated from the floor of the House by a low partition.

> . . . every now and then while the business of the House was going on and Webster speaking, a tremendous bustle and waving of feathers, and rustling of silks would be heard, and in came streaming a reinforcement of political beauties, and then would commence a jumping up, a sitting down, a squeezing through, and a how-d'ye-doing, and a shaking of hands. Then Senators would turn round, even Webster would hesitate as if

bothered by the row, and in short the whole thing was more irregular and unbusiness-like than anyone could have imagined.[29]

Fanny was particularly impressed by Webster, to whom she was introduced after the debate: 'He is very enchanting: I wish it had been my good fortune to see him oftener; one of the great men of this country, he would have been a first-rate man all the world over.'[30] Along with most of Washington's elite, Webster went to see her play: 'Fanny Kemble is here, turning everybody's head. I went to see and hear her last eve', and paid for it by a tremendous cold. I hear that the Venerable Judges go constantly.'[31]

Fanny found the little theatre rather cramped – a painted cloud tangled in her hair as she played Juliet on her balcony* – but she still managed to make the Chief Justice of the Supreme Court cry. Justice Marshall's colleague, Justice Joseph Story, reported to his wife that Miss Kemble played Mrs Haller, the heroine of *The Stranger*, 'with great propriety of manner, feeling, and power . . . she threw the whole audience into tears. The Chief Justice shed them in common with younger eyes.'[32] Story himself was moved to poetry:

Go, lovely woman, go! Enjoy thy fame!
A second Kemble, with a deathless name![33]

The attention paid Miss Kemble by the political elite was quite remarkable given the urgent affairs occupying their minds at the time. President Jackson, having won his second presidential term with a convincing majority, was in the midst of the Nullification Crisis. The Kembles were presented to an apparently unruffled President. Fanny described the White House as 'a comfortless,

*Watching her performing in the capital's little theatre during a later engagement, Philip Hone remarked that 'Fanny Kemble in the Washington Theatre is like a canary-bird in a mouse-trap', Tuckerman, Washington, 3 March 1834, p. 93.

handsome looking building' set in 'a withered grass plot enclosed in wooden palings in front and a desolate reach of uncultivated ground down to the river behind'. It was an open day and the public rooms were thronged with sightseers who snatched up the refreshments provided, put their feet on the furniture and climbed up on the mantelpieces to wave to their friends. The Kembles sat with the President for a quarter of an hour.

> His Excellency, Andrew Jackson, is very tall and thin, but erect and dignified in his carriage; a good specimen of a fine old well-battered soldier. His hair is very thick and grey, his manners are perfectly simple and quiet, therefore very good . . . He talked about South Carolina and entered his protest against scribbling ladies, assuring us that the whole of the present southern disturbances had their origin in no larger a source than the nib of the pen of a lady. Truly, if this be true, the lady must have scribbled to some purpose.[34]

The President may have made light of the crisis in conversation but profound issues were at stake. The pressure of the Union's rapid expansion was sharpening the demarcation between the interests of Northern and Southern states, throwing into relief the central unsettled dilemma embodied in the founding agreements of the American body politic: was the founding principle of the nation enshrined in the liberty of the States or in the Constitution that defined the contract made on behalf of the sovereign people across the whole federation?*

During the 1820s South Carolina had become increasingly dominated by the interests of cotton growers. As its power slipped

*The State Rights people held, along with Senator Robert Hayne of South Carolina, that 'the very life of the system is the independence of the States'. On the other side, unionists, such as Daniel Webster, contended: 'I go for the Constitution as it is, and for the Union as it is. It is, sir, the People's Constitution, the people's government, made for the people, made by the people, and answerable to the people.' – quotations from speeches made at a famous Senate Debate in January 1830.

in relation to the more densely populated and industrialized Northern States,* resentment solidified around the question of Federal Tariffs.† John C. Calhoun, Jackson's Vice-President during his first administration, came up with the notion of nullification as a mechanism to balance the effects of sheer majority rule. Arguing from the principle that the Constitution was a compact between sovereign states, the formula of nullification proposed that the state legislatures retained the right to rule whether an act of Congress was constitutional; the remedy for an act deemed unconstitutional being a nullifying state ordinance preventing its enforcement.

Jackson split with his Vice-President in 1831 and Calhoun resigned the post, remaining in Washington as Senator for South Carolina. In November 1832 the State Legislature of South Carolina passed a resolution nullifying the Federal tariffs and prohibiting the collection of customs duties within the state after 1 February 1833. Faced with this direct challenge to the authority of the Federal Government, Jackson ordered military preparations and the States Rights men prepared to do battle for their beliefs.

Charles Kemble had intended to perform in Charleston, but in January 1833 prospects looked so black that he abandoned the idea. Delayed in a snowstorm as they left the capital, Fanny wrote:

> It seems to me . . . that everything at this moment threatens change and disintegration in this country. It is impossible to imagine more menacing elements of discord and disunion than those which exist in the opposite and antagonistic interests of its

---

*South Carolina, along with its neighbours in the lower South, also faced increasing competition from producers in the more profitable lands of the South-West.

†These protectionist tariffs (or taxes) were imposed by the Federal Government with the ostensible aim of shielding emerging American industries from the competition of cheaper foreign goods. The tariffs impacted disproportionately on the rural Southern States as they were net importers of finished goods, and particularly on their main staple crop, cotton, which was sold as a raw material and re-imported as cloth.

> Southern and Northern provinces, and the anomalous mixture of aristocratic feeling and democratic institutions.[35]

At the last minute a compromise was brokered over the offending tariffs.* As spring approached, the crisis receded, but the threat of secession had been brought into vivid focus. Everyone knew that nothing had been settled. President Jackson's reported comment was that 'the next pretext will be the Negro or slavery question'.

The Kembles returned to Philadelphia to resume acting there – this time at the Walnut Street Theatre. To their dismay, they discovered that a scandal had followed them from the capital – a scandal that threatened to expand to serious proportions.

During their stay in Washington, Fanny had arranged to go riding with one Mr Adams. When Mr Adams arrived at the appointed hour, she found him accompanied by a Mr Fulton (a young relative of the steamboat engineer, Robert Fulton). Since she had never met Mr Fulton before, Fanny thought his inclusion in the party rather presumptuous, but he had brought her one of his own horses to ride and she was put in a difficult position.

> I did not think Mr Adams ought to have brought anyone to ride with me without my leave. However, as I was riding [Mr Fulton's] horse, I was just as well pleased that he was by, for I don't like having the responsibility of such valuable property as a private gentleman's horse to take care of. I told him this, alleging it as a reason for my preferring to ride an indifferent hack horse about which I had no such anxiety. He replied that I need have none about his. I told him laughingly that I would

*Congress enacted a Force Bill, authorizing the President to use the army and navy to collect duties, while at the same time passing a new Tariff Law, providing for a gradual scaling down of the offending taxes.

give him two dollars for the hire of it, and then I should feel quite happy, all of which nonsense passed as nonsense should without comment.[36]

A few days later, Charles Kemble was approached with the news that rumours were flying round Washington that Miss Kemble had disparaged American horses, their owners and even America itself,* and if a public apology was not made she would be hissed off the stage at her next performance. When some busybody attempted to impress upon her the seriousness of the affair, declaring that 'not less than fifty members of Congress have already mentioned the matter to me', Fanny exploded:

> Fifty gossiping women! Why, the whole thing is for all the world like a village tattle in England among half a dozen old wives round their tea pots. All Washington was in dismay, and my evil deed and words were the town talk – fields, gaps and marshes all rang with them . . . It were much to be desired that Americans had a little more national vanity or national pride. Such an unhappily sensitive community surely never existed in this world.[37]

In Washington, the anticipated hissing did not materialize, although the alarm severely dampened Fanny's performance as Beatrice in *Much Ado about Nothing*. But as they prepared to open at Walnut Street, Charles learned that pamphlets broadcasting the affair were being distributed in an attempt to rouse emotions against Fanny. Charles knew that if Fanny were to become the focus of nationalist outrage – given sensitivities in the wake of Mrs Trollope – it could cripple their money-making tour.

---

*The accusation, as related by Fanny, was that, 'during my ride with Mr Fulton I had said I did not choose to ride an American gentleman's horse and had offered him two dollars for the hire of his; that moreover I had spoken most derogatorily of America and Americans', *Journal*, 19 January 1833.

Miserable and tense, Fanny stepped on to the Walnut Street stage to open as Belvidera. She was taken aback by a tumultuous wave of applause. The Philadelphians had decided to discount the rumours and give her their backing. It was a turning point in her affections for the city.

> . . . they have behaved most kindly and courteously to us, and for mine own good part, I love the whole city of Philadelphia from this time forth for ever more.[38]

26

New England

In New York, that spring, Fanny heard a story about a print of Sir Thomas Lawrence's sketch. Carried by a pedlar into the wild interior beyond the Allegheny Mountains, it was said to have been bought –

> at an egregious price by a young engineer, who with fifteen others went out there upon some railroad construction business, and were bidding for it at auction in that wilderness, where they themselves were gazed at, as prodigies of strange civilization, by the half-savage inhabitants of the region.[1]

It was an intoxicating tale of fame; that romantic picture of her youthful self carried, like a talisman, deep into the raw back country to inspire a young engineer bringing civilization to the wilderness. No wonder the story 'touched and pleased me very much'.

Fanny's fame touched Pierce Butler too. Reports of the way she was received in Washington reached Philadelphia. Pierce Butler might be a man of consequence in his home town, but here was a woman received by the great men of the nation. When the Kembles moved back to New York, he followed. One night Fanny looked down from her stage to see 'that interesting youth' playing a flute along with the musicians in the orchestra pit.*

After seven months of hard touring Fanny was feeling the strain. One morning she was sitting in her New York drawing room entertaining Washington Irving, when the first mate of *The Pacific* called to present her with a box of English earth sent by his captain. This romantic gift caused Fanny to break down in floods of tears. It was an outburst of many things that had been piling up for weeks. She felt that her father was overworking them both, that their performances were suffering – the fine details coarsened and lost. (Charles Kemble had recently appeared drunk on stage, and he was to do so again. He covered himself well enough before the front of house, but in his heyday he would never have been so unprofessional.) Fanny was haunted by a sense of the years rushing by with no clear future for herself: 'As fast as I gather my wits together for any steady occupation, I am whisked off to some new place, and do not recover from one journey before I have to take another.'[2]

Charles Kemble assumed his daughter would do her family duty without complaint as he himself had done. Fanny confessed to Hal her fear that she would never be able to return to England. Despite their American profits,

> the state of my father's property in Covent Garden is such that it seems more likely that he may never be able to return to England without risking the little which these last toilsome years will have enabled him to earn for the support of his own and my mother's old age. He will be compelled, in all

---

*Pierce was well established among Philadelphia's amateur musicians. Fanny never seems to have questioned why he had the time to be so attentive. As an Englishwoman it was normal to her that a gentleman should be 'at leisure'. In America, however, even wealthy young men were expected to have a profession. 'Idlers' were seen as somehow unmanly and in the terms of his neighbours Pierce's lack of steady occupation was unusual.

likelihood, to settle and die abroad, as my Uncle John did, by the liabilities of that ruinous possession of theirs.[3]

Irving listened patiently to Fanny's stormy declaration of her dislike of her profession – how she was so 'dreadfully cramped for time' that her 'poor mind goes like a half-tended garden'.[4]

'You are living, you are seeing men and things,' he told her; 'you are seeing the world, you are acquiring materials and heaping together observations and experience and wisdom, and by and by, when with fame you have acquired independence and retire from these labours, you will begin another and a brighter course with matured powers. I know of no one whose life has such promise in it as yours.'

Maybe at twenty-three there were still better things to be looked forward to. 'I almost felt hopeful while he spoke to me.'[5]

It was in this frame of mind that Fanny began her acquaintance with the person she would always refer to as her 'first American friend': the successful New England novelist, Catharine Maria Sedgwick.

Fanny had collected Miss Sedgwick's nephew among her New York admirers. Theodore Sedgwick was a recent graduate from Columbia finding his feet in his Uncle Robert's New York law practice. His sober and upright father in Albany was moved to write to his firstborn, warning him against entanglements with actresses.[6] Young Theodore stoutly defended his admiration:

> Two or three notes, sundry visits, some prolonged almost to the next day, & much time spent in her company, talking, dancing & waltzing have altogether convinced me that she is the ablest woman I have ever seen . . . the most straightforward, masculine, controlling mind in a female head, & yet she is as feminine a creature in many things as I ever knew. In short, she is a vastly lovable person, & had I not Chancery bills to copy, a Book to finish, sundry reminiscences, & many hopes, I might have played the fool before this at her feet.'[7]

Theodore's work commitments and his father's disapproval may have kept him from declaring himself in any formal way, but in introducing Fanny to his famous aunt he formed a bond between them that would last the rest of their lives.*

In 1833 Catharine Sedgwick was forty-three years old and the best-known female American novelist of her day. She was a confirmed spinster, devoted to her three surviving brothers[8] and secure among their offspring as their beloved 'Aunt Kitty'.[9] She had published four successful novels, much praised for displaying 'the simple domestic virtues of the American home',† and she was beginning to be read across the Atlantic. The English writer and reviewer Harriet Martineau held Miss Sedgwick up as an example of the first generation of authentic New World writers, 'thoroughly American in . . . principles . . . intellectual and moral associations'.[10] A Philadelphian fan enchanted by Debby Lenox, the resolute Yankee spinster of Sedgwick's second novel, *Redwood*, wrote: 'The character . . . is to America what Scott's characters are to Scotland, valuable as original pictures, with enough of individual peculiarity to be interesting, and . . . sufficient . . . general characteristics to give them the philosophical merit of portraying a class.'[11]

Socially confident, cultivated, liberal, intellectual and publicly minded, the 'Sedgwicks of Stockbridge', the leading family of their particular New England valley in Berkshire, Massachusetts, embodied Fanny's ideal of nobility of mind: the charmingly civilized modern descendants of a 'pious, pioneering folk carving a

---

* Theodore suffered from ill health and was, perhaps, not the most dashing of suitors but in his constancy, intelligence and sympathetic understanding he might well have made a happy match for Fanny. A few months after that winter in New York he left for two years in France. On his return he married a woman said to be a model housekeeper and they had seven children together. He remained Fanny's faithful friend, acting as her lawyer and financial advisor for many years. At the end of an exemplary life, he was described as 'a man of methodical habits'.

† *A New England Tale* (1822), *Redwood* (1824), *Hope Leslie* (1827) and *Clarence* (1830). Severely affected by the death of her brother Harry at the end of 1831, Catharine Sedgwick struggled to produce her fifth novel. *The Lindwoods* eventually appeared in 1835 and many critics thought it her best, but Catharine would only publish one more novel, *Married or Single?* (1857), turning increasingly to the publication of highly popular moral tales.

new world out of the wilderness'. Their family's history was woven into the fabric of the Republic. Catharine's mother had been a Dwight, one of the distinguished families that settled the Connecticut River Valley and were nicknamed the 'river gods' in the eighteenth century. Her father had been a Federalist Judge who served as Speaker of the House of Representatives during the early days of the nation. Judge Sedgwick believed in the duty of the privileged to lead, teach and enlighten. All his life he referred to democrats as 'Jacobins' and 'miscreants' and raised his children by a creed of public service, lack of ostentation, and liberal-minded intellect.[12]

In the Sedgwick clan Fanny met her model of 'perfect love'; a family circle that demonstrated a working balance between men and women resting on mutual affection and respect for the intellect of both sexes. It was a New England version of the domestic harmony of Cousin Harriot and Fanny's Edinburgh days.

As their mother suffered from acute depression and their father was often absent in Washington, Catharine grew up sharing with her four brothers 'an intimate companionship and I think as true and loving a friendship as ever existed between brothers and sisters.' Every one of Catharine's four brothers was an enthusiastic supporter of her literary career. Her eldest brother, Theodore, while in many ways the most conservative of the set, counselled her against marriage, arguing that it would separate her from the support of her loving family and possibly extinguish her writing career when he looked 'forward to the exertion of your literary talents as a great national blessing'.[13] Henry Sedgwick, a passionate believer that 'the country must no longer neglect the genius of its women,'* arranged for his younger sister's poetry to be printed while she was still a

*Quoted Kelley p. 30. While he practised law in New York, Henry Sedgwick campaigned to give married women legal rights over the disposal of their own property - 'the advantages of which he was fond of illustrating by the marital law of Louisiana'. 'A zealous friend of universal freedom' he was known for boarding ships in the port of New York in pursuit of his determination to 'allow no escaped slave from the South to be sent back if he could prevent it'. He unfortunately developed his mother's malady and declined into mental illness in the late 1820s, dying – to Catharine's great loss and grief – at the end of 1831. Dewey p. 442.

teenager, encouraged her towards novel writing, and liaised on her behalf with publishers. Her brother Robert, in whose New York household Catharine spent her winters, was her 'kindred spirit' and managed her financial affairs; while the youngest brother Charles adapted his home in the mountain village of Lenox Massachusetts to create a special wing for her summer residence.

Catharine Sedgwick introduced Fanny to her sister-in-law, Elizabeth (wife of her youngest brother, Charles) and, as the years passed, the two women would become Fanny's American substitutes for Hal and Cousin Harriot,[14] and the Sedgwick clan her American family.

'I passed last evening with Fanny Kemble at Mrs Bells,' wrote Catharine Sedgwick in her diary on Valentine's Day 1833. 'She appears to me to love what is simple – to aim to be true – or to be so impulsively. She lives in a cloud of incense and yet seems not to be blinded and to be so accustomed to it that she sees truly through a false medium.'

The forty-something spinster responded so strongly to Fanny's youthful energy – the way she danced 'with the glee of unbroken youth' and sang with such 'dramatic effect' – that she wondered at her own infatuation.[15]

'I have never seen any woman on the stage to be compared with her,' Catharine wrote to a friend. 'She is most effective in a true woman's character, fearful, tender, and true. On the stage she is beautiful, far more than beautiful; her face is the mirror of her soul.'

At first concerned that she might find the real person disappointingly vulgar, Miss Sedgwick was delighted to discover Fanny 'a quiet gentlewoman in her deportment'.[16] Fanny in turn was drawn to the 'great simplicity and transparency of character'[17] of the slight, energetic, dark-haired authoress whose expressive face reflected 'intellectual keenness' and her 'acute sense of the ludicrous'. At last in America she had found a sympathetic woman friend, a public figure and a professional like herself, who related to her as a person of intellect and morals rather than as a mere performer. It was a refreshing contrast to all those celebrity hunters in pursuit of her stage persona.

One fine winter afternoon Pierce Butler and Fanny Kemble took the ferry to Hoboken and rode up the bluff above Weehawken. Across the Hudson River New York lay 'glittering like a heap of toys' in the clarified light. As the pair rode back through frosted woods, they fell to discussion of the different ways in which men and women experienced religious feeling.

> [He] agreed with me, that hardly one man out of five thousand held any distinct and definite religious belief. He said that religion was a sentiment, and that as regarded all creeds, there was no midway with them; that entire faith or utter disbelief were the only alternatives; for that displacing one jot of any of them made the whole totter, – which last is, in some measure, true, but I do not think it is true that religion is only a sentiment.[18]

It would appear from her journal that Fanny was flattered that Pierce should engage in such a serious discussion with her. She was not to know that his mother, Mrs Mease, had prided herself on being a free-thinker.* A querulous invalid, she had refused to allow the Bible into her house and was reported only to have given her children permission to attend the Unitarian Church on the principle that 'little or no religion was preached there'. Her Philadelphian neighbours had regarded her as eccentric to the extent that – as with Fanny's own mother – some hinted that she was mentally unstable.

The inflexibility of Pierce's stated views during that sunny winter ride might have given Fanny pause, but she was beginning to fall under the spell of physical attraction and in that condition none of us

---

*Pierce's mother died the year before he met Fanny.

are very analytical of each other's arguments. When Fanny's English friend Emily Fitzhugh eventually met Pierce, she would record her impression that he 'showed intelligence and a spirit of minute inquiry'. Pierce seems to have inherited a habit of focusing on detail from his father, who was a pedantic and opinionated man.*

Flirtation was beginning to blossom into courtship. The discussion evolved into a debate on women as the weaker sex; how God made them loving creatures of imagination and feeling: 'our capacities are inferior to those of men, – which I believe, as much as I believe our bodies to be inferior to theirs in strength, swiftness, and endurance'.[19] It is hardly surprising that a young man listening to such views might have been misled as to the character of the woman who expressed them with such passionate sincerity.

Charles Kemble at last settled his differences with the hard-bargaining Boston manager. On Sunday, 14 April 1833, the Kembles arrived in Boston to begin an engagement at the Tremont Theatre.

Fanny loved the city from the very first; from the solid wealth of its granite houses set back on avenues lined with handsome horse-chestnut trees, to the 'beautiful walk called the Common, the features of which strongly resemble the view over the Green Park just by Constitution Hill'. Their hotel, the Tremont House, was renowned for its size and splendour. With 170 well-appointed rooms, imported indoor water closets, marble floors and a dining room capable of seating 200, it introduced standards of luxury hitherto unknown in American hotels.† Even the theatre that stood across the street was delightful. It had 'the very prettiest collection of actresses' Fanny had ever seen and 'decidedly the best company I have ever played with anywhere out of London'.[20]

*Although qualified as a doctor, Dr Mease preferred to apply his time to composing monographs on a range of topics from the origins of Philadelphia through the treatment of hydrophobia to *Theoretical Observations as Connected with Navigation*. Philadelphians referred to him as 'distinguished', although he ceased to receive many social invitations after he published 'a malicious attack' against the Governor Thomas Mifflin.

†The Tremont House was a relatively new venture, having been opened in 1829.

Ticket sales were brisk. Fanny amused herself at her window watching the crowd assemble for the opening of the box office, the respectable customers jostled by ticket scalpers, their clothes smeared 'with molasses, sugar etc.' so that they could push to the front and buy up tickets for resale at considerable profit.[21]

In the course of their first morning in the city, the Kembles received fourteen visitors – among them Fanny's friends from *The Pacific*, William Hodgkinson and his sister Harriet. To her delight they took her out riding to see the latest novelty just beyond Cambridge. Newly opened in 1831, Mount Auburn Cemetery was a romantic landscape extending over more than a hundred acres embellished with fountains, chapels and elegant marble monuments to the dead.* Fanny was much taken with this melancholy pleasure-garden and much moved when Hodgkinson told her that he was buying a plot for the remains of an impoverished Englishman who had died without relatives to return him to his homeland for burial.

Hodgkinson was married to a pretty, somewhat older, wife. They lived with his sister in a large house resplendent with marble copies of 'Canova's dancing girls, the glorious Diana, a reclining figure of Cleopatra . . . [a] crouching Venus, and [a] lovely antique Cupid & Psyche'.[22] Mrs Hodgkinson was well-connected in New England and the couple's sponsorship no doubt helped the Kembles' introduction into Boston society. The warmth of their welcome was in startling contrast to their reception in Philadelphia.

'Crowds of strangers'[23] came to call, bearing invitations from the best homes in the city. The Bostonians were 'intellectual',[24] Fanny reported happily in letters. They displayed a 'general degree of cultivation . . . which renders their intercourse desirable and delightful'. Fanny and her father scarcely needed their letters of introduction from Edward Everett† calling them 'distinguished and amiable

*The success of Mount Auburn inspired a fashion for 'garden' cemeteries and encouraged the establishment of America's first public parks.

†Edward Everett (1794–1865), at that time Overseer of Harvard and a Member of Congress. According to Fanny he was also an eloquent Unitarian preacher. In 1836 he became Governor of Massachusetts.

strangers',[25] or Sir Charles Vaughn's* note to George Ticknor, Professor of Languages at Harvard, commending 'the distinguished support of the English stage Mr Charles Kemble and Miss Fanny Kemble . . . a new luminary . . . an authoress as well as an actress . . . [whose] play has at once placed her high in the literature of our country'.[26] The Wards, the Quincys, the Crowninshields, the Appletons, the Parkmans, were all happy to welcome such artists into their drawing rooms. Mrs Harrison Gray Otis got in first, organizing a party to follow Fanny's début in *Fazio*.

Fanny's opening night left a vivid impression on Anna Cabot Lowell Quincy, the younger daughter of the President of Harvard. A lively girl in her early twenties, Anna watched the performance with her friend Harriet Hodgkinson.[27] Anna was 'wild' to see Miss Kemble and she was not disappointed. 'The expression of her countenance, her shrieks, her starts, are admirable . . . and her laugh of agony and insanity was truly horrific.' Down in the pit, Henry Lee sat among a group of students from the Harvard Law School.

> We went out, transfixed with horror and fascination, into uttermost darkness, as when one passes an arc light on the road. We were all stricken, and only counted the hours and the cash which would bring us back again.[28]

Harriet and Anna were in such floods of tears by the time the curtain fell that they were hardly in a condition to present themselves at Mrs Otis's party, but they were determined to go. Miss Hodgkinson introduced her two friends and Miss Quincy was very agreeably impressed, finding Miss Kemble 'extremely modest and unassuming', a 'delicate, gentle, subdued, shadowy creature' who 'appeared like any other young lady, but had a very intelligent expression when she spoke'.

'Boston people are very ardent and enthusiastic,' Martha Ward

---

*British Minister to Washington.

wrote to her father, explaining the fuss over the Kembles; 'and when they admire a thing, they admire it with all their heart and soul.'[29]

For several days in a row Fanny woke to find a fresh bunch of flowers hung on the doorknob of her room. She lay in wait early one morning and pounced out to find Sarah Perkins, a blushing schoolgirl admirer of good family who had been leaving her tribute.* Up and down Chestnut Street young ladies started taking riding lessons and having copies made of the actress's military-style riding cap.† 'Every young girl who could sported Fanny Kemble curls. To be thought to look like Fanny Kemble was their aspiration.'[30] Every night Fanny performed, Harvard would empty of its students:

> So long as funds held out, there was a procession of us hurrying breathless over the road to Boston, as the evening shades came on, then a waiting in the narrow entrance alley, packed like sardines in a box, until at last we were borne along . . . into the pit, where we sat on the unbacked benches, absorbed, scarce knowing . . . where we were.'[31]

It was, declared Fanny, 'delightful to act to audiences who appear so pleasantly pleased with us.'[32]

Everyone wanted to dine with the English actors – even the former President John Quincy Adams‡ expressed himself floridly flattered to learn that Miss Kemble was 'desirous of being introduced' to him. 'As a sort of personage myself, of the last century,' he recorded, he was touched that 'this blossom of the next age' should wish to 'bestow some of her fresh fragrance upon the antiquities of

---

*The pair became friends and correspondents.

†Fanny congratulated herself on having introduced the beneficial concept of regular exercise to a class of women she considered over-delicate due to their unhealthy indoor lives. ''Tis quite entertaining,' she wrote to William Harness, 'to see how, before I have been a fortnight in a place, all the women are getting into riding skirts and up on horses. I have received ever so many thanks for the improved health of the ladies who, since my arrival, are horseback mad; and I truly think a good shaking does a woman good in every way.' L'Estrange, p. 68.

‡John Quincy Adams, (1767–1848), sixth President of the United States.

the past'.[33] Dr George Parkman arranged the dinner at his home on Walnut Street and Fanny found herself placed between Adams and Senator Daniel Webster. Her longed-for opportunity to see more of Webster, that 'first-rate' and 'enchanting' man, proved something of a disappointment. Webster's courtesy to Adams kept him silent during much of the meal, while the sixty-five-year-old Adams lived up to his nickname of 'old man eloquent'.

'Mr [Adams] began a sentence in assuring me that he was a worshipper of Shakespeare; and ended it by saying that *Othello* was disgusting, *King Lear* ludicrous, and *Romeo and Juliet* childish nonsense.'[34]

Adams lectured his dinner companion on the fact that she was too old to play Juliet,* before demanding rhetorically: 'Who can sympathize with the love of Desdemona? She falls in love and makes a runaway match with a Blackamoor for no better reason than that he has told her a braggart story.'[35] Desdemona's misfortunes, Adams concluded, 'with a most serious expression of sincere disgust', came 'as a very just judgement upon her for having married a nigger'.

'I swallowed half a pint of water, and nearly my tumbler too, and remained silent: for what could I say?'

It was all quite bewildering. 'Every hour, as it flies away, is filled with so much that must be done, letting alone so much that I would wish to do, that I am fairly out of breath, and feel as if I were flying . . . in a whirling high wind,' Fanny wrote to Mrs Jameson in a snatched half hour. 'If ever I stop for a moment, I shan't be surprised to find that I have gone crazy. I think I should like to spend a few days entirely alone in a dark room, secluded from every sight and sound.'[36]

The Kembles had been in Boston just three days when, on returning from a ride, Fanny ran into their hotel drawing room to find Pierce Butler sitting with her father.

'Quite a beau of hers,' gossiped Martha Ward. 'He rides with her, walks with her & waits on her most devotedly.'[37]

---

*Adams was insistent that Shakespeare's Juliet was a girl of fourteen.

When the Hodgkinsons took Fanny on excursions to Bunker Hill, to the beach toward Lynn, to Mount Auburn Cemetery, Pierce Butler went too. All those Harvard students who waited in Tremont Place to catch a glimpse of their idol at her window, or put their name down at the stables to hire Niagara, the horse she rode, were to be disappointed. It became very evident that Miss Kemble had a 'previous attachment'.

William Hodgkinson took Aunt Dall aside. He spoke 'guardedly and generally . . . tho' I suppose he knew much of Mr Butler's early career of profligacy'. His friendly warnings were in vain. Fanny 'was "in love & pleased with ruin" & paid little heed to his cautions'[38] relayed to her by her aunt. Through perfect spring weather the lovers galloped together over the hard-packed sands beside the sea at Nahant and wandered 'talking gravely of matters temporal and spiritual' through the romantic grounds of Mount Auburn. It was there, with the white monuments of the dead glinting discreetly in the distance, and apple blossom and lilacs blooming all around, that Pierce Butler and Fanny Kemble became engaged.[39]

Audiences at the Tremont Theatre were beginning to fall off. By the time of Fanny's farewell performance as Julia in *The Hunchback* the house was 'full but very unfashionable'.[40] It was time to move on. As Anna Quincy watched the curtain fall she meditated that:

> There is nothing in the world more beautiful, more striking, than such a gifted, graceful woman, yet while we feel proud of her powers, we cannot but regret to see them only employed in *acting*; however, if she is satisfied, we have no reason to wish it otherwise.[41]

Anna was not to know of Fanny's reading as she brushed her hair in the privacy of her room. 'I have finished Channing's sermons which are most excellent' ran one entry in her *Journal*. 'I think he is one of the purest English prose writers now living. I revere him greatly, yet I do not think his denial of the Trinity is consistent with the argument by which he maintains the truth of the miracles.'[42]

On arrival in Boston Fanny had been disappointed to discover that Dr William Ellery Channing, who was the Unitarian minister of the Federal Street Church, the favoured church of the city's elite, had been forced to go South for his health. She had been looking forward to reporting her impressions to Hal.* Catharine Sedgwick was a member of the Unitarian Church[43] and when the Kembles returned to New York in late May, the novelist took her young friend to visit the renowned preacher.

'His outward man bears but little token of his inward greatness,' Fanny wrote, rather disappointed. The fifty-three-year-old minister was a slight man with the delicate appearance of an habitual invalid. 'The eyes were small grey eyes, with an expression which struck me first as more akin to shrewdness of judgement than genius, and the loftier qualities of mind.'[44] Dr Channing engaged Fanny in a conversation about acting and the dramatic art, 'and, professing to know nothing about it, maintained some theories which proved he did not, indeed, know much'.

When Harriet Martineau met Dr Channing she particularly remarked on his academic habit of playing devil's advocate in order to get the measure of a person's opinions.[45] Fanny did not appreciate the technique. 'It appeared to me that . . . some of Dr Channing's opinions (with all respect be it spoken) betrayed an ignorance of human nature itself, upon which, after all, dramatic literature and dramatic representation are founded.'[46]

First he assaulted her convictions about the inner truth of her Shakespearean models, asking her, 'if at the present day and in our present state of civilization, such a character as Juliet could be imagined possible'; then compounded his offence by suggesting that the way to separate the intellectual pleasure of drama from the pernicious illusion of theatrical exhibition, was to extract a selection of the

---

*Dr William Ellery Channing (1780–1842) became known beyond Boston as an essayist. Fanny first came across his writing when, after a visit to Great Russell Street in December 1830, Miss St Ledger left behind copies of his essay on John Milton's 'Treatise on Christian Doctrine' and his review of Scott's *Napoleon*.

most powerful scenes to make readings for private assemblies. Fanny sputtered with outrage: 'To take one of Shakespeare's plays bit by bit, break it piecemeal, in order to make recitals of it! Destroy the marvellous unity of one of his magnificent works, to make patches of declamation!' She barely restrained herself from pronouncing the suggestion 'arrant nonsense', but no doubt her mobile features gave the sense for her.

From this unpromising encounter a formative relationship grew. Dr Channing became one of her moral mentors. First he followed up the visit by sending her Harriet Martineau's *Ella of Garvelock* – 'recommending it highly as an interesting story'* then in November that year he wrote:

> I trust that I shall yet have the opportunity of renewing the conversation, I will not call it controversy, which we had in New York. It does not trouble me at all to know that I did not convince you. In truth, I spoke of a subject on which I had not thought much – it is more than possible that my opinions needed not a little modification to make them strictly true. When we meet again, we will try to understand one another better, and I hope I shall not be slow to acknowledge my error if I have adopted one.[47]

During each of her subsequent Boston engagements, the minister came to call on Miss Kemble and she discovered that Dr Channing was moral, 'intellectual' New England personified.

'Everyone who converses with him,' testified Harriet Martineau a couple of years later, 'is struck with his natural, supreme regard to

*'. . . though he does not seem to think Miss Martineau's principles of political economy sufficiently sound . . . to do all the good which she herself evidently hopes to produce by these tales'. Letter to Hal begun 24 May 1833, *Records of Girlhood*, vol. III, p. 302. Hal too had pressed Harriet Martineau's tales on her friend. Fanny dutifully read what she was sent, admitting that 'for want of the habit of thinking and reading on such subjects I find the political economy a little stiff now and then, though the clearness and simplicity' of the story-telling itself was 'admirable'. Letter to Hal, April 1833, New York, vol. III, p. 289.

the true and the right; with the absence of all suspicion that any thing can stand in competition with these. In this there is an exemption from all professional narrowness, – from all priestly prejudice.'[48] Ever since she first read his essays back in Great Russell Street, Fanny had been drawn to Channing's fundamental belief in human goodness.[49] Certain that faith was 'a rational and amiable system, against which no man's understanding, or conscience, or charity, or piety, revolts', Channing's spirituality resonated with the creed of the Romantic poet articulated by Arthur Hallam, John Sterling and their friends. Intuition and sincerity became conscience.*

'We believe,' Channing wrote, 'that all virtue has its foundation in the moral nature of man, that is, in conscience, or his sense of duty, and in the power of forming his temper and life according to conscience.' His faith encompassed Fanny's essential conviction that 'to believe in and worship and obey something higher and better than itself' was native to human nature and that – as she once put it in a discussion with her brother, John Mitchell – 'rightly understood and lived up to, the only service of God . . . is intellectual freedom' and God's service 'moral freedom'.[50] Like poetry, Channing's theology spoke to all humanity, embracing women equally with men as active participants in God's mission on earth.

'I never was sensible of receiving such an impulse to my religious purposes and hopes,' Catharine Sedgwick wrote, after spending her first weeks in Channing's Boston circle in 1826.

> 'I have been much with those who dwell in light . . . Elsewhere I have seen the poor, the sick, and the afflicted detached from the world and turning to communion with the God of their spirits, but here I have met with some who have everything that the world can give, who feel that it is all very good, and yet their minds are intent on heavenly things. It seems to me that it

---

*As Fanny once wrote at the time of her discussions with the Apostles – 'the spiritual convictions, the intuitions of our souls, that lie upon their surface like direct reflections from heaven'.

would be impossible to live within the sphere of Mr Channing's influence without being in some degree spiritualized by it.'[51]

In Dr Channing Fanny met an apostle of the moral substance she had been seeking for so long.

27

Niagara Falls

'Our spring engagements are all over, and we are now going away from the hot weather to Niagara, into which, if all tales be true, I expect to fall headlong, with sheer surprise and admiration.'[1]

The Kembles set out from New York on the last day of June to visit Gouverneur Kemble at Cold Spring, his estate opposite West Point. On the steamboat they ran into Edward John Trelawny,* a fellow countryman. He was a drawing-room celebrity who traded heavily on fleeting friendships with the poets Byron and Shelley. A couple of years earlier, he had set himself before the public with a rollicking tale† called *The Adventures of a Younger Son*. Like Mrs Jameson, with her *Diary of an Ennuyée*, Trelawny published his

*According to her published letters, Fanny had noticed the romantic figure of Trelawny on another steamboat the previous winter. She had been introduced to him (she implies briefly) in New York.

†As Furnas points out, the style was probably inspired by *Tom Cringle's Log*, a successful series of overblown adventures set in the West Indies running in *Blackwood's Magazine* at the turn of the decade.

book anonymously as a novel, but played up the impression that the adventures were autobiographical.*

Deeply tanned, with thick curling black hair and a dashing moustache, Trelawny worked very hard to figure as the picture of Byron's Corsair.

> A savage . . . in some respects . . . a giant for strength . . . yet with the most listless indolent carelessness of gait . . . as if he didn't know where he was going, and didn't much wish to . . . a wild strange look about the eyes; . . . and a mark like a scar upon his cheek . . . The expression of his mouth is remarkably mild and sweet, and his voice is extremely low and gentle . . . he never profanes [his hands] with gloves, but wears two strange magical looking rings; one . . . made of elephant's hair.[2]

Look, pose, friendships – Trelawny's whole life was a determined essay in Romanticism; an effort to embody the drama of fiction in the flesh. Middle-age was beginning to tarnish his image. Depressed that he had turned forty, he was wandering around America living hand to mouth on the small proceeds of his book and the occasional article. The celebrated young actress's wide-eyed enthusiasm was a tonic to him.

---

*The 'Younger Son' is a midshipman in the Royal Navy during the Napoleonic Wars. He jumps ship in India to serve with the Dutch captain of a French privateer, becoming his lieutenant in several sea fights. On land he wrestles with tigers, fights hostile natives, rescues a lovely Arab maid of thirteen and marries her so that she can go privateering with him, whereupon she is poisoned and dies affectingly, leaving him conveniently free once more. Heartbroken, the narrator returns home to England to the life of a well-born but impoverished gentleman.

Trelawny, a younger son of a gentlemanly Cornish family, did serve in the Royal Navy and saw fighting in the Indian Ocean and the East Indies but he was discharged back into civilian life in England in the normal fashion. It is not established that the Arab girl ever existed, though he did claim to have married the young sister of a Greek chieftain, then divorced her, keeping their daughter, Zella, whom, in 1833, he boarded out with a succession of long-suffering women friends.

A sudden thunderstorm caught the pair on deck, soaking Fanny's light cotton gown. Trelawny accompanied her below to dry out by the boiler. 'Mr Trelawny . . . is sunburnt enough to warm one through with a look.'[3]

As the great wheel churned the water and the banks of the Hudson drifted by, Trelawny unfurled his best stories. He had been present when Shelley's drowned body was recovered, along with that of his sailing companion, after their yacht sank in a squall off Livorno. Trelawny described the corpses, battered and disfigured by the rolling surf, and how Shelley was identified by the book of Keats's poetry he carried in his jacket. He built the pyre on the beach before her, recounting how he stood watching with Byron and Leigh Hunt, and how Shelley's heart would not burn, so he, Trelawny, blistered his hand snatching it from the embers as a gift for the poet's wife. He told Fanny about his arrival in Greece to fight alongside Byron, but finding him dead of the fever, how he took up arms with Greek partisans and saw action in the mountains against the Turks.

Fanny relished the performance, although when Trelawny pressed her to read a piece of his personal correspondence, a letter from Claire Claremont,* she thought the letter notable only for unfeminine concision and had the wit to wonder whether he 'gave it me . . . on that account . . . or because it contained allusions to the wild and interesting adventures of his own'.[4]

For all his posturing, Trelawny was good company. Charles Kemble invited him to travel with them to see Niagara Falls. Trelawny, who could not bear to be thought lacking in any romantic experience, claimed that he had seen the Falls before,† but while 'almost all the wonders of the world were familiar to him . . . it was the only one that he cared much to see again'.[5] He gladly promised to meet them to continue North together after the Kembles had made their visit to Cold Spring.

---

*One of Byron's mistresses, mother of the poet's daughter, Allegra.

†This seems to have been poetic licence on Trelawny's part. According to surviving evidence it was his first trip to Niagara as it was the Kembles'.

Gouverneur Kemble gave his English 'kinsmen' an enthusiastic welcome at his handsome estate, laid out beside the ironworks where he made his fortune supplying ordinance for the US Army. Charles Kemble and Aunt Dall were left to rest on the veranda enjoying the view of the river dotted with white sails and the mountains beyond. Their host and his brother – knowing Fanny's special delight in waterfalls – took her on a walk up a nearby ravine where their local stream tumbled over three separate falls. Fanny was 'in perfect ecstasy'. Leaving her anxious host in charge of her parasol and bonnet below, she scrambled up, with William Kemble doing his best to guide her precarious progress over the damp leaves and slippery roots. 'At one moment . . . I swung over the water by a young sapling . . . by which I recovered footing . . . I was soaked through with spray . . . With my head bowed against the foam . . . I was feeling where next to tread.'

At last William Kemble managed to haul her up to the top. 'I wrang my handkerchief triumphantly at [Gouverneur Kemble] . . . literally dripping from head to foot, – no Naiad . . . could have taken more delight in a ducking . . . we presently all met on the dusty highway . . . and laughed very exceedingly at my soaked situation.'[6]

It was a most satisfactory visit. Their host sent his visitors off in style with a multi-gun salute – having timed the proving of his current batch of canons to mark Fanny's departure.

Trelawny met them on the steamboat, as arranged, and they all headed for Albany where Charles Kemble had fitted in a week's engagement at the local theatre. There they were joined by Pierce Butler. Waterfalls being the theme of the holiday, they made an excursion to Trenton Falls, at that time junior partner to Niagara in the list of sights for the romantic tourist in America.* It was a setting to delight Fanny's heart. Blithely ignoring the tension between Pierce and Trelawny she drank Trenton's cold, clear water from a bluebell cup and exalted: 'Oh fair world! Oh strange, and beautiful, and holy places, where one's soul meets one in silence.'[7]

---

*Before West Canada Creek was dammed to make electricity, the waters roiled over a succession of magnificent falls through the length of the gorge.

Pierce was none too pleased to discover that the intimate party had been invaded by such a glowingly romantic rival for his fiancée's attention. On the barge taking the group down the canal from Schenectady to Utica, Trelawny read aloud from *Don Quixote*, his voice resonating against the cool brick walls as they glided under the low bridges.[8] He greeted a spectacular sunset with eloquent reminiscences of Greece and an impromptu performance of Byron's 'The isles of Greece, The isles of Greece!'* He showed Fanny his journal. Edward Trelawny took every opportunity to ruffle Pierce Butler's composure.

Butler attempted to exert himself. Trelawny was holding a spirited debate with Charles Kemble on the merits of Edmund Kean in the coach one day, when Pierce began to relate to Fanny some entertaining incidents from the book he was reading. The book was *The Adventures of a Younger Son*. It seems too much to believe that Pierce did not know that the author was sitting in the carriage with him, but he talked on as if he did not. His intention was no doubt to expose his rival as a bragging liar. But the effect fell flat.

The weather grew extremely hot. When stormclouds finally cracked, the deluge forced the party to take shelter in a country inn for the night. The accommodation was very basic and Fanny was inclined to be difficult. Pierce quietly went to his luggage and produced some silver forks. Trelawny 'took out his pencil, and wrote upon a scrap of paper a very eloquent Mahomedan description of the attributes of God. I do not know whether it was his own, or an authentic Mahomedan document: it was sublime.'[9] Pierce could only retreat to sulk in his room.

Mr Butler of Philadelphia was not cosmopolitan enough to recognize that Trelawny was no real threat. For all he liked to portray himself as a superbly masculine adventurer,† there was something of

---

*'He recited with amazing vehemence and earnestness', observed Fanny. 'He reminded me of Kean several times; while he was declaiming he looked like a tiger.' *Journal*, 13 July 1833.
†When Mary Shelley, who was 'Englishing' his manuscript of the *Adventures of a Younger Son* (1831) for him, advised that it would be sensible to moderate his language or he would exclude a female readership, Trelawny replied: 'Dear Mary, I love women, and you know it, but my life is not dedicated to them; it is to men I write.' 19 January 1831, Forman, p. 141.

the neutered tomcat about the would-be Corsair. He liked to bask in the attention of certain women* – and the intelligent women he inclined towards recognized that he was both a compulsive wanderer and self-obsessed. Fanny soon had his measure. She recorded in her journal a walk where she found the footing difficult on a narrow path. She watched Trelawny stride ahead oblivious to everything save the sound of his own voice as he recited poetry to all who would listen. It was Pierce Butler who came up beside her to catch and steady her.

As they drove up to an inn for breakfast one morning their driver took too sharp a turn before the door and the coach overturned. Fanny found herself crushed under her father's bulk. Trelawny lay momentarily stunned. Pierce clambered out with no more than a cut finger. Aunt Dall was bleeding profusely from a nasty gash on her head, and people came from the tavern to carry her inside (such accidents were frequent in those primitive coaching days). Trelawny recovered to demonstrate his competence with field dressings, binding up Dall's wounds.

'Bruised, and aching, but still very merry, [we] sat down to breakfast . . . seeing it was no worse, we thanked God and devoured.'[10] Excited by the prospect of the romantic holy grail of Niagara ahead, Fanny failed to notice that her aunt was far from well.

They drove in an open carriage. The day was hot and bright and still.

> We stopped the carriage occasionally to listen for the giant's roaring, but the sound did not reach us until, within three miles over the thick woods which skirted the river, we saw a vapoury

*Mary Shelley and Claire Claremont were his favourite confidantes. 'The men I have linked myself to in my wild career through life,' he once wrote to Mary Shelley, 'have almost all been prematurely cut off, and the only friends which are left me are women, and they are strange beings. I have lost them all by some means or other; they are dead to me by being married or (for you are all slaves) separated by obstacles which are insurmountable.' Forman, p. 139–40.

silver cloud rising into the blue sky. It was the spray . . . When we reached what is called the Niagara House, a large tavern by the roadside, I sprang out of the carriage and ran through the house, down flights of steps cut in the rock, and along a path skirted with low thickets, through the boughs of which I saw the rapids running a race with me . . . and hardly faster than I did. Then there was a broad, flashing sea of furious foam, a deafening rush and roar, through which I heard Mr Trelawny, who was following me, shout, 'Go on, go on; don't stop!' I reached an open floor of broad, flat rock, over which the water was pouring. Trelawny seized me by the arm, and all but carried me to the very brink; my feet were in the water and on the edge of the precipice, and then I looked down. I could not speak, and I could hardly breathe; I felt as if I had an iron band across my breast. I watched the green, glassy, swollen heaps go plunging down, down, down; . . . I looked and listened till the wild excitement of the scene took such possession of me that, but for the strong arm that held me back, I really think I should have let myself slide down into the gulf. It was long before I could utter, and as I began to draw my breath I could only gasp out, 'Oh God! Oh God!' No words can describe either the scene itself, or its effect upon me.[11]

One wonders what went through Pierce's mind as he followed behind her at a decorous pace supporting Aunt Dall on his arm.

The Kemble party stayed for three days, during which Fanny spent the greater part of her time 'by the water, under the water, on the water and more than half in the water. Wherever foot could stand I stood, and wherever foot could go I went. I crept, clung, hung, and waded; I lay upon the rocks, upon the very edge of the boiling cauldron . . . with my feet naked for better safety . . . my delight was so intense that I really could hardly bear to come away.'[12]

The immensity of Niagara Falls – its all-encompassing sound, the light reflected off its myriad surfaces – for once met the intensity of Fanny's response to nature.[13]

They parted company with Trelawny at Niagara.* The rest of the trip went by in the enervated peace of anti-climax. They took the steamer across Lake Ontario and bumped† down the rapids of the St Lawrence in an open boat to Montreal, where Charles Kemble had arranged a few more performances, then on to Quebec for a fortnight's engagement. By 17 August Fanny was lying on the open deck of another steamboat reading the *Lady of Shalott* as the St Lawrence bore her back towards autumn and her second American season.

There was never any question that silver forks would win over impromptu translations of Islamic prayers. Fanny was in love with Pierce, caught in the electricity of physical attraction. The one lasting consequence of Trelawny's attentions was to leave Pierce all the more determined to win his prize. His pride had been challenged and young Mr Butler had a morbid fear of losing face.

'The whole world is talking of the engagement of Miss Fanny Kemble to Pierce Butler of Philadelphia,' Julia Kean wrote to her uncle in August. 'I believe there is little doubt of its existence and we shall probably see this celebrated actress placed in one of the most elegant establishments in our country and leading the circle which now scarcely deigns to notice her. It is certainly much to be regretted that we should fall into such bad European customs.'[14]

Marie-Thérèse Kemble was not in the habit of writing letters to her children, but word filtered across the Atlantic that she too was concerned. John Mitchell sent his sister wry congratulations: 'Do let me know, dearest Fan, when this terrible affair of marriage is to be . . . much righteous indignation has been excited . . . they say . . . that when you have a house and a nursery to look after, you will leave off writing plays.

---

*Left to himself, Trelawny nearly drowned trying to prove that he was still man enough to swim across a particularly dangerous stretch of river below the falls. He survived and lived on until 1881. He kept in touch with the Kembles (including Fanny's sister, Adelaide), and was a regular guest at their parties in London during the late 1830s and early 1840s.

†Fanny was disappointed at the lack of apparent peril, having been told that descending the rapids was dangerous.

'However, dearest girl,' he concluded, 'you will be happy if your husband only knows how to value you.'[15]

Charles Kemble was uneasy about his daughter's engagement. He proposed an extended trip down South to play New Orleans, a famously lucrative show-town, but a looming tragedy cancelled the plan. Aunt Dall's health was causing concern. The doctors blamed a concussion of the spine received in that holiday carriage accident. As the winter progressed the ever-reliable prop of the Kemble family became paralysed from the waist down and suffered convulsions.

Fanny was desperate. She performed her stage work and cared for her aunt as best she could in the temporary sickrooms she fashioned from a succession of hotel rooms.

'This is the only trial of the kind I have ever undergone,' she wrote to Anna Jameson from her aunt's bedside. 'This is my first lonely watching by a sick-bed, and I feel deeply the sadness and awfulness of the office . . . I am beginning to know what care and sorrow really are.'[16]

Charles Kemble closed down in frozen distress. Twenty-four years old, Fanny sat at her beloved aunt's bedside in a foreign land, powerless to do anything but watch her slip away. The Kembles managed to sustain their professional commitments until they reached Boston. There, where Fanny had been so happy the previous spring, they were forced to cut short their return engagement on 10 April 1834. Fanny's Boston fans gave her a rousing send-off:

> They shouted at us, they cheered us, they crowned me with roses. Conceive . . . the shocking contrast between this and the silent sick-room, to which I went straight from the stage. Surely, our profession involves more intolerable discords between the real human beings who exercise it and their unreal vocation, than any in the world!'[17]

A week later, as dawn broke into their room in the Tremont House Hotel, Adelaide Decamp died in her niece's arms. 'Her last words . . . after a night of angelic endurance . . . were, "Open the window, let in the blessed light".'[18]

Dr Channing came to offer what consolation he could. He too had recently lost a loved one, and Fanny was touched by the absolute faith with which he spoke of her. 'Gone! To the Author of all good. That which was good must return to Him. It is true, and I believe it, and know it; but at first I was lost.'[19]

Fanny had lost the linchpin of her daily life. 'There is no preparation for the sense of desolation which oppresses me . . . [it] is beyond words.' Aunt Dall had always been there – in the wings waiting to wrap her in a shawl, keeping her company, calming her nerves, mending her hems; they had shared absolute trust. And now Dall lay in a coffin as Fanny and her father folded stage costumes into their trunks in her aunt's bedroom.

Dall was buried in Mount Auburn Cemetery at a spot where Fanny and Pierce had courted the previous spring. 'I wished her to lie there, for life and love and youth and death have their trysting-place at the grave.'[20]

Ten days after the funeral Fanny was back on stage in New York feeling 'stunned and bewildered'.[21]

'I have almost cried my eyes out for the last three months,' she wrote to Hal, 'but that is over now.'

Without Dall, the whole 'charge of everything devolves entirely to me'. Fanny's father was 'deeply afflicted' and his only thought was to get his daughter back to England unencumbered. Pierce was pushing to marry Fanny that May. Charles Kemble now perceived that Pierce was a direct threat to his interests. The second season had not been as lucrative as the first. At the end of January 1834 *The Play-Goer*, an oracle of theatrical gossip in London, reported that the news from America was that 'the attraction of the Kembles . . . is entirely gone'.*

*This commentator added: '. . . we are not surprised by it. The enchantment of Miss

The Park Theatre in New York was out of fashion and the 'two last engagements of the Kembles' had been 'wretched'.

While Dall lay dying, Fanny wrote to George Combe:

> I did not expect to remain on the stage after the month of May when my marriage was appointed, and hoped to be free from a profession which has always been irksome to me, but it is otherwise. I shall return to England with my father in June and continue my labours for another twelve months either there or here. As I have seen good cause to adopt this determination, I shall not say anything more about it, for 'tis very vain to sit lamenting over a line of action which one had deliberately chosen as the most fitting to pursue.[22]

Charles needed to gather more money if he was to retire comfortably. As far as he knew he had secured their American earnings out of the reach of his English creditors. Fanny's share, some $35,000, had been invested in a New Orleans bank, while he had entrusted $20,000 on his own account to Nicholas Biddle's Second Bank of the United States. By 1834 Biddle's Bank was under siege. The previous September President Jackson had removed the federal funds to his network of 'pet banks'. Henry Clay, Daniel Webster and others were fighting a rearguard action in Washington to reverse the decision, but a cloud had settled around the Second Bank of the United States, adding to Charles Kemble's concerns.*

Fanny's father booked passages home for them for the end of June. 'How happy Fanny's friends will be to see her once more before she is married, won't they?' he wrote in typical style to William Harness. 'The legitimate drama will have another chance, I

Kemble's acting is not, we apprehend, such as to last anytime longer than a couple of seasons.' Cutting in Enthoven Collection.

*After lingering on through the waves of financial crisis that dogged the 1830s, the Second Bank of the United States finally crashed in 1841 amid accusations of fraud that discredited Biddle and his directors. Charles, like other investors in the bank, lost most of his money.

hope, of resuscitation; and we shall both at least take leave of the British stage in a manner worthy of the house of Kemble!'[23]

'Weak, and worn out, and good for nothing',[24] Fanny thought she could benefit from the enforced rest of an Atlantic crossing. She longed for her home and family, and as much as she looked forward to retiring from the stage, she agreed that she preferred to do so in London 'before my own people, who received my first efforts so kindly, and where I [stand] in the very footprints, as it were, of my kindred'.[25]

Charles Kemble expected to carry things off with his celebrated patrician charm. Pierce Butler would be forced to accept the prior claims of family; if Pierce was to wait a year or so while Fanny helped top up her parents' old-age security fund, then Charles guessed that Mr Butler would find other ladies to court.

He had underestimated the young Philadelphian. Pierce deployed all his powers of persuasion to convince Fanny that she must marry him *before* the Kembles sailed for England. This Romeo's pleadings were irresistible. Since marriage would mean that anything Mrs Butler earned would belong to her husband, Charles's reluctant consent was won by proposing that his daughter would set up a trust giving him life-interest in the $35,000 sitting in the New Orleans bank.*

''Tho I have but two minutes I must tell you how bright a ray of sunshine is parting my stormy sky,' Fanny reported to Catharine Sedgwick on 31 May.

> Pierce has behaved <u>most</u> nobly, and my Father most kindly – surely it is most noble to confess an error to a person that you do not like and whom you feel has committed an injustice towards you. We are together again nearly the whole day long, and on Saturday next before sailing for New York we <u>shall be married</u> so that you will never see <u>her, Fanny Kemble,</u> again.

---

*The New Orleans bank was not a random choice. Louisiana law, unlike that of most states, gave wives property rights and so long as the money stayed there, unless Fanny wished to surrender it to him, her new husband would have no legal right to touch it.

> Pierce has promised me that this shall not interfere with my departure or the discharge of my duties to my father, and relying implicitly as I do on his word, I could not resist his earnest entreaties to be his wife before I gave myself up to those chances which perhaps might never have suffered him to call me by that name. I cannot tell exactly whether I have done for the very best in this, because he implored me so that I do not believe I had much power of thought at the time, but I think now that it will be better that he should feel that I am his, fast for life, tho' at a distance, and I shall have reason without appeal for resisting any further claim which might hereafter be made upon me . . . I think seventeen happy days snatched on the very brink of bitterness and parting not to be denied to one who has followed my footsteps for a whole year with a hope which he now beholds defeated.[26]

Pierce's proposal was that they should take the opportunity of the Kembles's delayed engagement in Philadelphia to marry in his home town. Then they would catch a semi-honeymoon in intervals between the farewell engagements, before Fanny sailed for home with her father to carry out her family duties, a married woman, while he – her faithful American husband – waited for her return.

Fanny and Charles did not appreciate it yet, but far from being 'defeated', Pierce had won.

When Fanny's letter reached Catharine Sedgwick in the Berkshires she commented to her English correspondent, Mary Russell Mitford: 'Butler is a gentlemanly man, with good sense and amiable disposition, infinitely her inferior. Poor girl, she makes a dangerous experiment; I have a thousand fears for the result.'[27]

Neither of the Kembles seems to have questioned that Pierce would be content with a wedding night and a wife 'fast for life – tho' at a distance'. In their family's world, the stage always came first. Fanny wrote girlishly to her Boston friend, Saadi Perkins:*

---

*Sarah Paine Perkins (later Mrs Cleveland), the schoolgirl who had tied flowers to Fanny's door during her first visit to Boston.

> I am going to be married next Saturday, and after then you are not to imagine me in your mind's eye as Fanny Kemble racing along (Chekie) beach or dipping her feet into Jamaica Pond, but sober *Mrs Pierce Butler* with a ring on her third finger (bells on her toes, I suppose), and all the grave cares of matrimony in her mind and visage.[28]

She ended her note with a somewhat surprising request for Saadi to send her a pair of white satin shoes at once from Boston. In the past, perhaps, Dall would have seen to such things.

The financial agreements were signed and soon after eight o'clock on the morning of 7 June 1834 Fanny Kemble and Pierce Butler met at Christ Church, the venerable red-brick and white church in the centre of Philadelphia.* Fanny wore white, a blond lace veil covering her head and Saadi's satin shoes; the ceremony was conducted by an episcopalian bishop, and there were negro ushers at the door with smart white gloves – none of which could disguise the haste of the affair. The handful of friends and family who attended were outnumbered by the onlookers who gathered about the church door. Pierce's sister-in-law, the beautiful Mrs John Butler, was matron of honour, and at least one of Pierce's fabled aunts attended (she later gave Fanny a piano as a wedding gift). No surviving record of the ceremony mentions the presence of Charles Kemble.

The Boston Atlas's report described the groom speaking his part distinctly, while his bride was almost inaudible. As the bishop closed his prayer book, the new Mrs Butler burst into tears and collapsed on the shoulder of her new sister-in-law. Mid-morning the newlyweds were seen embarking on the New York-bound steamboat. Fellow

*Christ Church, Philadelphia, known as 'the Nation's Church' because of the famous leaders of the revolutionary-era who worshipped there, was the founding church of the Episcopalian Church (Anglican) in America. According to Robert Bernard Martin, Pierce had been christened in that church and many of his family were buried there. The fact that he arranged to be married there, instead of under the auspices of the Unitarian Church, to which he nominally belonged, may well suggest an attempt to add dignity and permanence to the event in the eyes of his Philadelphian neighbours.

passengers on board reported that the bride wept all the way to Burlington.

The Kembles's closing week at the Park Theatre in New York culminated in a last Benefit for Charles. In a tribute to her mother, as much as her new circumstances, Fanny played Lady Elizabeth Freelove in *The Day After the Wedding*. Twenty-six years before, Marie-Thérèse had adapted the French farce about the 'quick and irritable' bride so 'impatient of restraint' brought to heel by her authoritative spouse, as a playful tribute to her new husband. Now Charles stood in his part of Colonel Freelove admonishing his daughter as the new bride in those words written by her mother:

> 'Tis not an easy task to reform our characters suddenly; I expect to find you now and then relapsing into your former error: but you have experienced the evil effects of it; and reflection cannot fail to convince you, that affection and gentleness are the brightest ornaments of your sex, and the surest sources of Domestic Felicity.

Then Pierce brought the curtain down. Fanny's final performance on the American stage took place not in New York but in Philadelphia the following night in Mrs Inchbald's farce – *The Wedding Day*. Sometime in those last forty-eight hours, Pierce pronounced that he could not bear to be parted from his bride. After what must have been a harrowing scene, Charles Kemble boarded the ship for England alone and Pierce bore Fanny off to live with her new in-laws in Philadelphia.

Gossip flew everywhere. Rebecca Gratz, the well-connected doyenne of Philadelphia's small Jewish elite, reported:

> She had consented to another year's labour for her father . . . when the time arrived, her lover, who was prevented by a law suit from leaving the country, could not bear to part with her, without first securing her hand – and when married, could not consent to the separation or to her continuing on the stage – her

father was angry at losing the aid of her professional talents, considered himself wronged and deceived . . . since which it is reported that the Miss Butlers* have granted an annuity to her Mother, which secures her from any disappointment her daughter's retirement might have occasioned, and thus the good and talented Miss K. is rewarded for her filial piety, and it is believed she will be a very happy wife . . . The Butler family receive her very cordially.[29]

Pierce Butler had played his part very neatly. In the American papers he appeared in the guise of the gentlemanly hero outwitting a grasping father-in-law to rescue the pure, loving daughter. The story ran and ran. That October the *New England Galaxy* pronounced:

We have a high opinion of Mrs Butler, and believe her as eminently qualified to support the character of 'The Wife' in domestic life as on the stage . . . That filial affection which induced Mrs Butler to be so long obedient to a father whose avarice and other ungentlemanly, not to say mean, attributes rendered him so insupportably disagreeable – will prevent her from acknowledging, even to herself, that a release from even such a father's surveillance is a matter of congratulation. The blindness of a daughter to her father's faults, or at least her *apparent* blindness, is the best earnest she can give of her future duty to her husband.†

Democratic America had won the fair maiden; the immoral Old World father was roundly defeated.

---

*Pierce's two surviving aunts.

†Cutting in Enthoven collection, *New England Galaxy*, dated in ink 'Oct. 1834'. The American newspapers' resentment of Charles Kemble was fuelled by a lawsuit brought against Fanny's father by the manager of the Boston Tremont Theatre. Mr Dana accused Charles Kemble of cheating him by misrepresenting the terms on which the Kembles had previously been engaged in New York. In spring 1835 Mr Dana won his case and was awarded damages.

Fanny's childish dream of winning her father's company had proved a disappointment. As much as he indulged her in small things, Charles Kemble had proved himself an indifferent provider and a worse protector. She had chosen Pierce Butler, the wealthy gentleman who offered her marriage and the dignity of a private home, despite the knowledge that he would 'gain nothing from the worldly point of view' in taking her as his wife. She believed that Pierce and she were in love. But in making her choice she never dreamed she would suffer such a brutal parting from the father she adored. A couple of decades later, Fanny tried to write a 'short sketch of the circumstances of my engagement' for the young Sedgwicks but 'my heart failed me . . . it seemed to me too sad'.[30]

She had left the stage. She was a new bride stranded in a foreign land. She could only cling to the idea of Portia's 'generous self-denial'. 'Chance . . . gives [Portia] to the man she loves, a handsome, extravagant young gentleman, who would certainly have been pronounced by all of us quite unworthy of her, until she proved him worthy by the very fact of her preference for him.'

The London *Times* reported news of Miss Kemble's marriage on the last day of June. Eight weeks later, on 24 August 1834, Augustus Craven married Pauline de la Ferronnays in the chapel of the Acton Palace in Naples.

28

Slavery or a Wife's Duty

The tale of Fanny's marriage would fill another book (and indeed has filled several). When she was in her sixties, she attempted to sum up her life to William Dean Howells. 'I was engaged to be married,' she told him, 'and I came with my father to America for two years . . . my engagement was broken & I married Mr Butler – that is the whole story.'[1]

Her first attempt at published memoirs, *Records of a Girlhood*, ends abruptly. After the glories of the trip to Niagara there is one letter that speaks of Dall's illness six months later, a short harrowing one telling Hal of her aunt's death and the bare sentence: 'I was married in Philadelphia on the 7th of June, 1834, to Mr Pierce Butler, of that city.' The juxtaposition is eloquent. The tragic death of Dall led Fanny to surrender to Pierce and her marriage ended her youthful life.

Fanny and Pierce shared a passionate physical attraction that lasted some years. But as Fanny so wisely predicted when she was eighteen: 'I think I should be unhappy and the cause of unhappiness to others if I were to marry. I cannot swear I shall never fall in love, but if I do I will fall out of it again, for I do not think I shall ever so far lose sight of my best interest and happiness as to enter into a relation for which I feel so unfit.'

As she knew then, and would know again, 'independence of mind and body' were too important to her for her to make a happy wife.

The young couple began their wedded life in the Philadelphian home of Pierce's brother John.* Fanny had pictured herself with her garden, the domestic status she had always coveted, space to read and the improving society of a cultivated town. Having parted on bad terms with her father,[2] Fanny – traumatized, exhausted and in deep mourning – now discovered that Pierce Butler had, as yet, no house of his own.

Pierce was close to his elder brother. Intimate acquaintance with a lover's nearest relations is often a shock. John Butler, like his younger sibling, was known for his gentlemanly air; he fancied himself a crack rider and made much of his role in the local militia.† Apart from that, no one had much good to say of him.[3] He was given distinction in Philadelphian circles by his well-connected wife.‡ She was a dark beauty who carried off rich colours and gold turbans to great effect, but even Sydney Fisher – who much admired her – admitted that she had 'no mind'. Ella Butler was charming in her own way, with 'the ease & high breeding of the southern aristocracy',[4] but Fanny had little in common with her burnished sister-in-law.

In August 1834, a bored, bright sixteen-year-old from Boston, Fanny Appleton, who was staying in the fashionable resort of

---

*John, Pierce's elder by four years, had changed his surname to Butler in 1831 on their mother's death. By arrangement with his brother, he was later to divide their grandfather's legacy with Pierce. He lived in a town house in the centre of Philadelphia. 'Butler's is a fine establishment, built of Quincy Granite, and with a porte cocher, which I think very convenient. It is the only house so built in town,' wrote Philadelphian diarist, Sydney Fisher. 'It is very handsomely furnished,' Quoted Wainright, 24 January 1841, pp. 112–13.

†In fact, he was to become a casualty of the Mexican War – to which he volunteered, only to die of dysentery.

‡Gabriella Manigault Morris Butler was the granddaughter of Gouverneur Morris, a prominent statesman from the Hudson Valley; her middle name, Manigault, came from her connection to an aristocratic Charleston family.

Newport Rhode Island,* wrote home about her fellow guests:

> 'Mrs Pierce Butler . . . is so engaged in writing her book of travels that she only appears in the evening, when she is very gay, waltzing and gallopading most gracefully . . . I must say she is capable of being truly fascinating. I have got very well acquainted with her and feel myself bound by the spell which attracts every one to her . . . She allowed me to dress her hair the other day but was quite distressed because Pierce thought it becomed her. She clubs hers round in such a plain fashion from a principle that the form of the head should not be disfigured.'[5]

Having captured the embodiment of his generation's ideal of youthful womanhood, Pierce Butler was in for a rude awakening. Months before her marriage, Fanny had contracted with Henry Carey of Carey & Lea,[6] Philadelphian publishers, to print the journal she had kept since her arrival in America. The $2,500 Carey paid her was intended to provide an investment for Dall's old age.† In the storm of regret and mourning that followed her aunt's tragic death, the publication took on an emotional significance. Since she had failed her beloved Aunt Dall, Fanny was determined to carry out her pledge in the only way left to her – the money would be dedicated in Dall's memory to the support of her younger sister, Aunt Victoire, an equally impoverished spinster teacher.

Carey was eager to rush into print while the celebrity of the former Miss Kemble was still fresh in the public mind. Pierce did not

---

*'Here we are in this land of fog and windmills . . . freezing to death in this dreary, carpetless mansion, with a canopy of murky clouds overhead.' Fanny Appleton later married the poet Henry Wadsworth Longfellow. She and her sister, Mary, were family friends of Catharine Sedgwick, and came to know Fanny quite well during summers spent in Lenox, Massachusetts.

†Fanny was acutely conscious that her aunt, who had so dedicated her life to the happiness of others, had been left without provision.

see what Fanny was proposing to publish until late in the day. When he was at last given her manuscript to read, he was appalled to discover a text riddled with much 'unfit for the public eye'.[7]

Back in October 1833 the editor of the *Germantown Telegraph* had advised with sly foresight that 'he who weds [Miss Kemble] for an angel will discover, we opine, ere a fortnight that she is nothing more or less than a woman, and perhaps one of the most troublesome kind into the bargain.'[8] With the publisher pressing for copy to set up pages, the Butlers fought line by line.

'Any curtailment greatly irritated her,' Pierce recalled years later; 'she opposed the slightest alteration . . . Every sentence . . . was stoutly defended, and my suggestions made her very angry.'[9] Fanny's young husband even tried to buy Carey off, but the publisher, scenting a scandalous success, refused to allow the contract to be broken.

Fanny was living up to her part in *The Day After the Wedding*.* The single-mindedness with which Pierce had pursued his courtship now manifested itself in a stubborn determination to have her conform to his will. But, unlike her fictional counterpart, Fanny was not prepared to reform.

Philadelphian neighbours were scandalized by her 'singular' behaviour. Pierce recalled one incident when Fanny announced that she was going to explore the city's wharf district. He protested that 'a lady going there on horseback and alone, would attract great, if not rude attention, and cause unpleasant remarks.

'She replied by a few disdainful words, about my regard for what people said, dashed off, and took her ride along the wharves . . . one of the many instances of perverse self-will, in which she delighted.'[10]

*One well-connected Philadelphian, on first hearing of the engagement, had consulted Walter Stirling, a friend of Mrs Siddons. He had replied that Fanny's character was 'above question': 'she is a perfect lady . . . but she is troublesome and self-willed . . . despising all authority and advice . . . since infancy she has been the source of perpetual annoyance and anxiety – I am sure [her parents] will be glad when she is married but I pity the poor man . . . especially if he is so amiable a person as you think Mr Butler.' Quoted Furnas, p. 130.

Fanny was lonely and bored in Philadelphia.* Pierce seems to have had few respectable friends he might introduce to his wife and his desertion of Emily Chapman had blotted his reputation with Philadelphian hostesses.[11] The nearest thing Philadelphia had to intellectual women were Mrs T.I. Wharton, with her clique of 'mawkish, sentimental, would-be literary ladies',[12] and the retiring Miss Margaretta Morris of Germantown, whose diligent study of the Hessian fly led to a discovery of the 'utmost importance' to agriculture.[13]

'You can have no idea of the intellectual dearth and drought in which I am existing,' Fanny wrote to Hal, as her depression grew. Her manuscript, studded with stars marking passages censored by Pierce, was finally dispatched to the printers, leaving the Butlers' marriage tumultuous in its wake.

One dark winter evening, Fanny packed up her bags and walked out of John Butler's house. She left her luggage in a heap with a note on top requesting that the bags be surrendered to whoever she might send to fetch them. She enclosed a $20 bill to cover any petty debts she might have overlooked and directed that her pet bird, standing by in its cage, be given to Rose Sully, the painter's daughter.†

Three hours later she returned; went to her room and fell asleep on her bed without undressing.

Fanny had come face to face with the enormity of what she had

---

*As Sydney Fisher explained, 'The young men here spend their evenings not at parties or in the society of ladies, but at clubs, assignation houses and suppers, or else in the offices or counting rooms.' The diarist was damning about the 'want of high cultivation, of earnestness, of interest in elevated & important subjects of sincerity' among his patrician neighbours; writing about the 'selfishness, pretension, want of culture, of superior mental endowment combined with the conceit & claim of possessing both', and the 'narrow views & a life made up of a monotonous routine of nothings', quoted Wainright, 6 February 1839, p. 73 and 8 October 1843, p. 140.

†Thomas Sully, the Philadelphian portrait painter, was born in England and had studied with Sir Thomas Lawrence. He came to know the Kembles while sketching them for lithographs during their first American season. He went on to paint both Charles and Fanny several times, including producing one of the best portraits of Fanny (as Beatrice). Sully and his family became some of Fanny's first friends in Philadelphia.

done. Having made over to her father full life-interest in the $35,000 sitting in the New Orleans bank, she was entirely dependent on her husband.

Pierce treated her as a child-woman. He was indulgent, masterly, soothing. All she needed was a purpose and an establishment of her own. He arranged that they should move into Butler Place, the larger of two farms his aunt owned outside Germantown.

While workmen prepared the house for their reception Fanny applied her famous energy to the study of housekeeping manuals. She attempted to instruct herself in double-entry book-keeping. She took a close interest in the refurbishment of her new home, directing upholsterers and furniture makers.

The Pierce Butlers took possession of Butler Place on New Year's Day, 1835. To Pierce's delight, Fanny was carrying their first child. Now, he imagined, his highly strung wife would settle down to the life of a respectable mother in the country seclusion of his 'comfortable establishment'.

Four months pregnant, Fanny found herself isolated in a medium-sized farmhouse* in the midst of the Pennsylvania countryside. Butler Place stood on the west side of the turnpike six miles due north of Philadelphia's Market Street, on the outer edge of Germantown. The house was a plain, stone-built box, with a pitched roof set a few yards back from the road. Apart from a scattering of sparse trees, there was nothing to add interest to the flat, if fertile land, but barns and farm buildings. There were no cultivated 'grounds' and no deferential family retainers. The turnpike and paths about the farm were so bad as to be almost impassable in winter.

*As an old lady, Fanny told her grandson how one surprised British visitor described Butler Place as like a 'second-rate farmhouse in England, not like an English mansion or estate at all'. For the first few months of her life there Fanny insisted on heading her letters 'from the farm, Branchtown'.

> I live alone – much alone bodily, more alone mentally. I have no intimates, no society, no intellectual intercourse whatever.[14]

Fanny tried to behave as she imagined ladies were supposed to behave, but her notions were far too English. The Butler tenants were independent, comfortably-off farmers with a stiff sense of self-respect. She caused offence by offering to teach the small children of her gardener and the Butler Place farmer, along with any of the village children who might care to join them. 'My benevolent proposal excited . . . a sort of contemptuous amazement . . . the village school . . . for which they were obliged and willing to pay . . . fulfilled all their desires . . . These people and their children wanted nothing that I could give them.'*

She called in the Quaker dairymaid to request that her family should have fresh butter every day. The farmer's daughter heard her out in silence, then left with the remark: 'Well . . . don't thee fill theeself up with the notion that I'm going to churn butter for thee more than twice a week.'[15] Pierce had omitted to explain to his wife that the dairy and pastures were leased to the tenant on a contract detailing provision of fresh butter to Butler Place twice a week and no more.

Pierce's young English wife suffered the universally recognized 'servant problem' ten-fold.[16] A Philadelphian bride could at least hope to draw on her relatives' knowledge of reliable servants or at a pinch could borrow someone in an emergency. Fanny's first dinner party at Butler Place was ruined when her cook walked out, leaving her with a cold kitchen range and no help to prepare the food. And on top of this catalogue of domestic disasters, the newlyweds were dogged by the legacy of her public life.

---

*FK, *Records of a Later Life*, vol. I, pp. 7–8. On 4 July, she caused a minor local scandal by inviting all the members of the families farming Butler Place and York Farm to a celebration at which she served alcohol. The older generation were Quakers and staunchly teetotal. One guest went so far as to scold her for making them waste a good day idling instead of getting on with their work.

January had scarcely begun before someone leaked to the newspapers pages of Fanny's manuscript as it was before Pierce intervened.*

'The city is in an uproar,' reported Catharine Sedgwick from New York:

> Nothing else is talked of . . . in the counting houses . . . and Wall Street . . . people seem to think that there never was such ingratitude! – that coming as the Kembles did beggars to this country & leaving the stage enriched, Mrs B. should dare to say a word against us – This is arrant nonsense – they gave at least an equivalent . . . Nobody went to the theatre to do them a favour . . . But I do wonder that two years after – after having married an American & being two years older she should deliberately publish it . . . [it] shows a want of tact, judgement and good sense. I am very sorry she has done it tho' I expect it will appear much worse to those who do not know her than to us.†

The scandal made the *Journal* into a publishing success. One New York bookstore sold 800 copies on the first day. A rash of parodies appeared: *My Conscience! Journal of Fanny Thimble Cutler* (wife of

---

*'The tone of her remarks upon some of the most respected citizens by whom she was kindly received and entertained, but ill corresponds with the polite attentions bestowed,' stormed the New York *Commercial Advertiser*, 3 January 1835. 'We shall not repeat them – although it will be seen by one of the extracts that she very civilly informs her readers that "next to a bug, a newspaper writer is her disgust" . . . we marvel that she made the exception. The New York audience are too well paid for applauding her to the skies. She and her father were "CASTING PEARLS BEFORE SWINE".'

Pierce had cut the association of newspapermen and bugs; the lines as published being: 'A newspaper writer is my aversion.' Quoted Furnas, p. 150.

As the public storm grew, reaching across the Atlantic, the *Edinburgh Review*, July 1835, likened Fanny's 'declarations against the Press-gang' to the impulse 'under which foolish and fearless schoolboys provoke a nest of hornets.'

†Letter quoted by Furnas, p. 162. Catharine added that the *Journal* was like Fanny herself: 'glorious faculties, delightful accomplishments, immeasurable sensibility, and a half a hundred little faults'. Dewey, p. 240.

Fierce Cutler); *Outlines Illustrative of the Journal of F——A——K——*, a collection of scurrilous caricatures inspired by scenes from the *Journal*, and *Fanny Kemble in America*, a pamphlet that accused Fanny of getting drunk and consorting with stable boys. Satirical verses depicted Pierce proposing in an alcoholic haze and in New York, the Bowery Theatre put on a highly profitable burlesque *Bugs: Big and Little*, in which a popular knock-about comedian dressed up as 'Fanny Journaliana' to perform various acrobatics on horseback.

Pierce Butler loathed the publicity. He was cut to the quick by cartoons making mockery of his height next to representations of his wife as a rough-riding Amazon. This was not what he had bargained for.

While keeping up appearances before the world, privately the couple were at loggerheads. In a significant passage in a letter to George Combe, written on 20 March 1835, Fanny described the juxtaposition of their two characters:

> . . . myself and my husband act as mental moderators to each other. He is nothing if not mathematical, and in every subject whatsoever that comes under his contemplation, from the traditions of history, to the hypotheses of astronomical speculations, truth, reality, *fact* is the end upon which he fastens, and without a most palpable and solid body of fact there is no satisfying him. We are fortunately different in temper. He is cheerful and contented, exceedingly calm and self-possessed, and has an abundance of patience with my more morbid mental construction, without, however, quite understanding it.[17]

Heavily pregnant, Fanny: 'frequently [expressed] regret at having married'. She begged Pierce to release her and let her return home to England. Her young husband refused to take her seriously. 'I looked upon these expressions as merely perverse fancies, to be dispelled by the birth of her child; and I sometimes assured her that if she continued in the same mind after that event, I would not oppose her wishes, supposing that I should hear no more about it.'[18]

Pierce spent an increasing amount of time away from Butler Place.* Fanny relieved her feelings riding about the muddy lanes unattended in defiance of the doctor's misgivings. On 28 May 1835 she gave birth to a blue-eyed daughter; they called her Sarah after Pierce's mother.

Fanny enjoyed motherhood. In a letter written two weeks after the birth of her baby, she told Saadi Perkins:

> In the cares and interests and absorbing affections of maternity a woman finds . . . a safe and for some time at least happy channel for all those feelings which are too often miserably disappointed in the partner of her inconsiderate choice.[19]

Nonetheless, she decided her Philadelphian life was unbearable. She renewed her demands that Pierce carry out his promise to let her go home once the child was born.

> I am weary of my useless existence; my superintendence of your house is nominal . . . you will suffer no inconvenience from its cessation . . . procure a healthy nurse for the baby . . . provided she is fed, she will not fret after me. Had I died when she was born you must have taken this measure, and my parting from her now will be . . . as though she had never known me, and to me far less miserable than at any future time.'[20]

Fanny's desperate proposal ought to be seen in the light of her childhood, for her mother, Marie-Thérèse, had had little to do with her own early years; and, indeed, she and her sister had been happier by far with Dall.

Fanny's friends tried to rally her. Hal sent her consoling letters, proposing that she find another project and begin writing again. In late summer 1835 Catharine Sedgwick persuaded the young

*Supporters (in general male) of Pierce in later years said Fanny drove him away with unreasonable demands about his whereabouts and the company he kept.

mother to bring her new baby to visit her in the Berkshires.

That summer visit crystallized Fanny's lifelong friendship for the Sedgwick clan. She fell in love with their mountain valley home where the Housatonic River flowed through basalt gorges and upland pastures. 'A beautiful little river wanders singing from side to side in this secluded Paradise, and from every mountain cleft come running crystal springs to join it; it looks only fit for people to be baptized in.'[21]

Each summer Catharine Sedgwick occupied her own wing in her younger brother's house in the village of Lenox, Massachusetts. She, along with Charles Sedgwick and his wife, Elizabeth, were famous for their hospitality. Charles Sedgwick was a leading lawyer in Berkshire County. Elizabeth ran a well-regarded girls' school from their home, educating the offspring of the New England intelligentsia.* Fanny had never felt so at home in America before. Lenox, redolent with mountain streams and the good companionship of liberal-minded friends, came to embody Fanny's ideal of contentment. She once wrote,

> 'I cannot describe my delight in living water . . . The Swedenborgians consider water, when the mention of it occurs in the Bible, as typical of truth. I love to think of that when I look at it, so bright, so pure, so transparent, so temperate, so fit an emblem for that spiritual element in which our souls should bathe and be strengthened, at which they should drink and be refreshed . . . I believe the material element to be as potent in regenerating and healing the body, as the spiritual element its clearness dimly represents is to regenerate and heal the mind.[22]

The Sedgwicks, she wrote, were 'almost the only [Americans] among whom I have found mental companionship'.[23]

---

*Her pupils would include a daughter of Ralph Waldo Emerson, the future American sculptor Harriet Hosmer, and for a time Fanny's own daughter, Sarah.

Catharine's fame as a novelist brought a wide selection of writers and thinkers to the Sedgwicks' valley, helping to establish Berkshire County's reputation as an American version of the English Lake District. Washington Irving, the Appleton sisters – Fanny and Mary – Daniel Webster, Charles Sumner, and Oliver Wendell Holmes were all regular summer visitors. Anna Jameson and Harriet Martineau enjoyed the Sedgwick hospitality on their American tours, as did several other English writers. When the Sedgwick clan were assembled in Stockbridge,* recalled one friend,

> as they often were in summer days – and often with distinguished visitors from home and abroad – it would be difficult to find a family circle in which there was more good sense and good culture, more ease and freedom, or more gaiety and affection. Catharine was, perhaps, the central figure of the group, at least to strangers, but it was a circle in which every one had attractions, and it was emphatically a family of love.[24]

At the age of twenty-one Fanny had declared her opinion that intellect in a husband was not important. 'I do not think intellect excites love. I do not even think that it increases our love for those we do love, though it adds admiration to our affection.'[25] The contrast between the refreshing intellectual company of the Berkshires and the stultifying boredom of Philadelphia pointed up the fallacy of this statement. It was over points of intellect that she and Pierce divided, and the gulf between them was marked out by the issue of slavery.

The fact was that Fanny had married into tainted wealth. Pierce's grandfather, Major Butler, had possessed one of the largest holdings

*Stockbridge was the original Sedgwick family home, at this time occupied by eldest brother Theodore and his family; Lenox was a village a few miles higher up the road.

of slaves in the United States.* In the early 1800s he had purchased plantations in Georgia. These Sea Island plantations, 800 miles away from Philadelphia – Butler's Island, a rice plantation on the delta of the Altamaha River near Darien, and Hampton, or Butler Point, where cotton was grown on the north-west point of St Simons Island – formed the core of the Butler inheritance.

Fanny always maintained that she married Pierce ignorant of the source of his family's wealth.[26] Pierce Butler was not the kind of man to discuss his financial affairs with a young woman. It is possible that she never questioned the nature of the inheritance to be released to her fiancé on the death of his aunts; but she must have discovered the truth soon after her marriage.

The puzzle is why Pierce married her knowing her views. He had spent a year dogging her footsteps and Fanny had never made a secret of her opinion of slavery. Her feelings were openly displayed in her published *Journal*. After one discussion with Dr Charles Mifflin, during her first engagement in Philadelphia, she expressed her emotions with Old Testament fervour:

> Oh! What a breaking asunder of old manacles there will be some of these fine days, what a fearful rising of the black flood, what a sweeping away as by a torrent of oppressions and tyrannies, what a fierce and horrible retaliation and revenge for wrong so long endured – so wickedly inflicted.†

The only possible explanation appears to lie in Pierce's absolute conviction that as a man and the head of his household, the views of his hysterical wife did not count. Fanny, herself, after all, made much of the general rule that women were sup-

*Elected by the South Carolina legislature to the National Congress and later to the Constitutional Convention, Major Butler signed the Constitution for the state of South Carolina and was the author of its Fugitive Slave Law.

†One of the elements Pierce had insisted that Fanny cut from her published *Journal* had been a 'long and vehement treatise against Negro slavery'. (Her husband had managed to persuade her that its inclusion would risk bringing a mob out to burn Butler Place down.)

posed to be weaker than men, in intellect as much as in strength. Unfortunately, it soon became transparently clear that she did not believe Pierce's intellect *in particular* to be superior to *her* intellect.

At that time upper-class Northerners were by no means necessarily anti-slavery. Many a Beacon Hill fortune rested on the slave-grown cotton that supplied Northern mills. Brides from wealthy southern families were to be found adorning the first homes of New England, as they did in Philadelphia and New York. As a general rule, America's elite was uneasy at the violent tone of abolitionists such as William Garrison, who had begun his controversial publication, the *Liberator*, in January 1831. The Sedgwick family, however, had long been active proponents of emancipation.

An African-American woman, Mumbet (Ma-Bet), Elizabeth Freeman, had been a central figure of Catharine Sedgwick's childhood. After the Revolution, Elizabeth Freeman approached Catharine's father, then Berkshire County's most prominent lawyer. Acting as her counsel, in 1781, Theodore Sedgwick challenged the constitutionality of slavery in the courts of Berkshire County. Elizabeth Freeman's victory established a precedent for slavery's abolition throughout Massachusetts. Her freedom won, Mumbet joined the Sedgwick household in Stockbridge, becoming a substitute mother to the children during the lengthy periods of Pamela Sedgwick's illness.

As Catharine told her great niece, Alice, those 'who surround us in our childhood, whose atmosphere infolds us, as it were, have more to do with the formation of our characters than all our didactic and perceptive education'.[27] Catharine was profoundly inspired by Mumbet's 'incorruptible integrity', her strength of character, her love of justice and her 'intelligent industry'.

'Her character may be said to have been impressed by Divine influence, to have been God's gift – His image.'[28]

Mumbet died in 1829 but Catharine's affectionate reminiscences of this central figure in her childhood came to provide Fanny with an embodiment of the argument against slavery.*

By Catharine's account, Mumbet was a dramatic character:

> Her spirit spurned slavery. 'I would have been willing,' she has often said to me in speaking of the period when she was in hopeless servitude, 'I would have been willing if I could have had one minute of freedom – just to say "I am free"– I would have been willing to die at the end of that minute.' With this feeling ever alive she heard the Declaration of Independence read. 'If all are free and equal,' she said, 'why are we slaves?' and at her instance my father commenced a suit in the Supreme Court the result of which was (I do not understand the technical proceedings) that the blacks of the Commonwealth were restored to their natural rights – declared free.[29]

Here was 'nobility of mind' indeed; a nobility of mind to transform the world.

Dr Channing, Dr Charles Follen and various other leading lights of the Unitarian movement were frequent visitors to Stockbridge and Lenox, ministering in the summer to the small Unitarian congregation the Sedgwicks had planted amid the Calvinist villagers. It was in the Congregationalist church in Lenox that Dr William Ellery Channing delivered his much-discussed address on the anniversary of emancipation in the British West Indies, with its rousing conclusion: 'Come Father Almighty, and crown with Thine omnipotence the humble strivings of Thy children to subvert oppression and wrong, to spread light and freedom, peace and joy, the truth and spirit of Thy Son, through the whole earth.'[30]

By the early 1830s Dr Channing had begun to preach openly for emancipation. He argued that the worst evil of slavery was the moral corruption it inflicted on both slave and slave-holder. He granted that the general run of slave owners had a genuine desire to be free of the

---

*In fact, Fanny commemorated Mumbet, in barely fictionalized form, in the novel she wrote in her seventies, *Far Away and Long Ago*.

institution and believed that, with the proper encouragement, the Southern planters could be persuaded to prepare their slaves for freedom. He envisaged the benighted slaves being educated in self-respect and responsibility, until legal emancipation would follow naturally in recognition of an existing state of affairs. Few outside his inner circle thought Dr Channing's approach practical but it particularly appealed to women who were excluded from regular political discourse.

Since their marriage, both Fanny and Pierce had worshipped at the First Unitarian Church in Philadelphia. Fanny had become acquainted with the minister there, the Reverend William Henry Furness, who lived in Germantown in the summer, not far from Butler Place. Furness, a native of Boston, was a disciple and friend of Dr Channing's. He too was examining his conscience as to whether he should advocate emancipation, or even abolition, from his pulpit – an unpopular, and even dangerous position to take in Philadelphia at that time, given the strong trading and family ties with the South.

By early November, Fanny was back in Philadelphia. While the nursemaid played with baby Sarah in the background, she wrote to her Cousin Cecilia Combe:

> There is . . . a question now arising which will surely never again be suffered to rest, which in the opinion of the wise hereabouts threatens the Union far more closely than any previous one that has yet arisen. I speak of the slavery in the South, against which the people in the North are beginning to protest most violently. The evils of this system are horrible; not the positive evils endured by the wretched blacks alone, but the demoralization and degradation which exists wherever they exist, and which extends from the souls of men downward to their intellect, their body and the very soil they cultivate.[31]

Fanny had found her mission. She was aware of the dangers to her husband as well as herself. As she told Cecilia, if you abused slavery in the middle states 'they will cut you, and in the Southern ones they will lynch i.e. hang you, without a judge or jury'.[32] But, as she told Hal, 'we all have some appointed task . . . it can never be . . . that any one's duties are bounded by the half animal instincts of loving husband, wife or children'.[33]

Before she met Pierce Fanny had said she regarded a successful marriage as being 'like a well-arranged duet for four hands; the treble, the woman, has all the brilliant and melodious part, but the whole government of the piece, the harmony, is with the base, which really leads and sustains the whole composition and keeps it steady, and without which the treble for the most part runs to tune merely, and wants depth, dignity, and real musical importance'.[34]

Pierce had won her with the strong, dark and silent style of courtship that is curiously attractive to so many vivacious women. She had taken his willingness to weather the social opprobrium of marrying her as proof that he was a gentleman.* As a child she had perceived her own father's 'even temper' as the ideal buffer to the painful alarms and passionate freaks of her mother's temperament. For a time she mistook her husband's reticence for sincerity and his streak of stubbornness for the strength she had always looked for since Mrs Rowden – the rule over her self-destructive riot. But she had begun to suspect that her husband's 'taste' was a surface gentility with little of the 'nobility of mind' she had once expected of her Bassanio.

As one perceptive younger cousin put it, unchallenged, Pierce had the 'perfect amiability of a selfish man'.† Like his brother John, he had been raised in the notion that wealth, clothes and the outer man, made a gentleman. Sons of an eccentric mother and an ineffective father – unloved and untutored – the brothers combined little education with insecurity and arrogance.

---

*She was not to know at the time that in deserting Emily Chapman so publicly, he had probably irretrievably blotted his copy-book as far as a respectable Philadelphian marriage went.

†S. Weir Mitchell wrote that Pierce Butler was 'a person who always fascinated my youth on account of his singular beauty and a certain refined charm of manner. He had the perfect amiability of a selfish man', quoted Furnas, p. 122.

From Fanny's point of view, if Pierce was indeed the gentleman his manner and clothes proclaimed him to be, then he ought to have the self-possession to rise above what others thought of him. But Pierce was deeply conventional. The 'refined charm of manner' and the well-cut clothes were a veneer. Fanny's articulacy overwhelmed Pierce. For all his seeming composure he was stung by his wife's casual informality and teasing. Lacking her quick wit, he merely chose not to respond.

The couple's relationship was bedevilled by a mutual misunderstanding. Watching her devotion to her father, Pierce naturally expected that devotion to transfer to him once Charles Kemble was packed off to England. But to his disgust, his new English wife insisted 'that marriage should be companionship on equal terms – a partnership, in which, if both partners agree, it is well; but if they do not, neither is bound to yield – and that at no time has one partner a right to control the other.'[35] Pierce had grounds for believing that he had been wilfully misled. For all her professions of duty, his wife refused to recognize his God-given superiority as a man and the head of her household.

Fanny began to discover* in her husband's evasive manners a 'coldness' that concealed emotional inadequacy and moral indolence. The bald truth of the matter was that Fanny did not respect Pierce's intellect, and she lacked the tact to conceal the fact. Two years after their marriage, Fanny wrote to George Combe that although her husband was 'a person of no brilliancy of intellect', nevertheless, 'his moral faculties are strong and excellent'.[36] The issue of slavery shattered that fiction. Over that raw subject Fanny discovered that she could neither respect her husband for his intellect nor his morals.

*As her own mother discovered about her father.

29

Georgia

In Spring 1836 Pierce's last aunt died. In an act of nobility that did him much credit in the eyes of his neighbours, Fanny's husband rectified the injustice of his grandfather's will, making over a half interest in the Southern plantations to his brother John. Together the Butler brothers became co-owners of one of the largest slave properties in the South.

Before his aunt's death, in idle conversation, Pierce had told Fanny that the cotton lands in Georgia's Sea Islands were reaching exhaustion. New land was opening up further west in Alabama, where a proprietor with a sufficient number of negroes might realize an enormous fortune. He asked her 'jestingly' whether she would be willing to accompany him on such a venture.

> I replied, in most solemn earnest, that I would . . . if we might take that opportunity of at once placing our slaves upon a more humane and Christian footing . . . Though the blacks may not be taught to read and write . . . no law . . . can prevent one from . . . teaching them all . . . that personal example . . . can teach . . . I would tell them that in so many years I expected to be able to free them, but that those only should be liberated whose conduct . . . during that time would

> render their freedom prosperous to themselves, and safe to the community.[1]

Fanny was trying to be reasonable. She recognized the power of some of the arguments deployed by her husband. Pierce's position was that slavery might be offensive in an ideal world, but a practical man had to deal in facts. How were such large numbers of ignorant, unskilled, half-savages to be set free? In swathes of the South they outnumbered the whites ten-fold. What would happen if they were to be turned out without means of subsistence, or masters to control and care for them?

As winter approached, Pierce and his brother prepared to travel down to Georgia to inspect their inheritance. Fanny fought to go with them, but, backed by his brother, her husband refused to take her. Fanny expressed her frustration and disappointment to her new friend, Mrs Follen.

> I am not going to Georgia, I am not to accompany my husband in his expedition, I am not to open his mind to the evils of slavery, I am not to ameliorate the condition and enlighten the minds of those whose labour feeds me, nor am I to be *lynched*; alas! All of which I had so fondly anticipated. Dear Mrs Follen, I need not tell you what a disappointment it is to me not to be allowed to accompany my husband, but there is no house on our estate, and though I have offered, nay entreated, to be permitted to share any and every inconvenience to which Pierce might be subjected, and *even* to leave my child behind, the better to do so, he has deemed it expedient to determine otherwise, and I have no resource but to submit. I had hoped to have been the means of good, and I am sorry that I may not be so used . . . I pray God who is with each of us to do far better for my dear husband than I could have done, might I but have followed him.[2]

Pierce had been chosen as a delegate to the Pennsylvania State Constitutional Convention called for spring 1837, a commitment that would extend his absence from Philadelphia. He proposed that, while he was away, his wife should have her much-desired visit to her family in England and he would come to collect her after the Convention was finished.

Fanny, with her baby and her nurse, Margery O'Brien, sailed from New York on the packet *South America*, and arrived in Liverpool after a stormy crossing late in November.

Her family welcomed her with open arms, the old quarrel apparently forgotten. Mrs Butler settled down comfortably at her father's London residence in Park Place. Her mother was looking frail. Marie-Thérèse's health had declined and she was spending most of her time in Mrs Whitlock's cottage in Addlestone.* To their mutual pleasure, Fanny had arrived in time to witness Charles Kemble's formal farewell to the stage as Benedict in *Much Ado*. Her father was in fine spirits. He had just been appointed to the comfortably salaried post (much coveted by retired actors and theatre managers) of Licencer of Plays, and for the time being his finances were in order. John Mitchell, now married to a German wife, was working away at his Anglo-Saxon. Henry was with his regiment in the West Indies, but Fanny was able to give her parents some news of her younger brother, as he had dropped in to see her soon after her marriage. And sister Adelaide, looking very *soignée* and cosmopolitan after a couple of years training on the continent, was about to embark on a glowing career as an opera singer.

Fanny was delighted to be back among her 'own' people. There were soirées and parties and breakfasts and hours of intellectual banter. She was petted by Lady Dacre, Sydney Smith, the Ellesmeres, Samuel Rogers – all her old friends and more. She began to write again, setting to work on a new play. But she knew she was only visiting. She was still married to Pierce. 'We shall never desert America and the duties that belong to us there, and I should be the

---

*Mrs Whitlock had died that year, leaving her cottage to Charles Kemble so that Marie-Thérèse could continue to live there.

last person to desire that we do so,' she wrote to Anna Jameson, who was at that time travelling in Canada. 'Henceforth England and I are "Paradises Lost" to each other.'[3]

As May approached, Fanny stationed herself in Liverpool waiting for her husband to arrive. The Convention had been twice postponed. Pierce had left Georgia and was free to come and fetch his wife and child. Instead he wrote, apparently asking if the period of absence had mended the quarrels between them. Her answer carried echoes of Portia speaking from her stage.

> My dearest husband: You ask me if this separation has not strengthened our affection and our value for each other? If it has endeared me to you I ought to be grateful . . . it has led me to reflect upon some passages of our intercourse with self-condemnation, and a desire to discharge my duty to you more faithfully . . . Yet do not mistake me; you ask . . . how I like my independence, and whether I remember how vehemently and frequently I objected to your control . . . part of my regret . . . arises from the manner of my resistance, not the fact itself.
>
> . . . Neither my absence from you, nor my earnest desire to be again with you, can make me admit that the blessed and happy relationship, in which we stand to each other, is any thing but perfect companionship, perfect friendship, perfect love. For the existence of these, justice must also exist; and there is no justice in the theory, that one rational creature is to be subservient to another . . . dear Pierce, upon what ground should you exercise this control over me? Is it because having full power to withhold the gift, I freely gave myself to you, to add as much by my fellowship as I could to your happiness? Is it because you are better than myself? I am sure you will not say so, whatever I may think. Is it because you are more enlightened, more intellectual? You know that is not so, for your opportunities have not been the same. Is it because you are stronger in body? . . . If . . . you do not admit and respect the rights of your wife, how come it that she is at this moment an

> independent agent, having been so for upwards of six months, with the precious charge of your darling child, and the free and generous use of your means . . . I would rather hear you acknowledge a principle of truth, than enjoy the utmost indulgence that your affection could bestow upon me.[4]

Pierce let it be known that he was on his way to fetch her home. Contrary winds kept Fanny waiting with her small child and Margery in a scruffy beach resort outside the port, until Pierce finally arrived. There was a rushed introduction to Fanny's family in London and a couple of visits to his wife's aristocratic friends the Fitzhughs at Bannisters and Lord and Lady Dacre at the Hoo. They set sail for New York in the first week in September.

The crossing took thirty-seven days. By the time they landed in America, Fanny was pregnant again.

Back in Pennsylvania, as her mother had once done in similar circumstances, Fanny piled her energy into improving the house. She planted a fine double row of sugar maples to screen Butler Place from the road. She laid out flower beds and had a greenhouse built where citrus trees stood in tubs in the winter waiting to be put out when the warm weather came. The Butlers 'exist in the finest style', wrote one neighbour. 'In summer you can see the lovely English taste of Fanny in the embellishments . . . within doors all is comfort and opulence.'[5]

Pierce developed a form of rheumatism. He suffered periods of chronic invalidism and depression. He would fall into a stupor, keeping Fanny awaiting his pleasure interminably, only to whip into some action without forewarning. He had a streak of gambler's recklessness that worried Fanny. Through the repeated financial crises of the 1830s and 1840s, banks crashed, businesses went bankrupt and many a gentleman lost his fortune. Pierce Butler was repeatedly unlucky in his speculations.

As Fanny's second pregnancy advanced, communication between husband and wife deteriorated to the exchange of notes.

> You will oblige me by taking immediate means for my return to my own family . . . I will never be subject to rudeness and ill manners from any one . . . I will not return to the farm . . . but . . . remain here, at the corner of Chestnut and Eighth Streets [John Butler's], or go to an inn . . . If you do not choose to take these steps, I have my watch and gold chain . . . which will get me sufficient money to go home in some manner or other . . . There is abundance of time for me to reach England before my confinement; and if you will hereafter appoint means for your child's being brought over to you, I shall . . . observe them.[6]

Pierce ignored her 'freaks' and Fanny returned to 'the farm' to await her confinement. Lounging on her veranda, too big to risk going to church in Germantown, she whiled away the time sketching out improvements to the grounds and watching her toddler 'zigzagging like a yellow butterfly about the lawn' with Margery chasing after her.

On 14 May an association of Philadelphian abolitionists dedicated their new headquarters, Pennsylvania Hall, on the west side of Sixth Street. Three days later, a well-dressed mob stormed the building in broad daylight and burned it down. As the police stood by, the firemen were prevented from extinguishing the flames. 'So much for the supremacy of the laws, which cannot be executed in opposition to popular feeling,' meditated Sydney Fisher in his diary. 'To be sure there was great provocation. The cause itself is unpopular & justly so; the fanatic orators openly recommended dissolution of the Union, abused Washington etc. Black & white men & women sat promiscuously together, & walked about arm in arm. Such are the excesses of enthusiasm . . . There will be more trouble yet, I doubt not, from this prolific source. Such is the hatred to abolition here that many respectable persons, 'tho they do not defend these outrages, blame them faintly & excuse them.'[7] The lines were being drawn. The Reverend William Henry Furness made up his mind and preached emancipation from the pulpit of the First Unitarian

Church.* On little Sarah's third birthday, 28 May 1838, Fanny gave birth to her second daughter, her namesake, called Fan by the family.†

That summer there was a heatwave. The city emptied and the watering places were crowded to overflowing – 'people being willing to sleep in barns, in entries, on the floor, anywhere for the sake of breathing a cooler & purer atmosphere'.[8] For the first time in her life, Fanny's sturdy health gave way. She suffered from lingering complications after the birth of her baby. By the time the cooler weather came, Pierce was living in town. Fanny received the news that her mother, Marie-Thérèse, had died in the cottage in Addlestone with only John Mitchell and his German wife by her side.‡ It was perhaps the thought of how her mother had fretted the best part of her life away in an unsuitable marriage that prompted Fanny to challenge Pierce directly. 'You are now again relieved from my presence,' she wrote to her beleaguered husband.

> Take my advice and casting aside your regard for appearances . . . make some arrangements by which in future to be freed from it altogether . . . I believe you do not yourself think the state in which we live when on good terms . . . one of very intimate companionship or confidence; nature has . . . rendered the sympathy and communion of others totally unnecessary to you; and, were it otherwise, you are here in the midst of your own people . . . your own country . . . the case is the very reverse with me . . . In part this is my own fault; for I married you without for a moment using my own judgement or observation to ascertain whether . . . we were likely to be companions and fellows to each other . . . the sentiment which drew us together is waning and perishing away . . . There is,

---

*Pierce Butler was sitting in the front pew, Wister, p. 153.

†The coincidence of the two sisters' birthdays (both were born on 28 May) their mother said, showed 'an orderly, systematic, and methodical mode of procedure . . . creditable to me'.

‡Charles Kemble was abroad with Adelaide who was beginning her opera career with her first engagements in Italy.

however, one tie by which I am bound to you, that of utter dependence upon your means, and, therefore, of necessity, upon your will. Such a bond . . . though borne by many women, must needs be irksome to one who has the least feeling of pride; how doubly irksome then to me, who have had and still have the means of perfect independence . . . in the exercise of a distasteful profession . . . but . . . unfettered by the very odious restraint of obligation without affection. . . . I think your comfort will probably be increased by your absence from me.

These considerations . . . induce me to propose that we may henceforward live apart; my discontents will then no longer vex you, nor the restraints to which I am now subject, gall and irritate me.[9]

Pierce's response was to propose that they should go as a family to spend the winter in Georgia. He has left no record of why he took this bizarre decision. Possibly he too had reached the end of his tether and decided to get the confrontation over and see what came after. On the other hand, he may well have believed that when Fanny saw slaves in the flesh she would understand that there was no practical alternative; that it was impossible to countenance setting such childish savages free to roam about unmastered and unprovided for.

It was a fantastic undertaking. The journey was rough and demanding – let alone for a nursing mother with a baby and a toddler. The mansion that Major Butler had built on Hampton Point had fallen into ruin under the stewardship of Pierce's aunts. 'The common comforts . . . are so little known [down there] that we are obliged to ship a freight of necessary articles of food . . . Society, or the shadow of it, is not to be dreamed of . . . our residence . . . a half-furnished house in the midst of rice-swamps.'[10]

Fanny told Elizabeth Sedgwick that she had been warned against going down South 'prejudiced against what I am to find there'.

> I know not well how to answer . . . I am going prejudiced against slavery . . . Nevertheless, I go prepared to find many mitigations . . . much kindness on the part of the masters, much content on that of the slaves . . . you may rely upon the carefulness of my observation . . . certainly, on the plantation to which I am going, it will be more likely that I should some things extenuate, than set down aught in malice.[11]

She promised Elizabeth that she would keep a diary of her Southern experiences.*

Pierce fell into one of his stupors. 'We are . . . departing and not departing,' Fanny wrote in early December; '. . . indecision and procrastination entering largely into the . . . disposer of my destinies . . . after a week or ten days more of doubt and darkness [Pierce may well] get up and be going [in] the . . . abrupt summons which invariably terminates these seasons of weary waiting.'[12]

Two weeks later they finally set off for Georgia. The party comprised Pierce, his sister (who was travelling as far as Charleston with them), Fanny, her six-month-old baby and little Sarah, with Margery O'Brien, their Irish nurse. The journey South took ten days over half-made roads, newly laid railroad tracks, inland steamboats and wretched backwoods coaches.

As they forged deeper South, Fanny reported to Hal on the first 'real' slaves she had ever seen. In fact she had seen slaves before in Baltimore and Washington, but these looked like the degraded creatures she associated with the title. Poorly clothed, they looked 'horribly dirty'. Even their movements suggested to her 'a lazy recklessness . . . as they sauntered along, which naturally belongs to creatures . . . without responsibilities'.

The travellers suffered all sorts of trials, from the food – 'lumps of hot dough' and dirt-water tea – to airless, overheated railway carriages, inescapable dirt and fleas. They crossed terrifying, rickety

---

*The diary she would keep was in the traditional form of letters addressed to Elizabeth Sedgwick.

bridges where the passengers were sent ahead on foot to test that the slats would bear a coach's weight. They ploughed on through dark North Carolina pinewoods, crossing sand and swamps, rivers and waterlogged roads. One stretch of rail was so new, that theirs was only the third service ever to run on it. They arrived at the supposed railhead to find a solitary boxcar standing, abandoned in a clearing. It was a chilly winter day and night was coming on. A small crowd of locals appeared from the woods to watch them, a 'forlorn, fierce, poor, and wild-looking' set. The passengers eventually decided to look for shelter and food for the night. They found it, after a fashion, with a ramshackle 'Colonel', a widower served by a flock of black women (one of whom proudly informed Fanny that at least three of her fellows were the Colonel's daughters).

They arrived in Charleston on Christmas Day morning. Fanny liked the town's rubbed elegance – its 'genteel infirmity as . . . of a distressed elderly gentlewoman'. Charleston had a European air but it was a city under siege. Every evening the 'ominous tolling of bells and beating of drums' sounded the curfew. Twenty years previously an aborted slave uprising had left a simmering fear of arson and massacre. 'No doubt these daily and nightly precautions are but trifling drawbacks upon the manifold blessings of slavery . . . still, I should prefer going to sleep without the apprehension of my servants' cutting my throat in my bed.'[13]

Fanny's account of the rest of the journey portrays a descent into mud. The steamboat to Savannah took two nights and a day to make its way through 'cuts and small muddy rivers, where we stuck fast sometimes . . . a most dismal succession of dingy, low, yellow swamps and reedy marshes, beyond expression wearisome to the eye'. Savannah supplied a good hotel and a hot bath before they set off at night in another smaller steamboat. They woke the next morning as the boat entered the great Altamaha River. The channel wound between 'low, reedy swamps, rattling their brittle canes in the morning breeze'.[14] Darien appeared ahead. A scrubby, insignificant town (although Margery was cheered to see at least *one* other vessel tied up at the wharf).

Before the steamboat could dock, a couple of brightly painted boats came alongside, with black oarsmen whooping and calling out: 'Oh, massa! Oh, missis! Oh, lilli missis! Too glad to see you!' It was Sunday, a day off for the slaves, and so everyone on the secluded island had turned out to greet the owners coming to visit from the great world beyond.

> As we neared the bank, the steersman took up a huge conch, and . . . sounded out our approach . . . the wharf . . . began to be crowded with negroes, jumping, dancing, shouting, laughing . . . clapping their hands . . . using the most extravagant and ludicrous gesticulations to express their ecstacy . . . On our landing . . . the crowd thronged about us like a swarm of bees; we were seized, pulled, pushed, carried, dragged . . . They seized our clothes. Kissed them – then our hands, and almost wrung them off . . . not until we were safely housed, and the door shut . . . we indulged in a fit of laughing, quite as full, on my part, of nervousness as of amusement . . . Later . . . I attempted to take some exercise . . . but before I had proceeded a quarter of a mile, I was again enveloped in a cloud of these dingy dependents . . . clamouring welcome, staring at me, stroking my velvet pelisse, and exhibiting at once the wildest delight and the most savage curiosity. I was obliged . . . to return home.[15]

Home for the winter was the house that the Butlers were to share with the overseer. It was a building of no pretensions whatever; rough plaster walls and dirt floors, doors loosely fastened by the primitive wooden string latch. What furniture there was had been cobbled together by slave carpenters on the estate. There were three small, and three smaller rooms, two of the latter in which the overseer resided. Margery and the babies were given the upstairs. Meals were cooked by a male slave, Southern fashion, in a dingy shed separate from the main building. The only trees near to the house were the remnants of an orchard of orange trees blighted by a sharp frost some winters before.

The house servants were: 'generally barefooted, and always filthy both in their clothes and person . . . begrimed, ignorant, incapable poor creatures, who stumble about . . . in zealous hindrance of each other.'[16] Fanny had to 'wait upon myself more than I have ever done in my life before'.[17]

Cultivation in the Georgia Sea Islands was by big-gang slavery, unlike that of the thousands of much smaller cotton and tobacco farms to the North and West. Rice, in particular, demanded concentrated labour to maintain the network of ditches, dykes, locks and sluices that controlled the water levels in the rice fields. Among the Butler holdings the slave count, including children, was well over seven hundred.

The nearest towns – Darien and further away Brunswick – were bare settlements with a few churches, one or two general stores, whitewashed warehouses and loading docks for the vessels ferrying the rice and cotton to the outer world. Otherwise, the one link with civilization was the small steamboat that came down the sounds from Savannah carrying the mail and the odd passenger.

The only all-year-round inhabitants of the swampy plantations were slaves, bossed by drivers – also slaves – who worked to the orders of the white overseer. During the summer, the 'sickly season', even the white overseers retreated inland to higher ground to escape the malaria endemic to the swamps. The few white families were mostly interrelated by marriage. During the winter they would visit each other in boats rowed by slaves, to dine and gossip. As wife of Pierce Butler, Fanny was a figure in the small community. She made the requisite visits but she was not impressed by the local 'gentry'. She regarded the Sea Island ladies as languid and slovenly, and their drawling speech evidence of lazy minds. They in turn were shocked to see the mistress of Butler Island at times rowing her own skiff alongside a black oarsman as she went 'into town' across the creek on errands. Above all they remarked on her having a white nursemaid for her children. Fanny soon grew bored of their repeated exclamations of awe and envy.

On this waterlogged land, laced through with creeks, the ground underfoot was literally uncertain. Here there were none of the crystal streams of 'living water' Fanny loved so much.

> The land was in mere process of formation . . . [created by] a huge, rolling river, thick and turbid with mud . . . The river wants *straining* and the land wants draining, to make either of them properly wet or dry. A duck, an eel, or a frog might live here as in Paradise; but a creature of dry habits naturally pines for less wet . . . 'water, water everywhere'; indeed, in spring, the overseer tells me, we may have to go from house to house in boats, the whole island being often flooded.[18]

Man was in unsteady control of this slow, muddy, resistant nature. The swamp half-controlled by dykes and ditches, stretched out flat under intense sun, even in January. Everywhere there was the inescapable hugeness of the sky and the rattling of the reed beds.

On the few dryer stretches of higher ground there was rough pasture, but barely enough for horses and little firm ground to ride on. Spanish moss smothered the trees: 'Of all parasitical plants . . . the most melancholy and dismal . . . dark grey drooping masses, swinging in every breeze like matted grizzled hair . . . a naked cypress with its straggling arms all hung with this banner of death like a gigantic tree of monstrous cobwebs.'[19] Even walking was curtailed by the dense jungle of scrub and choking vegetation, at the margin of the rice fields.

'The strangeness of this existence surprises me afresh every hour . . . I [feel] like the little old woman whose petticoats were cut all round about. "O Lord a mercy, sure this is never I!"'[20]

Fanny and the nursemaid, Marjorie, were the only white women on the plantation; Fanny's husband and the overseer, the only white men, were occupied from dawn to dusk on their own business. Fanny, therefore, spent most of her time in the company of her husband's slaves.

Pierce gave her a boy called Jack, the son of a recently deceased head-driver, to run errands and keep her company. He was bright lad. Jack warned her about snakes, steered her clear of quicksands, and went fishing with her – offering useful advice about the poisonous barbs of catfish, and concocting local baits for her. They frequently went out together in a little boat Fanny christened *The Dolphin*. As they fished side by side they held long conversations about the great world outside the island that encompassed Jack's entire life.

> His questions, like those of an intelligent child, [were] inexhaustible; his curiosity about all things beyond this island, the prison-house of his existence, [was] perfectly intense . . .
>
> In the midst of his torrent of inquiries about places and things, I suddenly asked him if he would like to be free. A gleam of light absolutely shot over his whole countenance . . . [then he] became excessively confused, and at length replied, 'Free, missis! What for me wish to be free? . . . me work till me die for missis and massa.'[21]

Pierce and Fanny had arrived in Georgia at an important juncture in the history of the Butler properties. For more than fifteen years, the plantations had been managed by Roswell King Jnr., son of a co-founder of Darien who had helped Pierce's grandfather when he first organized his Georgia acquisitions. Now Mr King was relinquishing his management of the estate. He had bought land in Alabama and was heading down there with a gang of slaves to carve his own fortune out of the wilderness. He had hired a well-regarded replacement as overseer, a man who had worked on one of the better-run local plantations.

Fanny had been repeatedly assured that on the Butler plantations she would see 'the peculiar institution' of slavery shaped by the enlightened hands of good masters. King was not the average overseer. He was regarded as being on an equal social footing with the Butler brothers. The Kings, father and son, had made the Butler properties famous for production, discipline and enlightened management.* Their doctrine, according to the published views of the son, was that an 'overseer should be the kind friend and monitor of the slave, not the oppressor'.[22]

Fanny was eager to examine the evidence. Butler Island was organized into three separate 'camps' – self-contained villages. At Number One quarters she found the infirmary: 'a large two-storey building . . . of whitewashed wood [containing] four large-sized rooms.' The few glazed windows were dark with dirt; the unglazed ones covered with ill-fitting wooden shutters. There was an insignificant fire burning in a vast fireplace. Figures of women were crumpled on wooden settles:

> [Those] too ill to rise . . . lay . . . on the floor, without bed, mattress, or pillow, buried in tattered and filthy blankets . . . Here lay women expecting every hour the terrors and agonies of childbirth . . . others . . . groaning over the anguish . . . of miscarriages . . . some burning with fever, others . . . aching with rheumatism, upon the hard cold ground . . . this is the hospital of an estate where the owners are supposed to be humane, the overseer efficient and kind, and the negroes remarkably well cared for and comfortable.

Fanny was too courageous to turn and run. Her only weapons were cleanliness and order but she set to work to conquer dirt as best she could. She organized the able-bodied women to clean. Day after

---

*Ten years earlier, King had published an article in the *Southern Agriculturist* attributing his success to discipline; forbidding visiting back and forth between plantations and strict control of the drivers to reduce bullying. In the interests of health, he assigned pregnant women lighter field work, maintained infirmaries under the charge of slave midwives, ensured a certain amount of protein (salt beef, salt pork, salt fish) to complement the bulk rations of corn meal in the slaves' diet, and divided off the task of cooking the evening meal to old women who prepared the food for all. The burden of his message was that tyrannical overseers and corner cutting did the owners more harm than good. The slaves were 'the sinews of the estate' and it was sensible to look after them, just as a sensible farmer saw to the health of his draught animals. Furnas, p. 197.

day she returned home her clothes 'covered with dust, and full of vermin'. She rolled up her sleeves and stripped children of their rags. She showed their mothers how to give them their first all-over baths. Healthy babies were routinely left in charge of older children while their mothers worked in the fields. With these, Fanny tried bribery – offering a penny each day to any minder who brought their charge to her with clean face and hands.* The experiment worked, but before long she was running out of money.

'The black babies of a year or two old are very pretty,' she told Elizabeth. 'They have, for the most part, beautiful eyes and eyelashes.'

> And when the very unusual operation of washing has been performed, the blood shines through the fine texture of the skin . . . I have seen many babies on this plantation who were quite as pretty as white children, and this very day stooped to kiss a little sleeping creature that lay on its mother's knees in the infirmary – as beautiful a specimen of a sleeping infant as I ever saw. The caress excited the irrepressible delight of all the women present – poor creatures! Who seemed to forget that I was a woman, and had children myself.[23]

When she tackled the overseer, complaining about the state of the infirmary, he replied that he had mentioned the matter to John Butler the year before, and to Mr King, but their response led him to believe that it was 'a matter of indifference to the owners'. So he 'had left it in the condition in which . . . it has been for the last nineteen years'.

As word spread of the sympathetic new mistress, Fanny was besieged by petitioners – most of them women – asking her to inter-

---

*As she admitted satirically to Elizabeth: 'I have ingeniously contrived to introduce bribery, corruption, and pauperism, all in a breath, upon this island, which, until my advent, was as innocent of these pollutions, I suppose, as Prospero's isle of refuge.' – Georgia Journal, p. 77.

cede on their behalf with 'Massa'. Appalled by their tales of whippings, of miscarriages, of rheumatism and exhaustion, Fanny tried to become their advocate. Pierce told her that she did not understand, that they were 'shamming' and taking advantage of her good nature.

One day Margery* told Fanny that she had been approached by Psyche, a graceful mulatto woman in her early twenties with a sweet face, who was one of the house-slaves.

> The poor woman had inquired of her with much hesitation and anguish if she could tell her who owned her and her children. She has two nice little children under six years old, whom she keeps as clean and tidy, and who are as sad and as silent as herself.

Psyche had at one time been owned by Mr King, the ex-overseer who was now heading for the wild lands of Alabama. No one had bothered to inform Psyche whether she and her children were about to be wrenched from their home. Psyche was 'married' to another Butler slave, Joe – an 'excellent young man, whose whole family are among some of the very best specimens of character and capacity on the estate'.

Fanny waited for Pierce's return. The overseer came back to the house first. He, to her extreme surprise, informed her that he had recently purchased Psyche and her children from Mr King, who had offered them to him, saying that they would probably be 'troublesome' to take to Alabama. Fanny rushed to tell Psyche the glad news – but the drama was just beginning.

Fanny woke the next morning to hear loud voices coming from her husband's room. A man cried out in despair and she ran in to find Psyche's Joe:

> almost inarticulate with passion, reiterating his determination never to leave this plantation, never to go to Alabama, never to

---

*Margery, being a white woman, was regarded as a sort of junior wife to Pierce by the slaves.

leave his old father and mother, his poor wife and children, and dashing his hat, which he was wringing like a cloth in his hands, upon the ground, he declared that he would kill himself if he was compelled to follow Mr King.

Pierce leaned against a table with his arms folded, 'occasionally uttering a few words of counsel to his slave to be quiet and not fret, and not make a fuss about what there was no help for'.

Fanny went to find the overseer who informed her that Mr Butler, in gratitude for Mr King's service to his family, had 'made him a present' of Joe, who had just been told to get ready to leave with his new owner the next day.

It is possible that Pierce, thinking Psyche and her children were on their way to Alabama, had meant to keep the family together* but Fanny could only see the horror of the tragedy unfolding before her eyes. As soon as she found her husband alone, she deployed all her dramatic skills with a passion she had never felt on stage. She appealed to Pierce 'for his own soul's sake, not to commit so great a cruelty'.

> How I cried, and how I adjured . . . it seemed to me that I was imploring Mr Butler to save himself more than to spare these wretches.

Pierce refused to answer her. He left the room without a word.

Fanny stewed in her misery all day while her husband avoided her. That evening, the overseer came to work in the room where she sat. She asked him if he had seen Joe. Joe, the overseer replied, was a good deal happier than he had been in the morning. He was not going to Alabama after all. 'Mr King heard that he had kicked up a fuss about it and said that if the fellow wasn't willing to go with him, he did not wish to be bothered with any niggers down there who were to be troublesome, so he might stay behind.'

---

*The Butler management had always prided itself on preserving family units among their slaves.

Although she was relieved that Joe was safe, Fanny remained anxious for Psyche and her children. The next day, with Pierce still refusing to speak to her, she began counting up her valuables to see if she might be able to raise the price of Psyche and her children herself.

> For the last four years of my life that preceded my marriage I literally coined money, and never until this moment, I think, did I reflect on the great means of good, to myself and others, that I so gladly agreed to give up forever for a maintenance by the unpaid labour of slaves.

She went to the overseer and asked him whether, should he contemplate selling Psyche and her children, he would give her first refusal. He answered:

> Dear me, ma'am, I am very sorry – I have sold them . . . I didn't know, ma'am, you see, at all, that you entertained any idea of making an investment of that nature; for I'm sure, if I had, I would willingly have sold the woman to you; but I sold her and her children this morning to Mr Butler.

Pierce had heard her after all. 'Though he had, perhaps justly, punished my violent outbreak of indignation . . . by not telling me of his humane purpose,' she wrote to Elizabeth. 'He had bought these poor creatures, and so, I trust, secured them from any such misery in future.'

The moral boundaries were as confusing as the blurred demarcations of the intermixed land and water. Few of the white men Fanny encountered positively advocated slavery. Dr James Holmes, a Northern-born medic who treated the Butler slaves in extreme emergencies, for instance, professed to defend slavery only as a practicality.* Mr King and his successor, the present overseer, both

---

*In his informal memoirs, Holmes described Fanny as a 'hopeless monomaniac' on the subject of slavery and most unfair to what he considered the humanely run Butler Plantations. He added, however, that she was elegant and accomplished and he had 'respected her highly' and liked her 'social, companionable, and even playful ways'. Quoted Furnas, p. 209.

admitted slavery to be an inefficient system. They would prefer to work with free labour, they said. But slavery existed and there was no practical way to end it for the time being. 'I'll tell you why abolition is impossible,' one 'distinguished Carolinian' told Fanny: 'because every healthy negro can fetch a thousand dollars in the Charleston market at this moment.'

And yet, the more time Fanny spent with 'her' slaves, the more personable they became to her. 'I have found the slaves on this plantation intelligent and advanced beyond the general brutish level of the majority,'[24] she wrote to Elizabeth. One dramatic night crystallized her thoughts.

A valuable and skilled slave called Shadrach fell ill suddenly. Pierce did his best to save him. He called the doctor from Darien and even watched by the man's bedside himself, but Shadrach died. The funeral was held at night. It was officiated by a slave preacher, a cooper called London, who having learned somehow to read, had become 'a Methodist preacher of no small intelligence and influence among the people'.

Fanny and Pierce were the only white people present as the body, wrapped in a cotton winding sheet, was laid on trestles in front of the cooper's cottage. The congregation was large. A mass of slaves stood under the fitful light of pinewood torches.

> Presently the whole congregation uplifted their voices in a hymn, the first high wailing notes of which – sung all in unison, in the midst of these unwonted surroundings – sent a thrill through all my nerves.

They followed the coffin to the slaves' burial ground. With the sounds of the great river sweeping on in the darkness beyond the torchlight, London's voice proclaimed the words of the funeral service.

> I was . . . absorbed in the whole scene, and the many mingled emotions it excited of awe and pity, and an indescribable sensation of wonder at finding myself on this slave soil,

> surrounded by *my* slaves, among whom . . . I knelt while the words proclaim[ed] to the living and the dead the everlasting covenant of freedom, 'I am the resurrection and the life'.

Fanny knelt with the slaves, but Pierce 'alone remained standing in the presence of . . . the living God'.

When the coffin was lowered, the grave had begun to fill with muddy water.

By the time the Pierce Butlers left Georgia in May, Fanny had begun to appreciate the beauties of the Sea Islands: the lushness of the spring with its brilliant blossoms – a piece of sandy ground covered with hyacinths, double jonquils and snowdrops in early February. The river 'all burnished with sunset glories, and broken with the vivacious gambols of a school of porpoises';[25] or at night, being rowed home 'through a world of stars, the steadfast ones set in the still blue sky, and the flashing swathes of phosphoric light turned up by our oars and keel in the smooth blue water'. But as Fanny watched Pierce refuse a group of women petitioning for a reduction in their hard labour in the fields, she could no longer see the man she had once loved.

> Mr Butler seemed positively degraded in my eyes as he stood enforcing upon these women the necessity of their fulfilling their appointed tasks . . . setting forth . . . as a duty, their unpaid, exacted labour! I turned away in bitter disgust . . . the details of slavery holding are so unmanly . . . that I know not how any one with the spirit of a man can condescend to them.

That winter in Georgia confirmed once and for all the irreconcilable nature of the couple's disagreements. Years later Fanny told a friend that she had assured her husband that: 'If he could put his hand on his heart & say conscientiously that he thought himself right to hold slaves she would never say another word on the subject . . . He replied that he could *not* do so – & in her opinion it was acting against conscience which was the chief objection to it.'[26]

From Pierce's perspective that was not the point. He thought he was doing the best he could under the circumstances. The man of the mathematical and factual turn of mind would never appreciate his histrionic wife's sincerity.

Georgia divided Fanny from her husband as surely as Undine had been severed from her mortal lover: 'It is too intolerable to find myself an involuntary accomplice to this wickedness.'[27]

CONCLUSION

Consequences

> If I had my choice . . . I would rather live forwards, that is, have my head in my hand (martyr fashion, which is an allegorical representation of what befalls people with a propensity for living before their time), and carry it a little in advance of my body . . . the majority of people are so prejudiced in favour of the stupid, common usage, and so ill-natured towards those who depart from it.[1]

Fanny lost Pierce, who once made America home to her, the husband '*in whose companionship lies the best half of every pleasure*'.[2] Pierce Butler became fixed on the notion that the public submission of his wife was a measure of his manliness. After that winter in Georgia in 1838 he increasingly viewed Fanny's determination to advocate her own views as malicious and perverse.* The weight of her challenge dissolved his 'perfect amiability'. Towards her, at least, he displayed a resentful nature that harboured every slight.

The couple's relationship sank into acrimony. The dissolution of the marriage was news copy on both sides of the Atlantic. Pierce never forgave his actress-wife for setting herself above him before the world. As far as he was concerned, the law defined a wife as being without separate entity from her husband because God, nature

*Forty years later Fanny admitted that her views on slavery must have made her appear 'a mischievous madwoman' to the family she married into. *Records of a Later Life*, vol. I, p. 51.

and society had ordained that it was in her best interests to be ruled by him.

In March 1848, after a catalogue of domestic tyrannies,* Pierce Butler filed for divorce. He cited Fanny's vociferous arguments that marriage was a partnership between equals as the principal reason for terminating the relationship.

Pierce kept their two daughters. In her mid-30s Fanny was ejected from the domestic context which society judged so material to a woman's respectability. Symbolically, she was robbed of her womanhood and left exposed as an unnatural female. Fanny Kemble would never trust 'the whole government' of her life to anyone again.

Fanny never went back to the plantations. Pierce was forced to sell his slaves before the Civil War.† Having lost his fortune in a succession of bad speculations on the New York Stock Exchange, he sold hundreds of men, women and children born on the Butler Plantations in one of the largest slave auctions ever held in the United States in April 1859.

Fanny never understood Pierce's conception of honour: that code that made him share half his grandfather's fortune with his elder brother, and caused him to return to 'his' people after the war. Fanny's ex-husband ended his days in Georgia. After the Civil War, hearing that several of his erstwhile slaves had returned to the only home they had ever known, Pierce Butler went back to try to rebuild the plantations on a share-cropper basis. He was supported by his fervently loyal younger daughter, Fan. In August 1867 he died of

*He drove Fanny out of the house by having her sign specific terms and then entrapping her into breaking them. In one incident, having allowed her to stay under his roof on terms that included that she break off all correspondence with the Sedgwicks, he sent a servant to her with a letter from Elizabeth. Assuming that this meant she was allowed to open it, Fanny did so – whereupon Pierce attacked her for having deliberately broken their agreement. In the last phases of the terrible dispute, he prevented her from seeing her daughters; even going to the extent of having their governess make Sarah and Fan walk past her without speaking when she tried to talk to them in the street.

†As it turned out, one of his few pieces of good luck – financially speaking – since the Civil War, a few years later, would remove his right to call them property.

malaria, having been rowed across to Darien by one of his ex-slaves to find the white doctor. Fan took up her father's mission, as she saw it, and ran the plantations both by herself and – after she married a hearty English clergyman – for a time with her husband.

When the Civil War consumed the United States Fanny published her *Journal of a Residence on a Georgian Plantation* – that 'strong, insistent, one-sided' and 'most valuable account',[3] as Henry James called it. For years she had resisted the pressure of friends to publish, out of consideration for her estranged husband and daughters. However, in 1863, in the depths of the war, she felt it imperative to challenge the pro-Southern assumptions of the aristocratic ruling classes in England, several of whom were among her friends and acquaintances. While many in polite society objected that she had written of things no woman should articulate, in the long run the justification of the moral crusade against slavery contributed to her social redemption.

All her life Fanny remained convinced of the inner truth of her Shakespearean models. Emerson wrote that we are offered two choices: 'peace or truth'. Fanny certainly paid for her sincerity. Her younger daughter, Fan, for one never forgave her difficult mother for either her *Journal of a Residence* or for all the suffering she had caused her father – although in the end, it was in Fan's household in London that Fanny died, peacefully, in her sleep on 15 January, 1893, at the age of eighty-three.

After her ejection from Philadelphia and Butler Place in the early 1840s, Fanny tackled the challenge of providing for herself with the stoic professionalism she imbibed from her family, but her failed attempt to achieve the security of a domestic setting intensified the melancholy streak in her make-up. She spent her life looking for security, and she was never entirely satisfied that the only security she found was that which she won for herself. To the end of her days, she would complain about the lot of a woman having to cope on her own without the help and protection of a man, although she knew herself quite competent, and she could always call on a range of faithful male friends, both young and old.

Over the years Catharine Sedgwick, her brother Charles and his wife Elizabeth would participate in many of the ups and downs of Fanny's life. She bought a house in Lenox called The Perch, and became a resident in the Sedgwick 'paradise' for several happy years. Fredrika Bremer, the Swedish novelist, paints a picture of her in trousers, 'ranging about through wood and field . . . on one occasion she herself drove a cow home to Miss Sedgwick, who had lost hers, and who now received this as a present from her "sublime" Fanny'.[4]

Fanny only gradually gave up her early ambition to be a poet. It is an irony, given such a character and such a dramatic life, that poetry should bring out the banal in her. As Robert Browning said trenchantly to his wife of Fanny's first volume of collected verse: 'I had no conception Mrs Butler could have written anything so mournfully mediocre.'[5] In verse, Fanny's sincerity was markedly maudlin.* And, for all her outspoken determination not to be seduced by the ephemeral delights of celebrity, it betrayed her lingering wish for fame. 'I will not be forgot!' she wrote more than once.

Yet not in tears remembered be my name –
Weep over those ye loved: for me, for me,
Give me the wreath of glory and let fame
Over my tomb spread immortality![6]

Fanny found her purpose in what Henry James described as the 'only really secure happiness she knew', her love of Shakespeare. She explained to friends that Shakespeare had already said everything she would like to have expressed, in poetry she could never aspire to. In middle and later life she turned her considerable passion and poetic susceptibility to communicating that personal resonance.

In her readings Fanny picked up John Philip Kemble's tradition of

*Fanny Appleton Longfellow described her poems as 'rammed with life' and suffering, but 'too bitter and morbid for a Christian woman and wrong to publish, so many sickly souls will sharpen their griefs upon her thorns.' Wagenknecht, 15 May 1844, p. 111.

the Aristocracy of the Word, adapted for the Victorian era. Lifting drama free from the taint of the stage, she performed alone, seated at a desk, without props or costumes, in the polite setting of the drawing room or the didactic venue of the lecture hall. Her Shakespearean readings brought her substantial recognition in her own time. In the light of the lamps she became the embodiment of legend. 'What an abundance there is in her!' exclaimed Ralph Waldo Emerson after hearing her read in Boston in 1850 – 'She is Miranda, Queen Catherine, and many more in the same time!'[7] Fredrika Bremer agreed:

> No one can ever forget what he has once heard her read; she carries her audience completely into the world and the scene which she renders . . . I shall never forget her glowing, expressive countenance, when she as Henry V incited the army to heroic deeds . . . When Mrs Kemble steps before the audience, one immediately sees in her that powerful and proud nature which bows before the public in the consciousness that she will soon have them at her feet. And then, while she reads, she forgets the public and Fanny Kemble; and the listeners forget themselves and Fanny Kemble, too; and both live, breathe and are thrilled with horror, and bewitched by the great dramatic scenes of life which she conjures forth with her magic power.[8]

And yet, as Mrs Kemble, the Celebrated Reader, she was still only a player – even if as a votary of Shakespeare.

When she was in her sixties, her great friend and confidante Harriet St Leger sent her a box containing the thousands of letters Fanny had written over their forty-year-long friendship. Fanny used the letters as the backbone of what became a trilogy of three-volume memoirs – *Records of a Girlhood*, *Records of a Later Life* and *Further Records*.

If the aim of the Romantic artist was heroic sincerity – fashioning an epic out of personal talent, vision and experiences – then, after a lifetime of worrying about the ephemeral nature of her profession,

Fanny Kemble fulfilled the role of the Romantic Artist in her *Records* and journals.

Her early experience as a lay figure left her determined to preserve herself from being served up to posterity only as public entertainment. 'Few things have ever puzzled me more,' she once told her lifelong Boston admirer Henry Lee, 'than the fact of people liking me because I pretended to be a pack of Juliets and Belvideras, and creatures who were not me.'[9] Her *Records* are a chronicle of the sincerity of her feelings; an effort to explain – to justify – the private Frances Anne Kemble as against Fanny Kemble of the public prints. In so doing, she left in snatches of prose precisely what the Apostles intended in their poetry – a close-up of both a human being and an age. If the poetry of her day spoke 'unto the general mind'[10] then it is Fanny Kemble's records and journals that leave a close-up for posterity of the generation who embodied that mind.

Thomas Carlyle was convinced that democracy sounded the death-knell of genius and the end of heroes. Born into an aristocratic society, Fanny witnessed the advent of populist democracy, a model which presumes any elite to be oppressive of the majority. Democracy shrinks the image of the individual to one tiny and various part of the mass; the standard is the common man and respect for the individual signified by the possession of a vote.

The Romantic creed, bred out of an aristocratic society, applied intellectual belief in the value of the individual in a different way. In the face of the political and economic rubrics that would come to dominate the modern world, Romanticism embodied a conviction that the purpose of individual genius was to discern universal truths and communicate them for the enlightenment of all – so that the elite serves the mass.

The camera was invented when Fanny was in her middle age. In the few photographs that survive, she tends to present herself in profile, her eyes looking into some private middle distance. As she said herself: 'My face . . . never was intended for still life.'[11]

The photograph brings us face to face with the *image* of the individual; a face made up of eyes, mouth, expression. It transforms the close-up from something intimate into appearance. To quote Charles Lamb:

> We find to our cost that instead of realizing an idea, we have only materialized and brought down a fine vision to the standard of flesh and blood. We have let go a dream, in quest of an unattainable substance.[12]

Today we have what Fanny Kemble struggled against all her life. We are dominated by a celebrity culture, where artifice and the appearance of things serves for sincerity. In modern society the player has come to stand for Everyman. The close-up on a face, the movement of an eye, or the expression of a mouth communicates sensation rather than an idea. The risky, epic struggles of the artist to represent the essence and vitality of humanity are forgotten.* Whereas the mission of the Romantic Artist was to illuminate the life of Everyman so that each individual could live their life better, now the role of the star or celebrity is to make us all sit back, lusting after the illusion we poor mortals can only dream of sharing. One of the triumphs of populism is to make us all spectators.

A passage Fanny wrote to Hal towards the end of the time when she came nearest to living as a Miranda to her father's Prospero, echoes with her sense of fiction's power to communicate reflections from the elusive core of universal human experience:

> I so often contemplate in fancy that island, lost in the unknown seas, just in the hour of its renewed solitude, after the departure of its 'human mortal' dwellers and visitors, when Prospero and his companions had bade farewell to it, when Caliban was grunting and grubbing and grovelling in his favourite cave again, when Ariel was hovering like a humming-bird over the

*With the evolution of malleable digital photography, however, perhaps the cycle begins again.

flower draperies of the woods, where the footprints of men were still stamped on the wet sand of the shining shore, but their voices silent and their forms vanished, and utter solitude, and a strange dream of the past, filling the haunts where human life, its sin and sorrow, and joy and hope, and love and hate had breathed and palpitated, and were now forever gone. The notion of that desert once, but now deserted paradise, whose flowers had looked up at Miranda, whose skies had shed wisdom on Prospero, always seems to me full of melancholy. The girl's sweet voice singing no more in the sunny, still noon, the grave, tender converse of the father and child charming no more the solemn eventide, the forsaken island dwells in my imagination as at once desecrated and hallowed by its mortal sojourners; no longer savage quite, and never to be civilized; the supernatural element disturbed, the human element withdrawn; a sad, beautiful place, stranger than any other in the world. Perhaps the sea went over it; it has never been found since Shakespeare landed on it. I love that poem beyond words.[13]

NOTES

Introduction – A Reluctant Celebrity

1 F.A. Kemble (FK), letter to Harriet St Leger (Hal), 2 April 1831, *Records of a Girlhood* (RG), vol. II, p. 292.
2 Mathews, vol. IV, p. 39.
3 FK, RG, vol. I, p. 7.
4 FK, *Journal*, 12 January 1832.
5 James, p. 89.
6 Unidentified newspaper clipping – obituary of FK, 17 January 1893 in Enthoven collection.
7 E. Ritchie, p. 41.

PART I – THE IMPORTANCE OF BEING A KEMBLE

1 – The House that Jack Built

1 Details of 4 October 1809 and the Old Price Riots are drawn from several sources, the principal ones being – Stockdale; Saxe Wyndham, vol. I; Genest, vol. VIII; Boaden *Memoirs of the Life of J. P. Kemble*, vol. II and *Memoirs of Mrs Inchbald* vol. II; contemporary reports in *The Times* and playbills in the Garrick Club library.
2 FK, *On the Stage*.
3 Archer and Lowe, *Dramatic Essays of Leigh Hunt*, p. 11.
4 Oxberry, vol. I, no. VI, p. 97.
5 Quoted Baker, p. 5.
6 From letters of Ann Kemble Hatton held in the Folger Library, quoted Highfill et al vol. VIII, p. 389.
7 Kelly, vol. I, p. 345.
8 Guy Miege, quoted Bate, *Shakespearean Constitutions*, p.112.
9 *London Chronicle*, 3 January 1769, quoted Dobson, p.176.
10 Boaden, *Memoirs of Mrs Siddons*, vol. I, p. 8.
11 Published by John Bell, 1773–4.
12 From Dr Johnson's preface to his edition of Shakespeare's plays published in 1765, quoted Bate, *Shakespeare and the English Romantic Imagination*.

13 Robson, pp. 22–23.

2 – An Aristocracy of the Word

1 Schoch, p. 15.
2 Quoted Levy, p. 34.
3 Hazlitt, 'Mr Kemble's Retirement', *The Times*, 25 June 1817, quoted Archer and Lowe, *Dramatic Essays by William Hazlitt*, p. 138.
4 *True Briton*, 24 April 1798.
5 Boaden, *Memoirs of Mrs Inchbald*, vol. I, p. 352.
6 Boaden, *Memoirs of the Life of John Philip Kemble*, vol. II, p.210 n.
7 Herschel Baker, p. 217 – papers held in the Folger Library, Washington.
8 William Beloe, quoted Herschel Baker, p. 222.

3 – Covent Garden: The Kemble House

1 Quoted Schoch, p. 67.
2 Planché, vol. I, p. 54.
3 Ibid., vol. I, p. 52.
4 Mair (Mrs Siddons's granddaughter), p. 21.
5 Archer and Lowe, *Dramatic Essays of Leigh Hunt*, p. 7.
6 Hunt, 'An Essay on Invention in Pronunciation', Archer and Lowe, *Dramatic Essays of Leigh Hunt*, p. 118.
7 Young, p. 40.
8 Boaden, *Memoirs of the Life of John Philip Kemble*, quoted Saxe Wyndham, vol. I, p. 327.
9 Letter from Mrs Siddons, quoted Saxe Wyndham, vol. I, p. 328.
10 Quoted Bate, *Shakespearean Constitutions*, p. 43.
11 Oxberry, vol. II, p. 6. Oxberry's biographies were published after his death by his widow, Catherine, and her new husband, Leman Rede. Rede, who like Oxberry had been an actor and was also the author of a much reprinted handbook called *The Road to the Stage*, may have been the author of some of the gossip printed under Oxberry's name.
12 Boaden, *Memoirs of the Life of John Philip Kemble*, vol. II, p. 493.
13 Boaden, *Memoirs of Mrs Inchbald*, vol. II, p.143.
14 Quoted Saxe Wyndham, vol. I, p. 345.

4 – 'To Charm the Sportive Throng'

1 Letter from Lord Harcourt to the actor R.W. Elliston, Raymond, p. 60.
2 FK, RG, vol. I, pp. 2–3.
3 Ibid., p. 12.
4 Ibid., p. 3.
5 Kelly, vol. I, p. 225. Kelly, reminiscing about working with Gluck in Vienna in the 1780s, recalled that 'the ballet master was Monsieur De Camp, the uncle of that excellent actress, and accomplished and deserving woman, Mrs Charles Kemble'.

6 Details of the Decamp and Simonet families are drawn from the impressive collection of articles in Highfill et al.
7 From an obituary of Mrs Charles Kemble printed in an unidentified newspaper clipping dated in pencil 'Sept 9 1838', Smith, vol. II, p. 110.
8 Ibid., vol. II, p. 110.
9 FK, RG, vol. I, pp. 6–7.
10 La Roche, p. 94.
11 Quoted Highfill et al.
12 Edward Fitzgerald to W.B. Donne, 19 November 1862, Terhune, vol. II, p. 461.
13 Printed in the London press, 27 January 1795.

5 – Thérèse and Charles: A Melodrama

1 Porter, 12 March 1801.
2 Williams, *The Pin Basket to the Children of Thespis*.
3 Donne, p. 608.
4 Peachum in Gay's *The Beggar's Opera* – 'If the wench does not know her own profit, sure she knows her own pleasure better than to make herself a property.' (Act I, Scene I).
5 Kelly, vol. II, p.146.
6 Grimaldi in pantomime at Sadler's Wells in 1809, Speaight, p.102.
7 Archer and Lowe, *Dramatic Essays of Leigh Hunt*, p.108.
8 Robson, pp. 47–48.
9 John Philip Kemble's private apology to Miss Decamp, quoted Highfill et al in the article on Marie-Thérèse Decamp.
10 Porter, 9 February 1801.
11 Ibid., 22 April 1801.
12 Ibid., 5 February 1801.
13 Ibid., 13 May 1801.
14 Saxe Wyndham, vol. I, p. 303.
15 Porter, 22 April 1801.
16 *Morning Herald*, 3 July 1806, quoted Williamson, p. 57.
17 Kelly, vol. II, p. 229.
18 Smith, vol. II, p. 110.
19 Quoted Blainey, p. 8.

PART II – CONFESSIONS

6 – Childhood

1 Mathews, vol. III, p. 174.
2 Letter from Charles Kemble, dated 17 June 1812, Enthoven Collection, V & A.
3 Saxe Wyndham, vol. I, p. 357.
4 FK, RG, vol. I, p.15.
5 Pollock, p. 59.

6 FK, RG, vol. I, p. 26.
7 Ibid., pp. 23–4.
8 Ibid., p. 41.
9 Catherine Macdonald Maclean in her foreword to Hazlitt, *The Round Table & Characters of Shakespeare's Plays*.
10 Keats reviewing Edmund Kean in *The Champion*, 21 December 1817.
11 Lennox writing about Edmund Kean as Richard III, *Celebrities I Have Known*, vol. I, p. 284.
12 Young, p. 55.
13 Coleridge, 27 April 1823.
14 Robson, p. 113.
15 Mair, p. 20.
16 Julian Charles Young recounting a story from Charles Mathews who claimed to be with Wewittzer at the time, Young, p. 57.
17 Robson, p. 249.
18 Letter from Mr Poole to Mr Charles Mathews, quoted Mathews, vol. III, p. 317.
19 Marston, p. 149.
20 Mair, p. 56.
21 FK, *Far Away and Long Ago*, p. 48.
22 Hazlitt, *A View of the English Stage*.
23 Lennox, *Celebrities I Have Known*, vol. I, p. 286.
24 Bunn is something of a prejudiced witness, and he is the only source that mentions this quarrel, but he was a good friend of Henry Harris and was in a position to have the inside gossip. Bunn vol. I, p. 13.

7 – 'Cette Diable de Kemble'

1 FK, RG, vol. I, p. 43.
2 Ibid., p. 51.
3 Smith, vol. II, p. 110.
4 Lennox, *Fifty Years of Biographical Reminiscences*, vol. II, p. 39.
5 Adelaide 'Dall' Decamp's entry in Highfill et al – Adelaide was apprenticed to a Mr Percy – who, the article's author suggests, was John Percy, a violinist and popular composer. Information based on a report written by Mrs Jeanne Decamp in 1795 to the Royal Society of Musicians.
6 Genest, vol. IX, pp. 10–11.
7 Smith, vol. II, p. 110.
8 FK, RG, vol. I, p. 53.
9 Ibid., p. 66.
10 Quoted St Aubyn, p. 56.
11 FK, RG, vol. I, p. 63.
12 Saxe Wyndham, vol. II, p. 1.
13 Review of John Philip Kemble in *King John*, first published 8 December 1816. Hazlitt.
14 FK, RG, vol. I, p. 69.

8 – The Schoolgirl

1 Stodart, Mary Ann, 'Female Writers: Thoughts on Their Proper Sphere and on Their Powers of Usefulness', quoted Helsinger et al, p. 20.
2 FK, RG, vol. I, p. 82.
3 Edward Bulwer-Lytton, quoted Helsinger, p. 7.
4 FK, RG, vol. I, p. 94.
5 Ibid., p. 99.
6 Ibid., p. 110.
7 Ibid., p. 104.

9 – The Forging of a Masculine Mind

1 Blainey, p. 27.
2 FK, 'Lines in Answer to a Question', *Collected Poems*.
3 Mary Russell Mitford to Sir William Elford, December 1813, Chorley, p. 102.
4 FK, RG, vol. I, pp. 130–31.
5 Ibid., p. 82.
6 Planché, vol. I, p. 45.
7 Robson, p. 48.
8 Young, p. 53.
9 Planché, vol. I, pp. 56–7.
10 FK, RG, vol. I, p. 158.
11 Planché, vol. I, p. 80.
12 FK, RG, vol. I, p. 164.
13 Saxe Wyndham, vol. II, p. 41.
14 FK, RG, vol, I, p. 134.
15 Ibid., p. 135.

10 – 'The Glad Sunlight of Clear Thought'

1 Quoted Furnas, p. 35.
2 Power Cobbe, vol. I, p. 198.
3 An anonymous critic's tart description of Priscilla Kemble as an actress in *Candid and impartial strictures on the performers belonging to Drury-Lane, Covent-Garden and the Haymarket Theatres, etc.*
4 FK, RG, vol. I, p. 166.
5 FK on Hal's mental state, reproduced in Clinton.
6 In the dismissive phrase of the hostile critic Genest.
7 Egan, p. 245.
8 Gay, act I.
9 Letter from Edward Fitzgerald to FK, 27 February 1872, quoted Terhune, vol. III, p. 331.
10 FK, RG, vol. I, p. 140.
11 Ibid., p. 143.
12 Ibid., p. 217.

13 Letter from FK to Hal, ibid., p. 179.
14 Jameson, from the preface to *The Diary of an Ennuyée*.
15 Jameson, *The Diary of an Ennuyée*, quoted Thomas.
16 FK, RG, vol. I, pp. 202–3.

11 – Mothers and Daughters

1 Arthur Hallam to William Ewart Gladstone, Saturday, 8 November 1828: 'Kemble, who is a kind of Pericles, or rather Cleon in the Union, did not please me much.' The distinction being between Cleon, the fifth-century BC Athenian demagogue and Pericles the fifth-century BC statesman. Kolb, pp. 244–5.
2 Ibid., pp. 244–5.
3 Merivale, p. 59.
4 FK, RG, vol. I, p. 183.
5 John Sterling to his brother, 10 November 1829 – 'I had seen some beautiful verses of hers long before she was an actress' – quoted Carlyle 'Life of Sterling', *Works*.
6 FK, RG, vol. I, p. 187.
7 Quoted Highfill et al., vol. VIII, pp. 310–11.
8 FK, letter to Hal, RG, vol. I, p. 194.
9 Doran, quoted Saxe Wyndham, vol. II, p. 49.
10 Edward Fitzgerald reminiscing to W.F. Pollock, 11 May 1871, Terhune, vol. III p. 285.
11 FK, RG, vol. I, p. 190.

12 – Head, Heart and Literary Talent

1 On a holiday trip down the Rhine in 1827 Planché records that of the two questions 'eagerly asked wherever we landed' the first was always 'was the Thames Tunnel finished?' – Planché, vol. I, p. 142.
2 FK, RG, vol. I, pp. 195–8.
3 Ibid., p. 201.
4 Thomas, p. 36.
5 FK, RG, vol. I, p. 211.
6 Ibid., p. 200.
7 Ibid., pp. 216–17.
8 Ibid., pp. 215–16.
9 Ibid., pp. 220–21.

13 – Honourable Conduct and the Acting Profession

1 FK, letter to Hal, RG, vol. I, p. 222.
2 Archer and Lowe, *Dramatic Essays of Leigh Hunt*.
3 FK, RG, vol. I, pp. 220–30.
4 Littell, vol. III, issue 32, 21 December 1844.
5 FK, 'Lines in Answer to a Question', *Collected Poems*.

6 FK, RG, vol. I, p. 261.
7 Ibid., p. 271.
8 Ibid., pp. 241–2.
9 Ibid., p. 252.
10 Ibid., p. 258.
11 Ibid., p. 260.
12 Mair, letter 1, p. 4.
13 FK, 'To Miss Sarah Siddons', *Collected Poems*.

14 – Miranda and Prospero

1 Letter from Arthur Hallam to his father, Henry Hallam, 15 February 1829, Kolb p. 274 and p. 275n.
2 FK, RG, vol. I, p. 291.
3 FK, RG, vol. II, p. 7.

15 – Selling Juliet

1 Horne, R.H., *A New Spirit of the Age* (1844), quoted Nicoll, p. 171.
2 FK letter to George Combe, 7 September 1830, quoted Wister, p. 46.
3 Jameson, *Visits and Sketches at Home and Abroad*, vol. III, pp. 23–4.
4 FK, RG, vol. II, p. 11.
5 Brookfield, p. 164.
6 FK, RG, vol. II, p. 41.
7 Unidentified newspaper cutting in the Theatre Museum personal file for FK.
8 FK, RG, vol. II, p. 59.
9 *The Times*, 6 October 1829.
10 Unidentified newspaper cutting dated 11 October 1829, Enthoven collection, Theatre Museum.
11 For an account of the performance see Archer and Lowe, *Dramatic Essays of Leigh Hunt*, 'Miss Kemble as Juliet'.
12 FK, *Journal*, vol. II, p. 125.
13 Letter from Richard Milnes to his mother, late October or November 1829, Kolb, p. 350 n.
14 Press cutting dated 11 October 1829, Enthoven Collection, Theatre Museum.
15 Ibid.
16 Ibid.
17 FK, RG, vol. II, p. 62.
18 John Sterling (1806–1844) became editor of the *Athenaeum*. Quoted Carlyle 'Life of Sterling', *Works*.
19 FK, RG, vol. II, p. 67.

PART III – A QUEST FOR SUBSTANCE

16 – Artists and Lay-Figures

1 FK, letter to Hal, 14 December 1829, RG, vol. II, p. 64.

2 FK, RG, vol. II, p. 68.
3 Ibid., p. 83.
4 Ibid., pp. 83–4.
5 FK, letter to Hal from New York, 24 May 1832, *Journal.*
6 FK, letter to Sir Thomas Lawrence, autumn 1829, quoted Somes Layard, pp. 220–1.
7 FK, RG, vol. II, p. 44.
8 Sir Thomas Lawrence to Mrs Hayman, 4 January 1830, quoted Somes Layard.
9 FK, RG, vol. I, p. 26.
10 FK, *Journal*, vol. II, p. 124
11 FK, RG, vol. II, p. 97.
12 Ibid., p. 16.
13 Ibid., pp. 331–2.
14 Ibid., p. 61.
15 Ibid., p. 87.
16 Ibid., pp. 91–2.

17 – 'One of Shakespeare's Women'

1 Quoted Kolb, p. 350.
2 W.B. Donne to Richard Trench, December 1829, quoted Johnson, p. 4.
3 FK, RG, vol. II, p. 106.
4 W.B. Donne to Richard Trench, 29 April 1830, quoted Johnson, p. 5.
5 Arthur Hallam to Robert Robinson, 14 March 1830, quoted Kolb, pp. 356–7.
6 Merivale, looking back in later years with a certain affectionate contempt for their youthful arrogance, quoted Brookfield, p. 10.
7 'O! There is union, and a tie of blood/With those who speak unto the general mind' – verses by Arthur Hallam, quoted ibid., p. 363.
8 Verse by James Spedding – quoted ibid., p.259.
9 Quoted ibid., p. 309.
10 Letter from Emily, Lady Tennyson, 23 November 1889, quoted Kolb, p. 581n.
11 FK, RG, vol. II, p. 1.
12 Ibid., pp. 1–2.
13 John Sterling to his brother, 10 November 1829, quoted Carlyle 'Life of Sterling', *Works.*
14 FK, RG, vol. II, pp. 102–3.
15 Shakespeare, *Much Ado about Nothing*, Act I, Scene I.
16 Arthur Hallam in the sonnet he dedicated to Fanny – 'To An Admired Lady'.
17 Quoted Brookfield, p. 164.
18 Description of Mrs Beverley in *The Gamester.*
19 FK, RG, vol. II, p. 105.
20 Ibid., p. 108.

18 – Revolution and Railways

1 FK, RG, vol. II, pp. 110–11.
2 FK to Hal, 2 May 1830, RG, vol. II, pp. 114–15.
3 FK to Hal, 2 May 1980 – uncut version published *Atlantic Monthly*, September 1876, pp. 330–1.
4 Ibid., p. 127–8.
5 Andrew Combe to FK, quoted Furnas, p. 68.
6 FK, RG, vol. II, p. 137.
7 Ibid., p. 152.
8 FK, 'A Promise', *Poems*.
9 FK, RG, vol. II, p. 170.
10 Ibid., pp. 183–4.
11 Ibid., pp. 163–4.

19 – An Introduction to Silver Forks

1 FK, RG, vol. II, p. 72.
2 Ibid., p. 186.
3 Quoted Bishop, vol. I, p. 61.
4 FK, RG, vol. III, p. 106.

20 – Living on the Highway

1 Leigh Hunt's review in *The Examiner*, 5 October 1830, Archer and Lowe, pp. 147–8.
2 FK, RG, vol. I, p.202.
3 Fraser, vol. II, no. X, pp. 458–66.
4 Ibid., p.461.
5 FK, RG, vol. II, p. 209.
6 Ibid., p. 214.
7 FK, RG, vol. III, p. 12.
8 'From the extravagance of praise to the extravagance of censure is little more than a step, and that step was made by Miss Fanny Kemble in her provincial tour', Fraser, vol. II, p. 46.
9 Ibid., p. 464.
10 FK, RG, vol. II, p. 216.
11 Ibid., p. 215.
12 Arthur Hallam to Richard Chenevix Trench, 2 December 1830, Kolb, p. 387.
13 Ibid., p.388–9n.
14 Mair, p. 82.

21 – Looking for Bassanio

1 FK, RG, vol. II, p. 229.
2 Jameson, 'Essay on Portia', *Shakespeare's Heroines*, p. 1.
3 '. . . the outward shows be least themselves/The world is still deceived with

ornament' – Bassanio, *Merchant of Venice*, Act III, Scene I.

4 '. . . the full sum of me/Is sum of something which, to term in gross,/Is an unlessoned girl, unschooled, unpractised,/Happy in this, she is not yet so old/ But she may learn; happier than this,/She is not bred so dull but she can learn;/ Happiest of all is that her gentle spirit/Commits itself to yours to be directed/As from her lord, her governor, her king/Myself and what is mine to you and yours /Is now converted. But now I was the lord/Of this fair mansion, master of my servants,/Queen o'er myself; and even now, but now,/This house, these servants, and this same myself/Are yours, my lord's.' – ibid., Act III, Scene I.

5 Jameson, *Shakespeare's Heroines*, pp. 14–15.

6 FK, RG, vol. II, p. 300.

7 'It is worthy of note that Bassanio, who is clearly nothing remarkable, is every inch a gentleman, and in that respect no unfit mate for Portia.' Ibid., p. 303.

8 Ibid., p. 255.

9 Ibid., p. 263.

10 Ibid., p. 335.

11 Ibid., p. 286.

12 Ibid., p. 300.

13 FK, RG, vol.III, p. 3.

14 Shakespeare, *Merchant of Venice*.

15 FK, RG, vol. III, p. 7.

22 – Augustus

1 FK, RG, vol. III, p. [illegible].

2 FK, RG, vol. II, p. 295.

3 Quoted Bernard Martin.

4 FK, RG, vol. III, p. 16.

5 Ibid., p. 12.

6 FK, letter to Hal, 29 May 1831, ibid., p. 3.

7 Ibid., p. 39.

8 Ibid., p. 27–8.

9 Ibid., p. 34.

10 Ibid., p. 35.

11 Ibid., 6 June 1831, p. 42.

12 'I could not be much grieved for myself, for of course I had had but little intercourse with her, though she was always very kind to me when I saw her.' Ibid., 8 June 1831, p. 43.

13 Ibid., p. 44.

14 Ibid., p. 48.

15 Ibid., p. 51.

16 Ibid., p. 53.

17 Ibid., p. 61.

18 Ibid., p. 76.
19 'I have no joy of this contract to-night;/It is too rash, too unadvised, too sudden,' *Romeo and Juliet*, Act II, Scene II.
20 Bishop vol. I, p. 10.
21 Her account of the 'perfect' love of her brother Albert, who died young, displaying a 'devotion to something afar' all of which gave scope for tasteful meditations on death – as well as the edifying record of his Lutheran wife converting to Catholicism. The core group of Pauline's brother Albert, his wife, Alexandrine, and her younger sister Eugenie, all of whom were to die young, came to be known through Pauline's *Le Récit d'une soeur* as 'i santi' – the saintly ones.
22 As his wife's biographer M. Bishop put it – 'To belong to the old English Catholic families was in itself a singularity; to be a convert was a strange weakness amounting to disloyalty.' Bishop, vol. 1, p. 35.
23 Duff, vol. I, p. 25.
24 Ibid., p. 434.
25 'Old Woman's Gossip', XIV *Atlantic Monthly*, September 1876, p. 333.
26 'His career was of social incident and success. To have been the husband of Pauline de la Ferronnays was no mean title to consideration,' Bishop, vol. I, p. 263.
27 Ibid., vol. I, p. 263.
28 FK to Hal, undated letter – circa November 1832, RG, vol. III, p. 268.

23 – Exile

1 FK, letter to Hal, 31 July 1831, from Exeter, RG vol. III, pp. 83–4.
2 FK, journal, 7 July 1831, from Bristol, ibid., p. 61.
3 FK, letter to Hal, 7 March 1831, RG, vol. II, p. 280.
4 FK, letter to Hal, 31 July 1831, from Exeter, RG, vol. III, p. 85.
5 FK, letter to Hal, 12 October 1831, ibid., p. 116.
6 FK, letter to Hal, 3 October 1831, ibid, pp. 110–11.
7 'The Kembles have called, John yesterday, Henry today – he is a dear fellow and we talked about nothing but you and the theatres – the two things I like best in the world . . . Sunday . . . have had the Kembles to breakfast. John stayed with me til five o'clock, that is til three when we set forth on a walk – I like him better, but he seems to me a very forced plant – in reading thinking & conversation beyond his natural growth. We went round the Regent's Park and he had the talk to himself; it was agreeable enough about his Spanish adventures & his friend General Torrijos's exploits.' Thackeray to Edward Fitzgerald, letter written over 16–23 November 1831, Ray, pp. 172–3.
8 FK, letter to Hal, 18 December 1831, RG, vol. III, p. 134.
9 Ibid., p. 130.
10 Ibid., p. 133.
11 FK, letter to Hal, 29 December 1831, ibid., p. 152.
12 FK, diary entry, December 1831, ibid., p. 121.

13 'With my scheme of going to America, I think I can look the future courageously in the face' – FK, letter to Hal 31 January 1832, from Great Russell Street, ibid., p. 178.
14 FK, RG, vol. III, p. 149. Henry had once wanted to go to sea. His mother, who had a phobia about drowning, squashed the idea and after that he never expressed the slightest preference for any other profession: 'They may put me at a plow-tail if they like.' He did persuade his father not to go to the expense of sending him to Cambridge, arguing that 'he was sure he would only waste money, and do himself and us no credit.'
15 'I am engaged at this moment in editing "Beowulf", the oldest, finest, and hardest of the Anglo-Saxon poems; and one peculiarly valuable as being the only hero-poem they have left us, of any length. It is so mythic, that from that and other circumstances I am inclined to think it must have accompanied our forefathers into England' – J.M. Kemble to W.B. Donne, January/February 1832, quoted Johnson, p. 13.
16 Although Fanny did arrange a deal with her publisher, Murray, to bring out her brother's book on a profit-share basis. J.M. Kemble's *The Anglo-Saxon Poems of Beowulf* was published in 1833.
17 FK, RG, vol. III, p. 154.
18 Ibid., p. 142.
19 FK, RG, vol. II, pp. 255–6.
20 FK, RG, vol. III, p. 183.
21 Ibid., p. 192.
22 Ibid., p. 196.
23 Ibid., p. 204.
24 J. Spedding, letter to W.B. Donne, quoted Brookfield, p. 262. Arthur Hallam focused on the language rather than the content – 'I like it much and certainly think it very remarkable to have been written at seventeen. The language is very pure, free, elegant English & strictly dramatic. There is none of that verbiage called "mere poetry." She must have nourished her childhood with the strong wine of our old drama.' – Hallam writing to Tennyson from London, 10 April – quoted Kolb p. 549.
25 *The Hunchback*, along with other plays by Sheridan Knowles, became particularly popular in the United States. The American critic R. Shelton Mackenzie, writing in 1838, claimed that the Irish playwright 'is inferior only to Shakespeare. He equals him in originality of thought and expression. It is no hyperbole to say that, since Shakespeare, no dramatist save Knowles has written so much *from* and *to* the heart.' Quoted Foulkes, p. 164.
26 'Old Woman's Gossip', XXI, *Atlantic Monthly*, April 1877, pp. 432–3.
27 'Very good, and a great success. Miss Fanny Kemble acted really well – for the first time, in my opinion, great acting. I have not seen anything since Mrs Siddons (and perhaps Miss O'Neill) so good.' Reeve, 8 April 1832.
28 Letter from Arthur Hallam to Emily Tennyson, 5 May 1832, Kolb, p. 569.

29 Letter from Thackeray to Edward Fitzgerald, 20 to 21 April, Ray, pp. 239–40.
30 Published 16 April 1832.
31 21 April 1832, Kolb, p. 554.
32 Arthur Hallam to Alfred Tennyson, London 30 April to 6 May 1832, Kolb, p. 562.
33 FK, journal, RG, vol. III, p. 183. 'I am always a little disappointed with the exterior of our poet when I look at him, in spite of his eyes, which are very fine; but his head and face, striking and dignified as they are, are almost too ponderous and massive for beauty in so young a man; and every now and then there is a slightly sarcastic expression about his mouth that almost frightens me, in spite of his shy manner and habitual silence. But, after all, it is delightful to see and be with any one that one admires and loves for what he has done, as I do him.'
34 Ibid., p. 208.
35 Ibid., p. 211.
36 Edward Spedding to William Bodham Donne, 27 June 1832, Kolb, p. 602n.
37 FK, RG, vol. III, pp. 213–14.
38 Ibid., p. 218.
39 Ibid., pp. 220–21.
40 FK, letter to Anna Jameson, 22 July 1832, RG, vol. III, p. 227. 'The little sketch on that leaf differs from the design you had described to me some time ago, and I felt the full meaning of the difference.'
41 Ibid., p. 227.
42 FK, *Journal*, 1 August 1832.

24 – That 'Big Bragging Baby'

1 Preface to the English edition of FK's *Journal*, p. v.
2 *The Times*, 3 January 1846, quoted Mullen, p. 7
3 FK, *Journal*, 23 August 1832.
4 Ibid., 19 August 1832.
5 Ibid., 25 August 1832.
6 Ibid., 3 September 1832.
7 Ibid., 4 September 1832.
8 From Catharine Sedgwick's journal, 11 May 1833, Kelley, p. 133.
9 FK, RG, vol. III, p. 224.
10 Durang, quoted Furnas, pp. 113–14.
11 FK, *Journal*, 7 and 15 September 1832.
12 Tuckerman, 15 September 1832.
13 Ibid., 15 September 1832.
14 *New York Mirror*, 19 September 1832, quoted Wister, pp. 86–7.
15 *New York American*, 19 September 1832, Theatre Museum archive.
16 See cutting in Enthoven Collection, Theatre Museum: 'Theatrical Chit Chat' dated in pencil, 12 November 1832: 'It appears by letters received from New York on Saturday, by Mr Kenneth, the Theatrical Agent, dated the 15th of October, that the Park Theatre had, from its opening been very successful. The

Kembles had averaged 1,400 dollars per night.'

17 'The system upon which theatrical speculations are conducted in this country,' Fanny wrote in her *Journal* on 1 October 1832, 'is having one or two "stars" for the principal characters, and nine or ten sticks for all the rest. The consequence is that a play is never decently acted, and at such times as stars are scarce, the houses are very deservedly empty. The terrestrial audiences suffer much by this mode of getting up plays, but the celestial performers, the stars propped upon sticks, infinitely more.'

18 FK, RG, vol. III, p. 242.

19 Henry Berkeley, letter to Pierce Butler, quoted Bernard Martin.

20 FK, letter to Hal, 16 September 1832, RG, vol. III, p. 243.

21 FK, letter to Hal, September 1832, ibid., p. 248.

22 FK, 'Lines to Miss St Leger', *Poems*, p. 106.

23 FK, *Journal*, 22 September 1832.

24 FK letter to Hal from New York, September 1832, RG, vol. III, p. 246.

25 From FK's *Journal* for 20 September 1832, quoted Wister, p. 87.

26 FK, letter to George Combe, 29 September 1832, quoted Wister p. 81–2.

25 – Enter Pierce Butler – American Gentleman

1 Henry Berkeley to Pierce Butler, 23 September 1832, Historical Society of Pennsylvania, Wister Family Collection.

2 FK, letter to Hal from Philadelphia, 10 October 1832, RG, vol. III, p. 258.

3 FK, *Journal*, 9 October 1832.

4 Sydney George Fisher, 9 February 1837, quoted Wainright, p. 21.

5 FK, letter to Hal from Philadelphia, 10 October 1832, RG, vol. III, p. 256.

6 FK, *Journal*, 13 October.

7 HSP, letter from Henry Berkeley to Pierce Butler, 3 October 1832, Wister Family Collection.

8 In the archives of the Historical Society of Pennsylvania there is a letter dated a year before Pierce met Fanny, in which his spinster Aunt Eliza takes him to task, hearing of his behaviour in New York. She is 'more distressed than I can express to you at hearing what is said of you . . . The Shadow of a young lady who treats you with the greatest contempt . . . Butler, whose Feelings I have always believed to be so exalted – so correct – so alive upon all occasions – devoting Himself to a Lady whose manner toward Him is marked contempt! . . . It is not possible that I could have so mistaken Butler's Character and Heart.' 7 November 1831.

9 FK, *Journal*, 2 November 1832.

10 Ibid., 21 September 1832.

11 Ibid., 28 October 1832.

12 Ibid., 27 October 1832.

13 Ibid., 18 October 1832.

14 FK, letter to Hal, 10 October 1832, RG, vol. III, p. 255. Daniel Webster (1782–1852), the Senator for Massachusetts, had acquired an international

reputation as an orator, while Miss St Ledger much admired the writings of Dr William Ellery Channing, (1780–1842), the Unitarian preacher and essayist.

15 'The Boston manager it seems does not approve of our terms, and after bargaining till past two o'clock last night with my father, the latter, wearied out with his illiberal trafficking and coarse vulgarity of manner, declined the thing altogether, so unless the gentleman thinks better of the matter, we shall not go to Boston this winter.' FK, *Journal*, 16 October 1832.

16 FK, letter to Hal from Philadelphia, 22 October 1832, RG, vol. III, p. 262.

17 FK, letter to Hal, 2 November 1832, ibid., p. 266.

18 Quoted Wister, p. 100.

19 FK, *Journal*, 17 October 1832, note.

20 Quoted Wister, p. 101.

21 FK, *Journal*, 5 November 1832.

22 Armstrong, pp. 210–11.

23 FK, *Journal*, addition opposite vol. II, p.14, Columbian University edition.

24 Quoted Bernard Martin.

25 FK, *Journal*, quoted Wister, p. 106.

26 'This is the newest-looking place we have yet visited, the youngest in appearance in this young world.' FK, letter to Hal, Baltimore, January 1833, RG, vol. III, p. 275.

27 Ibid., vol. III, p. 275.

28 Henry Wikoff wrote of his first visit to the capital in late autumn 1831: 'I must confess that the appearance of Washington contrasted ludicrously with what my fancy painted it. Consisting chiefly of the long, broad, unpaved street known as Pennsylvania Avenue, occupied by straggling houses of mean aspect, some of wood and some of brick, with cross-streets of immense width, dotted here and there with houses of various sizes and styles, it literally fulfilled the description of Randolph, 'a city of magnificent distances'. The public buildings, constructed of brick, with no pretensions to architecture, and of insignificant proportions, fell far short of my inflated expectations. The White House was much the most imposing edifice of the soi-disant city, with the exception of the Capitol. That, indeed, owed more to its site than its own merits.' Wikoff, pp. 31–2.

29 FK, *Journal*, 14 January 1833, quoted Wister, pp. 107–8.

30 FK, *Journal*, vol. II, pp. 151–2.

31 Quoted Biddle and Fielding.

32 Quoted Clinton, p. 59.

33 Story, pp. 116–7. When asked, by one of his students at Harvard, how he could reconcile the pleasure he took in Fanny's performances with his Puritanism, Judge Story was said to have replied: 'I don't try to. I only thank God that I am alive in the same era with such a woman.'

34 FK, *Journal*, 17 January 1833.

35 FK, letter to Hal, 21 February 1833, RG, vol. III, p. 286.

36 Quoted Wister, p. 109.

37 FK, Journal, 19 January 1833, quoted Wister pp. 110–11.
38 Ibid., pp. 111–12.

26 – New England

1 FK, letter to Hal, New York, 3 April 1833, RG, vol. III, p. 288.
2 As Fanny wrote to Mrs Jameson: ''Tis not with me now as in the fortunate days when, after six rehearsals, a piece ran, as the saying is, twenty nights, leaving me all the mornings and three evenings in the week at my own disposal. Here we rush from place to place, at each place have to drill a new set of actors who have not even had the conscience to study the words of their parts, all the morning. All the afternoon I pin up ribbons and feathers and flowers, and sort out theatrical adornments, and all the evening I enchant audiences, prompt my fellow mimes, and wish it had pleased Heaven to make me a cabbage in a corner of a Christian kitchen-garden.' Baltimore, 11 January 1833, ibid., vol. III, p. 281.
3 FK, letter to Hal, February/March 1833, ibid., p. 285.
4 FK, letter to Hal, from Boston, 16 April 1833, ibid., p. 293.
5 FK, letter to Hal, from Boston, 16 April 1833, ibid., p. 294–5.
6 Theodore Sedgwick, the elder, a prominent lawyer in Albany, wrote to his son: 'I have not the least fear, that Miss K[emble] will make a fool of you, or that My Son is in danger of marrying an Actress, who may not be half worthy of him . . . but this I will say, that any man's reputation depends upon consistency and upon his acting with a just respect for himself . . . which I think was not the case when last fall you permitted half your friends to believe that Miss K. had turned your head. A Man of Sense neither suffers his head to be turned, nor does he let the world believe that it can be.' Sedgwick papers, 25 February 1833.
7 Theodore Sedgwick to his sister, Sedgwick papers, 8 March 1833.
8 Catharine's eldest brother Theodore, who was some ten years her senior, was her nephew Theodore's father. Their brother Harry died at the end of 1831. Catharine's closest relationship was with her brother Robert. After Robert's death in 1841 his place was taken by the youngest brother Charles, who, with his wife Elizabeth, became Fanny's particular friends, providing her with regular refuge at their home in Lenox, Massachusetts.
9 As Catharine Sedgwick once wrote, surveying her life from old age, she had 'boarded round . . . in so many houses and so many hearts' that her life had been 'so woven into the fabric of others that I seem to have no separate, individual existence'. Letter to William Minot, 5 October 1851, CMS Papers, Massachusetts Historical Society.
10 Martineau, 'Miss Sedgwick's Works', *London & Westminster Review*, pp. 42–65.
11 May 1825 – A Philadelphian correspondent of Miss Maria Edgworth who forwarded the comment to Catharine Sedgwick, Dewey, p.169.
12 Writing of her brothers and father in her autobiography, Catharine recollected how: 'Their "talk was <u>not</u> of beeves", nor of making money; that now universal passion had not entered into men and possessed them as it does now . . . My father

was richer than his neighbours. His income supplied abundantly the wants of a very careless family and an unmeasured hospitality, but nothing was ever given to mere style, and nothing was wasted on vices.'

13 Theodore Sedgwick to Catharine Sedgwick, Stockbridge, November 1827, Dewey p. 189.

14 The American poet, William Cullen Bryant, a family friend, wrote of Miss Sedgwick's 'unerring sense of rectitude, her love of truth, her ready sympathy, her active and cheerful beneficence, her winning and gracious manners, the perfection of high breeding'– a description reminiscent of Fanny's own estimation of her Cousin Harriot. Memorial of Catharine Sedgwick, quoted Dewey, p. 446.

15 'Am I wrong in giving so much time and thought to her? My conscience is <u>not easy</u> – and yet I think that she who kindles the evening with the brightness that lit up the morning of life, who brings a melting influence to the frigid of forty, is an enchantress not to be resisted.' Catharine Sedgwick's journal, 14 February 1833, quoted Kelley, p. 132.

16 Letter from Catharine Sedgwick to Mrs Frank Channing, New York, 12 February 1833, quoted Dewey, p. 230. The well-bred Catharine, who had been concerned that Miss Kemble might be too apparently an actress off the stage, was pleased to meet her and her aunt dressed soberly in 'good old-fashioned muffs & tippets'.

17 FK's memoir of Catharine Sedgwick, Dewey, p. 416.

18 FK, *Journal*, 23 March 1833.

19 Ibid., 23 March 1833, note.

20 Ibid., 15 April 1833, note.

21 FK, letter to Mrs Jameson, from Boston, 21 April 1833, RG, vol. III, p. 297.

22 FK, *Journal*, 20 April 1833.

23 FK, letter to Hal, from Boston, 16 April 1833, RG, vol. III, p. 293.

24 Fanny informed William Harness that Boston was 'the most blue* town in the Union as well as the most aristocratic' (*i.e. favourable to intellectual ladies), L'Estrange, pp. 67–8.

25 Quoted Furnas, p. 125.

26 Ibid., p. 125.

27 That spring Anna Quincy happened to be writing a journal for the entertainment of her elder sisters who were away from home on a visit down South. DeWolfe Howe.

28 Memoir of FK, Lee.

29 Quoted Furnas, p. 126.

30 Lee.

31 DeWolfe Howe.

32 Letter to Mrs Jameson, from Boston, 21 April 1833, RG, vol. III, p. 296.

33 Quoted Bernard Martin.

34 FK, *Journal*, May 1833.

35 FK, *Journal of a Residence on a Georgian Plantation in 1838–1839* (Georgia Journal), p. 86.

36 FK, letter to Anna Jameson, 21 April 1833, RG, vol. III, p. 295.

37 Quoted Furnas, p. 129.
38 FK, *Journal*, addition opposite vol. I, p. 49, Columbian University edition.
39 Ibid., the addition opposite vol. II, p. 186, reads: 'We were engaged before we left Boston.'
40 Quincy, 13 May 1833.
41 DeWolfe Howe, p. 102.
42 FK, *Journal*, quoted Wister, p. 119.
43 Dr Channing began his ministry as a Congregationalist but, rebelling against the Calvinist doctrine of human depravity, he applied Enlightenment values to his theology, arguing from a belief in human goodness and the importance of the application of reason in matters of faith. Denounced by his Orthodox former co-religionists as 'Unitarian', Channing was forced to defend the label or disown his faith. His sermon, 'Unitarian Christianity', delivered at an ordination in Baltimore in 1819, became the defining text of a movement. Rather reluctantly (since he considered 'orthodoxy' of any kind oppressive to true faith) Channing found himself the guiding light of a new denomination. Other liberal ministers rallied to his cause, organizing themselves to form the American Unitarian Association in 1825.

Catharine Sedgwick had grown up in the pious atmosphere of a Calvinist New England village. She first met Dr Channing at the time of her father's final illness. Judge Sedgwick found much consolation in the minister's spirituality. The novelist's brothers, Henry and Robert, were among the founders of the first Unitarian Church in New York and in 1821 Catharine formally separated herself from the Calvinistic Church to join 'the new communion'. Dewey, p. 93
44 FK, letter to George Combe, quoted Wister, p. 118.
45 'This method of conversation is not to be defended even on the ground of expediency, for a person's real views are not to be got at in this way, no one liking to be managed.' Martineau went on to reassure her readers that in fact Dr Channing laid 'up what he obtains for meditation; and it reappears, sooner or later, amplified, enriched, and made perfectly his own'. Martineau, vol. III, pp. 72–91.
46 FK, RG, vol. III, p. 300.
47 William Ellery Channing to FK, 7 November 1833, quoted Wister, p. 120.
48 Martineau, vol. III, p. 85.
49 When her friend Emily Fitzhugh talked of human souls as 'vile', Fanny gave her friend Channing's 'The moral argument against Calvinism' to read. 'She liked it very much, but said that his view of man's nature was not that of a Christian; I think her contempt for it still less such. As we are immortal in spite of death, so I think we are wonderful in spite of our weakness, and admirable in spite of our imperfections, and capable of all good in spite of all our evil.' FK, letter to Hal, 2 April 1831, RG, vol. II, p. 292.
50 FK, 21 December 1831, RG, vol. III, p. 141.
51 Catharine Sedgwick to Charles Sedgwick, from Boston, 4 November, 1826, Dewey p. 181.

27 – Niagara Falls

1 FK to Mrs Jameson, from New York, 24 June 1833, RG, vol. III, p. 302.
2 FK, *Journal*, 6 July 1833.
3 Ibid., 2 July 1833.
4 Ibid., 6 July 1833.
5 FK, letter to Hal, written on the steamboat *St Patrick* on the St Lawrence, 17 August 1833, RG, p. 582.
6 FK, *Journal*, Sunday, 30 June 1833.
7 Ibid., 12 July 1883.
8 'I like travelling by canal boats very much. Ours was not crowded; and the country through which we passed being delightful, the placid . . . gliding through it, at about four miles and a half an hour, seemed to me infinitely preferable to . . . the jerking of bad roads . . . The only nuisances are the bridges over the canal, which are so very low, that one is obliged to prostrate one's self on the deck of the boat, to avoid being scraped off it . . . Mr Trelawny read *Don Quixote* to us. He reads very peculiarly; slowly, and with very marked emphasis. He has a strong feeling of humour, as well as poetry.' Ibid., 10 July 1833.
9 Ibid., 14 July 1833.
10 Ibid., 16 July 1833.
11 FK, letter to Hal, 17 August 1833, RG, vol. III, pp. 309–11.
12 FK, RG, vol. III, p. 311.
13 'If you fancy the sea pouring down from the moon, you still have no idea of this glorious huge heap of tumbling water.' FK, letter to Emily Fitzhugh, from Montreal, 24 July 1833, ibid., p. 305.
14 Julia Kean to her uncle, John Cox Morris, Ballston Spa, August 1833, Armstrong, p. 217. Philip Hone noted in his diary after seeing Fanny play Mrs Haller in New York: 'This will probably be her last engagement, if the report is true that she is married already, or about to be, to Mr Pierce Butler, of Philadelphia.' 30 September 1833, Tuckerman, p. 79.
15 Letter from the Folger collection, quoted Furnas, p. 140.
16 FK, letter to Anna Jameson, from Boston, 16 April 1834, RG, vol. III, p. 319.
17 Ibid., p.319.
18 FK, letter to Hal from New York, 24 April 1843, RG, vol. III, p. 40.
19 FK, RG, vol. III, pp. 320–1.
20 Ibid., p. 321.
21 Ibid., p. 320.
22 FK, letter to George Combe, from Boston, 11 April 1834, quoted Wister, p. 134.
23 Furnas, p. 143n.
24 FK, letter to Mrs Jameson, from New York, 15 October 1833, RG, vol. III, p. 316.
25 FK, letter to Mrs Jameson, from New York, 15 October 1833, ibid., p. 316.
26 Quoted Wister, p. 189.
27 Quoted Furnas, p. 144.
28 FK, letter to Miss Sarah Paine Perkins, quoted Wister, p. 139.

29 Furnas, p. 145.
30 Papers in the Huntington Library, San Marino, California, quoted Furnas, p. 146.

28 – Slavery or a Wife's Duty

1 Quoted Bernard Martin.
2 Lady Dacre wrote to John Murray reflecting the storms in the Kemble household back in London: [Fanny] 'cannot be so wrong toward her parents; as in all quarrels both are to blame . . . and there are two violent tempers . . . we are pretty well assured', quoted Furnas p. 146.
3 Sydney Fisher described John Butler as 'a mere idler . . . a hard, selfish, profligate fellow, totally without education or intellect . . . [but] the manners of a gentleman and . . . great taste in dress, house and equipment.' Fanny's only recorded comment about her brother-in-law was the story of how, when they first went riding together, he rode hell-for-leather and when asked why, confessed that he had heard such reports of her style that he felt honour bound to give a good show.
4 Quoted Wainright, 24 January 1841, pp. 112–3.
5 Fanny Appleton, letter to Susan Benjamin, from Newport R. I., 19 August 1834, quoted Wagenknecht, pp. 13–14.
6 Carey & Lea were the American publishers of a range of prominent authors, including Sir Walter Scott, Washington Irving and Thomas Carlyle. Fanny concluded a second agreement for a London edition with John Murray.
7 Butler, p. 22.
8 Quoted Gibbs, p. 129.
9 Butler, pp. 22–3.
10 Ibid., p. 48.
11 Poor Emily Chapman had made a rushed marriage barely six weeks before Pierce wed Fanny. It was only years later that Fanny caught up on the full story. She made a note in the margin of the annotated copy of her Journal about the 'most cruel and dishonourable' conduct of her husband towards the jilted Emily.
12 They reminded Sydney Fisher of 'Les precieuses ridicules' of Molière, quoted Wainright, 28 December 1838, p. 67.
13 'She has found out that the Hessian fly deposits its eggs in the grain and not in the stalk as has been supposed. So that it is only necessary to use grain for seed from a part of the country where the wheat has not been attacked to escape its ravages,' quoted ibid., 20 December 1840, p. 107
14 Quoted Wister, p. 149.
15 FK, *Records of a Later Life*, vol. I, p. 10.
16 Fanny wrote to her Cousin Cecilia Combe, that she had six servants at Butler Place and that 'it requires all the energy I possess and a great deal more knowledge than I possess to keep them to the proper fulfilment of their duty . . . .Here there is but one way of being well served – you must deal with your servants as your equal; that is, as conscientious and rational beings having duties and responsibilities to fulfil towards you as you towards them. Nothing but this and a good deal of firmness and withal

constant attention will keep them in order.' FK to Mrs George Combe, 8 November 1835, quoted Wister, p. 155.

17 Quoted Wister, p. 150.
18 Butler, p. 24.
19 FK, letter to Sarah Perkins, 11 June 1835, quoted Wister, p. 152.
20 Butler, p. 24–5.
21 FK, *Records of a Later Life*, vol. I, p. 31.
22 FK, *A Year of Consolation*, vol. I, pp. 124–5.
23 FK, *Records of a Later Life*, vol. I, p. 159.
24 Revd Dr Dewey's memorial letter, Dewey, p. 435.
25 FK, letter to Hal, 29 January 1831, RG, vol. II, p. 245.
26 'When I married . . . I knew nothing of these dreadful possessions . . . and even if I had I should have been much puzzled to have formed any idea of the state of things [on the Butler's Island plantation].' FK, Georgia Journal, p. 138.
27 Quoted Kelley, pp. 15–16.
28 Catharine Sedgwick's diary, 29 November 1829.
29 Quoted Kelley, pp. 125–6.
30 Quoted Sedgwick, p. 555.
31 Quoted Wister, pp. 155–6.
32 FK, letter to Cecilia Combes, 8 November 1835, quoted Wister, p. 154.
33 FK, letter to Hal, spring 1836, *Records of a Later Life*, vol. I, p. 30.
34 FK, journal entry, 27 January 1832, RG, vol. III, p. 175.
35 Butler, p. 9.
36 FK, letter to George Combe, 6 January 1837, quoted Bernard Martin.

29 – Georgia

1 FK, *Records of a Later Life*, vol. I, p. 48.
2 FK to Mrs Charles Follen, late autumn 1836, quoted Wister, p. 156.
3 FK, *Records of a Later Life*, vol. I, p. 81.
4 Butler, pp. 9–11.
5 Willis Gaylord Clark, p. 36.
6 Butler, pp. 26–7.
7 Wainright, 19 May 1838, p. 49.
8 Ibid., 30 July 1838, p. 55.
9 Butler, pp. 27–9.
10 FK, *Records of a Later Life*, vol. I, p. 169.
11 FK, Georgia Journal, p. 11.
12 FK, letter to Sarah Perkins, 4 December 1838, quoted Furnas, p. 195.
13 FK, letter to Hal, *Records of a Later Life*, vol. I, p. 203.
14 Ibid., vol. I, p. 213.
15 Ibid., vol. I, pp. 216–17.
16 Ibid., vol. I, p. 223.
17 FK, Georgia Journal, p. 61.

18 FK, *Records of a Later Life*, vol. I, p. 219.
19 Ibid., vol. I, pp. 215–16.
20 Ibid., vol. I, p. 222.
21 FK, Georgia Journal, p. 84.
22 Roswell King Jnr., article *Southern Agriculturist*, December 1828, quoted Furnas, p. 198.
23 FK, Georgia Journal, p. 78.
24 For the story of Joe and Psyche, see chapter X in the Georgia Journal.
25 FK, Georgia Journal, p.174.
26 Letter from Eliza Middleton Fisher to her mother, from Philadelphia, 10 February 1845, Cope Harrison, pp. 427–8.
27 FK, Georgia Journal, p. 190.

Conclusion – Consequences

1 FK, 'Old Woman's Gossip', IX, *Atlantic Monthly*, April 1876, p. 459.
2 FK, letter to Mrs Carl Follen, late autumn 1836, quoted Wister, p. 156.
3 James, p. 113.
4 Bremer, letter XI, from New York, 2 March 1850, vol. I, pp. 240–43.
5 Robert Browning to Elizabeth Barrett Browning, from London, 2 August 1846, Kelley and Lewis, vol. XIII, letter 2520.
6 FK, 'A Wish', *Poems*.
7 Bremer, letter 19 February 1850, vol. I, p. 230.
8 Benson, pp. 75–6.
9 Lee, p. 667.
10 From verses by Arthur Hallam, quoted Brookfield, p. 363.
11 FK, letter to Hal, 2 April 1831, RG, vol. II, p. 292.
12 Lamb.
13 FK, letter to Hal, 2 November 1832, from Philadelphia, RG, vol. III, pp. 266–7.

BIBLIOGRAPHY

A Note on Sources

The following is by no means a comprehensive bibliography. In researching *Fanny Kemble: A Reluctant Celebrity* I tried as far as possible to concentrate on the letters and diaries left by contemporaries. The following bibliography focuses on works I found particularly interesting and those from which I have taken direct quotations.

Principal Publications of Frances Anne Kemble Butler

JOURNALS AND REMINISCENCES

Journal (2 vols) (Philadelphia: Carey, Lea & Blanchard, 1835)

Where an 'addition' is mentioned in the Notes, this refers to a copy Fanny Kemble gave to Charles Sedgwick in which she has written by hand on pages which have been stitched into the book. This copy is held in Columbia University's collection.

A Year of Consolation (2 vols) (London: Edward Moxon, 1847)

Journal of a Residence on a Georgian Plantation in 1838–1839 (New York: Harper & Brothers, 1863). This is referred to in the Notes as Georgia Journal.

'Old Woman's Gossip', a series of articles published in *Atlantic Monthly* 1875–1877

Records of a Girlhood (3 vols) (London: Richard Bentley, 1878). This is referred to in the notes as RG.

Records of a Later Life (3 vols) (London: Richard Bentley, 1882)

Further Records (New York: Henry Holt, 1882)

PLAYS

Francis I: An Historical Drama (London: John Murray, 1832)

The Star of Seville (London: John Murray, 1837)

An English Tragedy, Mary Stuart (translated from the German) and *Mademoiselle de Belle Isle* (translated from the French) (London: Longman, 1863)

POETRY

Poems (Philadelphia: John Penington, 1844)

Collected Poems (London: Richard Bentley, 1883)

Bibliography

DRAMATIC CRITICISM

On the Stage, (London: Cornhill Magazine, 1863)

Notes Upon Some of Shakespeare's Plays (London: Richard Bentley,1882)

NOVELS

Far Away and Long Ago (London: Richard Bentley, 1889)

The Adventures of Mr John Timothy Homespun in Switzerland (London: Richard Bentley, 1889)

Biographies of Fanny Kemble

Armstrong, Margaret – *Fanny Kemble: A Passionate Victorian* (New York: Macmillan, 1938)

Bear Bobbe, Dorothie De – *Fanny Kemble* (London: Elkin Mathews & Marrot, 1931)

Blainey, Ann – *Fanny and Adelaide: The Lives of the Remarkable Kemble Sisters* (Chicago: Ivan R. Dee, 2001)

Clinton, Catherine – *Fanny Kemble's Civil Wars* (New York: Simon & Schuster, 2000)

Craven, Pauline – *La Jeunesse de Fanny Kemble* (Paris: Didier, 1880)

Driver, Leota Stultz – *Fanny Kemble* (Chapel Hill: University of North Carolina Press, 1933)

Furnas, J.C. – *Fanny Kemble, Leading Lady of the 19th Century Stage* (New York: Dial Press, 1982)

Gibbs, Henry – *Affectionately Yours, Fanny: Fanny Kemble and the Theatre* (London: Jarrolds, 1945)

Marshall, Dorothy – *Fanny Kemble* (London: Weidenfeld & Nicolson, 1977)

Pope-Hennessy, Una – *Three English Women in America: Fanny Trollope, Fanny Kemble and Harriet Martineau* (Benn, 1929)

Ransome, Eleanor – *The Terrific Kemble: A Victorian Self-Portrait* (London: Hamish Hamilton, 1978)

Rushmore, Robert – *Fanny Kemble* (London: Crowell-Collier Press, 1970)

Wister, Fanny Kemble (ed.) – *Fanny, the American Kemble: Her Journal and Unpublished Letters* (privately published, Tallahassee: 1972)

Wright, Constance – *Fanny Kemble and the Lovely Land* (London: Robert Hale & Co., 1972)

General Bibliography

Anonymous – *Candid and Impartial Strictures on the Performers Belonging to Drury-Lane, Covent-Garden and the Haymarket Theatres, Etc.* (London: Martin & Bain, 1795)

Archer and Lowe (eds) – *Dramatic Essays by William Hazlitt* (London: Walter Scott Ltd, 1895)

Archer and Lowe (eds) – *Dramatic Essays of Leigh Hunt* (London: Walter Scott Ltd, 1894)

Armstrong, Margaret – *Five Generations, Life and Letters of an American Family 1750–1900* (New York: Harper Brothers, 1930)

Baker, Herschel – *John Philip Kemble* (Cambridge, Mass.: Harvard University Press, 1942)

Baker, Michael – *The Rise of the Victorian Actor* (London: Croom Helm, 1978)

Bate, Jonathan – *Shakespearean Constitutions* (Oxford: Clarendon Press, 1989)

——, *Shakespeare and the English Romantic Imagination* (Oxford: Clarendon Press, 1986)

Bell, Malcolm – *Major Butler's Legacy, Five Generations of a Slaveholding Family* (Athens, Ala.: University of Georgia Press, 1987)

Bellamy – *London Theatres* (London:1795)

Benson, Adolph (ed.) – *America of the Fifties: Letters of Fredrika Bremer* (New York: American–Scandinavian Foundation, 1924)

Bernard Martin, Robert – Manuscript of an unfinished biography of Fanny Kemble

Biddle, Edward and Mantle Fielding – *The Life and Works of Thomas Sully* (New York: Kennedy Graphics, 1970)

Bishop, M.A. – *Mrs Augustus Craven* (2 vols) (London: Richard Bentley, 1898)

Blainey, Ann – *Fanny and Adelaide: The Lives of the Remarkable Kemble Sisters* (Chicago: Ivan R. Dee, 2001)

Boaden, James – *Memoirs of the Life of John Philip Kemble* (2 vols) (London: Longman & Co., 1825)

——, *Memoirs of Mrs Inchbald* (2 vols) (London: Richard Bentley, 1833)

——, *Memoirs of Mrs Siddons* (2 vols) (London: Henry Colburn, 1827)

Bremer, Fredrika – *Homes of the Americans* (3 vols) (Howitt translation) (London: Virtue & Co., 1853)

Brookfield, Francis – *The Cambridge 'Apostles'* (London: Pitman & Sons, 1906)

Brown, Eluned (ed.) – *The London Theatre 1811–1866: Selections from the diary of Henry Crabb Robinson* (London: Society for Theatre Research, 1966)

Bunn, Alfred – *The Stage: Both Before and Behind the Curtain* (3 vols) (London: Richard Bentley, 1840)

Butler, Pierce – *Mr Butler's Statement* (Philadelphia: J.C. Clark, 1850)

Carlyle, Thomas – *Works* (London: Chapman & Hall, 1857)

Cathcart, Mary – *An Illustrated Guide to London 1800* (London: Robert Hale, 1988)

Chorley, Henry (ed.) – *Letters of Mary Russell Mitford* (London: Richard Bentley, 1872)

Clinton, Catherine – *Fanny Kemble's Civil Wars* (New York: Simon & Schuster, 2000)

Coleridge, Henry Nelson (ed.) – *Specimens of the Table Talk of the Late Samuel Taylor Coleridge* (London: John Murray, 1851)

Cope Harrison, Eliza (ed.) – *Letters of Eliza Middleton Fisher and her Mother, Mary Hering Middleton, from Charleston, Philadelphia and Newport, 1839–1846* (South Carolina: University of South Carolina Press, 2001)

Cundee, James (publisher) – *Thespian Dictionary or Dramatic Biography* (London, 1805)

Dewey, Mary (ed.) – *The Life and Letters of Catharine M. Sedgwick* (New York: Harper & Brothers, 1871)

Dobson, Michael – *The Making of the National Poet* (Oxford: Clarendon Press, 1992)

Duff, Mountstuart Elphinstone Grant – *Notes from a Diary 1892–1895* (2 vols) (London: John Murray, 1904)

Dunlop, L.W. (ed.) – *The Letters of Willis Gaylord Clark and Lewis Gaylord Clark* (New York: 1940)

Egan, Pierce – *The Life of an Actor* (London: Pickering & Chatto, 1892)

Fisher, Joshua Francis – *Recollections of Joshua Francis Fisher* (privately printed 1929)

Fitzball, Edward – *Thirty-Five Years of a Dramatic Author's Life* (London: T.C. Newby, 1859)

Forman, H. Buxton (ed.) – *Letters of Edward John Trelawny* (Oxford: OUP, 1910)

Foulkes, Richard (ed.) – *Shakespeare and the Victorian Stage* (Cambridge: CUP, 1986)

Genest, John – *Some Account of the English Stage from the Restoration in 1660 to 1830* (10 vols) (Bath: H.E. Carrington, 1832)

Hazlitt, William – *A View of the English Stage* (London, 1818)

——, *The Round Table & Characters of Shakespeare's Plays*, foreword by Catherine Macdonald Maclean (London: Everyman, 1964)

Helsinger et al. – *The Woman Question*, vol. III (New York: Garland Publishing, 1983)

Highfill et al. – *Biographical Dictionary of Actors, Actresses, Musicians, Dancers, Managers and Other Stage Personnel in London 1660–1800* (14 vols) (Illinois: Southern Illinois University Press,1975–1993)

James, Henry – 'Frances Anne Kemble', *Essays in London and Elsewhere* (London: Osgood & Mclloaine, 1893)

Jameson, Anna – *The Diary of an Ennuyée* (London: Colburn, 1826)

——, *Shakespeare's Heroines: Characteristics of Women, Moral, Poetical and Historical* (London: Dent & Son, 1910)

——, *Visits and Sketches at Home and Abroad* (4 vols) (London: 1834)

Johnson, Catharine (ed.) – *W. B. Donne and his Friends* (London: Methuen, 1905)

Kelley, Mary (ed.) – *The Power of her Sympathy (the Autobiography and Journal of Catharine Maria Sedgwick)* (Massachusetts: Massachusetts Historical Society, 1993)

Kelley & Lewis (eds) – *The Brownings' Correspondence* (Kansas: Wedgestone Press, 1995)

Kelly, Michael – *Reminiscences* (2 vols) (London: Colburn, 1826)

Kemble, Frances Anne & Frances A. Butler Leigh – *Principles & Privilege: Two Women's Lives on a Georgia Plantation* (Michigan: University of Michigan Press, 1995)

Kolb, Jack (ed.) – *The Letters of Arthur Henry Hallam* (Ohio: Ohio State University Press, 1981)

La Roche, Sophie von – *Sophie in London 1786; being the diary of Sophie v. la Roche* translated from the German by Clare Williams (London: Jonathan Cape, 1933)

Lennox, Lord William Pitt – *Celebrities I have Known* (2 vols) (London: Hurst & Blackett, 1876)

——, *Fifty Years of Biographical Reminiscences* (2 vols) (London: Hurst & Blackett, 1863)

L'Estrange, A.G. – *The Literary Life of the Rev. William Harness, Vicar of All Saints, Knightsbridge, and Prebendary of St Paul's* (London: Hurst & Blackett, 1871)

Levy, Michael – *Sir Thomas Lawrence 1769–1830* (London: National Portrait Gallery, 1979)

Mair, Elizabeth H. – *Recollections of the Past* (privately printed, R & R Clark, 1877)

Marston, John Westland – *Our Recent Actors* (2 vols) (London: Sampson & Low & Co., 1888)

Martineau, Harriet – *Retrospect of Western Travel* (3 vols) (London: Saunders & Otley, 1838)

Mathews, Ann – *Memoir of Charles Mathews, Comedian* (4 vols) (London: Richard Bentley, 1838)

Merivale, J.A. (ed.) – *Autobiography of Dean Merivale*, (London: E. Arnold, 1899)

Mullen, Richard – *Birds of Passage: Five Englishwomen in Search of America* (London: Duckworth, 1994)

Nicoll, Allardyce – *A History of Early Nineteenth Century Drama* (Cambridge: CUP, 1930)

Oxberry, William – *Dramatic Biography and Historical Anecdotes* (7 vols) (London: Virtue, 1825–27)

Palmer, Beverley Wilson (ed.) – *A Woman's Wit & Whimsy: The 1833 Diary of Anna Cabot Lowell Quincy* (Boston: Northeastern University Press, 2003)

Planché, J. R. – *The Recollections and Reflections of J. R. Planché* (London: 1872)

Pollock, Frederick (ed.) – *Macready's Reminiscences & Selections from his Diaries and Letters* (New York: Macmillan & Co., 1875)

Porter, Jane – *The Diary of Jane Porter 1801–1803*, (MS Folger Shakespeare Library, Washington)

Power Cobbe, Frances – *Life of Frances Power Cobbe* (2 vols) (London: Richard Bentley, 1894)

Presley, Felma (ed.) – *Dr Bullie's Notes: Reminiscences of Early Georgia and of Philadelphia and New Haven in the 1800s by James Holmes* (Atlanta: Cherokee Publishing Co., 1976)

Ray, Gordon N. – *The Letters and Private Papers of W.M. Thackeray* (4 vols) (Cambridge: Harvard University Press, 1945–46)

Raymond, George – *The Life and Enterprises of Robert William Elliston* (New York: G. Routledge, 1857)

Reeve, Henry (ed.) - *The Greville Memoirs* (8 vols) (London: 1888)

Ritchie, Emily – *From Friend to Friend* (London: John Murray, 1919)

Ritchie, Hester Thackeray (ed.) – *Thackeray and His Daughter: The Letters and Journals of Anne Thackeray Ritchie with Many Letters of William Makepeace Thackeray* (New York: Harper & Brothers, 1924)

Roberts, Diane – *The Myth of Aunt Jemima* (New York: Routledge, 1994)
Robson, William – *The Old Playgoer* (London: Centaur Press, reprinted 1969)
Rowell, George – *The Victorian Theatre 1792–1914* (Cambridge: CUP, 1978)
——, *Victorian Dramatic Criticism* (London: Methuen, 1971)
Saxe Wyndham, H. – *Annals of the Covent Garden Theatre* (2 vols) (London: Chatto & Windus, 1906)
Schoch, Richard – *Shakespeare's Victorian Stage* (Cambridge: CUP, 1998)
Shepherd, Thomas – *London and its Environs in the Nineteenth Century* (London: 1829)
Smith, C.B. – *Original Letters of Dramatic Performers*, papers held at the Garrick Club
Somes Layard, George (ed.) – *Sir Thomas Lawrence's Letter-Bag* (1906)
Speaight, George (ed.) – *Memoirs of Charles Dibdin the Younger* (London: Society for Theatre Research, 1956)
St Aubyn, Fiona (ed.) – *Ackermann's Illustrated London* (Herts.: Wordsworth Editions, 1985)
Stockdale, J. – *The Covent Garden Journal* (2 vols) (London: 1810)
Stodart, Mary Ann – *Female Writers: Thoughts on their Proper Sphere and on Their Powers of Usefulness* (London: Seeley & Burnside, 1842)
Story, William (ed.) – *Life and Letters of Joseph Story* (Boston: 1851)
Summerson, John – *Georgian London* (London: Pimlico, 1988)
Terhune, A.M. & A.B. (eds) – *The Letters of Edward Fitzgerald* (4 vols) (Princeton: Princeton University Press, 1980)
Thomas, Clara – *Love and Work Enough: The Life of Anna Jameson* (London: Macdonald, 1967)
Trewin, J.C. – *Mr Macready: A Nineteenth-century Tragedian and His Theatre* (London: Harrap & Co., 1955)
Tuckerman, Bayard (ed.) – *The Diary of Philip Hone* (2 vols) (New York: 1889)
Wagenknecht, Edward (ed.) – *Selected Letters and Journals of Fanny Appleton Longfellow* (London: Peter Owen,1959)
Wainright, Nicholas B. (ed.) – *A Philadelphia Perspective: The Diary of Sidney George Fisher* (Pennsylvania: The Historical Society of Pennsylvania, 1967)
Weightman, Gavin & Steve Humphries – *The Making of Modern London 1815–1914* (London: Sidgwick & Jackson, 1983)
West, Shearer – *The Image of the Actor* (London: Pinter Publishers, 1991)
Wikoff, Henry – *Reminiscences of an Idler* (New York: Fords, Howard & Halbert, 1880)
Williams, D.E. (ed.) – *The Life and Correspondence of Sir Thomas Lawrence* (2 vols) (London: Colburn,1831)
Williams, John – *The Pin Basket to the Children of Thespis* (London, 1796)
Williamson, Jane – *Charles Kemble, Man of the Theatre* (Nebraska: University of Nebraska Press, 1964)
Young, Julian – *Memoir of Charles Mayne Young* (London: Macmillan, 1871)

PLAYS

Anonymous (Marie-Thérèse Decamp Kemble) – *The Day After the Wedding, or A Wife's First Lesson* (London: 1808)

Gay, John – *The Beggar's Opera* (London: Goulding and D'Almaine, first performed 1728)

ARTICLES

Anonymous – 'The Sock and the Buskin' – *Fraser's Magazine for Town and Country*, November 1830, vol. II, pp. 458–66

Dewolfe Howe, M.A. – 'Young Fanny Kemble as seen in an Old Diary', *Atlantic Monthly*

Donne, W.B. – 'Obituary of Charles Kemble', *Fraser's Magazine for Town and Country*, December 1854, vol. L

Lamb, Charles – 'On the Tragedies of Shakespeare', *The Works of Charles Lamb* (1811)

Lee, Henry – Frances Anne Kemble obituary, *Atlantic Monthly*, vol. LXXI, issue 427, May 1893

Littel – *The Living Age*, vol. III, issue 32, 21 December 1844

Martineau, Harriet – 'Miss Sedgwick's Works', *London & Westminster Review*, October 1837, section III, VI & XXVIII, no. 1

Sedgwick, Henry Dwight – 'Reminiscences of Literary Berkshire', *The Century*, vol. XXVIII

INDEX